STUDIES IN DEUTERONOMY

SUPPLEMENTS

TO

VETUS TESTAMENTUM

EDITED BY
THE BOARD OF THE QUARTERLY

J.A. EMERTON – PHYLLIS A. BIRD – W.L. HOLLADAY
A. VAN DER KOOIJ – A. LEMAIRE – R.E. MURPHY – B. OTZEN
R. SMEND – J.A. SOGGIN – J.C. VANDERKAM – M. WEINFELD
H.G.M. WILLIAMSON

VOLUME LIII

C.J. Labuschagne

STUDIES IN DEUTERONOMY

IN HONOUR OF C.J. LABUSCHAGNE
ON THE OCCASION OF HIS 65TH BIRTHDAY

EDITED BY

F. GARCÍA MARTÍNEZ, A. HILHORST
J.T.A.G.M. van RUITEN, A.S. van der WOUDE

E.J. BRILL
LEIDEN · NEW YORK · KÖLN
1994

The paper in this book meets the guidelines for permanence and durability of the Committee on Production Guidelines for Book Longevity of the Council on Library Resources.

BS
1275.2
.S78
1994

Library of Congress Cataloging-in-Publication Data

Studies in Deuteronomy : in honour of C.J. Labuschagne on the occasion
of his 65th birthday / edited by F. García Martínez ... [et al.].
       p.   cm. — (Supplements to Vetus testamentum, ISSN 0083-5889 ;
v. 53)
    Includes bibliographical references and indexes.
    ISBN 9004100520 (alk. paper)
    1. Bible. O.T. Deuteronomy—Criticism, interpretation, etc.
I. Labuschagne, C. J. II. García Martínez, Florentino.
III. Series.
BS1275.2.S   1994
22'.1506—dc20
                                         94-4098
                                          CIP

ISSN 0083-5889
ISBN 90 04 10052 0

PRINTED IN THE NETHERLANDS

CONTENTS

PREFACE

The present *Festschrift* was conceived, prepared and brought to publication as an expression of gratitude to a respected scholar and a dear colleague and friend. The book was presented to him on the occasion of his 65th birthday, a few years after his retirement as Professor of Old Testament at the State University of Groningen.

In the last decades, Professor Casper Jeremiah Labuschagne has dedicated his scientific research especially to the book of Deuteronomy. The hitherto published volumes of his Dutch commentary on this Old Testament writing (*Deuteronomium* IA, IB, II) have been welcomed as a major contribution to its interpretation. The editors decided therefore to honour Labuschagne's scholarly achievements by the publication of a collection of essays devoted to this important biblical book. During his academic study at the University of Pretoria Berend Gemser and Adrianus van Selms were his most influential teachers. Theodorus C. Vriezen had a comparable impact upon him during the happy time that Cas and his wife Lenie spent in Groningen in the mid-fifties. After his career as a minister at Wolmaransstad he returned to the University of Pretoria as a lecturer in Old Testament. In those years, marked by the strict politics of apartheid and by the conservative stance of the majority of his colleagues, he courageously joined Dr. Beyers Naudé in opposing what he considered an intolerable oppression of human rights and a fatal threat to the destiny of his native country. Furthermore, he sided with Professor Geyser by defending the latter against allegations of heresy. In 1968 he accepted the invitation of the faculty of theology at the State University of Groningen to join its ranks. There he taught until his retirement in 1991, highly respected by his colleagues and beloved by his students. Impressed by the work of Claus Schedl, he enthusiastically propagated his conviction that the biblical writings are numerical compositions, a thesis which he regards as a sound and promising alternative to the prevailing literary critical analyses of the Old Testament. Next to his scholarly publications, he significantly contributed to the spread of the results of academic biblical studies by the publication of works comprehensible to a large audience. They proved to be a salutary eye-opener to many of his readers but at the same time arroused fierce opposition among conservative circles in the Netherlands.

Cas Labuschagne excels as a gifted Old Testament scholar, an advocate of a critical treatment of the biblical tradition and a champion of an up-to-date reception of the truth embedded in Israel's holy writings. It is a great pleasure to dedicate this *Festschrift* to him as a tribute to a friend and colleague who in his personal and academic life did not shrink from drawing dramatic conclusions from what he considered to be essential to human well-being and faithful allegiance to God.

The editors

ABBREVIATIONS

AB	The Anchor Bible, Garden City N.Y.
ACEBT	*Amsterdamse cahiers voor exegese en bijbelse theologie*, Amsterdam
ADPV	Abhandlungen des deutschen Palästina-Vereins, Wiesbaden
AJSL	*American Journal of Semitic Languages and Literature*, Chicago
ARN	Abot de Rabbi Nathan
ASTI	*Annual of the Swedish Theological Institute in Jerusalem*, Leiden
AnBib	Analecta Biblica, Roma
AOAT	Alter Orient und Altes Testament, Neukirchen-Vluyn
ATANT	Abhandlungen zur Theologie des Alten und Neuen Testaments, Zürich
ATD	Das Alte Testament Deutsch, Göttingen
ATS	Arbeiten zu Text und Sprache im Alten Testament, St. Ottilien
b	talmud babli
ber	(tractate) Berakot
BASOR	*Bulletin of the American Schools of Oriental Research*, New Haven
BBB	Bonner Biblische Beiträge, Bonn
BETL	Bibliotheca Ephemeridum Theologicarum Lovaniensium, Leuven
BFCT	Beiträge zur Förderung christlicher Theologie, Gütersloh
BHS	Biblia Hebraica Stuttgartensia, Stuttgart 1977
Bib Or	Biblica et Orientalia, Roma
BKAT	Biblischer Kommentar Altes Testament, Neukirchen-Vluyn
BN	*Biblische Notizen*, Bamberg
BTB	*Biblical Theology Bulletin*, Roma
BVSAW.PH	Berichte über die Verhandlungen der sächsischen Akademie der Wissenschaften zu Leipzig, Philologisch-historische Klasse
BWANT	Beiträge zur Wissenschaft vom Alten und Neuen Testament, Leipzig, Stuttgart
BZ	*Biblische Zeitschrift*, Paderborn
BZAW	Beihefte zur Zeitschrift für die alttestamentliche Wissenschaft, Giessen, Berlin
CAT	Commentaire de l'Ancien Testament, Neuchâtel
CB	Coniectanea Biblica, Lund
CBC	The Cambridge Bible Commentary, Cambridge
CBQ	*Catholic Biblical Quarterly*, Washington
CD	Damascus Document
CSS	Cursus Scripturae Sacrae, Paris
DBAT	*Dielheimer Blätter zum Alten Testament*, Heidelberg
DBS	*Dictionnaire de la Bible. Supplément*, Paris
Deut r	Midrash Deuteronomy Rabbah
DJD	Discoveries in the Judaean Desert, Oxford
EB	Die Echter Bibel, Würzburg
Eccl r	Midrash Ecclesiastes Rabbah
Eccl z	Midrash Ecclesiastes Zuta
EdF	Erträge der Forschung, Darmstadt
EH	Exegetisches Handbuch zum Alten Testament, Münster

ETL	*Ephemerides Theologicae Lovanienses*, Leuven
ETR	*Études théologiques et religieuses*, Montpellier
ETS	Erfurter theologische Studien, Erfurt
EVV	English Versions
EvTh	*Evangelische Theologie*, München
Ex r	Midrash Exodus Rabbah
FJB	*Frankfurter Judaistische Beiträge*, Frankfurt a. M.
FRLANT	Forschungen zur Religion und Literatur des Alten und Neuen Testaments, Göttingen
GAS	Grundrisse zum Alten Testament, Göttingen
Gen Rabbati	Genesis Rabbati
GCS	Die griechischen christlichen Schriftsteller, Leipzig
GK	W. Gesenius - E. Kautzsch, *Hebräische Grammatik*, Leipzig 1909²⁸
HAR	*Hebrew Annual Review*, Colombus (Ohio)
HAT	Handbuch zum Alten Testament, Tübingen
HBT	*Horizons in Biblical Theology*, Pittsburg
Hev	Hever
HK	Göttinger Handkommentar zum Alten Testament, Göttingen
HKAT	Handkommentar zum Alten Testament, Göttingen
HSAT	Die Heilige Schrift des Alten Testaments, Bonn
HSM	Harvard Semitic Monographs, Cambridge (Mass.)
HTR	*Harvard Theological Review*, Cambridge (Mass.)
HTS	Harvard Theological Studies, Cambridge (Mass.)
HUCA	*Hebrew Union College Annual*, Cincinnati
IAA	Israel Antiquities Authority
ICC	The International Critical Commentary, Edinburgh
IDC	Inter Documentation Company, Leiden
IEJ	*Israel Exploration Journal*, Jerusalem
Int	*Interpretation. A Journal of Bible and Theology*, Richmond (Virg.)
JBL	*Journal of Biblical Literature*, Philadelphia
JCS	*Journal of Cuneiform Studies*, Chicago
JETS	*Journal of the Evangelical Theological Society*, Wheaton (Il.)
JJS	*Journal of Jewish Studies*, Oxford
JNES	*Journal of Near Eastern Studies*, Chicago
JNSL	*Journal of Northwest Semitic Languages*, Stellenbosch
Joüon	P. Joüon, *Grammaire de l'hébreu biblique*, Roma 1947²
JQR	*Jewish Quarterly Review*, Philadelphia
JSJ	*Journal for the Study of Judaism in the Persian, Hellenistic and Roman Period*, Leiden
JSOT	*Journal for the Study of the Old Testament*, Sheffield
JSOTS	Journal for the Study of the Old Testament Supplement Series, Sheffield
KAI	H. Donner - W. Röllig, *Kanaanäische und aramäische Inschriften*, I-III, Wiesbaden I 1979⁴, II 1973³, III 1976³
KAT	Kommentar zum Alten Testament, Leipzig, Gütersloh
KEH	Kurzgefasstes exegetisches Handbuch zum Alten Testament, Leipzig
KHC	Kurzer Hand-Commentar zum Alten Testament, Tübingen, Leipzig
KRI	K.A.S. Kitchen, *Ramesside Inscriptions* V/1-2, Oxford 1970-72.

KS	A. Alt, *Kleine Schriften zur Geschichte des Volkes Israel*, 3 Vol., München 1953-1959.
LeDiv	Lectio Divina, Paris
Lev r	Midrash Leviticus Rabbah
LXX	Septuagint
Mas	Masada
Med	Medinet
Mek	Mekilta de Rabbi Yismael
MMT	Miqṣat Ma'aśeh ha-Torah
M Ps	Midrash on Psalms (Shoher Tob)
MRS	Mekilta de Rabbi Simeon ben Yohai
MSU	Mitteilungen des Septuaginta-Unternehmens, Göttingen
MT	Massoretic text
Mur	Muraba'at
NBL	M. Görg - B. Lang (eds.), *Neues Bibel-Lexikon*, Zürich 1988ff.
NCBC	The New Century Bible Commentary, Grand Rapids, London
NEB	Die Neue Echter Bibel. Kommentar zum Alten Testament mit der Einheitsübersetzung, Würzburg
NEngB	New English Bible
NICOT	New International Commentary on the Old Testament, Grand Rapids (Mich.)
NS	New Series
NTT	*Nederlands Theologisch Tijdschrift*, Wageningen
OBO	Orbis Biblicus et Orientalis, Freiburg - Göttingen
OLP	*Orientalia Lovaniensia periodica*, Leuven
OLZ	*Orientalische Literaturzeitung*, Berlin
Or	*Orientalia*, Roma
OTS	*Oudtestamentische Studiën*, Leiden
PAM	Palestine Archaeological Museum (= Rockefeller Museum)
Pes	(tractate) Pesahim
Pes r	Pesiqta Rabbati
PJB	Palästinajahrbuch, Berlin
POS	Pretoria Oriental Series, Leiden
POT	De Prediking van het Oude Testament, Nijkerk
PP	Pentateuque paraphrase
PRE	Pirqe de Rabbi Eliezer
PS	Pentateuque Samaritain
PSBA	*Proceedings of the Society of Biblical Archaeology*
Q	Qumran
QD	Quaestiones disputatae, Freiburg B.
RB	*Revue Biblique*, Paris
RevQ	*Revue de Qumran*, Paris
Sanh	(tractate) Sanhedrin
SB	Subsidia Biblica, Roma
SBA	Stuttgarter Biblische Aufsatzbände Altes Testament, Stuttgart
SBL	Society of Biblical Literature, Decatur (Ga)
SBS	Stuttgarter Bibelstudien, Stuttgart
Se	Seiyâl
SER	Seder Eliyahu Rabbah
SHANE	Studies in the History of the Ancient Near East, Leiden - New York - Köln
Sifre Deut	Sifre Deuteronomy

Song r	Midrash Song of Songs Rabbah
SP	Samaritan Pentateuch
STDJ	Studies on the Texts of the Desert of Judah, Leiden
Suk	(tractate) Sukkot
SVT	Supplements to Vetus Testamentum, Leiden
SWBA	Social World of Biblical Antiquity, Sheffield
Tanh B	Tanhuma (ed. Buber)
TB	Theologische Bücherei. Neudrucke und Berichte aus dem 20. Jahrhundert, München
THAT	E. Jenni - C. Westermann (eds.), *Theologisches Handwörterbuch zum Alten Testament*, I-II, München 1971-76
THGD	J. W. Wevers, *Text History of the Greek Deuteronomy* (MSU 13; Göttingen, 1978).
ThR	*Theologische Revue*, Münster
ThZ	*Theologische Zeitschrift*, Basel
TLZ	*Theologische Literaturzeitung*, Berlin
TM	Texte massorétique
TOB	Traduction Oecuménique de la Bible, Paris
TRu	*Theologische Rundschau*, Tübingen
TUAT	O. Kaiser et al. (eds.), *Texte aus der Umwelt des Alten Testaments*, Gütersloh 1982ff.
TWAT	G. J. Botterweck - H. Ringgren (eds.), *Theologisches Wörterbuch zum Alten Testament*, I- , Stuttgart 1970-
UBL	Ugaritisch-Biblische Literatur, Münster
UF	*Ugarit-Forschungen*, Neukirchen-Vluyn
VT	*Vetus Testamentum*, Leiden
WBC	World Biblical Commentary, Dallas Texas
WMANT	Wissenschaftliche Monographien zum Alten und Neuen Testament, Neukirchen-Vluyn
WTJ	*Westminster Theological Journal*, Philadelphia
y	talmud yerushalmi
ZÄS	*Zeitschrift für Ägyptische Sprache und Altertumskunde*, Berlin, Leipzig
ZAW	*Zeitschrift für die alttestamentliche Wissenschaft*, Giessen, Berlin
ZDPV	*Zeitschrift des deutschen Palästina-Vereins*, Stuttgart, Wiesbaden
ZWT	*Zeitschrift für wissenschaftliche Theologie*, Jena, Halle, Leipzig

1994: A SIGNIFICANT ANNIVERSARY IN THE HISTORY OF DEUTERONOMY RESEARCH

CHRISTOPHER T. BEGG

Washington, D.C., U.S.A.

1994 marks the 65th birthday of a foremost contemporary commentator of Deuteronomy, C.J. Labuschagne. But this year is also the centennial of a pair of publication by two young German scholars, Willy Staerk and C. Steuernagel, which, once for all, focussed scholarly attention on the import of the *Numeruswechsel* phenomenon in Deuteronomy.[1] In this essay I purpose then to examine and compare the treatment of the *Numeruswechsel* in the two works within the context of their overall conceptions of the formation-history of Deuteronomy. In addition, I shall attempt to relate these *Erstlingsarbeiten* to their authors' later publication history and to trace the outlines of the century-long discussion to which they gave rise. I do so in hopes of furthering appreciation of the historical dimension of a problematic which no Deuteronomy exegete of the hundred years since Staerk and Steuernagel wrote has been able to ignore and to which Labuschagne's own commentary makes ample reference.

W. Staerk

I begin with Staerk as the older of our two authors.[2] By 1894 Staerk (born Dec. 13, 1866 in Berlin) at age 28, had already published both his Halle "philosophical" dissertation on Zechariah 9-14[3] as well as three scholarly articles on a range of OT topics.[4] The next in his series

---

[1] The phenomenon had received some sporadic attention prior to 1894, see C.T. Begg, "The Significance of the *Numeruswechsel* in Deuteronomy: the 'Pre-History' of the Question", *ETL* 55 (1979), 116-24.

[2] On Staerk, see his self-presentation, "Willy Staerk", in E. Stange (ed.), *Die Religionswissenschaft der Gegenwart in Selbstdarstellungen* (Leipzig, 1929), 159-206.

[3] *Untersuchungen über die Komposition und Abfassungszeit von Zach. 9-14 mit eingehender Berücksichtigung der neuesten Hypothesen* (Halle, 1891).

[4] "Der Gebrauch der Wendung באחרית הימים im alttestamentlichen Kanon", *ZAW* 11 (1891), 247-53; "Zur Kritik der Psalmenüberschriften", *ZAW* 12 (1892), 91-151; "Die alttestamentlichen Zitate bei den Schriftstellern des Neuen Testamentes", *ZWT* 35 (1892), 464-85; 36 (1893), 70-98.

of early writings is the one which concerns us here, i.e. *Das Deutero-nomium. Sein Inhalt und seine literarische Form. Eine kritische Studie* (Leipzig: Hinrichs, 1894).[5] In an intellectual self-portrait penned many years later, Staerk tells us that this study was inspired by the recent monograph of B. Baentsch - later to be his friend, scholarly confederate and predecessor in the OT chair at Jena - on the *Bundesbuch*,[6] and was written without knowledge of Steuernagel's similar and simultaneous work at Leipzig.[7]

Staerk's monograph opens with a *Vorbemerkung* whose first paragraph deserves citation in full since already here he sets out the understanding of Deuteronomy's *Numeruswechsel* which will guide the whole subsequent investigation:

> Der Ausgangspunkt der vorliegenden Untersuchung über das Deuteronomium ist die bislang wohl angedeutete, aber zu wenig als kritischer Kanon verwertete Tatsache, dass in dieser ... Schrift die Hörer bald als ein einzelnes Individuum mit 'Du', bald als eine Mehrheit von Personen mit 'Ihr' angeredet erscheinen. Kommt das nun auch sachlich auf dasselbe hinaus, so ist es doch formell als schriftstellerisch mindestens sehr ungeschickt, wenn nicht unmöglich zu bezeichnen und bildet ein starkes Präjudiz für die schon von anderen auf anderm Wege gefundene Einsicht, dass das jetzige Deuteronomium, wenigstens in seinem Einleitungs- und Schlussreden, einen literarischen Prozess durchgemacht hat. Aber auch für die eigentliche Gesetzgebung lässt sich eine solche Mehrheit von Händen auf demselben Wege erweisen.[8]

The above remarks are all the more to be kept in mind in that they constitute Staerk's one and only "statement of principle" on the phenomenon.

In the body of his study Staerk devotes two chapters apiece to the "Code" of Deuteronomy 12-26 and its framework chaps. 1-11 and 27-34. Staerk's initial chapter on the Code treats in turn its cultic and "secular" provisions. Several questions guiding Staerk's reading of Code may be identified: Is the text of a given law an original unity?

---

[5] This volume represents an expanded version of Staerk's Halle theology dissertation titled *Beiträge zur Kritik des Deuteronomiums* for which E. Kautzsch (1841-1910) was the *Doktorvater*, see the article cited in n. 2, p. 171 and *Orientalische Bibliographie* 8 (1894), 283.

[6] *Das Bundesbuch Ex. XX.22-XXIII.33. Seine ursprüngliche Gestalt, sein Verhältnis zu den es umgebenden Quellenschriften und seine Stellung in der alttestamentlichen Gesetzgebung* (Halle, 1892). On Staerk's relationship to Baentsch (1859-1908), see the article cited in n. 2, 174-176.

[7] See the work cited in n. 2, p. 171 where Staerk states: "Dass Steuernagel zu gleicher Zeit an dem Thema arbeitete, wusste ich natürlich nicht".

[8] *Deuteronomium*, p. 1. Note the vagueness with which Staerk refers to previous scholarly treatment of the *Numeruswechsel* phenomenon here. On the subject see my article cited in n. 1.

What was its likely original context? How probable is it that such a law constituted part of Josiah's lawbook?[9] For our purposes, it is of special interest to see how Staerk handles occurrences of the *Numerus-wechsel* in Deuteronomy 12-26. That chap. 12 is "anything but a unity" is evident already from the contrast between the (predominantly) plural vv. 1-12 and the singular vv. 13-28. Within the former segment, in turn, Staerk eliminates the singular concluding words of vv. 5 and 7 with the observation that these "ungeschickt nachschleppen" (p. 3). In the basically singular passage 13:2-19, he qualifies the phrase *'šr sbybtykm* of v. 8 as "at least superfluous", while the likewise plural vv. 4b-5 are "alien to the context". In v. 6, on the other hand, the plural phrase "against the Lord *your God who brought you out* of the land of Egypt" is to be emended to the singular in accord both with the LXX and the parallel phrase of v. 11 (p. 6). Similarly, Staerk emends the opening plural *w'śytm* in 19:18 in line with the singular address of the remainder of 19:16-20. Finally, the plural forms of 20:18 "already indicate" that it is a "secondary addition by another hand" (p. 20), just as the oscillation in the form of address in 24:8-9 "proves" that its text "cannot be original" (p. 26). Thus in chaps. 12-26, instances of (purported) textual corruption aside,[10] Staerk consistently finds the change of number indicative of a variation in authorship in accord with the statement of his *Vorbemerkung* about the Code (see above). Staerk concludes his analysis of the code with an appendix on "the form of the laws in Deut 12-26". Here, he notes that whereas most of the plural items within the segment show themselves to be either textually corrupt or later additions (glosses) to the singular laws, e.g., in the case of the centralization law of chap. 12, one finds self-contained plural prescriptions. This observation would in turn suggest that "already earlier on" the Code existed in both forms of address, although only the singular version has come down to us more or less intact (p. 27).

Staerk devotes his second chapter ("Deuteronomy and the Legislation in JE") primarily to an attempted reconstruction of the original content and distribution of the material of the *Bundesbuch* as the long-recognized "source" of the Deuteronomic Code in order thereafter

---

[9] In answering this question, Staerk identifies a whole series of Deuteronomic prescriptions which could not have been part of Josiah's book (e.g., 17:14-20 and 20:1-9, 10-20, see pp. 19-21) since the lack of sense for political / military reality they reflect could only have emerged once Israel has ceased to be a state, i.e. in the (post-)exilic period.

[10] In the case of both 13:6 and 19:18 (see above) Staerk's proposed emendations seem to go against the *lectio difficilior* principle which would support the extant MT readings as "disharmonious" with the context.

4 CHRISTOPHER T. BEGG

to use this reconstruction as a key to identifying which of the (singular) laws in chaps. 12-26 did in fact stand in the original Code.

Staerk's third chapter focusses on the material that now precedes and follows Deuteronomy 12-26. Following the present sequence of the material, he attempts to determine what in a given chapter did or did not belong together originally. As his *Vorbemerkung* already suggests, Staerk makes consistent use of the *Numeruswechsel* "canon" in carrying out this endeavor. In the majority of instances, shorter or longer passages in a number divergent from their context, are declared, with (or sometimes even without) appeal to confirmatory contentual and stylistic considerations, to derive from another hand. Thus, e.g., the singular 2:7 is "a disruptive insertion" within a plural sequence which "with its cheerful parenesis is not at all appropriate in its context" (p. 59). Again, the singular half-verse 1:31a appears readily dispensible given the smooth connection between the plural 1:30 and 3lb (p. 58). On the other hand, Staerk rather regularly has recourse to the readings of LXX or conjecture in order to eliminate problematic number changes. Given, e.g., the necessity of Moses' command reported in 1:21 as preparation for what follows, he proposes to substitute LXX's plural for MT's singular in the latter (p. 58), just as he ascribes the opening plural *wbqštm* in 4:29 to dittography with the following *mšm* (p. 63).

At the same time, Staerk, it should be observed, is not proposing anything so simple or straightforward as a partition of the framework chapters between two hands, one using the singular, the other the plural address. Repeatedly, he distinguishes several strata with segments favoring one or other number. In chap. 28 (singular except for vv. 62-63*, 68*) for instance, he reduces the original "curse section" to those items having a pendant in the blessings of vv. 1-14, while identifying a whole series of secondary amplifications of the former in the extant vv. 15-68 (pp. 70-72). It is not, however, only within segments utilizing a given number that Staerk disallows single authorship. He does so also where it is a question of the literary relationship of such segments among themselves. Chaps. 1-3, 5, and 9:7bβ-10:11, e.g., are all predominantly plural in number. Given, however, that whereas in the first of these units the "you" addressed is the post-Exodus generation, in the latter two it is rather the Exodus generation itself, Staerk concludes that they cannot be the work of the same author (see pp. 64, 67).

Basing himself on the "analysis" of chap. 3, Staerk proceeds in his chap. 4 to a "synthesis". In particular, he attempts to reconstruct the original content and sequence of what once constituted introductions to and conclusions of independent editions—whether singular or plural—

of the Code, but which have now been dispersed throughout chaps. 1-11, 27-34. From out of the plural materials in these chapters, Staerk assembles three such longer "framework" speeches:

1) 4:45-46; 1:6-4:2*; 4:10-14* (11:31-32?) [+ a plural code]; 4:5-8; 29:9 ... 29:13-14 ... 29:8 ... (28:62-63*?) ... (27:1ff.*?) ...;
2) 5:1-28*; (5:29?) ... 6:1 [+ a plural code]; (27:1ff*?) ... 32:45-47(?) ... 28:69(?);
3) 29:1, 4 ... 29:3; 9:7b-24 ... 10:(15)-19 ... 7:7-8 ... 11:2-25* [+ a plural code] ... (4:15-19?) ... 4:25-28 ... 11:21-28? ... (27:11-28?).

The first two of these sequences are pre-exilic, while the third stems from the Exile (pp. 86-87). Staerk fails to find sequences of comparable length in the extant singular material of chaps. 1-11, 27-34. Rather, he distinguishes the fragmentary remains of numerous singular "speeches", some pre-exilic, but most Exilic, which once "framed" distinct editions of the Code. Of these, he gives particular attention to the sequence 7:12b-24 which, as its parallelism with the parenetic conclusion of the *Bundesbuch* (Exod 23:20-33) suggests, originally constituted part of a closing speech to an edition of the Deuteronomic law-book (pp. 88-89).

In his final, fifth chapter, Staerk presents his conclusions regarding the makeup of *Urdeuteronomium*. Decisive for this reconstruction is his conception of the original content, context, and placing of the *Bundesbuch* as incorporated into the work of the earlier Elohist (E^1). Adopting (and adapting) the proposals of such scholars as A. Kuenen and H. Holzinger, Staerk suggests that in E^1 the *Bundesbuch* was promulgated by Moses at that juncture Deuteronomy itself now stands, i.e. at the end of the desert wanderings, directly before Israel's entry into the land. In that context the laws of the *Bundesbuch* were preceded by a historical retrospective - currently preserved in Jos 24:2-14* - and followed by the blessings and curses of Exod 23:20-33 plus an account of a covenant-making on the basis of the laws and their writing down now constituting Exod 24:4-8*. The foregoing reconstruction of E^1's *Bundesbuch* and its framework furnishes Staerk with his key for recovering content, sequence, and mode of formulation of the original Deuteronomy. Thus, like the (original) laws of the *Bundesbuch*, *Urdeuteronomium* would have employed the singular address. Like the E^1 *Bundesbuch* as well, its legal core would have been preceded by an historical introduction (Staerk finds remnants of this in the singular elements of Deuteronomy 2-3) and followed by a series of blessings and curses (Staerk identifies this element with Deut 7:12b-24) plus a record of covenant making and writing down of the law (equated by Staerk with Deut 27:9-10, 1ff.*). The widegoing parallelism between the two reconstructed documents further suggests, according to Staerk, that *Urdeuteronomium* was composed as a replacement for E[1]'s *Bundesbuch* "complex" (p. 109) Rather quickly, however, the former came to stand on its own. This now independent document generated a number of distinct editions, one of which was "discovered" in Josiah's time (in an appendix, pp. 111-119 Staerk prints a translation of "das mutmassliche Gesetzbuch des Königs Josia a. 621" in which he drastically rearranges the extant order of Deuteronomy's legal material, bringing together laws of related content into a continuous sequence).

Staerk continued to write prolifically for some 45 years after 1894 (he died Dec. 3, 1946 in Jena). He did so in a wide range of scholarly issues, including, e.g., Biblical theology, the Elephantine and Geniza discoveries, the Psalms, the Suffering Servant and post-Biblical Jewish literature.[11] Within this impressive corpus, Deuteronomy studies have, however, a rather minor place, being represented only by a brief monograph[12] and a follow-up article to this[13] in which he argues (against his own earlier supposition) in support of T. Oestreicher's[14] contention that Deuteronomy (12:5 excepted) does not enjoin a centralization of the cult at a single site. In addition, it is of interest to note that Staerk came to have increasing doubts about the validity of the literary-critical approach pursued so confidently in *Das Deuteronomium*[15] just as he ended up deploring that work's "-theological" character[16]. It thus appears that in later years Staerk looked back on his

---

[11] See the bibliography appended to the article cited in n. 2, pp. 203-06. This bibliography covers Staerk's output for the years 1891-1929. He continued to produce books and longer articles, primarily on questions of biblical theology and *Religionsgeschichte*, throughout the 1930's.

[12] *Das Problem des Deuteronomiums. Ein Beitrag zur neusten Pentateuchkritik* (BFCT 29:2; Gütersloh, 1924).

[13] "Noch einmal das Problem des Deuteronomiums", *Ernst Sellin Festschrift. Beiträge zur Religionsgeschichte und Archäologie Palästinas* (Leipzig, 1927), 139-50.

[14] *Das Deuteronomische Grundgesetz* (BFCT 27:4; Gütersloh, 1923).

[15] On this point, see the sceptical comments with which he concludes his reviews of F. Puukko, *Das Deuteronomium* (BWANT 5; Leipzig, 1910), in *OLZ* 13 (1910), cc. 499-500 and of J. Hempel, *Die Schichten des Deuteronomiums* (Leipzig, 1914), in *OLZ* 18 (1915), cc. 277-278. Both these works attempt to carry further Staerk's (and Steuernagel's) literary-criticism of Deuteronomy. Note too Staerk's remark on his own 1894 work in the article cited in n. 2, p. 171: "... von unzureichenden formal-ästhetischen Geschichtspunkten her [arbeitete ich] an den sehr problematischen Rahmen der Schrift [i.e. Deuteronomy]".

[16] See his comment in the piece cited in n. 2, p. 171: "Ich selbst würde heute solch eine, wesentlich auf Formales und Historisches gerichtete Dissertation nicht als theologische Arbeit gelten lassen, denn Theologie darf sich nicht in Literargeschichte auflösen, auch nicht in Gattungs- und Stilgeschichte. Ihr Gegenstand darf nie von der Bibel als dem Zeugnis der Offenbarung Gottes so absehen, dass er in profangeschichtlicher Isolierung erscheint".

publication of 1894 as a kind of "youthful indiscretion" from which he increasingly distanced himself.

C. Steuernagel

Our second work for consideration was its 25 year old's author's very first scholarly publication. Entitled *Der Rahmen des Deuteronomiums. Literar-kritische Untersuchung über seine Zusammensetzung und Entstehung* (Halle: Wischan & Wettengel, 1894), the work represents Steuernagel's dissertation at the Philosophical Faculty of the University of Leipzig.[17] One half the length of Staerk's volume, Steuernagel's monograph, as its title indicates, confines itself to the framework chapters of Deuteronomy.[18] More specifically, as Steuernagel himself points out (p. iv), it focusses on chaps. 5-11 with more cursory attention to the remaining material. Steuernagel begins his investigation of Deuteronomy 5-11 with a critical survey of previous views on the unity of these chapters and their relation to other segments of the book. It is this connection that Steuernagel comes to cite (p. 4) the *"höchst befremdlich"* change of number in the chapters under review, where, in contrast to its occurrences in the Code and Deuteronomy 27-34, it had not hitherto provoked scholarly attention. Nonetheless, as Steuernagel goes on to remark, the change, also in chaps. 5-11 themselves, can hardly be "accidental" given that the change coincides, in 5:1-10:11 (at least) with a content difference, i.e. "narrative" segments in these 5 1/2 chapters employ the plural address, while in their "parenetic" passages the singular predominates. In light of this consideration, Steuernagel proposes to develop a new analysis of Deuteronomy 5-11 *"nach dem Merkmal des Numerus"* (Ibid.), treating 5:1-10:11 and 10:12-11:32 (where the *Numeruswechsel* has a different character) separately.

Steuernagel commences his treatment of 5:1-10:11 with the two longer plural (narrative) segments 5:1-6:1 and 9:8-10:11. On various grounds, he first eliminates much of these units' present content as

---

[17] Steuernagel was born Feb. 17, 1869 at Hardegsen near Göttingen. On him, see: W. Schmauch, "In Memoriam Carl Steuernagel", *TLZ* 83 (1958), 547-50; M. Noth, "Carl Steuernagel", *ZDPV* 74 (1958), 1-3.

[18] According to the "Vorwort" of his later study, *Die Entstehung des deuteronomischen Gesetzes kritisch und biblisch-theologisch untersucht* (Halle, 1896) Steuernagel only came to know Staerk's work when he had "basically" completed this new monograph. He comments further: "In der Beobachtung des Einzelmaterials, das den Ausgangspunkt meiner Untersuchungen bildet, bin ich vielfach mit Staerk zusammengetroffen ... Die Verwertung desselben jedoch weicht von der Staerks beträchtlich ab, so dass ich hoffen darf, die Veröffentlichung meiner Arbeit sei doch einigermassen gerechtfertigt." (Ibid).

secondary, e.g., the Decalogue of 5:6-20 is a post-Deuteronomistic composition (p. 6), while 5:29-6:1 shows itself to be largely formulaic (p. 7). He finds what remains (i.e. 5:1-4, 20-21a, 22*, 23-28; 9:8-10, 12-17, 21, 25-29; 10:1-5, 10-11) to constitute a continuous sequence in which 9:8ff. picks up where 5:28 leaves off and 5:21 and 9:26 share the rather unusual noun *gdl* (p. 9). He next proceeds to the predominately singular section 6:2-9:7. From this sequence Steuernagel eliminates, *inter alia*, formulaic elements (e.g., 6:2-3) as well as the recurring plural verses or verse parts. On the other hand, he views the stray plural form *bkm* in 7:4 as a textual error, occasioned by the preceding plural verb *w'bdw* (p. 11). By such a "process of elimination" Steuernagel arrives at an original parenetic discourse in 6:2-9:7* (i.e. 6:4, [5], 10-13, 15; 7:1-4, 6, 9, 12b-16aα, 17-21, 23,24; 8:7-10, 12-18; 9:1-4a, 5-7a). This sequence evidences a coherent line of thought wherein two thesis affirmations about *Yhwh* (see 6:4 and 7:9) each give rise to a double admonition (p.16).

Deut 10:12-11:32 preserves the "transitions" to the Code itself of the two sequences previously isolated by Steuernagel in 5:1-10:12. Again taking the form of address as his analytic key, Steuernagel now endeavors to identify which elements within the former segment might represent the continuations of 5*; 9:8-10:11* and 6:2-9:7*, respectively. As in the previous segment, much material within the longer plural or singular passages of 10:12-11:32 is adjudged to be secondary by Steuernagel on grounds of its formulaic character, (momentary) shift to the other form of address, or lack of content coherence with the context. The conclusion of this analysis is that Pl.'s transition to the Code (i.e. 10:16-17a; 11:2-5, 7, 8aα,8b-9, 10aβ, 11, 13-14a, 16-17, 22-28) has been more completely preserved than that of Sg. (i.e. 10:12aα, 14-15, 21-22; 11:10aαb, 12, 14b-15 [+ 11:18-20 in their originally singular form and 6:20-25?]), see pp. 20-22.

Having now completed his reconstruction of two distinct introductory discourses of chaps. 5-11, Steuernagel proceeds to point out that these differ not only in their form of address, but also in *Sprachgebrauch*, sources used and the moment at which they represent Moses as promulgating the Deuteronomic Code (in "Pl." this is shortly after the departure from Horeb, in "Sg." rather in Moab), see pp. 22-28.

As noted above, Steuernagel offers an admittedly cursory treatment of the remaining framework materials of Deuteronomy. He assigns chaps. 1-3* (shorn of the singular insertions) to a later author who wished to "fill in the gap" concerning the years between the people's departure from Horeb (with which Pl.'s narration terminates) and their arrival in Moab (where Sg.'s parenesis is situated), p. 34. Chap. 4 (in which Steuernagel follows LXX [and/or Sam] where its form of address differs from that of MT, in vv. 3, 10, 25, 29, 34) comprises 5 distinct units of which the first, vv. 1-4 may represent the continuation of 1-3* (pp. 34-36).

In chaps. 27-34, Steuernagel identifies mostly (exilic) redactional amplifications, e.g., the self-contained piece 28:69-29:28* (p. 49). Sg. finds its conclusion in 26:17-19*; 28:1-44*; 30:15-20*; (31:9aα, 24-25a, 10, 11b, 12b-13?), while to Pl. pertains only 32:45-47 (p. 53).

Steuernagel concludes his study with a consideration of the date of the two strata distinguished by him and of the subsequent formation-history of Deuteronomy. Both Pl. and Sg. stem from Manasseh's reign. The same would be the case for "D'", the redactor who combined the two complexes, while also inserting much, mainly formulaic, material of his own between and within their component parts. Still prior to the Exile another Deuteronomic author prefaced the corpus 5-31* with the review of events from Horeb to Moab, 1:6-4:4 (see above). In the exilic/post-exilic period "Deuteronomy" was combined with JE, and passages like 30:1-10 were inserted into the former.

By way of conclusion to my review of Steuernagel's work, I would call attention to some similarities and differences between its approach/findings and those of Staerk. In general the two authors have in common their systematic application of the "number criterion" to the analysis of Deuteronomy's framework chapters; thereby they arrive at their shared notion of these chapters as preserving the opening and concluding discourses of several distinct editions of the Code. This commonality constitutes, at the same time, the most original feature of their respective works and the one which was to have the most lasting influence on subsequent scholarship. On the other hand, both are also ready to "correct" MT number changes in a whole series of instances (e.g., in Deuteronomy 4), mostly with appeal to LXX, in a way that appears text-critically questionable. Staerk and Steuernagel also arrive at some common conclusions on matters of detail. Both, e.g., ascribe 1:6-4:4* to an (preexilic) author other than the writer(s) of the plural material in chaps. 5, 9-10 on the grounds of the difference of generation being addressed, see above. Both also attempt to reconstruct an originally parallel set of blessings and curses in Deuteronomy 28. On the other hand, several substantive divergencies between the two scholars' conclusions should not be overlooked. Thus, while Staerk holds (see above) that the original Deuteronomy was written to substitute for E's *Bundesbuch*, Steuernagel denies this (p. 25). While Steuernagel assigns both 5:1-28* and 9:8-10:11* to his (preexilic) "Pl.", Staerk attributes the former to a preexilic, the latter to an exilic author.

They likewise differ in their conceptions of the function of the sequence 1:6-4:4*; for Staerk this originally constituted the introduction to yet another, freestanding "plural" introduction to the Code, whereas Steuernagel sees it as a prefatory supplement to the already combined Sg. and Pl., see above. Also with respect to the singular materials of chaps. 5-11, our two authors diverge notably: Steuernagel reconstructs a fairly extensive and continuous discourse ("Sg.") here where Staerk finds only a heap of fragmentary singular sequences, of which, e.g., 7:12b-24 once functioned as the concluding discourse to an edition of the Code.

A final difference to be noted concerns the place and "fate" of the two works treated in the lifetime scholarly output of their respective authors. We noted above that after 1894 Staerk wrote relatively little on Deuteronomy and came to have considerable reservations about the validity and adequacy of the approach adopted by him in his work of that year. In both these respects, Steuernagel's post-1894 scholarly career offers a marked contrast. First of all, he continued to write extensively on Deuteronomy over a thirty-year period.[19] Moreover, Steuernagel (d. March 4, 1958 in Greifswald) retained a lifetime confidence in the legitimacy of the literary-critical approach as utilized in his *Der Rahmen* in general and, contrary to what one sometimes reads, of the "*Numeruswechsel* criterion" in particular.[20] If then, in its author's own estimation, Staerk's *Das Deuteronomium* appears as a sort of "youthful indiscretion", Steuernagel's contemporaneous production constitutes a clear intimation of a major thrust of his lifework as a scholar.

---

[19] See: *Die Entstehung des deuteronomischen Gesetzes* (1896, cf. n. 18); *Das Deuteronomium* (HKAT 1:3; Göttingen, 1898; 2nd significantly revised edition, 1923); *Lehrbuch der Einleitung in das Alte Testament* (Tübingen, 1912), 172-203. For a general bibliography of Steuernagel, see "Bibliographie Carl Steuernagel", *TLZ* 74 (1949), cc. 113-15.

[20] For an extensive review of Steuernagel's post-1894 writings on Deuteronomy as cited in n. 19, see my unpublished Leuven dissertation of 1978, *Contributions to the Elucidation of the Composition of Deuteronomy with Special Attention to the Significance of the* Numeruswechsel, Vol. I, 467-85, 592-608. Here it might be noted that over time Steuernagel's analysis of Deuteronomy underwent a variety of changes. E.g., *à la* Staerk he eventually recognized Deut 1:6-4:2* as the opening of a *Sonderausgabe* of the book rather than as a supplement to the combined "Pl." and "Sg." as he had argued in 1894. These changes are cited in detail in the above dissertation. On the (erroneous) assertions made by various authors concerning Steuernagel's latter hesitations concerning or even abandonment of the *Numeruswechsel* criterion, see my Vol. V, 1546-1547, n. 931 where these are cited and refuted.

Conclusion

We stated above that the 1894 works of Staerk and Steuernagel focussed subsequent scholarly attention on the *Numeruswechsel* phenomenon in Deuteronomy in remarkably perduring fashion; they made the phenomenon one of the great, inescapable questions about the book in 20th century exegesis. Of course, the specific approach taken by them to Deuteronomy's change of number has been controverted right from the start. That approach continues to find its advocates up till today, notably in the 1991 work of R. Achenbach, *Israel zwischen Verheissung und Gebot* (Frankfurt a. M., 1991) whose very subtitle, *Literarkritische Untersuchungen zu Deuteronomium 5-11* puts one in mind of the title and focus of Steuernagel's study of almost a century before. Over against the use of the *Numeruswechsel* as a key for reconstructing the formation-history of Deuteronomy as first systematically applied by Staerk and Steuernagel stands the understanding of the phenomenon as a rhetorical device of a single author. This alternative approach to the *Numeruswechswel* was put forward already a few years after the appearance of Staerk's and Steuernagel's monographs by e.g., A. Bertholet and E. König. More recently, it has been championed especially by N. Lohfink and G. Braulik.[21] It is with this alternative approach that the jubilarian aligns himself as well in the numerous references which he makes to the *Numeruswechsel* throughout the three published volumes of his POT commentary where he brings the feature into connection with the numerical patterns of Deuteronomy which are his primary concern. In one of these references, Labuschagne announces that the whole problematic of the change of number will receive a systematic treatment in the final volume of his commentary.[22] As one who spent several years of his youth laboring over the history of the question, the author looks forward with great anticipation to the appearance of this discussion and the enlightenment it will undoubtedly offer.

---

[21] For a discussion of the treatment of the *Numeruswechsel* phenomenon by the four above authors, see my dissertation cited in n. 20, Vol. I, 327-54; III, 935-46, 1058-65.

[22] C.J. Labuschagne, *Deuteronomium deel IA* (POT; Nijkerk, 1987), 63.

THE DANGERS OF DEUTERONOMY
A PAGE FROM THE RECEPTION HISTORY OF THE BOOK

FERDINAND E. DEIST
Stellenbosch, South Africa

This contribution is about the reception of concepts and portions from the book of Deuteronomy by the majority of South African Dutch Reformed theologians from about 1930 to 1960, the time during which the policy of apartheid was invented, formulated and defended.[1] It is hoped that this tragic history will encourage biblical scholars to become critically aware of the profound influence exerted on the "meaning" of a biblical passage by their hermeneutical presuppositions, epistemological choices, and their historicity as readers of texts.

In their discussion of reception aesthetics Fokkema & Ibsch[2] remark that, since reception aesthetics accepts the mutability of an aesthetic object, it "cannot avoid discussing problems of historical and cultural relativity, [and] taking a stand on the questions of understanding and the 'fusion of horizons'..." One's own epoch, they assert, is an essential element in the constitution of the aesthetic object. This insight has also been emphasized by deconstructionists.[3] Ideology criticism would share these views. But being aware as it is of readers' vested interests in the meanings generated in the reading process, it would be sceptical of the "neutrality" and harmlessness of the input of the relevant "epoch" and "historicity" in the production of meaning. Accordingly, knowledge of the historical circumstances and mind-set of pro-apartheid readers of Deuteronomy could enhance insight not only into the contribution of their historicity to their construction of Deuteronomy's meaning (their *aesthesis*), but also uncover their interests in the meanings generated (their *ideology*).

---

[1] All translations from Afrikaans documents are my own.

[2] D. Fokkema & E. Ibsch, *Theories of Literature in the Twentieth Century* (New York, 1979), 137-138.

[3] J. Degenaar, "Deconstruction - the celebration of language", *The Reader and Beyond. Theory and Practice in South African Reception Studies*, edit. B.C. Lategan (Pretoria, 1992), 204-205.

1. *The readers*

1.1 *The socio-economic background*

As a consequence of, *inter alia*, the devastation brought about by the
Anglo-Boer War (1899-1902), the influence of the two World Wars,
prolonged droughts, epidemics, and the great depression, the period
1920 – 1950 saw the rapid urbanisation of the Afrikaans speaking
section of the South African population.[4] During the decade 1936 –
1946 the number of urban Dutch Reformed congregations in the
provinces of Transvaal and Natal increased by 51% and 68% respectively, while the number of church members in the Johannesburg area
increased by 111% in roughly the same period.[5] According to an
investigation conducted in 1945 in the urban area of Boksburg only
16% of the resident Dutch Reformed members had been born in the
town. The rest migrated there from rural areas.[6] Between 1926 and
1936 the number of Afrikaans speaking people earning a living from
agriculture increased by a mere 2%, while the number employed by
industries increased by 46%.[7]

Afrikaners, who had for centuries been independent farmers and land
owners with a culture of their own suddenly became urban day labou-
rers and found themselves in a foreign culture and at the bottom of the
social ladder. Already in 1935 Afrikaans speaking people made up
85% of the unskilled labour force.[8] By 1945 only 9% of them owned
property in the towns and cities, compared to 71% of their families in
rural areas[9], while 10 000 Afrikaans speaking children lived in orphan-
ages, 6000 were in foster-care, 50% of the aged had no pension and
300 000 families were classified as "poor whites". Family life started
falling apart and the number of divorces, something seldomly heard of
earlier, soared while cases of alcohol abuse and family neglect
increased dramatically. Most of these people adopted an attitude of
resignation, while some tried to imitate their much more successful

---

[4] P.A.H. Grobler, [Letter to the Editor], *Die Kerkbode* 26 June 1949, 1539;
EDITORIAL, "Die Boerplaas bedreig", *Die Kerkbode* 21 June 1950, 1259.

[5] P. du Toit, "Ons Jaarboek van 1950", *Die Kerkbode* 1 February 1950, 205.

[6] J.H. Roos, "'n Kerklik-sosiologiese opname van 'n stadsgemeente", *Die
Kerkbode* 20 February 1946, 171-172.

[7] P.J. Pienaar, "Die armblankevraagstuk nie armesorg nie", *Die Kerkbode* 22
September 1943, 254-255.

[8] J.R. Albertyn, "Die Kerk en sy stadsmense", *Die Kerkbode* 10 May 1950,
928-930.

[9] J.R. Albertyn, "Kerklike sensus van Augustus", *Die Kerkbode* 2 January 1946,
10-11.

English speaking neighbours.[10] Large numbers started deserting the church.[11] No wonder Albertyn found that the total character of the Afrikaans community was rapidly changing[12] and complained (1946: 10-11) that the Dutch Reformed Church was no longer the "Boerekerk" (Church of the Boers).[13]

The Afrikaans Churches were unprepared for this sudden change, but realised that something had to be done for their members. In 1949 the regular column "Uit die Transvaal" ("From the Transvaal") of the official Dutch Reformed weekly, *Die Kerkbode*, urged the Dutch Reformed Church to ensure that social justice be done to these people and to protest against all oppressive measures putting them at a disadvantage.[14]

This "disadvantage" refers mainly to an influx of black people into the cities, resulting in their competing with Afrikaans speaking people for low cost unskilled employment, especially on the mines. Moreover, the black migrants were also eager to get an academic education. For example, by 1949 black pupils already outnumbered white pupils by nearly two to one.[15] Afrikaans speaking people felt themselves threatened by these circumstances and insisted that the principle of "no equalization" (*geen gelykstelling*) between black and white people had to be applied.[16]

1.2 Self-understanding

By the time Afrikaans speaking people were being forced from rural areas into the towns and cities the idea of "no equalization" referred to in the previous paragraph had already had a long history behind it.

The Boers who in the nineteenth century's Great Trek left the Cape Colony for the Orange Free State and the Transvaal understood themselves as God's chosen people escaping out of Egypt (British oppression) to the Promised Land.[17] The names of rivers and towns along

---

[10] Anonymous, "Toestande van die stadskerk", *Die Kerkbode* 28 November 1945, 274-275.

[11] F.J. Minnaar, "Wat haper daar aan ons stadsgemeentes?", *Die Kerkbode* 18 June 1947, 1162-1163.

[12] J.R. Albertyn, "Uiterstes ontmoet mekaar. Instroming van stadsidees in ons plattelandse lewe", *Die Kerkbode* 25 January 1950, 144-146.

[13] J.R. Albertyn, "Kerklike sensus van Augustus", 10.

[14] Anonymous, "Die Kerk en die arbeider", *Die Kerkbode* 4 May 1949, 1066-1067.

[15] Editorial, "Die Kleurlingonderwys", *Die Kerkbode* 20 June 1956, 1124.

[16] Cf. F.E. Deist, "Aufstieg und Niedergang der Apartheid", *Politische Studien* (Sonderheft 2), 1986, 19-30.

[17] F.A. van Jaarsveld, *Lewende Verlede* (Pretoria, 1961), 234-235.

their route today still reflect that belief: Bethlehem, River Jordan, Jericho, Nylstroom ("River Nile"), etc. On this route the Bible served as their source of self-interpretation and information regarding their future and fate. Consequently, the indigenous black people among whom they now found themselves represented for them the Canaanites who served foreign gods and with whom "Israel" should not intermarry.[18] Already in 1858 this attitude resulted in a clause in the constitution of the *Zuid-Afrikaanse Republiek* stating that "the people" ("het volk") did not want "gelijkstelling" (equalization) of black and white, neither in the Church nor in the State." As a result the Reformed Church (Gereformeerde Kerk) some twenty years later found it necessary to remind congregations to ensure that blacks and whites were not educated or allowed to conduct church services in the same buildings.[19]

This spontaneous, though naive, identification with Israel was romanticized,[20] endorsed and encouraged during the fourth and fifth decades of the twentieth century.[21] Consider, for instance, the parallel Kritzinger[22] drew in a sermon on occasion of a commemoration of the Day of the Covenant (16 December) between ancient Israel and the Afrikaans speaking section of the population.

---

[18] Lion Cachet, a popular Dutch minister of the time who later became a teacher at the Reformed Church's theological seminary, wrote in this regard, "The Boers want to guard against the mixing of which Moses and Joshua warned the children of Israel. Consequently, the Boers, surrounded by black people (*kaffers*, i.e. "heathens") keep themselves apart, so that a Boer-Kaffir bastard is a rare sight". (Quoted by T.J. Kotzé, "Eerbiedige bewaring en navolging van die ideale van ons voorgeslag - op die pad van Suid-Afrika", *Die Gerefomeerde Vaandel* 6/11, 1938, 332.)

[19] W.J. van der Merwe, "Die sendinggesindheid van die Voortrekkers", *Die Kerkbode* 23 January 1935, 168-170.

[20] For a modern example of an overevaluation by posterity of their ancestors' knowledge of and insight into the Bible, see M.E. Marty, "The Bible and American cultural values", *New Theology Review* 2/1 (1989), 6-15.

[21] For examples, see J.A. Loubser, *The Apartheid Bible* (Cape Town, 1987), 25.

[22] Kritzinger, *Die Kerkbode* 1936, 163-165.

Israel	Afrikaners
Went from Palestine to Egypt	Went from Europe to Africa
Suffered under foreign rulers	Suffered under British rulers
Escaped from Egypt to Canaan	Escaped from the Cape Colony to the north
Considered the nations as numerous and strong	Considered black people as numerous and strong
Miraculously received a new land	Miraculously received a new land
Made a covenant with God	Made a covenant with God
Erected memorial stones	Erected the Cilliers memorial church
Fathers recounted their history to posterity	Fathers recounted their history to posterity

Dutch Reformed ministers prided themselves that their Church was the custodian of this ancient tradition. In a published sermon of the 1930's on 1 Kings 20:23 the Rev. C. R. Kotzé said,[23]

> Our ancestors were against equalization, the mixing of blood and mixed marriages. *Our church is steadfast and upholds the colour line* ... But other churches are for equalization ... and we are being mocked and blamed for our convictions. *Here in the church we are strong and we uphold our convictions. But in the field of commerce, where our young people are in need and looking for employment, they are forced to work shoulder to shoulder with black people. They (i.e. the liberalists) fight us on the plains.*

1.3 *The hermeneutical background*

Groenewald is correct when he says, "After 1900 South Africans (i.e. Afrikaans speakers - F.E.D.) found a spiritual home in the Free University of Amsterdam. Up to this day it remained the only true home for our young theologians. This university has consequently exerted a strong influence on the theological climate in our land, especially since it had professors of exceptional format ... [like] A. Kuyper and H. Bavinck."[24] The influence on Afrikaner thinking of Kuyper's cultural philosophy, with its emphasis on "the people" ("het volk"), cannot be overestimated, although one should hasten to add that it was a thoroughly reduced and *adapted* Kuyper that featured in South African publications of the time. That is why Groenewald[25] was proud of the Reformed theology developed by South Africans, "a theology that emerged from our own soil and the history of our own people" and

---

[23] M.H. van Zijl-Kotzé, *Die Bybel en ons Volkstryd* (Bloemfontein, 1955), 4.
[24] E.P. Groenewald, "Die stand van die teologiese wetenskap in Suid-Afrika", *Die Kerkbode* 12 March 1952, 508.
[25] *op. cit.*, 509.

Erasmus[26] could say of the South African brand of Calvinism that it
neither bore the mark of importation, nor wished to imitate the Calvinism of other countries or to voice any overseas form of Calvinism, but,
adapted to the national temperament, history and circumstances,
followed its own "Boer" road to prevent "our people from anglicization
and interbreeding".

"Boer Calvinism"[27] was a mixture of Kuyperian cultural philosophy[28] and Princetonian fundamentalism[29] both of which had their
foundation in common sense realism,[30] and could perhaps best be
described with Shepard's term "neotraditionalism".[31] While Kuyper
insisted that political decisions as well as true scholarship should be
founded on *Christian* insight and Christian insight on *the Bible*, the
fundamentalists heavily emphasized the "plain sense" of the Bible.[32]
Machen, for instance, was particularly suspicious of any form of
"interpretation": The human mind should not be allowed to *impose* its
categories on reality and Scripture, but should merely discover the
truth that was revealed by the plain sense of things, events and Scripture.[33] *Anybody* perceiving society and reading the Bible in its plain

---

[26] D.F. Erasmus, "Ons eie Calvinisme", *Die Gereformeerde Vaandel* 14/11,
1946, 11-12.

[27] A term coined by the Calvinists themselves. See D.G. Franzen, "Die A.N.S en
die Boerevolksbeweging", *Wapenskou* 3/3, September 1942, 3.

[28] See E.E. Ericson, "Abraham Kuyper: cultural critic", *Calvin Theological
Journal* 22 (1987), 210-227.

[29] F.E. Deist, "Notes on the context and hermeneutic of Afrikaner civil religion",
Missionalia 18/1 (1990), 124-139; "Objektiewe Skrifuitleg? Kanttekeninge by
Skrifuitleg in die Ned Geref Kerk 1930-1990", *HTS* 47/2 (1991), 367-385.

[30] For a discussion, see W.S. van Heerden, *Die interpretasie van die boek Jona
in die Nederduitse Gereformeerde Kerk*, Unpublished D.Th. thesis, University of
South Africa, 1988, 147-174. Also P. Helm, "Thomas Reid, common sense and
Calvinism", *Rationality in the Calvinian tradition*, edit. H. Hart, J. Van derHoeven
& N. Wolterstorff (Lanham, 1983), 71-92.

[31] W. Shepard, "'Fundamentalism' Christian and Islamic", *Religion* 17 (1987),
355-378. As a result of its politically involved nature "Boer Calvinism" had much
in common with the kind of radicalism Shepard ascribes to Islamic neotraditionalism.

[32] The strongest fundamentalist influence on the Dutch Reformed Church was
exerted by people like Machen, Wilson, Warfield and Hodge, whose writings were
eagerly studied. See, in this regard, J.H. Moorhead, "Joseph Addison Alexander:
common sense, romanticism and biblical criticism at Princeton", *Journal of
Presbyterian History* 53/1 (1975), 51-65. However, Kuyperian theology was not
altogether free from fundamentalist suppositions. See R.B. Gaffin, "Old Amsterdam
and inerrancy", *WTJ* 44 (1982), 250-289 and *WTJ* 45 (1983), 219-272.

[33] One of the major proponents of common sense philosophy, T. Reid, *An
inquiry into the human mind* (Chicago, 1813 [Reprint 1970]), 4, would say, "Conjectures and theories are the creatures of men, and will always be found very unlike
the creatures of God. If we would know the works of God, we must consult

sense could thus know the will of God directly, that is, without prior "interpretation".[34] If Laudan is correct that rationality has much to do with people's "most preferred intuitions",[35] their circumstances convinced these theologians that a common sense based hermeneutic was the only really *rational* position to hold.[36] Any effort at "interpreting" either their circumstances or the Bible, and especially any critical handling of the Bible, consequently became taboo.[37] Small wonder, then, that Malan,[38] appealing to Kuyper's rejection of the spirit of revolution and emphasis on authority, argued strongly against the "revolutionary spirit" of historical criticism.[39] The South African brand of Calvinism became, to employ a term coined by Troffler,[40]

---

themselves with attention and humility, without daring to add any thing of ours to what they declare. A just interpretation of nature is the only sound and orthodox philosophy: whatever we add of our own, is apocryphal, and of no authority."

[34] For a contemporary example of the same conviction, see L.J. Hoppe, "The Bible tells me so", *BTB* 29 (1991), 278-283.

[35] B. Laudan, *Progress and its problems* (Berkeley, 1977). A. van Schalkwyk, "Wêreldbeeld en kulturele omgewing", *Die Gereformeerde Vaandel* 20 (1952), 127-135, expressed a similar view in explaining why suddenly in the nineteenth century evolutionism was acceptable: "a doctrine is only seized upon ... when it supplies some great need, emotional as well as intellectual, in the life of man."

[36] T. Reid, *Philosophical Works*, Vol I (Hildesheim, 1895 [Reprographic offprint 1967]), 425 would argue, "It is absurd to conceive that there can be any opposition between reason and Common Sense. It is indeed the first-born of Reason.... We ascribe to reason two offices, or two degrees. The first is to judge of things self-evident; the second to draw conclusions that are not self-evident from those that are. The first of these is the province, and the sole province, of Common Sense; and, therefore, it coincides with reason in its whole extent, and is only another name for one branch or degree of reason." For a discussion of Reid's concept of rationality, see N. Wolterstorff, "Thomas Reid on rationality". For the effect of common sense rationality on Calvinism, see P. Helm, "Thomas Reid, common sense and Calvinism", *Rationality in the Calvinian tradition*, edit. H. Hart, J. Van derHoeven & N. Wolterstorff (Lanham, 1983), 43-69.

[37] In his "Intellectual powers" T. Reid (*Philosophical Works*, Vol I [Hildesheim, 1895, Reprographic offprint 1967], 234-236) maintains, "[W]hatever is built upon conjecture is improperly called science, for conjecture may beget opinion, but cannot produce knowledge.... Although some conjectures may have a considerable degree of probability, yet it is ... uncertain. ...What can fairly be deduced from facts duly observed or sufficiently attested, is genuine and pure; it is the voice of God, and no fiction of human imagination."

[38] D.G. Malan, "Waar dryf ons heen?", *Het Zoeklicht* 4 (1926), 18.

[39] In 1932 the Dutch Reformed Church fired professor J. du Plessis because of his advocacy of historical criticism. This trial made it clear that the Dutch Reformed Church preferred its brand of Calvinism with its foundation in common sense realism to any critical theory.

[40] On this term and its relation to reception of literary texts, see C. Malan, "Metodologiese aspekte van navoring oor literêre en teaterresepsie: Die geval Poppie", *The Reader and Beyond. Theory and Practice in South African Reception*

the "gatekeeper" guarding against the reception of the Bible in any sense other than in its "common sense" meaning. Moreover, alongside the socio-economic conditions Calvinism itself became an intermediary[41] text exercising censure on the meanings constructed from Bible reading. There was no way in which critique would be allowed to question the application of a naively interpreted Bible to the common sense interpretation of Afrikaners' socio-political situation.

2. A naive realist reading of Deuteronomy

2.1 The basis for a naive reading of Deuteronomy

2.1.1 A shared sense of promise

The book of Deuteronomy presents itself as Moses' final address to the Israelites just before they moved into the promised land. Its Afrikaans readers of the 1930's and 1940's also viewed themselves as an oppressed people on the verge of a new era. Sermons and official publications of the Dutch Reformed Church kept reminding them of this *kairos*. De Beer wrote, "The 1938-festivities [accompanying the symbolic ox-wagon trek commemorating the Great Trek of 1838] reflect the people's urge for unity... Can we afford not to use this God-given opportunity to establish one people's church (volkskerk)?"[42] In an editorial under the heading "We are rapidly coming of age" the editor of *Die Kerkbode* (5 February 1936) wrote, "We already have our own flag, our own anthem with its own melody, our own Bible and shortly also our own hymn book. We produce our own literature and we are commemorating the history of our people with monuments." The suggestion is clear: the day of complete equality and liberation is around the corner. In a sermon delivered just before the election of 1943 the Rev. Kotzé pleaded, "O, Afrikanerdom, if you would only recognize on this your day the things that will serve your peace! ... This is the day of decision. Will there be a white South Africa for our children? ... *This will be decided today.*"[43]

2.1.2 A shared sense of anxiety

In spite of the promising future suggested by its introduction the

Studies, edit. B.C. Lategan (Pretoria, 1992), 13-27.

[41] See C. Malan, *ibid.*

[42] D.F.B. de Beer, "Kan ons die drie Afrikaanse Kerke verenig?", *Die Kerkbode* 15 February 1939, 298.

[43] H. van Zijl-Kotzé, *op. cit.*, 66.

content of Deuteronomy reflects what Stuhlman fittingly describes as "a great deal of *internal* anxiety and a marked sense of vulnerability".[44] Afrikaners, too, experienced their situation as dangerous. A professor of theology warned against "the powerful temptation of intellectualism, modernism, humanism, personalism and moralism" of his day furthered by the dangerous currents of "rationalism, naturalism, materialism, Baalism, atheism, totalitarism, and communism",[45] a list often occurring in writings of the time. The Afrikaner theologians were anxious about all these threatening ideologies. That they also experienced their own situation as vulnerable, will be understandable in view of the exposition of their socio-economic situation presented above.

2.1.3 A shared need for strict obedience to God's prescripts

Like the Moses character in Deuteronomy, Afrikaners were convinced that their only hope of survival in this hostile, though promising, environment lay in them strictly keeping God's commandments, which they found in the Bible and to which they turned for direction. The most important and instructive access for ordinary people to these prescripts was the expositions of the Bible given to them by their preachers and leaders. And A.B. du Preez, a professor of theology, assured them that only an "objective" reading of the Bible would provide them with the correct answer to their questions:[46]

> We cannot and may not propagate the policy of apartheid or any other policy on mere "practical grounds" ... This would boil down to petty, selfish attempts at self-preservation based on human considerations foreign to the will of God. So completely should we subject ourselves to God's revealed will that, should it become clear from Scripture that complete equality and mixing of blood, even the extinction of the white population, is the will of God, we should accept it with our whole heart and demonstrate the moral courage to acknowledge that the idea of apartheid had been born from sinful unbrotherliness, and then oppose as contrary to the will of God every effort to give effect to apartheid.

While the boldness of the professor's statement most probably flowed from the fact that he knew in advance that he would be able to present

---

[44] L. Stuhlman, "Encroachment in Deuteronomy: an analysis of the social world of the D code", *JBL* 109 (1990), 626. This feature of the book is overlooked by G. Braulik, "Die gesellschaftliche Innerseite der Kirche", *BK* 43 (1988), 134-139, who produces a fairly romantic interpretation of Deuteronomy.

[45] D. Lategan, "Toespraak by die opening van die Teologiese Seminarie 26 Februarie 1937", *Die Gereformeerde Vaandel* 5/3 (1937), 87-89; Idem, "Die Gees van Elia", *Die Gereformeerde Vaandel* 12/3 (1944), 10-14.

[46] A.B. du Preez, "Die Skrif en rasseverhoudinge", *Die Kerkbode* 15 March 1953, 502.

a common sense reading of the Bible that would support apartheid, ordinary, fairly uneducated people, who accepted the Bible as their norm for moral conduct, would be convinced by the appeal to objectivity in this argument. Moreover, their preachers constantly reminded them, "what is ethically correct, must be possible sociologically"[47] or, "according to the Calvinist view of life and the world we maintain that the light of God's Word should also shine on racial theory in order to give us direction".[48] It was in showing the "objective ethical way" and in "shedding its light" on the relevant racial theory that the naive reading of the book of Deuteronomy played an enormous role in the establishment of the policy of apartheid.

2.2 *Appealing themes and concepts in the book of Deuteronomy*

2.2.1 The notion of a divinely instituted natural order

In Deuteronomy 32:8 the authors seem to have demythologised an earlier concept[49] according to which Elyon, in dividing the nations according to the number of gods, allotted Israel to Yahweh. The result of the editorial reworking does not make very good sense, but retains the idea of a divinely instituted division of nations and a special, pre-ordained and unbreakable bond between Yahweh and Israel. These ideas were strengthened by the concept of Israel's special calling (14:2), which made them different from all other nations (4:37-38; 7:7-8; 10:14-15).

These ideas supplied the apartheid readers of Deuteronomy with the notion of divinely ordained divisions among nations that directly conflicted with the idea of "internationalism". If God separated the nations, then no human being had the right to unite them.[50] In expounding the "Scriptural" foundation of the policy of apartheid the popular Reformed theologian J.D. du Toit (Totius) wrote with reference to

---

[47] Anonymous, "Die invloed van die Kerk op ons volkslewe", *Die Kerkbode* 13 November 1935, 951.

[48] L.A.D. Roux, "Die rassevraagstuk", *Die Gereformeerde Vaandel* 15/4, 1947, 14.

[49] That is, in an effort to reinterpret Elyon's sharing out of the nations among the gods during a meeting of the divine council. See P.D. Miller, "Cosmology and world order in the Old Testament. The divine council as cosmic-political order", *HBT* 9/2 (1987), 53-78.

[50] See, for instance, J.H. Kritzinger, a professor of Old Testament at the University of Pretoria, in an article in *Op die Horison* of March 1947, 22-31, and E.P. Groenewald, a professor of New Testament at the same institution in his "Apartheid en Voogdyskap in die lig van die Heilige Skrif", *Regverdige Rasse-Apartheid*, edit. G. Cronjé (Stellenbosch, 1947), 52-53.

Deuteronomy 22:9-11:[51]

> Firstly, what God united, no one may divide. This is the basis of our plea for
> unity among Afrikaners. ...Secondly, we may not unite what God has divided.
> The council of God is realized in pluriformity ... Consequently we do not want
> any equalization or bastardization.

Deuteronomy's suggestion of divinely ordained territories for various
nations supplied the motivation for Calvinists' insistance that other
people should also be urged to become obedient to God (as Calvinists
understood his will). Venter[52] explained:

> In society, so Calvin, there is a clear God-willed ordering system uniting right
> with responsibility... Individuals do not live for themselves. As members of the
> ordered whole they ought to apply their talents to the honour of God and the
> prosperity of the whole. Calvin does not understand "the whole" to refer to
> humanity, also not (like Luther) to the church, but to the *populus*, the *people* ...
> The idea of an organism is very much in his mind here. It is to this idea of an
> organism that Calvin links the principle of authority.

Every such organism (i.e. ethnic group) should consequently be
allowed to choose a governmental system that would best fit its
character and be "in accordance with the principles of Scripture".[53]
Since common sense observation (confirmed by Scripture) showed that
every "people" (i.e. ethnic group) exhibited characteristics distinguishing it from other peoples, Calvinists insisted on separate *governmental*
systems for each group. Loots wrote[54] (my emphasis),

> From this *reformed principle* of separate, independent groups within the kingdom
> [of God] flows our policy of apartheid in church and state. This is a universal
> principle (*lewensbeginsel*) which was, according to *Scripture and Nature*,
> instituted by the great Creator and which the Afrikaner people and the Church of
> the Boers have to defend to the utmost, especially against modern liberalism's
> policy of equalization.

---

[51] J.D. du Toit, "Die godsdienstige grondslag van ons rassebeleid, *Inspan* 4/3
(1944), 7-17.

[52] E.A. Venter, "Die moderne kapitalisme", *Die Gereformeerde Vaandel* 14/9
(1946), 7.

[53] E.A. Venter, "Gedagtes oor 'n Christelike staatsleer", *Die Gereformeerde
Vaandel* 9/12 (1941), 358. C.R. Kotzé, "Kalvinisme en politiek", *Die Gereformeerde Vaandel* 3/9 (1935), 272 would say, "God in his providence gives to every
people that form of government which fits that people". However, Calvinists had to
reject liberal democracy. In their view this system of government was founded on
the *unscriptural* principles of revolutionary lawlessness and the sovereignty of the
people which subject the individual conscience to the arbitrary decisions of the
masses (so E.A. Venter, "Gedagtes oor 'n Christelike staatsleer", 359; "Die totale
staat", *Die Kerkbode* 27 April 1949, 1400-1401; cf, also C.R. Kotzé, "Kalvinisme
en die politiek", *Die Gereformeerde Vaandel* 3/11, 1935, 335).

[54] P.J. Loots in a letter to the editor, *Die Kerkbode* 18 August 1957, 527.

And Potgieter added, "Like Kuyper opposed the ideal of uniformity of the French Revolution we are being called upon today to counter the slogans of the Liberalists who are the children of this Revolution. Over against their self-fabricated idea of equality we have to put Scriptural pluriformity".[55]

2.2.2 The legality of discrimination

Whether or not one accepts Weinfeld's dating of the book of Deuteronomy his analysis of the differences between Priestly and Deuteronomic views of Israel's identity remains valid.[56] He says, "According to Deuteronomy, the laws of the Torah apply only to the true Israelites, that is members of the Israelite nation by blood and race, whereas the resident alien is not deemed to be a true Israelite ..." It was these authors who coined the description of Israel as a holy and elected *people* (*'am*).[57] Consequently, while the priestly writers distinguished between "natives" and "foreigners", the social polarity in Deuteronomy is between "brother" and "foreigner" in the same geographical area.[58]

Deuteronomy's special brand of social polarity allows, further, for legal discrimination between "brother" and "foreigner". It is, for instance, not permissible for a "brother" to eat something that died of itself, but permissible to give such meat to the "foreigner" (Deut. 14:21; compare, however, Lev. 17:15). Special provision is also made for the poor *Israelite* (Deut. 15:7-15). While the law allows for the charging of interest on loans to foreigners, it forbids the same to be done in the case of "brothers" (Deut. 15:3; 23:19-20).[59] The law protects the human dignity of brothers, but does not specify what the situation has to be in regard of foreigners (Deut. 24:10-13). Stuhlman[60] correctly observes that D attempted to produce a programme in

---

[55] F.J.M. Potgieter, *Veelvormige Ontwikkeling: die Wil van God* (Bloemfontein, 1958).

[56] M. Weinfeld, *Deuteronomy and the Deuteronomic School* (Oxford, 1972), 225-232.

[57] See E.A. Speiser, "People and nation of Israel", *JBL* 79 (1960), 157-163.

[58] H. Eilberg-Schwartz, "Creation and classification in Judaism: From Priestly to rabbinic conceptions, *History of Religions* 26 (1986/7), 357-381. For a wider perspective on Old Testament attitudes towards other cultures, see E. B. Smick, "Old Testament cross-culturation: Paradigmatic or enigmatic?" *JETS* 32 (1989), 3-16.

[59] Cf. M.L. Chancey, "Debt easement in Israelite history and tradition", *The Bible and the Politics of Exegesis. Essays in Honor of Norman K. Gottwald on his sixty-fifth birthday*, edit. D. Jobling, P.L. Day & G. T. Shepard (Cleveland, 1991), 127-139.

[60] *ibid.*

which the integrity of Israel's inner boundaries is (re)established and clarified in order to protect insiders from potentially harmful outsiders, especially *indigenous* outsiders.[61]

Given their own tradition, self-understanding and socio-economic position Afrikaans speaking theologians easily identified with these sentiments. Appealing to Scripture's "teaching" on "the *inequality of people*" Venter[62] said, "It not even is humiliating for a whole people ... to be in a subservient position to another people for many centuries". Because of these sentiments Calvinists were as a rule feverishly against capitalism and for socialism. "Modern capitalism," wrote Venter, "derives its principles from the French Revolution... Every effort towards reforming the socio-economic situation should, in my opinion, go back in history to the time before that revolution interrupted the historical continuity, that is, to the time before the liberalist degeneration had set in."[63] It is therefore not surprising that leaders of the people's movement of the time openly encouraged some form of socialism. C.H.J. de Wet[64] said the capitalist system had to be uprooted and destroyed and advocated a system of "limited private initiative". When the Nationalist Party came to power in 1948 a form of socialism close to these ideals, but with a strong bias towards the "brothers", was instituted.

2.2.3 Prohibition against "mixing" with other groups

Deuteronomy is explicit in its prohibition of Israelites mixing with the indigenous people (7:3-4).[65] It furthermore prohibits the "mixing" of a

---

[61] For a further development of this interpretation, see F.E. Deist, *Revolution and reinterpretation. Chapters from the history of Israel*, edit. F.E. Deist & J.H. le Roux (Cape Town, 1987), 91-97; S.D. McBride, "Polity of the covenant people: the Book of Deuteronomy", *Interpretation* 41 (1987), 229-244; E. Nicholson, "Deuteronomy's vision of Israel", *Storia e Tradizioni di Israeli. Scritti in onore di J. Alberto Soggin*, edit. D. Garrone & F. Israel (Brescia, 1991), 191-203. It is difficult to concede to the view of J.M. Cohen, "Polarization in the Mosaic period", *Dor le Dor* 16 (1987/8), 263-266 that Deuteronomy seeks a kind of middle way between avoiding contact with foreign cultures and compromise. The boundaries between "brother" and "foreigner" are drawn too clearly for such a mild interpretation.

[62] E.A. Venter, "Die Apartheidsvraagstuk", *Die Gereformeerde Vaandel* 18/1 (1950), 9.

[63] E.A. Venter, "Die moderne kapitalisme", *Die Gereformeerde Vaandel* 14/9 (1946), 7.

[64] C.H.J. de Wet, "'n Skoon republiek en die weg daarheen", *Wapenskou* 3/3, September 1942, 45.

[65] For a perspective on the Jewish interpretation of these laws, see S.J.D. Cohen, "From the Bible to Talmud: the prohibition of intermarriage", *HAR* 7 (1983), 23-39. For a literary analysis of Deut. 7 as a whole and the place of this chapter in its

number of other entities of different kinds (22:5. 9-11). Whether or not Deuteronomy really or only ideally regulated Israelite life[66] this kind of Deuteronomic legislation supplied the "scriptural basis" for the now scrapped clause in the South African immorality act prohibiting mixed marriages.[67] "The people" had to be kept "pure".

It is, of course, true that a book like Nehemiah (displaying similar sentiments) also played a major role in South African politics of the time. It is also true that many politicians, community leaders and quite a number from the ranks of the clergy were also heavily influenced by naked racist theories and sentiments of Nationalist-Socialism and some American sociological theories of the time. But while these sentiments formed part of their receptive framework the *religious* justification of much of the system of apartheid was founded on a naive reading and application of concepts from the book of Deuteronomy to the South African situation.[68] It was with explicit reference to Deuteronomy's concept of "purity" and its prohibition of mixing with foreign nations (Deut 7:1-6) that theologians insisted that they had "scriptural ground" for identifying Afrikaners with Israel[69] and could declare the notion of the "calling of the Afrikaner nation" a "scriptural truth".[70]

Of particular interest are Deuteronomy's graded tolerance in respect of the admittance of foreigners into the "congregation" and its rather harsh legislation regarding "bastards" (23:2-8). The translation of the Hebrew *mamzer* with "baster" ("bastard") in the old Dutch as well as the first Afrikaans translation of the Bible (1933) caused great harm in South Africa. Apart from the fact that the meaning of the Dutch term underwent a major shift in Afrikaans (i.e. from "a child born out of

---

wider literary context, see R.H. O'Connell, "Deuteronomy vii, 1-26: asymmetric concentricity and the rhetoric of the conquest", *VT* 42 (1992), 248-265.

[66] See, in this regard P.E. Dion, "Deuteronomy and the gentile world: a study in biblical theology", *Toronto Journal of Theology* 1 (1985), 200-221.

[67] E.P. Groenewald, "Apartheid en voogdyskap".

[68] Most Calvinists were convinced that the real reason for their political stance was obedience to the Bible. Even a philosopher of the format of H.G. Stoker (in an article in *Woord en Daad* of 17 August 1960) maintained that the Calvinists' refusal to give the vote to black people was "basically religious" and based on the Afrikaners' divine calling in South Africa. This statement merely echoed earlier views. Referring to the symbolic ox-wagon trek H.P. Blom, "Eeufeesoordenking", *Die Kerkbode* 22 February 1939, 365-368 said, "This centenary tells the Afrikaner that ... we have to trek away from everything that could bastardize the pure blood which, by the grace of God, flows in our veins and continue on the tracks of the Voortrekkers who, surrounded by black nations, kept their blood clean."

[69] H.J. Strauss, "Calvinistiese volksbeskouing", *Die Gereformeerde Vaandel* 15/4 (1947), 12.

[70] F.J.M. Potgieter, "'n Opspraakwekkende vergadering oor die C.N.O. op Stellenbosch", *Die Gereformeerde Vaandel* 17/4-5 (1949), 12.

wedlock" to "a child born from parents of differing races"), the translation itself is wrong.[71] However, ordinary people had no access to the
Hebrew text or Hebrew dictionaries and took biblical words in their
ordinary sense and as they were being explained by their preachers.
The consequence of this very unhappy translation was a particularly
strong resistence against church unity between "coloured" and "white"
churches.[72]

2.2.4 Ownership of the land

The authors of Deuteronomy persistently describe the Israelites as a
minority who, through divine miracles, came into possession of the
land (4:6-8, 32-34, 37-38; 7:17-18; 9:1-3). They do not seem to have
been bothered in the least by the fact that Canaan (according to the
Deuteronomistic picture) had been taken from the indigenous people by
force. Deuteronomy even prescribes the application of *cherem* (7:1-2)
and the destruction of the indigenous culture (7:5-8). For these authors
the Israelite possession of the land was the result of a divine act that
had to be accepted in faith and could only be celebrated. As such it
formed an integral part of common sense knowledge that could not be
questioned along ordinary historical lines.

South African Calvinists accepted their ownership of the whole land
with a similar matter-of-factness and viewed it as an indisputable
divine right. If anybody would query the validity of such a sweeping
presupposition their standard answer would be *contra principia negantem non est disputandum* or *contra principia negantem disputari non
potest*.[73] Consequently the (white) occupation of South African land
formerly possessed by other (black) people has not, until very recently,
become an issue in South Africa, while some circles still bluntly refuse
to discuss the matter.

3. *Conclusion*

It is, of course, easy to tear the sketched naive reading of the Bible
apart and to laugh or scorn at the people who facilitated this impos-

---

[71] Against J. Levitsky, "The illegitimate child (*mamzer*) in Jewish Law", *Dor le
Dor* 18/1 (1988/9), 6-12, although he is quite correct that later rabbinical interpretation took *mamzer* to refer to an illegitimate child.

[72] For examples, see A.J. Botha, *Evolusie van 'n Volksteologie: 'n historiese en
dogmatiese Ondersoek na die Samehang van Kerk en Afrikanervolk in die teologie
van die N.G. Kerk, met besondere verwysing na die apartheidsdenke wat daaruit
ontwikkel het.* D.Th. thesis, University of the Western Cape, 1984, 258.

[73] P. de B. Kock, "Calvinisme en etiek", *Die Gereformeerde Vaandel* 4/3 (1936),
85.

sible "fusion of horizons". But one has to bear in mind that the "gate-keeping" fundamentalist and Kuyperian inspired hermeneutic encouraged and prescribed precisely such a naive reading and prevented any critical investigation into the reading process or the text itself.[74] Moreover, the circumstances in which the readers found themselves made their approach and interpretation of the book appear self-evidently rational. From their perspective those who understood the Bible and the situation differently and kept referring to "interpretation" simply *had* to be biased by some or other ideology preventing them from seeing the obvious state of affairs or *must* have had a hidden agenda and *had* to be ostracized, because they obviously did not accept the authority of the plain sense of the Bible.

The great Wellhausen once said, "Verstehen ist noch lange nicht billigen". Accounting for the naive reading of Deuteronomy in support of apartheid does not excuse or mend the suffering and dehumanization of millions of South Africans over the last five decades. Many were locked up in prisons, many became exiles or died as a result of their resistance to the ideology. And even though the consequences of the two forms of resistance are not in the least comparable, there were also a number of academics, including Cas Labuschagne, who contributed their share in countering the naive reading and application of the Bible sketched above. Having attacked the very religious (or mythological) basis of the ideology they often had to bear the consequences of their own form of resistance.

The country is presently paying a very high price for apartheid. Moreover, as a result of the consequences of the ecclesiastical Biblical interpretation of the past sixty years outlined above, the Dutch Reformed Church has lost its credibility for and the Bible its appeal to many Afrikaans speaking and black people.[75] Apart from the loss of human dignity, this is perhaps our most costly spiritual loss. It will be an uphill battle to convince people that the Bible and the gospel of Jesus Christ have anything to contribute to their humanity and self-understanding. The whole exercise was an enormous disaster.

Perhaps Deuteronomy *does* contain dangerous ideologies and therefore might very well *be* a dangerous book. But the greater danger lies

---

[74] For a worrying modern revival of this stance, see D. Bergant, "Fundamentalists and the Bible", *New Theology Review* 1/2 (1988), 36-50; R. Oberforcher, "Fundamentalistische Textauslegung als Feindbild der historisch-kritischen Bibel-wissenschaft", *Una Sancta* 44 (1989), 200-207.

[75] For some of the cultural consequences of such a development, see E. A. Wcela, "Who do you say that they are? Reflections on the biblical audience today", *CBQ* 53 (1991), 1-17.

in its (uncritical) *readers*. In so far as the tragic history of South Africa and the still threatening national disaster have been the result of Biblical interpretation, this tragedy is the consequence not so much of wrong or dangerous exegetical *methods* (about which scholarship seems to be arguing for ever) but the result of a lack of critical self-awareness on the part of the *exegetes*. The South African experience points to the critical importance of a heavy emphasis on reader oriented hermeneutical approaches and the creation of a critical consciousness of the historicity of *any* piece of literature and *any* form of interpretation, and therefore on the ethics of interpretation.[76]

---

[76] See E. Schüssler Fiorenza, "The ethics of Biblical interpretation decentering Biblical scholarship", *JBL* 107 (1988), 3-17; S.E. Fowl, "The ethics of interpretation, or what's left after the elimination of meaning", *The Bible in three Dimensions*, edit. D.J.A. Clines (JSOTS 87; Sheffield, 1990), 379-398.

THE ONE GOD AND ALL ISRAEL
IN ITS GENERATIONS

KAREL A. DEURLOO

University of Amsterdam

I

The sample issue of the new journal *Biblical Interpretation* contains an interesting article by R. Rendtorff, describing the situation of Old Testament scholarship as a crisis of the paradigm: the former things have come to pass, the new things have not yet arrived. Rendtorff expresses his fears about the modern tendencies towards late dating of biblical texts and his hopes in connection with the synchronic approach which has come to manifest itself so broadly: "It is because here the text is taken as it is." It is important "to interpret the text as we have it before us, in its given form".[1] The meanings and messages of many texts from the Hebrew Bible do not depend on the information we have about their dating; we have to learn to take biblical texts seriously, from whatever period and in whatever context they appear. In many ways this article reminds us of what M. A. Beek wrote as early as 1968:[2] "The science of Introduction has come to a standstill", and therefore it is useful "to go back to the starting-points adopted by Buber and Rosenzweig": the letter R, "redactor", should be read as "Rabbenu". In his conclusion, however, Rendtorff is more outspoken

---

[1] R. Rendtorff, "The Paradigm Is Changing: Hopes—and Fears", *Biblical Interpretation*, Sample Issue (1992), 1-20. Oddly enough, he fails to include among the "Spätdatierer" the Old Testament scholar B. J. Diebner of Heidelberg who for many decades has been advocating a new approach of the science of Introduction in *DBAT*.

[2] M. A. Beek, "Verzadigingspunten en onvoltooide lijnen in het onderzoek van de oudtestamentische literatuur", *Vox Theologica* 28 (1968), 2-14. An English translation of this article will soon be published ("Saturation Points and Incomplete Lines in the Study of Old Testament Literature", in: M. Kessler [ed.], *Voices from Amsterdam. A Modern Tradition of Reading Biblical Narratives* [Semeia Studies; Atlanta, in the press]). The original article was written at the request of the editorial staff of *Vox Theologica* after the publication of several dissertations prepared under Beek's supervision that had provoked a discussion on method, described in: R. Oost, *Omstreden bijbeluitleg. Aspecten en achtergronden van de hermeneutische discussie rondom de exegese van het Oude Testament in Nederland* (Kampen, 1987).

than Beek was able to be at the time: "The paradigm is changing. I
believe it has changed already."[3] This is indeed clear from the publications of Labuschagne, especially from his commentary on Deuteronomy, not least because of his logotechnical structural analysis. In the
introduction to his commentary[4] he argues that the *literary* analysis of
the form and structure of a text should be clearly distinguished from
the *historical* research of the history of its development, in conformity
with the principles outlined by Schedl: 'vorerst vom diachronistischen
Aspekt des literarischen und geschichtlichen Werdeganges der Schrift
abzusehen und die Schrift als synchronistisch-literarische Ganzheit zu
erfassen".[5] At this point, Labuschagne's pupil Nobel has noted that
one should nevertheless be careful not to neglect the historical dimension of the text.[6] Accordingly Labuschagne not only promises to offer
a diachronic discussion at the end of his book, but he is aware throughout of the question of the dating of the final redaction of the text and
its historical *Sitz im Leben*. He even argues explicitly and with a fair
amount of detail that in connection with the special place of Deuteronomy within the great biblical narrative—the threshold situation before
the conquest of the land—one should give due consideration to historical reality. The book of Deuteronomy is the blueprint for a fresh start
for one of the waves of exiles returning to Palestine from Babylonia
and elsewhere. The priestly-prophetic author encourages them to set
foot on the land of their ancestors again.[7]

In this respect on the basis of the final redaction there is sufficient
reason to assume a first stage of "restoration" in the exile (e.g. in 4:
25-31; 30:1-10). This, however, only gives us a *terminus a quo*. The
redaction *may* have taken place around the end of the *Babylonian
Exile*.[8] At the same time one should realize that the commonly used
terms 'late exilic' or 'post-exilic' refer to this particular period of the
sixth century BCE. The *golah* or diaspora in itself has never come to
an end. On the contrary: in addition to the golah in Mesopotamia one
has to take into account a growing Egyptian diaspora in the centuries
following this period. The author of Deuteronomy may have been
consciously avoiding the name of Babel in his book. Only incidentally,
in connection with the figure of Balaam, does one find the name of
Aram Naharaim (23:4; cf. Num 22:5). Does "Egypt" have to serve as a

---

[3] Rendtorff, "Paradigm", 20.
[4] C. J. Labuschagne, *Deuteronomium* (POT; Nijkerk, I[A] and I[B] 1987, II 1990).
[5] C. Schedl, *Baupläne des Wortes. Einführung in die biblische Logotechnik* (Vienna, 1974), 28.
[6] H. Nobel, *Gods gedachten tellen. Numerieke structuuranalyse en de elf gedachten Gods in Genesis-2 Koningen* (Diss. Groningen, 1993), 40.
[7] Labuschagne, *Deuteronomium* I[A], 18ff.
[8] B. J. Diebner, NBL, *sub voce* Exil, Babylonisches.

pseudonym for Babel, on account of the literary "threshold situation" in Moab after the Exodus and prior to Moses' death?[9] Yet the place of the diaspora is described as covering a remarkably large area. The people is not only "cast into another land" (29:27), brought back in ships to Egypt (!) (27:68), but also scattered among the peoples (4:27), so that YHWH will have to gather them from there (30:3).

According to its setting, Deuteronomy is a book of restoration. But does this mean that the author can be characterized as "the spokesman of the deuteronomistic restoration movement"?[10] Does not the book rather give the impression of being an exponent of a rigorous *reform* movement? Where else is the motif of "YHWH alone" elaborated with such fervour and in such minute detail?

It is indeed YHWH alone who ties Israel together as one people in all its generations: the Exodus-generation, the "Moab"-generation and the future generations both in the land and in the diaspora.[11]

II

In the debate about monotheism set in motion especially by B. Lang,[12] it would be advisable not to focus exclusively on attributing the invention of monotheism to Israel's religious genius nor on provid-

---

[9] Th. Römer, *Israels Väter. Untersuchung zur Väterthematik im Deuteronomium und in der deuteronomistischen Tradition* (OBO 99; Freiburg-Göttingen, 1990), 393.

[10] Labuschagne, *Deuteronomium* I^A, 18. Early datings will increasingly have to be justified by external evidence. Cf. such recent publications as Th. L. Thompson, *Early History of the Israelite People. From the Written and Archeological Sources* (Leiden, 1992) and N. P. Lemche, *The Canaanites and Their Land. The Tradition of the Canaanites* (JSOTS 110; Sheffield, 1991). These were preceded by the contributions of B. J. Diebner and H. Schult in *DBAT* 8 and 10 (1975) and B. Zuber, *Vier Studien zu den Ursprüngen Israels* (OBO 9; Freiburg-Göttingen, 1976). On the basis of internal evidence one may assume the exilic period (6th century BCE) as a global *terminus a quo* for the final redaction of Deuteronomy. A *terminus ad quem* is more difficult to determine. With the necessary caution one might suggest the 3rd century, this being a period before the schism of the Proto-Samaritans. The peoples "hated" by Jesus Ben Sira (Sir 50:25—the Philistines must stand for the Hellenists—) are not yet mentioned in Deuteronomy. The absence of missionary features such as found in Deutero-Isaiah need not be an argument in favour of (problematic) earlier or (more plausible) later dating. It can also be attributed to a "school" or "denomination".

[11] "... alle Andersartigkeit und Eigentümlichkeit Israels ist nichts anderes als ein gekennzeichnet sein durch die Eigenart seines Gottes." J. Heller, *An der Quelle des Lebens* (Beiträge zur Erforschung des Alten Testaments und des antiken Judentums 10; Frankfurt-am-Main, 1988), 263.

[12] B. Lang (ed.), *Der einzige Gott. Die Geburt des biblischen Monotheismus* (Munich, 1981). B. Lang, *Monotheism and the Prophetic Minority* (SWBA 1; Sheffield, 1983).

ing modern confessions with a historical foundation.[13] From a religious-historical and theological point of view, the "incomparability of Yahweh"[14] implied in the Old Testament texts is of far greater interest.

On historical issues Labuschagne mostly agrees with Lang. He sketches briefly the development of an YHWH-alone-movement (Elijah, Elisha) struggling against Canaanite polytheism and resulting through Hosea and the "Deuteronomy-movement" in the final redaction of Deuteronomy during the last stage of the Babylonian exile: one people, one god, one land, one place of worship, one teacher, with one teaching tradition which is adequately and absolutely guaranteed (4:2).[15] Lang's argument, too, undeniably possesses a certain consistency, but one may wonder whether it is not merely a historian's construction built on the consistency that was woven into the texts. Veijola rightly observes that the texts adduced by Lang are "quellenkritisch zweifelhafter Natur".[16] Such sources Thompson qualifies as being not "earlier than the Persian period, and possibly as late as the Hellenistic period".[17] Everything that in conformity with the actual meaning of the texts is presented as "restoration" is really a radical "reform". Thus Diebner, instead of seeing the concept of "exile" as a historical category referring to a specific period of Israel's existence, would prefer to interpret it as a "sociological" category, namely as a general term for the Judaism of the centuries after the Persian period defining itself by the writings of the Old Testament, partly in opposition to the people who stayed behind in the land, the "Canaanites".[18] Not only the fervid polemics, but also the "Hear, Israel!" (6:4) can be explained from this background. In the syntactical and religious-

---

[13] E. Haag (ed.), *Gott, der einzige Zur Entstehung des Monotheismus in Israel* (QD 104; Freiburg-Basel-Vienna, 1985). Does dogmatic theology really profit from an early dating of YHWH's claim to exclusivity? At Von Rad's statement that "right from its beginning ... Yahwism's claim to excusivity did not tolerate peaceful co-existence with other cults", Lang notes: "Such a statement would be quite fitting for a Karl Barth, but can it be accepted as a historian's judgement?" (*Monotheism*, 16). In saying this, Lang incidentally displays a considerable lack of understanding of Barth's theology.

[14] C. J. Labuschagne, *The Incomparability of Yahweh in the Old Testament* (Leiden, 1966).

[15] Labuschagne, *Deuteronomium* I^A, 19f.

[16] T. Veijola, "Höre Israel! Der Sinn und Hintergrund von Deuteronomium vi 4-9", *VT* 42 (1992), 528-541: 541.

[17] Thompson, *History*, 356.

[18] B. J. Diebner, "Anmerkungen zur hermeneutischen Funktion des 'Exils' für das Verständnis des Kanons der Biblia Hebraica (TNK)", *DBAT* 26 (1989/90), 173-184: 178, 181.

historical debate over this confession I would agree with Labuschagne: YHWH's uniqueness can be traced back to his incomparability, and hence it can be inferred that he is the only God.[19] The interpretation of this is an essential matter. Despite the fact that *'ḥd* is a numeral, and despite connotations of polemics against polytheism and poly-yahwism Veijola argues convincingly that *yhwh 'ḥd* should be taken to mean not only "ein(er)", but also more specifically "(ein) einzig(er)". "Der Nominalsatz 'Jahwe ist einzig' will natürlich nicht im Sinne des absoluten Monotheismus verstanden werden, sondern im Horizont der vorangehenden, parallelen Aussage ('Jahwe ist unser Gott') schlicht besagen, daß Jahwe *unser* einziger Gott sei."[20] More fitting than the term "monotheism" is therefore "henotheism", "monolatry" being too weak, as all other "gods" pale beside YHWH.

Only one of the gods is mentioned by name besides the one God: the Baal of Peor (4:3). He is given a prominent place at the beginning of the speech in which Moses outlines the essential contents of the book. That which happened recently at the same location to the generation hearing Moses' speech is to be the introduction of what follows. His hearers are thus made to listen as eyewitnesses. Moses is speaking in the valley opposite Beth-peor (3:29), on the future site of his grave (34:7). This lends additional weight to the exemplum (1:22). By a reference to Joshua's seeing it with his own eyes (3:21), the people have just been reminded of what YHWH did to the two kings: so YHWH will also do to all the kingdoms in the land. Moses' hearers have seen with their own eyes what YHWH did near Baal-peor, destroying from among them all those who followed the Baal of Peor: in the same way their descendants will be destroyed if they act likewise in the land (4:26). Only by following YHWH—in the diaspora by turning back to YHWH on account of his mercy (4:30-31)—can Israel exist at all. Of this the Baal of Peor is the sign. Meanwhile the peoples

---

[19] Labuschagne, *Deuteronomium* I[B], 78. Cf. N. Lohfink, *Studien zum Deuteronomium und zur deuteronomistischen Literatur* II (SBA 12; Stuttgart, 1991), 42ff.

[20] Veijola, "Höre Israel", 533f. He enters into a discussion with, among others, N. Lohfink, G. Braulik, A. Dillmann, E. Nielsen ("Weil Jahwe unser Gott ein Jahwe ist", polemics against the local shrines), P. Höffken; see 529f. To these one may add: P. A. H. de Boer, "Some Observations on Deuteronomy vi 4 and 5", in: P. A. H. de Boer, *Selected Studies in Old Testament Exegesis* (ed. C. van Duin), OTS 27 (1991), 203-210. On the basis of e.g. Gen 40:5 (*the same night*), Gen 2:24 (*a close unity*), and 1 Kings 5:2 (*a whole day*) he advocates the following paraphrase: "(the term) *Yhwh our god* (means) *Yhwh on its own*" (210). Also J. Heller, "Sjema als fundament van 'monotheïsme'?", *ACEBT* 10 (1989), 37-44: 43. As if monotheism were the highest aim to be achieved, R. E. Clements (*Deuteronomy* [Sheffield, 1989]) writes: "Without yet reaching to a full and complete monotheistic universalism" (58).

are not referred to in a negative way. They acknowledge Israel's
greatness, which consists exclusively in the keeping of YHWH's
commandments (4:6) and is therefore a gift from him rather than an
innate quality. The seeing of the events of Baal-peor is in contrast with
the not-seeing of a form at Horeb and the hearing of words. Accordingly Israel's identity will be defined by the fact that it will not represent YHWH by earthly shapes nor bow down to heavenly bodies. Of
the passage 4:15-19, Fishbane observes "that it precisely reiterates the
creation sequence of Gen 1-2:4a — but in reverse order! This creation
account has thus been subtly used to 'carry' a midrashic teaching
...".[21] YHWH has allotted (*hlq* 4:19, cf. 32:8f., in contrast to his taking
[*lqh*] of Israel [4:20]) to the peoples the *visible* heavenly bodies for
worship. By contrast, in the diaspora *Israel* will have to serve wood
and stone (4:28). In this connection Labuschagne points out the comparative respect with which this chapter speaks of the peoples.[22] This
is due to the fact that they are "the peoples everywhere under heaven"
rather than the Canaanites, the Perizzites, etc., with whom Israel will
indeed have to deal in the land. The former category is granted space
(it could hardly have been otherwise); the latter is deprived of it. The
former category may praise YHWH's people (32:43); the latter is fated
to disappear gradually from the land (7:22). At this Van Seters rightly
comments: "The conquest theme is invoked in terms of the extermina-
tion of the original inhabitants of the land as a basis for maintaining
the purity of worship and religious devotion to Yahweh alone."[23]
Whoever deems this aspect of the message of Deuteronomy offensive,
should realize that those among the people who incite others to serve
other gods will suffer a similar fate (cf. ch. 13). Such people are
expressly (12:29ff.; 8:19) associated with the "original inhabitants".
Labuschagne's observation that in Deuteronomy matters are really
quite simple ("The enemies are to be defeated, and the brother peoples
to be spared") refers to the "real" brother peoples: Edom, Ammon and
Moab, in contrast to the "autochthons". The comfort Lemche offers
with regard to the latter is that the Canaanites "are not historical
persons, but actors in a play in which the Israelites have got the better,

---

[21] M. Fishbane, "Tora and Tradition", in: D. A. Knight, *Tradition and Theology
in the Old Testament* (London, 1977), 275-300: 278f. Cf. M. Fishbane, "Varia
Deuteronomica", *ZAW* 84 (1972), 349-356: 349.

[22] Labuschagne, *Deuteronomium* I^A, 242, 265. It is doutbtful whether with this
"allotment" to the peoples the author as an "arch-monotheist" creates room for a
theologia religionum, for a form of knowledge of God among all peoples everywhere under heaven.

[23] J. Van Seters, *Prologue to History. The Yahwist as Historian in Genesis*
(Westminster, 1992), 232.

or the hero's part."[24] It would even be better to say that this aspect of the message of the book is intrinsically related to its central confession— *yhwh 'ḥd* —, which is to control life in the one country. It allows no room for the followers of other gods, regardless whether they are "Israelites" or "Canaanites". The Baal of Peor is the sole other God mentioned by name, who in the threshold situation in Moab provides the cautionary example; Moses' untraceable grave is situated "opposite Beth-Peor" (34:6)! With the other peoples—which include not only the brother peoples, but also the "Egyptians"—with these "peoples under heaven" matters are different. YHWH, the one God, who holds a unique position in the world of the gods, has acquired a people of his own which as such holds a unique position in the world of the peoples[25] and as such commands the peoples' respect (4:6ff.). This exceptional position is Israel's "to be or not to be", as *gwy 'ḥd* (2 Sam. 7:23), as a confessional community. In all its generations, all Israel—in Deuteronomy never "the house of Israel" but always "children of Israel"[26]—is constituted by the statement *yhwh 'ḥd*.

III

In Deuteronomy the 'generation of Moab' is addressed by Moses. The assumed background of this is the theme of the two generations in Numbers, which inspired D.T. Olsen's non-geographical division of this book. The parallel formulations of Num 1:1ff. and 26:1f. mark the two main parts. Both in the first and in the second census one finds the expression "from twenty years old and upward, everyone in Israel able to go to war". It comes back in the decisive divine judgment after the story of the spies: "Your dead bodies shall fall in this very wilderness; and of all your number, included in the census, from twenty years old and upward" (Num 14:29), excepting Caleb and Joshua. Accordingly, the second census is concluded with the following statement: "Among these there was not one of those enrolled by Moses and Aaron the priest, who had enrolled the Israelites in the wilderness of Sinai" (Num 26:64). Starting from the divine judgment, the text offers "the portrait of the second generation as a paradigm for all succeeding gene-

---

[24] Lemche, *Canaanites*, 155. Did Deuteronomy contribute to an unhappy relationship between the Jews and other inhabitants of Palestine after the Babylonian Exile (Labuschagne, *Deuteronomium* I[B], 112) or is this situation reflected in it?

[25] Labuschagne, *Deuteronomium* I[B], 110ff.; id., *Incomparability* 149ff.

[26] H. D. Preuss, *Deuteronomium* (EdF 164; Darmstadt, 1982), 182: "das neue Israel ... zu entwerfen und zu gestalten."

rations".[27] Also with regard to Deuteronomy, it fits likewise "die Exilsgemeinde als durch das Gericht hindurch geretteten 'Rest'"[28] of the days since the beginning of the Persian period.

The forty years in the desert remain notably unfilled, perhaps less owing to a lack of tradition material[29] than because of the need to treat the topic of a "new generation". Deut 2:13ff. turns it into a geographically marked moment: the crossing of the Wadi Zered, the borderline between Edom and Moab, mentioned three times. The threefold '*br* is combined with the threefold *tmm* of the warriors from the camp (vv. 14, 15), from among the people (v. 16). The words "warriors" and "camp" "define in a military way the adult males",[30] reminding us of Num 12 and 14, and foreshadowing the struggle during the conquest of the land. This is underlined by the statement that the period between Kadesh and Zered lasted thirty-eight years, which is forty years less the two years till Horeb. "Les défaitistes sont enfin morts, l'histoire peut reprendre son cours, et la promesse se réaliser"[31]—a striking characterization, provided it is interpreted thematically rather than historically.

Within Deuteronomy this text should be read against the background of 1:34-40, a passage of which the structure has been made beautifully clear in Labuschagne's logotechnical analysis.[32] In the menorah-form of the text the ban on Moses' entering the land constitutes the central branch. Moses is flanked by Caleb and Joshua. These two are flanked in their turn by the ban imposed on the old generation and the permission given to the new one. This whole complex is enclosed by YHWH's reaction to the people and YHWH's command to the people. Almost in the manner of a litotes, all Israel is standing around Moses despite the setting of wrath and judgment. Even though the contemporary people (the old generation) is addressed, the new generation of hearers can recognize themselves in the little children and the sons who on account of their age cannot yet bear responsibility. Moses is flanked by Caleb as the sole exception of the old generation and by Joshua as the future leader of the new generation. In the land promised

---

[27] D. T. Olsen, *The Death of the Old and the Birth of the New* (Chico, California, 1985), 149.

[28] Preuss, *Deuteronomium*, 183.

[29] G. von Rad, *Das fünfte Buch Mose. Deuteronomium* (ATD 8; Göttingen, 1964), 31.

[30] M. Weinfeld, *Deuteronomy 1-11* (AB; New York, 1991), 163.

[31] P. Buis and J. Leclercq, *Le Deutéronome* (Sources Bibliques; Paris, 1963), 46.

[32] Labuschagne, *Deuteronomium* I^A, 130ff. Cf. appendix "Logotechnische analyse" 10. Cf. also C. J. Labuschagne, "Divine Speech in Deuteronomy", in: N. Lohfink (ed.), *Das Deuteronomium* (BETL 68; Louvain, 1985), 111-126: 129ff.

to the patriarchs, Caleb will inherit Hebron as the representative of the South[33] and Joshua will be buried in the mountains of Ephraim as the representative of the North. The whole land, both the North and the South, is in sight. As the one place of worship is not mentioned, the Tora and especially Deuteronomy can be read and handed down not only in the Judaean community of Jerusalem, but also in the "proto-Samaritan" community of Mount Gerizim.[34] Moses is the link between all the sons of Israel. He will die "because of you" (*bgllkm* 1:37), that is, because of the old generation. "Er haftet wie sonst ein altorientalischer Herrscher für sein Volk",[35] even though he is not guilty. He will be able to *see* the land (albeit in a different way from Caleb), but he will not enter it. He will, however, cross the Zered with the new generation, to let them hear his last words, from the site of his future grave. He is even allowed to *see* the beginning of YHWH's work, the defeat of Sihon and Og (3:23), but his last request for permission to cross the Jordan is turned down "on your account" (*lm'nkm*, 3:26), that is, on account of the new generation. Moses' death makes room for a new period in the land.

IV

The theme of the two generations as used in Numbers and Deuteronomy is continued in the book of Joshua in a combination of both. In preparation for the Passover celebration in the land, Joshua is ordered to circumcise the Israelites "a second time". The questions arising from this expression[36] can be explained from the fact that the circumcision described in Joshua 5 is confession-related: circumcision as a shibboleth for the exilic community. It is used to explain that "all the people who came out had been circumcised"[37] and that "all the people born on the journey through the wilderness ... had not been circumcised"

---

[33] Perlitt assumes that the form of Deut 1:37 is to be explained from Josh 16:6-15 (L. Perlitt, *Deuteronomium* [BKAT V 2], 117f).

[34] B. J. Diebner, "Gottes Welt, Moses Zelt und das salomonische Heiligtum", in: Th. Römer (ed.), *Lectio difficilior probabilior?* (Festschrift Fr. Smyth-Florentin. DBAT-Beiheft 12; Heidelberg, 1991), 127-154: 131. He also believes that one of the reasons for Moses' death before the entry into the land and his unknown grave in Moab must be connected with the prevention of rivalry between the two communities of Israel (lecture Herlíkovice, Czechia 14.04.1993).

[35] G. Braulik, *Deuteronomium 1-16,17* (NEB; Würzburg, 1986), 28.

[36] "Ne semble pas avoir beaucoup de sens ici", J. A. Soggin, *Le livre de Josué* (CAT Vᵃ; Neuchâtel, 1970), 57.

[37] The variant textual tradition of the Septuagint (cf. E. Tov, *Textual Criticism of the Hebrew Bible* (Minneapolis, 1992), 327-332) mentions uncircumcised people at the exodus from Egypt, which is interesting from a historical point of view.

(5:5). They are connected by the fact that "the sons of Israel travelled forty years in the wilderness" (5:6). That the exodus-generation did not "listen to the voice of YHWH" (5:6) is physically visible in the case of the new generation, who being uncircumcised cannot take part in the celebration of the Passover, for "no uncircumcised person shall eat of it" (Exod 12:48). At that moment, on the tenth day of the first month (Josh 4:19), the day on which the lamb is to be set apart (it is lacking here, as this is not the one place chosen by YHWH), after the people had come up out of the Jordan, Joshua circumcised them, so that the three days before the festival would give them time to be healed. Thus at Gilgal YHWH rolls away (*gll*) the "disgrace of Egypt" (Josh 5:9). This "disgrace" implied that YHWH would not have been able to bring the people into the land (cf. Num 14:11-16).[38]

The passage calling to mind the judgment after the story of the spies, runs as follows:

> For the sons of Israel travelled forty years in the desert,
> until all the nation perished,
> the warriors who came out of Egypt,
> who had not listened to the voice of YHWH,
> to whom YHWH swore
> that he would not let them see the land
> that YHWH had sworn to their fathers
> to give us,
> a land flowing with milk and honey. (Josh 5:6)

The texts from Numbers alluded to read:

> As I live ...
> none of these men ...
> *who ... have not listened to my voice,*
> *shall see the land*
> *that I swore to give to their fathers.* (Num 14:21)

They will never arrive in the land *flowing of milk and honey* (Num 14:8):

> Your dead bodies shall fall in this wilderness,
> your *sons* shall be wanderers *in the wilderness for forty years,* ...
> in this wilderness they shall all *perish,*
> and there they shall *die.* (Num 14:32-35)

In addition, however, the version given in Deuteronomy is also important; in particular the term "warriors", which in Josh 5:4 is used as a

---

[38] K. A. Deurloo, "Om Pesach te kunnen vieren in het land", in: M. Boertien (ed.), *Verkenningen in een stroomgebied* (Festschrift M. A. Beek) (Amsterdam, 1974), 41-50.

specification of "all the nation ... who came out":

> And the length of time ... (from Kadesh-barnea until the Wadi Zered) was thirty-
> eight years,
> until the entire generation of warriors
> had *perished from the camp*,
> as YHWH had *sworn* concerning them,
> ... to root them out *from the camp*,
> until all had *perished* ...
> ... all the warriors ... (Deut 2:14ff.)

The major term connecting Numbers and Deuteronomy is the verb *tmm* (to "finish" or "perish") with reference to the old generation. It is also important in Joshua 4 at the crossing of the Jordan: "the entire nation *finished* crossing over the Jordan" (Josh 3:17; 4:1.10.11). It is the new generation which, being the "sons", marks the new beginning in the land, once the old generation has "perished" before the crossing of the Zered:

> It was their sons, whom he (YHWH) raised up in their place,
> that Joshua circumcised,
> for they were uncircumcised,
> because they had not been circumcised on the way.
> When all the nation had *finished* being circumcised,
> they sat in the camp in their place[39]
> until they were healed. (Josh 5:7-8)

All the warriors had perished "from the camp" (Deut 2:16). After their *end* and after the *end* of the circumcision the living sons have occupied *their place*. The addition to "all the people who had come out of Egypt", namely "the males" (Josh 5:4) and the double mention of "the warriors" (Josh 5:6) can be explained from this context. The old generation did not risk the battle for the land. When their sons are no longer uncircumcised, the latter "sit" in the camp in their place. Moses had already spoken threateningly to Reuben and Gad in a similar way:

---

[39] Translations and commentaries often neglect the word *taḥtam* (e.g. R. G. Boling, *Joshua* [AB; New York, 1982], 183), or apply it to the circumcised sons themselves (e.g. M. Görg, *Josua* [NEB; Stuttgart, 1991], 25: "blieb man an Ort und Stelle"). The reason for this is that the circumcision is in itself seen as the subject of this passage, possibly as an aetiological narrative in connection with the information about the special location (following B. Stade, "Der 'Hügel der Vorhäute', Jos. 5", *ZAW* 6 [1886], 132-143), rather than the circumcision as a sign in connection with the new generation. It seems more plausible to interpret the the unidentified Hill of the Foreskins as belonging to the world of narrative geography. Boling (*Joshua*, 194) even concludes from the text "that some of the earliest Israelites knew of adult circumcision." In making this observation he is not thinking of e.g. Acts 16:1ff.

"All the generation that had done evil ... had *perished*. And now you ...
have risen *in place of* your fathers" (Num 32:14). Their solidarity with
the brothers of all Israel foreshadowed the conquest of the land, which
is now going to take place, starting from the Passover celebration. The
death of the Exodus-generation (Josh 5:4) is transformed into the life
of the generation who will enter the land (Josh 5:8: until they were
healed; lit.: "until they lived [again]").

The story of the fathers thus serves to encourage the sons "that they
should not be like their fathers, a stubborn and rebellious generation"
(Ps 78:8). The actual link with the exilic community is made in Ps
106:24-27 which says of the generation of Numbers 13 and 14:

> Then they despised the pleasant land,
> having no faith in his promise.
> They grumbled in their tents,
> and did not listen to the voice of YHWH.
> Therefore he raised his hand and swore to them
> that he would make them fall in the wilderness,
> and would disperse their descendants among the nations,
> scattering them over the lands.

To the continuity between the wilderness-generation and the diaspora-
generation stressed in this text certain 'homiletic' objections can be
raised. These are obviated in Psalm 106 by the theme of YHWH's
mercy, so that the psalm can end with the prayer: "Gather us from
among the nations". At such a moment of return it would be incon-
ceivable not to refer to a positive continuity with the ancestors, because
without it "restoration" in the sense of renewal would not be possible.
In the book of Joshua, too, the new generation replaces the old one,
"all the people that came out of Egypt and had been circumcised".
Thus the disgrace is "rolled away" that Egypt made the inhabitants of
the land listen to: "It is because YHWH was not able to bring this
people into the land he swore to give them that he has slaughtered
them in the wilderness" (Num 14:16; cf. Deut 9:28).

V

In a negative setting, all Israel figures in the menorah-structure of Deut
1:34-40, where the old generation is addressed: "As for you, turn about
and march into the wilderness." Listening to Moses' speech, the new
generation is also allowed to hear this. It is the new generation which
after the crossing of the Wadi Zered went through a second selection at
Baal-Peor, to prepare them for living in the land. The people addressed
are those who "held fast" to YHWH their God and are "all alive
today" (4:4). This Moab-generation has seen with their "own eyes"

(4:3.9) that part of YHWH's work which was the judgment at Baal-Peor, and implicitly also what Joshua's "own eyes" saw, namely what YHWH did to the two kings (3:21, cf. 23). But these two aspects of the recent past, of which the people of the Moab-generation were literally eyewitnesses, provide insufficient basis for building a community; a connection must be established with the Exodus-Horeb-generation. The decisive events at Horeb are really of overriding importance, and therefore the thirty-eight years between Kadesh and the Wadi Zered must be bridged.

Once the most essential matters have been set out in Deuteronomy 5 ff., Moses can say: "It is you who must acknowledge ...' (11:2), and after a brief summary: "It is your own eyes that have seen every great deed that the Lord did" (11:7). The Moab-generation is supposed to identify with the Horeb-generation, with regard to the guilt of their seeing without perceiving and hearing without listening: "You have seen all that YHWH did before your eyes ... your own eyes saw ... But to this day YHWH has not given you a mind to understand, or eyes to see, or ears to hear" (29:1-3). This is said to those who belonged to the little ones and minors at Kadesh (1:39), but it includes, of course, also the *two witnesses* linking the two generations: Caleb (1:36) and Joshua (1:38). I. L. Seeligmann's statement that the contrast of two generations such as found in Numbers 14 returns with particular frequency in the book of Deuteronomy[40] must be qualified first of all by distinguishing between the contrast habitually made between parents and children (Ps 78:5ff.) and the unique contrast between the Exodus-generation and the generation which entered the land. Also, in Deuteronomy this contrast is not without nuance. The Moab-generation and the Horeb-generation are the same in their failure to perceive and listen. They are also equals with respect to their decisive turning to YHWH at Horeb: "YHWH our God made a covenant with *us* at Horeb. Not with our fathers did the Lord make a covenant, but with us, who are all of us here alive today" (5:2.3). Labuschagne rightly observes that we have here a dialectic negation: not so much ... as. The rules of the covenant were of course important to the generation that had perished, but they are now relevant to the coming Moab-generation.[41]

---

[40] I. L. Seeligmann, "Erkenntnis Gottes und historisches Bewußtsein im Alten Israel", in: H. Donner etc. (eds.), *Beiträge zur alttestamentlichen Theologie* (Festschrift W. Zimmerli) (Göttingen, 1977), 414-445: 437.

[41] Labuschagne, *Deuteronomium* I[B], 24. Lohfink's view that the text is about "alle Vorfahren aller denkbaren Generationen" before the present generation, which is then described as a combined Exodus-Horeb-Moab-generation, is to be rejected (N. Lohfink, *Die Väter Israels im Deuteronomium. Mit einer Stellungnahme von Thomas Römer* [OBO 111; Freiburg-Göttingen, 1991], 23).

In the summarizing introduction of Deuteronomy 4 to the theophany of the next chapter there is a shift from *seeing* to *hearing*.[42] All the signs, including the one of Baal-Peor, are seen, but at the crucial moment there is only the Voice in the event. Nowhere else in the O.T. is there so much emphasis on the not-seeing of a form of YHWH.[43] In this connection even the term theo*phany* is questionable. The idea that "to see God is to die" is here changed to: "Today we have seen that God may speak to someone and the person may still live." Has anyone ever experienced this, to have "heard the voice of the living God speaking out of fire, as we have, and remained alive?" (Deut 5:24.26). This fundamental experience of God turns the people into Israel, into a confessional community, the Horeb-generation, "who are all of us here alive today" (5:3). The experience of the voice is preserved in the Ten Words that are written down, and in the words that Moses will write down. On account the "Hear, Israel" the Moab-generations know these words, but this does not apply to their children (11:2), so that the confessional community will also have to become a catechizing community (cf. 6:20ff.).[44]

In the future there will again be "eyewitnesses" of the signs performed by YHWH. If their children and children's children fail to listen, the people will have to live in the diaspora (cf. 4:25ff.). With the eyewitnesses of that future moment, the hearers are also identified: "(You shall be) driven mad by the sight that your eyes shall see" (28:34; cf. 28:67). In ch. 29, under the heading of the identification of the covenant made in Moab with the one made at Horeb (18:69), the opposite applies.[45] Parallel to "Not with our fathers ..., but with us"

---

[42] That "das Temporell-Geschichtliche" rather than "das Räumlich-Kosmische" dominates the O.T., is reflected in the polemics of Deut 4:16-19 against the deified, visible terrestrial and celestial phenomena. "The covenantal history related in the biblical texts does not take place in the light of the surrounding cosmos, but conversely the cosmos is seen in the light of the covenantal history taking place in it" (F. H. Breukelman, "Het scheppingsverhaal als onderricht in bijbelse hermeneutiek", in: K. van der Horst etc. [eds.], *Voor de achtste dag* [Festschrift J. P. Boendermaker] [Kampen, 1990], 19-34: 29).

[43] Cf. S. Terrien, *The Elusive Presence. Toward a New Biblical Theology* (New York, 1978), 202. Emphasis is put on "the sense of hearing" in connection with "cultic anamnesis".

[44] One can observe here the continual contrasting of two generations (Seeligmann, "Erkenntnis", 444f.). It is not so much a "historisches Bewusstsein" as a religious identification which is at issue. Cf. D. N. Freedman, J. Lundblom, *TWAT* II, s.v. *dwr*, 193ff.

[45] G. Braulik, *Deuteronomium* II (NEB; Würzburg, 1992), 214: "die späteren Generationen", "Auf analoge Weise 5:3, frühere Generationen". Cf. A.D.H. Mayes, *Deuteronomy* (NCBC; Grand Rapids, 1981), 165, 362.

(5:3) in connection with Horeb, in Moab we hear the words: "I am making this covenant, sworn by an oath, not only with you who stand here with us today before YHWH our God, but also with those who are not here with us *today*" (29:13-14). After this the prospect of the destruction of the land and the exile of the people is sketched: "as is now the case" (29:26). The future teachers of the book[46] are allowed to identify with the Moab-generation. For them, the book is what it tends to be on the whole: a book of *tšwbh* in a twofold sense, return and conversion. This is underlined by the elaborate play on the verbal stem *šwb* at the beginning of the next chapter. Everyone in the exilic community can feel personally addressed. The great change will take place "as you have turned back and listen to the Voice of YHWH" (30:8). The Moab-generation is the point of identification linking the Horeb-generation with the generation of the exile. Of the latter it is said that YHWH will *turn back* to them and rejoice over them as he rejoiced over their forefathers,[47] so that the circle of all Israel is made full (30:9).

In conclusion it may be said that the the covenant-related motto "YHWH alone" defines a confessional community with highly intro-spective features in the situation of the exile. There are hardly any signs of a missionary interest. Instead, there is all the more emphasis on personal engagement (e.g. 7:10) and responsibility for the teaching of future generations (e.g. 6:20ff.). "All Israel" is a favoured expression and "suits well Deuteronomy's exclusive concern with this people."[48] The audience addressed by the book is supposed to be part of an extensive Golah. The "original inhabitants" of "Canaan" are excluded rigorously, just as are the "Israelites" associating with the religion of the "Canaanites". This confessional community is apparent-ly forced to pursue zealously the purity of its exclusive faith.

The suggested frame of reference is the Moab-generation listening to

---

[46] C. Schäfer-Lichtenberger, "Göttliche und menschliche Autorität im Deuterono-mium", in: C. Brekelmans and J. Lust (eds.), *Pentateuchal and Deuteronomistic Studies. Papers Read at the XIIIth IOSOT Congress Leuven 1989* (BETL 94; Louvain, 1990), 125-142. Moses has a successor with regard to his leadership rather than with regard to the Tora. For the latter the book will take over. "Die Relation JHWH-Mose/Israel wird für das Alltagsleben im Lande durch die Relation JHWH-Torabuch-Israel abgelöst" (137). Through his death Moses makes room for the book; a living reality for the exilic community.

[47] On the basis of Deut 28:63, the most likely association seems to be that of the generation that entered the land. The unspecified term "forefathers" is open to a variety of interpretations. In Deuteronomy, the patriarchs are only present in outline. (Cf. the debate between Lohfink and Römer in: Lohfink, *Väter*.)

[48] Mayes, *Deuteronomy*, 113.

Moses in the book. In the threshold situation before the conquest of the land, they constitute the literary "Israel" purified after Baal-Peor, and thus the ideal point of identification. Yet behind this audience the mystery of the confession was to be presented as ancient and impenetrable. The re-articulation of existing vocabulary was able to adapt YHWH's revelation in a way that did not detract from the reliable "age" of the origins. The Voice at Horeb, the *words* spoken by YHWH and Moses can be heard through the book: "O that today you would listen to his voice!" (Ps. 95:7).

At the rephrasing of the motif of the two generations—so well suited for liturgical-cultic purposes—the purified Moab-generation, contrasting with the "evil generation" (1:35) of Kadesh, was able to serve as a mirror for the reform-generation of the exile, contrasting with the generation that preceded it. At the same time, the loyalty and mercy of YHWH, "der alles überragende und Israel gegen Israel liebende Gott",[49] could be preached.

The *tšwbh*-community is formed by those who take to heart (lit.: let *turn* into their hearts) (30:1) the words of this book and identify with the Moab-generation, which in its turn can be identified with the Horeb-generation. Just as the Song of Moses will not be lost from the mouths of future generations and will preserve Israel (31:21), so the entire book of Deuteronomy will bring the generation that keeps on reading *in statu confessionis*.[50] Because the one God defines Israel in all its generations, a new generation will recognize its place in the menorah-structure of all Israel hidden behind Deut 1:34-40 and so elegantly described in Labuschagne's logotechnical analysis.[51]

---

[49] Lohfink, *Studien* II, 42 ("Gott im Buch Deuteronomium", 25-53).

[50] In that sense Van Goudoever is justified in calling Deuteronomy "the most liturgical book of the Bible" (J. van Goudoever, "The Liturgical Significance of the Date in Dt 1,3", in: N. Lohfink (ed.), *Das Deuteronomium* (BETL 68; Louvain, 1985), 145-148: 148.

[51] I owe a debt of gratitude to P. J. Booij MA for his translation and general advice.

DEUT 34, DTR HISTORY AND THE PENTATEUCH

FÉLIX GARCÍA LÓPEZ

Salamanca, Spain

1. *Presentation[1]*

Chapter 34 of Deuteronomy occupies a strategic position, because it is not only the end of one book, but also the conclusion of one whole block and a bridge reaching out towards another. In Deut 34 many strands are interwoven and tangled together; some are difficult to identify and unravel.

In the analysis which follows we will, firstly, present the history of the research, highlighting those opinions which offer the most significant data for the interpretation of Deut 34. In the second place, we will give a description of the text in its final form, concentrating on its general framework and its most significant component parts. Next, we will turn our attention to the vision of Moses and the speech of Yahweh (v. 1b-4),[2] key elements in the understanding of the text. Finally, we will outline a sketch of the formation process of Deut 34, within the framework of current debates on the Pentateuch.

Thus, we will go from the final text to its process of formation, from a vision which is synchronic to one which is diachronic, in a critical and integrating approximation. In current exegesis the need is felt to combine efforts and make best use of the achievements of different methods, in order to respond more adequately to the challenges raised by the text.

2. *Deut 34, in the light of critical exegesis*

2.1 *The first critical observations* on the Pentateuch targeted chapter 34 of Deuteronomy. Against Jewish and Christian tradition which defended the Mosaic authenticity of the Torah,[3] the *Talmud* indicates

---

[1] I would like to thank Denis E. Carlin of the Scots College, Salamanca, for his help in the translation of this article.

[2] Above all, we would like to acknowledge the works on 'divine speech' published by Prof. C.J. Labuschagne to whom we dedicate this study (cf. *VT* 32 (1982), 268-96; N. Lohfink (ed.), *Das Deuteronomium* (BETL 68; 1985), 111-26.

[3] Josephus (*Ant.* IV, viii, 48) and Philo (*Vita Moysis* II, 51) specifically state that Moses wrote the whole Torah, including the account of his own death.

that Deut 34:5-12 might possibly have been added by Joshua.[4] Bigger cracks in the said tradition however would appear from the 15th century onwards. Among the pioneers mention must be made of Alfonso de Madrigal, nicknamed Tostado (circa 1410-1455) who defended with vigour and conviction the position that Moses could not be the author of the account of his own death. Later Karlstadt took up this same position. With these authors the critical question of the Pentateuch was already clearly posed.[5]

2.2 In *historical-critical exegesis,* the greater part of ancient authors who tend towards the documentary theory are convinced that none of the sources of the Pentateuch would have omitted the account of the death of Moses. These same authors however differ when they identify the said sources of Deut 34.[6] The most common opinion from the end of last century until little more than a decade ago was that which holds that in Deut 31 and 34 narrative elements from the sources of the Pentateuch are quoted, interwoven with other Dtr elements. Normally v. 1*.2-3.5-6 are attributed to J; v. la*.7a.8-9 to P and v. 4.10-12 to Dtr. The combination of these elements, one with another, would be brought to term with the incorporation of Deut into the Pentateuch.[7]

2.3 Among *recent critical exegetes* who re-examine the classical critical theory one must single out Rendtorff and Blum.

Rendtorff, in his critical observations on the sources of the Penta-teuch, adverts to the absence of the account of the death of Moses in J,

---

[4] *bBaba Bathra,* 14b.

[5] Alphonsi Tostati, *Commentaria in Deuteronomium,* III/2 (Coloniae, 1613), 317-19; A.B. Karlstadt, *De canonicis scripturis libellus,* 1520, quoted by H.-J. Kraus, *Geschichte der historischkritischen Erforschung des Alten Testaments* (Neukirchen-Vluyn 1982³), 30. Immediately after outlining the opinion of Tostado, H. Cazelles concludes: "La question critique était posée" (H. Cazelles (ed.), *Introduction à la Bible, II. Introduction critique à l' Ancien Testament* [Paris, 1973], 111).

[6] Cf. A. Bertholet, *Deuteronomium* (KHC V; Freiburg i.B.-Leipzig-Tübingen, 1899), 111-112, which offers a panoramic vision of the principal divisions of sources in Deut 34 from Bacon to Wellhausen.

[7] Cf. H.D. Preuss, *Deuteronomium* (EdF 164; Darmstadt, 1982), 164. Some authors however attribute set verses to E: thus, among older authors, J.E. Carpen-ter-G.H. Battersby, *The Hexateuch* I (New York-Bombay, 1900), 278 (Deut 34:1dr.4: J; Deut 34:lb.2.5a.6r.10-12: E; Deut 34:lac.5b.7-9: P) and, among the more recent, L. Ruppert, *Wort und Botschaft* (Würzburg, 1967), 387 (Deut 34:lb-4: J; 5-6(10): E; l.a.7-9: P). Finally some exegetes prefer to class as JE those verses commonly attributed to J and to E: see, for example, R.E. Friedman, *The Exile and Biblical Narrative* (HSM 22; Harvard, 1981), 118 (Deut 34:1-6: JE; 7-9: P; 10-12: Dtr).

while, at the same time, noting the uncertainty among authors on this point; moreover, he highlights the discussion about the end of P: does it end with the death of Moses (Deut 34) or does it continue into Joshua? In his opinion, Deut should not be separated too emphatically from the Tetrateuch, given the link between the announcement of the death of Moses in Num 27:13-23 and its statement in Deut 34. In their turn, neither the last chapters of Numbers nor the present Deut can be separated from Jos-2 Kings. This problem—he adds—cannot be solved by appealing to a redaction of the Pentateuch, as Noth does, basing himself on the pre-supposition that a perfectly worked out P-narrative exists as a basis for such a redaction. The fact that it should be Dtr— and not P—which calls the tune in the account of the death of Moses (Deut 34) invites us to think, according to Noth, that we are dealing with a late redaction. In the judgement of Rendtorff, however, this argument is irrelevant if we do not recognise the existence of a fully worked out P-narrative. For suddenly the information about the death of Moses in Deut 34:7 appears formulated in a unique way without parallel in the rest of the Pentateuch.[8]

In the opinion of Blum, in Gen-Deut independent and parallel sources do not exist but rather *two post-exilic compositions* which have reunited or elaborated *traditions* or older texts: KD, a pre-priestly composition of deuteronomic type, and KP, a composition of the priestly school. The Pentateuch is the result of the integration of KD into KP.

KD starts with Abraham (Gen 12s) and goes as far as Num. KD relies on the existence of DtrH. Both works—KD and DtrH—join up in the last chapters of Deut. The conclusion of KD coincides with the death of Moses: Deut 34 is an open conclusion; KD is only relatively independent of DtrH, as Deut 31:14-15.23 and 34:10 show. When it comes to the relationship between KD and Deut, KD knows the ancient texts as well as Deut and elaborates them according to it. Like DtrH, KD places the prophets in the wake of Moses, but does not discard the possibility of a rivalry and a pre-eminence of Moses in relation to the prophets. With regard to its dating, KD is situated in the first generation of the return, a generation which is trying to re-orga-nise itself, seeking support in the promises to the patriarchs and in the exodus. In the tradition prior to KD there existed a long text from the time of the fall of Samaria, which began with the Exodus and finished with the death of Moses, although this last datum is less certain.

---

[8] R. Rendtorff, *Das überlieferungsgeschichtliche Problem des Pentateuch* (BZAW 147; Berlin-New York, 1976), 92. 112. 161, n.7. 166f.

KP is neither a source nor a redaction. Its horizon is limited to the Pentateuch. Against a global composition which goes from Gen to Jos is the reference in Num 27:12s to the death of Moses and its resumption in Deut 32:48-52, which along with Deut 1:3 and 34:1*.7-9 have the function of incorporating Deut into KP.

The Pentateuch is the result of a historical compromise, reached in the Persian epoch, between two different tendencies (KD and KP) represented by two dominant groups in the community of the second temple. Some texts were added after this compromise. No "final form" exists, but rather a complex amalgam which cannot be the product of a single intention.[9]

2.4 Clines and Childs start from methodological presuppositions which are different from each other's, and different again from those of Rendtorff and Blum, although they are related and coincide in some points.

Clines' analysis of the Pentateuch has a methodological and thematic approach. It is fundamental for his method to start with the final form of the Pentateuch. In this view one seeks the theme of the Pentateuch. Throughout the first five books of the Hebrew Bible — he says — we note a progression, in time and in space, with an objective and a direction. From where does this movement derive its impetus? Without doubt — he replies — from the promise to the patriarchs: in the first place from Gen 12:1-3. The theme of the Pentateuch is the partial fulfilment of the promise to the patriarchs. In Gen 12:1-3 an arch is opened which closes — but only partially — in Deut 34. Deut stands between the promise and its fulfilment. The presence at the end of the Pentateuch of a book with these characteristics serves to highlight the open ended nature of the promise. In Deut 31:3.7.20 it is taken for granted that the promise of the land will be fulfilled, and in 34:9 the loyalty which Israel owes to Joshua is underlined. The death of Moses provides a formal end to the Pentateuch, but the death of the hero cannot complete the story. The Pentateuch is pushing further, towards an objective which is still seen as future.[10]

Childs presents his canonical method as a post-critical alternative to historical-critical methods. Canonical form plays a determining role,

---

[9] E. Blum, *Studien zur Komposition des Pentateuch* (BZAW 189; Berlin-New York, 1990), 5.102ff (esp. 76-88.106-11.194-97). 221ff (esp. 227f); Id., "Gibt es die Endgestalt des Pentateuch?" in: J.A. Emerton (ed.), *Congress Volume: Leuven 1989* (SVT 43; Leiden-New York-Köln, 1991), 46-57.

[10] D.J.A. Clines, *The Theme of the Pentateuch* (JSOTS 10; Sheffield,. 1978), 10. 25-29. 95f. 106.

given that "the formation of a Pentateuch established the parameters of Israel's understanding of its faith as Torah (...) The fundamental theological understanding of God's redemptive work through law and grace, promise and fulfilment, election and obedience was once and for all established". In agreement with Rendtorff, Childs holds that in the present form of the Pentateuch there exist some elements, like the expression "the land which he swore to Abraham, to Isaac and to Jacob", which offer "a holistic reading of the entire Pentateuch in terms of promise which goes beyond the individual sources ..." With regard to the "Canonical Shape of Deut", Childs singles out chapters 31-34 as "an important example of canonical shaping of the final form of ancient tradition". Deut consists of a series of speeches of Moses to the people, to which chapters 31-34 are added, introducing "a different narrative framework, namely the imminent death of Moses and the appointment of a successor (chapter 31) ... and the report of the death of Moses (34)".[11]

2.5 Within the framework of modern literary criticism of synchronic type, Polzin analyses the book of Deut, focusing on the hero (Moses) and the "author" of the book (the deuteronomic narrator). Seen from this angle, Deut is the speech of the deuteronomic narrator, who quotes two figures directly: Moses and God. Given that Moses, in his turn, frequently quotes God, Deut turns into a complex mosaic of quotes within quotes, of manifestations of God within the manifestations of the narrator. Apart from Moses, the only person who quotes God directly is the narrator (five times in total: 31:14b.16b.21.23b; 32:49-52; 34:4b).

Deut 34:1-12 has the function of presenting Moses as a pre-eminent figure, as the greatest prophet of Israel (34:10-12). There is a certain tension however between the voice of Moses and that of the narrator. With the report of the death of Moses in 34:5 the voice of Moses is stilled, but not that of the narrator who can "now take centre stage in the history". The narrator is a privileged observer and a reporter of the words of Moses and of God.[12]

---

[11] B.S. Childs, *Introduction to the Old Testament as Scripture* (Philadelphia, 1979), 127. 131f. 211. 219; also see 221-224.

[12] R. Polzin, *Moses and the Deuteronomist. A Literary Study of the Deuteronomistic History. I. Deuteronomy. Joshua, Judges* (New York, 1980), 25-72, especially 26f. 29f. 35-37. 72. Id., "Reporting Speech in the Book of Deuteronomy: Toward a Compositional Analysis of the Deuteronomic History", in: B. Halpern - J.D. Levenson (es.), *Traditions in Transformation. Turning Points in Biblical Faith* (Winona Lake, Indiana, 1981), 193-211; Id., "Deuteronomy", in: R. Alter - F. Kermode (eds.), *The Literary Guide to the Bible* (London, 1987), 92-101.

3. General framework and principal components of Deut 34

3.1 In *v. 1-6* five wayyiqtol come one after another, heading a series of propositions of a distinctly formal and thematic tenor. Two of them have Moses as their specific subject: *wy'l mšh - wymt šm mšh* (v. 1a.5); another two have Yahweh as their explicit subject: *wyr'hw yhwh - wy'mr yhwh 'lyw* (v. 1b.4a). The fifth, on the other hand, lacks a specific subject (*wyqbr:* v. 6a) so that it can be interpreted as Yahweh (*Yahweh* buried him) or as an indeterminate subject (he was buried).[13] In the phrases in which Yahweh is the subject, Moses functions as the direct or indirect object, thus constituting a factor of cohesion in the whole.

v. 1a.5*.6a give short and summary news of Moses going up a mountain and of his death and burial there. v. 1b-4, on the contrary, contain full and prolix descriptions of the land which Yahweh made Moses see, as well as the divine speech to Moses. In this regard, v. 1b-4 are in contrast to v. 1a.5*.6 (the indication of v. 6b does not square with the information in v. 6a about the place where he was buried).

3.2. In *v. 7-9* some significant syntactical-stylistic changes are effected from v. 1-6. Above all, the series of wayyiqtol mentioned above is interrupted. v. 7a and 9a contain two nominal propositions which are very similar in construction, referring to Moses and Joshua respectively. For their part, v. 8 and 9b use two more wayyiqtol which have the Israelites as their subject: *bny yśr'l*, an expression that appears here for the first time in chapter 34 and which will not reappear. The points of formal correspondence between v. 7a + 8a.8b on the one hand and 9a + 9bα.9bβ on the other seem undeniable:

wmšh bn-x ...	//	*wyhwš' bn-x...*
wybkw bny yśr'l ...	//	*wyšm'w bny yśr'l ...*
wytmw ...	//	*wy'św ...*

The references to Joshua in v. 9 also introduce something new in these verses with respect to what has gone before and what will follow. Nevertheless, v. 7-9 open and close with the name of Moses: *wmšh - 't-mšh*. This series of characteristics produces the impression that v. 7-9, with the exception of v. 7b, have a certain unity in themselves, without this preventing their connection with the rest of the chapter.

---

[13] Cf. C. Steuernagel, *Das Deuteronomium* (Göttingen, 1923), 183.

3.3. *v. 10-12* are distinguished from the earlier verses by a series of formal characteristics and by their content. Neither wayyiqtol nor nominal propositions, but rather a *wl'* + qal to open v. 10, which closes with a relative proposition. The title *nby'* applied to Moses is surprising, specially for the contrast it supposes with *'bd yhwh* of v. 5.; a contrast which is accentuated if compared to Jos 1:1.2.7, the continuation of Deut 34, where Moses continues to be given the title of *'bd yhwh*.

After the reference to Joshua in v. 9, we return to Moses in v. 10-12 to pay him final homage. His prophetic function and great actions on behalf of his people are exalted. Israel and Moses / Moses and Israel (these verses do not speak of *bny yśr'l* but simply of *yśr'l*) appear closely united in each expression, situated at the beginning and end of 34:10-12 in chiastic form: ... *byśr'l kmśh --- mśh l'yny kl-yśr'l*.

3.4. Deut 34 narrates, in first place, the last events of Moses life (v. 1-4), in order to tell later of his death-burial (v. 5-6) and of the mourning that the Israelites made for him (v. 8). His figure and his actions live on in memory, and v. 7.10-12 give good evidence of this.

Moses is present, directly or indirectly, in the whole chapter. Without doubt he is the central figure of the account (Joshua is only mentioned briefly to say that the Israelites obeyed him as they did Moses, but his leadership is not emphasised: in this respect, the contrast between 34:9 and 31:3.23 is manifest). The multiple references to Yahweh in Deut 34 serve, in a kind of a way, to exalt the figure of Moses.[14] The sight that Moses has of the promised land (v. 1b-4) acquires particular importance by the very fact that it is Yahweh who shows it to him. Similarly, the accompanying divine speech gives the act a profundity and prominence that elevates it, in a certain sense, to the edge of the transcendent. However the narrative does not limit itself to quoting the words of Yahweh (v. 4); it states, in addition, that specific things happened just as Yahweh had told / ordered Moses: *'l py yhwh / k'śr ṣwh yhwh* (v. 5.9).[15] The narrative highlights in the same way the intimacy Moses had in dealing with God and the incomparable nature of his actions, achieved through the power of God: *'śr šlḥw yhyh l'śwt* ... (v. 10b-11). In a word, the greatness of Moses has its source in Yahweh.

Behind Moses and Yahweh—and, in a certain sense, above them—

---

[14] On the pre-eminence of Moses, cf. F. García López, "El Moisés histórico y el Moisés de la fe", *Salmanticensis* 36 (1989), 5-21.

[15] On the significance and parallelism of these two formulas, cf. F. García López, "*paeh*", *TWAT*, VI, 522-33, esp. 528.

hides the omniscient narrator, who not only knows what Moses does but also knows what Yahweh does and says. In reality, his voice outlives that of Moses, but he only uses it to exalt him above everyone else: "there has not arisen since a prophet in Israel like Moses" (v. 10). Moreover, the narrator quotes the words of Yahweh (v. 4), he being the only person—except Moses—to whom this privilege is accorded in the Book of Deut.

From the preceding observations one can infer that Deut 34 is basically composed of three pieces, three small "units" (v. 1-6. 7-9. 10-12) which together make up a single narrative.

4. *The vision of the land and the speech of Yahweh: 34:1b-4*

In the present text the components of Deut 34 are found linked together in such a way that one cannot exclude that their union is redactional, fruit of a literary composition. Theoretically at least, v. 1a and 5* could function independently of v. 1b-4 (but these could not with respect to v. 1a). The narrator might well have limited himself to saying: "Moses went up to X and died there". In the parallel case of Aaron this is the type of information we are given.

Num 33:38a: *wy'l 'hrn hkhn*   *'l-hr hhr ... wymt šm*
Deut 34:1a,5*: *wy'l mšh m'rbwt mw'b*   *'l-hr nbw   ... wymt šm ...*

In both cases the sequence *wy'l* x *'l* x *wymt šm* would coincide. This simple statement makes clear the possible independence of v. 1a.5* from v. 1b-4. These last named moreover enjoy a certain formal unity in themselves to judge from their structure: *wyr'hw - wy'mr - hr'ytyk*. In the middle of the verb *r'h*, situated at the beginning and end of v. 1b-4, is the verb *'mr*, with which the vision of Moses (v. 1b-3) and the speech of Yahweh (v. 4) appear closely linked.

The union of a vision account with a divine speech, expressed through the verbs *r'h* (in Hifil, which is much less frequent than in Qal and also in Nifal) and *'mr*, Yahweh being the subject of both, is used particularly in prophetic literature. We single out here, for their greater formal closeness to Deut 34:1b-4, the passages from Amos 7:7s.; 8:1s. and Jer 24:1-3.[16] The sequence *r'h* (Hifil) + *wy'mr* appears in all three with Yahweh as subject. The change from first person (Amos and Jer) to third (Deut) is explained because in Deut the narrator is speak-

---

[16] One can also see Jer 1:11-13; Zac 3:1; 4:1s.; 5:1s.; cf J.L Ska, *'Our Fathers Have Told Us'. Introduction to the Analysis of Hebrew Narratives* (SB 13; Roma 1990), 73s.

ing. As is logical, the object of the vision and the content of the divine speech also vary. In this sense, Deut 34:1b-4 is closer to some texts of the Abraham story and also to Deut 3:23-29. The introduction of the oath of Yahweh with *l'mr* in Deut 34:4 suggests, in the first instance, that it could be quoting Gen 12:7:[17]

> Deut 34:4: *z't h'rṣ   'šr nšb'ty l-X wl-X wl-X l'mr lzr'k 'tnnh*
> Gen 12:7: *lzr'k 'tn 't-h'rṣ hz't*

There exist moreover implicit references to Gen 12:1 and 13:14f., texts closely related between themselves.[18] In these three texts from the beginning of the Abraham story both formulas (*'mr* and *r'h*) are combined together with the theme of the land, as occurs in Deut 34:1b-4. Nonetheless some differences are noted between Gen 12f and Deut 34: in Gen 12:1 the sequence *r'h - 'mr* is inverted; in 12:7 *r'h* is in Nifal and the object of the vision is not the land, but rather Yahweh himself, and in 13:14s. *r'h* is used in Qal in the expression *ś'-n' 'ynyk wr'h*. In this last text the vision of the land is very similar to that expressed in Deut 34, not only along general lines, but also in many particular characteristics. Yahweh commands Abraham to raise his eyes towards the north and south, towards the east and west (Gen 13:14), and adds: *ky 't-kl-h'rṣ 'šr 'th r'h lk 'tnnh wlzr'k 'd-'wlm* (13:15). The expression *'t-kl-h'rṣ*, which appears here for the first time in the Pentateuch, is the same one which is pronounced for the last time in Deut 34:1b. Moses also glances at the four cardinal points of the promised land, described in more detail than in the case of Abraham.[19] For its part the description of the land is summed up in the formula *'t-kl-h'rṣ* and the gift of the land is expressed in the same way in both texts: *'tnnh*. The difference between Moses who will not enter the land (*l' t'br*: Deut 34:4) and Abraham who will (*wy'br 'brm b'rṣ*: Gen 12:6), emphasises—by contrast—the similarities in the texts of Gen 12-13*

---

[17] Cf. T. Römer, *Israels Väter. Untersuchungen zur Väterthematik im Deuteronomium und in der deuteronomistischen Tradition* (OBO 99; Freiburg-Göttingen, 1990), 254.

[18] Cf. M. Köckert, *Vätergott und Väterverheissungen. Eine Auseinandersetzung mit Albrecht Alt und seinen Erben* (FRLANT 142; Göttingen, 1988), 250-55.

[19] For an analysis of the expressions to describe the land in Deut 34:1b-3, cf. S.R. Driver, *Deuteronomy* (ICC; Edinburgh, 1895), 417-23; it is worth noting here, as an interesting detail, the term *ś'r*, which in the BH is only represented in Gen 13:10; 14:2.8; 19:22s. (all texts from the Abraham story) 30:2; Deut 34:3; Is 15:5; Jer 48:34.

and Deut 34:1b-4.[20]

From what has been said one can deduce that Deut 34:1b-4 is due, at least in part, to an author who knows the story of Abraham, especially Gen 12:1-4a.6-8 and 13:14-17, passages which belong to the same literary composition.[21]

5. The formation process of Deut 34

To clarify the formation process of a text like Deut 34 right down to the last details is an extremely difficult, if not impossible task. If we have been treating this chapter in its final form, it is not because we think that it is homogeneous, rather the reverse. In spite of this, we have no intention—in the brief space of this analysis—to enter into all the complications of the text. We simply want to enter the current debate, offering some personal points of view which might assist the interpretation of some aspects which are still obscure.

5.1. *Deut 34:1-6* has always been the focal point for exegetes without them reaching a satisfactory solution as to its development. In the first epoch of source criticism, these verses used to be shared out between J, E and P. Since Noth many authors have attributed these verses to DtrH,[22] without however reaching a consensus, except up to a point, about v. 4. Echoing this situation, Perlitt wrote in 1988: "Zahle ich richtig, so bleibt erfreulicherweise immerhin V. 4 für Dtr".[23] Perlitt however did not take account of all the authors earlier than himself,[24]

---

[20] Cf. S. Tengström, *Die Hexateucherzählung. Eine literargeschichtliche Studie* (CB 7; Lund, 1976), 147. This same author indicates that the expression *nšbʿty* of Deut 34:4 goes back to Gen 22:16, a text which is attributed by E. Blum to the KD composition, *Die Komposition der Vätergeschichte* (WMANT 57; Neukirchen-Vluyn, 1984), 363ff.

[21] Cf. M. Köckert, *Vätergott* (n. 18), 250-66. See also M. Collin, "Une tradition ancienne dans le cycle d'Abraham? Don de la terre et promesse en Gn 12-13", in:P. Haudebert (ed.) *Le Pentateuque. Débats et Recherches* (LeDiv 151; Paris, 1992), 209-28, especially 217f., who distinguishes a primitive "itinerant tradition" (Gen 12:1a.4a; 13:3*.14s.17), earlier than the oldest Deut texts, and a "very close to Deut tradition" (Gen 12:6s.; 13:7-11), earlier than the priestly tradition.

[22] M. Noth, *Überlieferungsgeschichtliche Studien* (Tübingen, 1967³ [1943¹]), 213 n. 1 thinks that Deut 34:1aβbα. 4-6 is DtrG, 34,1aα is due to P and that 34:1bβ is a "clarifying addition". Other opinions, cf. supra, n. 7.

[23] L. Perlitt, "Priesterschrift im Deuteronomium?", *ZAW* 100 (1988), 77 n. 29.

[24] Cf. D.E. Skweres, *Die Rückverweise im Buch Deuteronomium* (AnBib 79; Rome, 1979), 91: "Es fällt auf, dass Dtn 34:4 einen anderen Sprachgebrauch aufweist als die übrigen Dtn-Texte".

nor was the "consensus" to last long after him.[25]

After so much reshuffling, can one still say something new about these verses? If we start off once again from the final form of the text, we agree with Polzin that Deut 34:4 is one of those rare examples in the Book of Deut in which the narrator quotes God in a direct address (§2.5). In the Appendix to chapters 31-34, where the traditions/redactions of the Pentateuch and the Dtr history join up, one finds five texts in which the narrator presents a speech of Yahweh: in four of them (31:14.16.23; 34:4) he is introduced by the formula *wy'mr yhwh 'l-mšh / 'lyw*.[26] Without reference to this datum—important, in our opinion—Blum, based only on other observations, attributes Deut 31:14.15.23 to its KD composition, while he considers, as does Noth, that Deut 34:4 is DtrH.[27] As we see it, Deut 34:4 is rather due to the same "author" as Deut 31:14.15.23; an author whom—for want of a better name—we could classify as KD (following the terminology employed by Blum for the texts of chapter 31), but not as DtrH.[28] To support this interpretation one must stress in the first place that Deut 34:4 does not fit in with the deuteronomic or Dtr current.[29] In a recent analysis of texts relating to "the Promise of the Land as Oath", Boorer has identified "a standard formulation in Deuteronomy", represented by numerous passages from Deut and from the rest of the Pentateuch. It is clear however that, in this analysis, texts such as Gen 50:24; Ex 33:1; Num 32:11 and Deut 34:4 do not easily fit into the stereotypes proper to the above mentioned formula.[30] So one confirms, from another angle, that Deut 34:4 belongs neither to the deuteronomic nor the Dtr current, but rather has to be attributed to a different redaction. If one thinks, on the other hand, that even Blum

---

[25] T. Römer, *Israels Väter* (n. 17), 254 writes: "34:4 gehört zur (oder in die Nähe der) Endredaktion des Pentateuch"; see the reply of N. Lohfink and the counter-reply of Römer in *Die Väter Israels im Deuteronomium* (OBO 111; Freiburg-Göttingen, 1991).

[26] In Deut 34:23 one can deduce clearly from the immediate context that it is Yahweh who addresses Moses. With regard to the fifth text, Deut 32:48-52, cf. *infra*, § 5.3.

[27] E. Blum, *Die Komposition* (n. 20), 374 n. 87; Id., *Studien* (n. 9), 76-88.

[28] The attribution of Deut 34:4 to KD does not necessarily imply that Deut 1:8; 6:10; 9:5 etc. must be attributed to the same composition. For one thing, in none of these texts does the narrator introduce God's direct speech, as he does in Deut 34:4.

[29] Cf. A. Dillmann, *Die Bücher Numeri, Deuteronomium und Josua* (KEH; Leipzig, 1886²), 433; also see Skeweres, n. 23 and Römer, *Israels Väter* (n. 17), 252.

[30] S. Boorer, *The Promise of the Land as Oath. A Key to the Formation of the Pentateuch* (BZAW 205), Berlin, New York 1992, 112-118.

attributes Gen 50:24; Ex 33:1 and Num 32:11 to KD,[31] it appears logical—if not obligatory—to attribute Deut 34:4 to this same composition. The coincidences between Deut 34:4 and Ex 33:1 certainly support such an interpretation. In a word, the reasons furnished in part 4, together with those we have just noted in this part, endorse the view that Deut 34:4 belongs to the same literary composition as Ex 33:1; Deut 31:14.15.23 etc.

When it comes to *Deut 34:1b-3*, closely linked to 34:4 (§4), one ought to make some distinctions. In the opinion of Noth, 34:1bα would belong to the DtrH, while 34:1bβ would be an addition (n. 22). In favour of this opinion, one can adduce the fact that 34:1ba, referring to the vision of the land, is prepared by other Dtr texts, particularly by Deut 3:23-29. On the other hand, 34:1bβ-3 does not fit in with some Dtr texts round about it, especially not with Jos 1:4.[32] Consequently, Deut 34:1bβ has to be attributed to another author or redactor, probably the same one who composed 34:4. The repetition of the verb *r'h* at the end of v. 4 could be interpreted as a wish of the aforementioned redactor to tie up more closely the links between v. 4 and v. lb-3. Such an interpretation would be strengthened by the comparison between Deut 34:1b-4 with Gen 12s. The use of the formula *wšmh l' t'br*, with which Deut 34:4 ends, would point in the same direction (cf. *supra* §4). This redactor would, in his turn, be one who elaborated Deut 34:10(-12), as we will see shortly. We are dealing with an author / redactor who was not so much concerned with the connection of his work with Dtr History (hence the fact that neither 34:1bβ-3 nor 34:10-12 fits in well with the Dtr beginning of Joshua)[33] as with the History of Abraham (and because of this has composed his text, while keeping Gen 12s in mind).

5.2. *Deut 34:10* belongs, according to Blum, to KD, a composition particularly interested in prophecy. In this composition Moses is placed in the orbit of the prophets, without losing his pre-eminence. One can deduce this from Deut 34:10: "and there has not arisen a prophet since

---

[31] E. Blum, *Studien* (n. 9), 58ff.72ff.

[32] According to M.A. O'Brien, *The Deuteronomistic History Hypothesis: A Reassessment* (OBO 92; Freiburg-Göttingen, 1989), 27-29. 64-66, the DtrG version of Deut 3:23-28 is continued in Deut 31:7f.9a.24-26; 34:1-6*, while 31:2-6. 14-15. 23 are the fruit of a later elaboration. On the Dtr character of Jos 1:1ff, cf. M. Noth, *Das Buch Josua* (HAT 7; Tübingen, 1971³), 27ff.

[33] J. Blenkinsopp comments: "That the opening verse of the Former Prophets (Jos 1:1) follows on more naturally after Deut 34:6 or 34:9 confirms our impression that it (= 34:10-12) is a relatively late statement ...", *Prophecy and Canon. A Contribution to the Study of Jewish Origins* (Notre Dame IN-London, 1977), 85f.

in Israel like Moses, whom the Lord knew face to face". In this passage, which was surely acquainted with Deut 18:15-22, regarding prophets of the mosaic type,[34] the fact that Moses deals with God "face to face" (cf. Ex 33:1; 34:5ff.29; Num 12:8) shows his intimacy with Him and, at the same time, his superiority over other prophets.[35] In this perspective, one can well understand the divine speech and the vision of Deut 34:1b-4, whose formal connections with some prophetic accounts of visions we have already mentioned (§4). It seems normal that the editor who wants to conclude the Pentateuch by exalting the prophetic figure of Moses tries to bolster this figure by using a divine speech and a vision with certain prophetic characteristics. The KD composition begins with the figure of Abraham, who in Gen 20:7 also receives the title of *nabî* and who in Gen 15:1-6 is considered as a seer,[36] and reaches its highest point with Moses, the greatest of the prophets (Deut 34:10).

Whether or not *Deut 34:11-12* belongs to KD is a question that Blum does not tackle. Commentators often note that these verses do not sit well with v. 10. Steuernagel comments briefly: "11-12 schliessen schlecht an", but hesitates to classify them later as a secondary addition, but rather he simply adds: "sind also *vielleicht* (my underlining) ein Zusatz".[37] In my opinion, from the formal point of view there is no shortage of characteristics which invite us to think of the unity of 34:10-12 (cf. §3.3). From the thematic point of view also, there exists a coherence in these verses, because in them the superiority and incomparability of the prophetic figure of Moses is given prominence, through the remembrance of the wonders worked by him in Egypt. These are not alien to his prophetic condition. On the contrary, they endorse and enhance it: "By (one) prophet Yahweh brought Israel up from Egypt (cf. Hos 12:10; 13:4): this is Moses (Deut 18:15; 34:10)", is the comment of Andersen-Freedman.[38] The promises to the patriarchs and the events of the exodus make up the pillars on which the first generation to return from exile bases itself. It is precisely within this framework that the work KD fits (§2.3). Would this not be

---

[34] Cf. F. García López, "Un profeta como Moisés. Estudio crítico de Deut 18,9-22", en: N. Fernández Marcos et al. (eds.), *Simposio Bíblico Español* (Madrid, 1984), 289-308.

[35] Cf. J. Blenkinsopp, *Prophecy and Canon*, (n. 33), 89ff; E. Blum, *Studien*, (n. 9), 76ff.194ff.

[36] Cf. W. Zimmerli, "Der 'Prophet' im Pentateuch", in: G. Braulik (ed.), *Studien zum Pentateuch (Fs. W. Kornfeld)* (Wien-Freiburg-Basel, 1977), 197-211.

[37] C. Steuernagel, *Das Deuteronomium* (n. 13), 183.

[38] F.I. Andersen - D.N. Freedman, *Hosea* (AB 24; Garden City, N.Y., 1980), 621.

a magnificent conclusion to the whole KD composition—I wonder—:
the references to the patriarchs (Deut 34:4), in the first place, and to
the exodus (34:10-12) as the ultimate glorification of Moses? Just as
what Yahweh did was seen by the prophetic eyes of Moses (hr'ytyk
b'ynyk: 34:4) one could add that what the great prophet Moses did was
done before the eyes of all of Israel. (l'yny kl-yśr'l: 34:12).

5.3. Most exegetes interested in the formation process of Deut 34 agree
in attributing v. 1*.7a.8-9 to P (§2.2). Recently Perlitt has called into
question whether these belong to P^g.[39] These positions, however
distant and different they might be or appear, can be brought much
closer together by attributing these verses to a redactor of the priestly
current on the one hand who, on the other hand, would be later than
KD; such a person could be the post-exilic editor (author/redactor) who
composed KP (cf. supra, §2.3).

The central piece of this composition in Deut 34 is found in v. 7a +
8a.8b and 9a + 9bα.9bβ whose syntactic-stylistic parallelism we have
already mentioned (§3.2).[40] This same "editor" would have composed
some minor pieces with the intention of better slotting his own text
into the chapter, or of strengthening and complementing the existing
text. Thus, the use of the expression b'rbwt mw'b in v. 8 would lead
him to add m'rbwt mw'b in v. 1, thus showing the differences from the
expressions of v. 5-6 referring to Moab. At the end of v. 5 he would,
in like manner, add the expression 'l py yhwh, parallel to k'šr ṣwh
yhwh which finishes v. 9.[41]

Finally, KP would be responsible for Deut 32:48-52 (§2.3). Deut
32:48 is one of those five passages in Deut into which the narrator
introduces a divine discourse (§5.1). The formula used here differs
from that of the other four texts already examined. Even if the narrator
is still the same, the editor or redactor is not. Deut 32:48-52 was
certainly added by KP to provide a bridge between Deut 31* and 34*
where, possibly, we must seek the primitive conclusion of DtrH and
KD.

---

[39] L. Perlitt, "Priesterschrift im Deuteronomium?", ZAW 100 (1988), 65-88.

[40] Deut 34:7b does not fit in with either the syntactical-stylistic structure of v.
7a.8-9 or with the language proper to the priestly current.

[41] Cf. supra §3.4 on the significance and parallelism of these expressions; see
also F. García López, "ṣwh", TWAT, VI, 936-59.

6. *Conclusion*

Referring to "the Canonical Shape of the Pentateuch", Childs writes: "Any attempt to offer a different approach to the study of the Pentateuch which does not take into account the achievements of historical critical scholarship over the last two hundred years is both naive and arrogant".[42] This statement has been amply demonstrated by our analysis of Deut 34. We have come a long way from the former historical type criticism of the Pentateuch to the new criticism of a literary character. Our study has benefited as much from the historical-diachronic studies as it has from the literary-synchronic ones.

Deut 34 can be read as *one single narrative,* in which the last information on the life of Moses is given, his death is related and his figure exalted. A figure which achieves prominence thanks to Yahweh.

Deut 34 can also be read at three successive levels which complement and enrich each other. At the first level, represented by *DtrH (34:1*. 2aα.5.6a)*, the story is told of Moses' ascent to the summit of Pisga, his vision of the promised land and his death and burial there. Moses is presented as the "servant of Yahweh" in keeping with the Dtr current of Jos 1:1ff. This presentation is prepared by Deut 3:23-29 (DtrH). At the second level, *KD (34:2aβ- 4.10-12)* goes deeper into the mission and importance of Moses, presented as the greatest of the prophets. The divine speech, with reference to the promise to the patriarchs, closely linked to the quasi-prophetic vision of the land and the allusions to the exodus events also connected with Moses as prophet, contributes to this. This composition is not so much concerned with the continuation in Jos 1 as it is with crowning the whole work with a conclusion in keeping with its beginning (Gen 12s.). Finally, at the third level, *KP (34:1*.5b*. 7a.8-9),* some data referring to Moses are completed or emphasised, while mention is made of Joshua, the principal character in the next book. If in DtrH Moses is the "servant of Yahweh" and in KD is the prophet *par excellence*, in KP he appears as the "hander on" of his leadership to Joshua.

A personage as outstanding as Moses could not disappear completely from the scene: his works remain, as do the successors in his enterprise. The voice of the narrator integrates all the different voices into one single narrative. With it, the full stop is put on the Pentateuch in an "open ended" conclusion.

Open also is the conclusion of this study of ours; we do not claim to have settled any question but we hope through it to contribute to the clarification of some problems discussed in current exegesis.

---

[42] B.S. Childs, *Introduction* (n. 11), 27.

LES MANUSCRITS DU DÉSERT DE JUDA ET LE DEUTÉRONOME

F. GARCÍA MARTÍNEZ

Qumrân Instituut-RUG

Avec la publication de *The Dead Sea Scrolls on Microfiche*[1] il est finalement possible d'arriver à une vision d'ensemble des apports des manuscrits du Désert de Juda à l'étude du Deutéronome. Pour cette vision d'ensemble il est nécessaire d'étudier au moins six sortes de données provenant de divers types de manuscrits:

— les apports des manuscrits proprement bibliques, c'est-à-dire des copies du livre de Deutéronome;

— les apports des tefillim et des mezuzot qui contiennent des extraits de Deutéronome;

— les apports des citations explicites du Deutéronome qui se trouvent dans divers manuscrits qumrâniens[2] et de bien plus nombreuses allusions, références, etc., qui nous montrent l'influence et l'assimilation du Deutéronome au début de l'ère chrétienne;

— les apports de toute une série de manuscrits trouvés à Qumrân qui se placent aux frontières du texte biblique, manuscrits que l'on classe dans le groupe des paraphrases bibliques, mais qui pour une grande partie au moins nous transmettent une (autre) forme du texte biblique:[3]

— les apports des textes halachiques qui nous offrent des réélabora-

---

[1] E. Tov with the collaboration of Stephen J. Pfann (eds.), *The Dead Sea Scrolls on Microfiche. A Comprehensive Facsimile Edition of the Texts from the Judean Desert* (Leiden, 1993).

[2] Par exemple dans le Document de Damas, où on trouve les citations suivantes du Deutéronome: Deut 5:12 dans CD x,16-17; Deut 7:9 dans CD xix,1; Deut 9:5 dans CD viii,14-16; Deut 9:23 dans CD iii,7; Deut 17:17 dans CD iv,19-v,2; Deut 23:24 dans CD xvi,6-7; Deut 32:33 dans CD viii,9-23.

[3] Par exemple 4Q158 et 4Q364-367, sur lesquels voir E. Tov, "The Textual Status of 4Q364-367 (4QPP)", J. Trebolle Barrera - L. Vegas Montaner (eds.), *The Madrid Qumran Congress* (STDJ XI,1; Leiden-Madrid, 1993), 43-82. 4Q364 contiendrait d'abondants fragments de Deut 1-14, 4Q365 aurait préservé uniquement une partie des chapitres 2 et 19 de Deut., et 4Q366 seulement des chapitres 14 et 16. La partie conservée des autres deux copies de l'œuvre, 4Q158 et 4Q367, ne comprennent pas de restes du Deutéronome. Par contre, le seul fragment préservé de 6Q20 pourrait être une paraphrase du Deutéronome.

tions des lois du Deutéronome:[4]

— les apports de certains textes, comme le *Rouleau du Temple*, qui sont en grande partie une réécriture du texte même du Deutéronome.

Il est clair que nous sommes encore très loin d'une telle vision d'ensemble, qui prend en considération toutes ces données. Un bon nombre d'études préparatoires doivent être auparavant réalisées. Dans cette contribution en l'honneur de C.J. Labuschagne, qui a tant œuvré pour améliorer notre connaissance de ce texte biblique,[5] je voudrais collaborer à ce travail préparatoire par rapport notamment à la première des six sortes de données mentionnées en présentant d'abord une transcription des quelques copies du Deutéronome encore inédites et en dressant une liste complète des passages du Deutéronome qui se trouvent dans la totalité des manuscrits bibliques provenant du Désert de Juda.

1. *Copies du Deutéronome provenant du Désert de Juda*

Un parcours rapide du *Companion Volume* de l'édition en microfiche et du *Dead Sea Scroll Inventory Project*[6] permet de reconnaître comme restes de copies du Deutéronome les manuscrits suivants (avec, entre parenthèses, leur lieu d'édition):

1Q4	[1QDeut^a]	(*DJD* I,[7] pp. 54-57, pl. IX)
1Q5	[1QDeut^b]	(*DJD* I, pp. 57-62, pl. X)
2Q10	[2QDeut^a]	(*DJD* III,[8] p. 60, pl. XII)
2Q11	[2QDeut^b]	(*DJD* III, pp. 60-61, pl. XII)
2Q12	[2QDeut^c]	(*DJD* III, pp. 61-62, pl. XII)
4Q28	[4QDeut^a]	(White,[9] *JBL*, 23-28)
4Q29	[4QDeut^b]	(Duncan,[10] Diss., 14-31, fig. 1-4, pl. I)

---

[4] 4QMMT, par exemple, cite expressément le Deutéronome.

[5] Voir son monumental commentaire, C.J. Labuschagne, *Deuteronomium* I^a, I^b et II (POT; Nijkerk, 1987 et 1990).

[6] Stephen A. Reed, *Dead Sea Scroll Inventory Project: Lists of Documents, Photographs and Museum Plates*. Fascicle 7: Qumran Cave 4 (4Q1-127) Biblical (Claremont, 1992).

[7] D. Barthélemy - J.T. Milik, *Qumrân Cave 1* (DJD I; Oxford, 1955).

[8] M. Baillet - J.T. Milik - R. de Vaux, *Les 'Petites Grottes' de Qumrân* (DJD III; Oxford, 1962).

[9] S.A. White, "Three Deuteronomy Manuscripts from Cave 4, Qumran", *JBL* 112 (1993), 23-42.

[10] J.A. Duncan, *A Critical Edition of Deuteronomy Manuscripts from Qumran, Cave IV: 4QDt^b, 4QDt^e, 4QDt^h, 4QDt^j, 4QDt^k, 4QDt^l* (Harvard University, 1989).

4Q30	[4QDeut^c]	(White,[11] Diss., 19-127, pl. 128-132)
4Q31	[4QDeut^d]	(White, *JBL*, 28-34)
4Q32	[4QDeut^e]	(Duncan, Diss., 39-49, fig. 5-9, pl. II)
4Q33	[4QDeut^f]	(White, Diss., 155-210, pl. 211-214)
4Q34	[4QDeut^g]	(White, *JBL*, 35-42)
4Q35	[4QDeut^h]	(Duncan, Diss., 58-77, fig. 10-16, pl. III)[12]
4Q36	[4QDeut^i]	(White, Diss., 241-261, pl. 262)
4Q37	[4QDeut^j]	(Duncan, Diss., 89-114, fig. 17-26, pl. IV-VII)
4Q38a	[4QDeut^{k1}]	(Duncan, Diss., 140-145. 151-152, fig. 27-28. 34-36, pl. VIII)
4Q38b	[4QDeut^{k2}]	(Duncan, Diss., 146-150. 154, fig. 29-33. 37, pl. VIII)
4Q39	[4QDeut^l]	(Duncan, 163-168, fig. 38-44, pl. IX)
4Q40	[4QDeut^m]	Inédit, PAM 42.714
4Q41	[4QDeut^n]	(White, Diss., 263-296, pl. 297-299)
4Q42	[4QDeut^o]	Inédit, PAM 43.055
4Q43	[4QDeut^p]	Inédit, PAM 43.063
4Q44	[4QDeut^q]	(Skehan,[13] *BASOR*, 12-15)
4Q45	[4QpaleoDeut^r]	(*DJD* IX,[14] 131-152, pl. XXXIV-XXXVI)
4Q46	[4QpaleoDeut^s]	(*DJD* IX, 153-154, pl. XXXVII)
4Q122	[4QLXXDeut]	(*DJD* IX, 195-197, pl. XLIII)
5Q1	[5QDeut]	(*DJD* III, pp. 169-171, pl. XXXVI)
6Q3	[6QpapDeut?]	(*DJD* III, pp. 106-107, pl. XX)
11Q3	[11QDeut]	(van der Ploeg,[15] *RevQ*, 10)
Mas1c	[MasDeut]	Inédit, IAA 302376
Mur2	[MurDeut]	(*DJD* II,[16] pp. 78-79, pl. XXI)
XHev/Se3	[HevDeut]	Inédit, PAM 42.187

---

[11] S.A. White, *A critical edition of seven manuscripts of Deuteronomy: 4QDt^a, 4QDt^c, 4QDt^d, 4QDt^f, 4QDt^g, 4QDt^i, and 4QDt^n* (Harvard University, 1988).

[12] Un petit fragment additionnel a été dernièrement publié par E. Eshel - M.E. Stone, "A New Fragment of 4QDeut^h", *JBL* 112 (1993), 487-489.

[13] P.W. Skehan, "A Fragment of the 'Song of Moses' (Deut 32) from Qumran", *BASOR* 136 (1954), 12-15 et "The Qumran Manuscripts and Textual Criticism", *Volume du Congrès. Strasbourg 1957* (SVT 4; Leiden, 1957), 150, n. 1, où Skehan annonce la découverte d'un autre fragment et modifie l'arrangement stichométrique du texte. Voir PAM 42.164.

[14] P.W. Skehan - E. Ulrich - J.E. Sanderson, *Qumran Cave 4 - IV. Palaeo-Hebrew and Greek Biblical Manuscripts* (DJD IX; Oxford, 1993).

[15] J.P.M. van der Ploeg, "Les manuscrits de la grotte XI de Qumrân", *RevQ* 12/45 (1985), 3-15.

[16] P. Benoit - J.T. Milik - R. de Vaux, *Les Grottes de Murabba'at* (DJD II; Oxford, 1961).

En tout, donc, 32 copies plus ou moins fragmentaires du Deutéronome ont été récupérées. La grande majorité provient des grottes de Qumrân, surtout de la Grotte 4 (presque deux tiers). De ces 32 copies cinq seulement, à ma connaissance, restent encore inédites: 4QDeut^m, 4QDeut^o, 4QDeut^p, MasDeut et ḤevDeut.

1.1 *4Q40 [4QDeut^m]*

De ce manuscrit trois fragments ont été préservés: le premier et le plus ample est formé d'un assemblage de quatre morceaux, dont la grande pièce que l'on trouve encore plissée dans plusieurs photographies (PAM 41.423; 42.632, par exemple), deux petites pièces raccordées à distance, et une autre avec un joint matériel direct au niveau de l'insertion interlinéaire.

L'écriture est de type hasmonéen, avec des lettres pas encore bien calibrées et quelques formes archaïques, et pourrait être datée vers la fin du deuxième siècle avant J.-C.

Le texte a été copié dans le système défini par E. Tov comme "Qumran system"[17] et emploie régulièrement les formes כול, לוא (כיא n'est pas attesté dans le texte préservé), ainsi que les formes longues soit des pronoms indépendants, soit des suffixes pronominaux de la deuxième et troisième personne. Son orthographe est pleine, au moins en ce qui concerne l'emploi du *waw* (נותן, אלוהיכמה, אבוד, לכלותמה).

Transcription:[18] PAM 42.714. Autres photographies: PAM 41.423, 41.939, 42.632.

Frag. 1

]לאמור יהוה אלוהי[	] לרשתה [	[1
		ושפכ]
]ישראל כול בן	]יכמה ומ[ ]יכ[ ]]ידעתו	[2
		אלו היכמה
]ר נתתי ל[ ]]א[ן]ר יניח יהוה לאחיכמה ככמ]		[3
]ה את הא[ן] אלוהיכמה נותן להמה בעבר הי[ן		[4
]את יהושוע צויתי בעת ההואה לא[ן		[5

---

6 [ ] לשני המלכים האלה כן יע[ן

7 [ ] ה ולוא תיראום [

Frag. 2

1 [ ] ה למן [

2 [ ] הנהיה כדבר [

3 [ ]ר שמעתמה א[ן

4 [ ] ובמ[ן

Frag. 3

1 [ ]יכן

2 [ ]יד החזקה [

3 [ ]ה אלוהיכה לכול העמים א[ן

4 [ ] במה עד אבוד הנשא[ן

5 [ ] בקרבכה אל גד[ן

6 [ ]וכל לכלוותמ[ן

Reconstruction:

Frag. 1: Deut 3:18-22

[בעת ההואה]לאמור יהוה אלוהי[כמה נתן לכמה את הארץ הזואת] לרשתה [הלוצים]
[וטפכ]מה[

[תעברו לפני אחיכמה בני] ישראל כול ב[ני חיל רק נש]יכמה ומ[ן]קנ[י]כ[מה] ידעתי
אלו היכמה

[כי מקנה רב לכמה ישבו בעריכמה אש]ר נתחי ל[כמה עד] א[ש]ר יניח יהוה לאחיכמה ככמ[ה
[וירשו גם המ]ה את הא[רץ אשר יהוה] אלוהיכמה נותן להמה בעבר הי[רדן ושבתמה]
[איש לירושתו אשר נתתי לכמה ו]את יהושוע צויתי בעת ההואה לא[מור עיניכה]
[הרואות את כול אשר יהוה אלוהיכמה] לשני המלכים האלה כן יע[שה יהוה]
[לכול הממלכות אשר אתה עובר שמ]ה ולוא תיראום [כי יהוה אלוהיכמה הואה]

Le fragment contient deux insertions interlinéaires. La première (si *vera lectio*), serait l'insertion de וטפכמה juste au-dessus de ידעתי. La lecture est incertaine, mais les traces conservées au bord du fragment semblent correspondre mieux à ce mot, avec *waw*, que à ומקנכמה. En tout cas, il est clair que le scribe avait écrit au début uniquement deux des trois catégories qui devaient rester dans les villes (femmes, enfants et troupeaux), et qu'après il en a ajouté une troisième. Le Pentateuque Samaritain (PS) inverse ici l'ordre du TM et de la LXX mentionnant en premier lieu les enfants, avant les femmes. Malheureusement, l'état de notre manuscrit ne nous permet pas d'être sûrs de la lecture, mais plutôt qu'à une variante, je pense que nous avons à faire à une insertion hors de place.

La deuxième insertion est de lecture certaine, bien que le mot se trouve séparé par la hampe du *lamed* de la ligne inférieure.

Mis à part les variantes orthographiques et l'emploi des formes longues des suffixes, le fragment ne nous offre que deux variantes réelles par rapport au TM: l'insertion אלוהיכמה après יהוה dans la ligne 3, en accord avec la LXX contre TM et le PS, et l'addition du *waw* en ולוא de la ligne 7, une addition propre à notre manuscrit qui ne se trouve nulle part ailleurs.

Frag. 2: Deut 4:32-34

[להמה כי שאלו נא לימים ראשונים אשר היו לפניכמ]ה למן [היום אשר ברא אלוהים]

[אדם על הארץ ולמקצה השמים ועד קצה השמים] הנהיה כדבר [הגדול הזה או הנשמע]

[כמוהו השמע עם קול אלוהים מדבר מתוך האש כאש]ר שמעתמה א[תמה ותחיו או הנסה]

[אלוהים לבוא לקחת לו גוי מקרב גוי במסות באותות] ובמ[ופתים ובמלחמה וביד]

L'identification de ce petit fragment avec Deut 4:32 semble s'imposer grâce aux mots clairement visibles dans la ligne 2, הנהיה כדבר (les lectures des lignes 1 et 4, ne sont que des conjectures, plus ou moins raisonnables). Mais cela implique une variante dans la ligne suivante. La lecture du verbe à la deuxième personne du pluriel, contre la deuxième personne du singulier des autres témoins (שמעת אתה du TM et PS, ἀκήκοας σὺ de la LXX) est certaine. Uniquement la version Syriaque et le Targum Palestinien lisent le verbe (et le pronom suivant) au pluriel, comme notre manuscrit. Notre texte semble prolonger ici une tendance que l'on trouve déjà dans les autres témoins (dans 4:25.29 et 37, par exemple), ce qui montrerait le caractère secondaire de cette variante, mais qui nous oblige aussi à reconstruire le verbe au pluriel dans la ligne 1, en accord avec le Targum Palestinien et la version Syriaque.

La reconstruction du verbe suivant est plus problématique. TM lit le verbe à la troisième personne du singulier (ויחי), en prenant comme sujet le 'peuple'; la LXX et la version latine représentent une lecture ותחי, deuxième personne du singulier, avec 'toi' (Israël) comme sujet;[19] la version syriaque et le Targum palestinien prennent aussi le pronom comme sujet et conséquemment portent le verbe à la deuxième personne du pluriel. En vue de l'accord de notre manuscrit avec le Targum et la version Syriaque dans le pluriel du verbe précédent, la reconstruction du pluriel ici aussi, semble la plus logique.

---

[19] C'est un des rares cas dans lesquels C. Labuschagne s'éloigne de la lecture de TM et suit la lecture de la LXX, *Deuteronomium deel IA*, 286.

Frag. 3: Deut 7:18-22

[זכור תזכור את אשר עשׂה יהוה אלוה]יכ[ה לפרעה ולכול מצרים המסות הגדולות אשר]

[ראו עיניכה והאותות והמופתים וה]יד החזקה [והזרוע הנטויה אשר הוצאכה יהוה]

[אלוהיכה כן יעשה יהו]ה אלוהיכה לכול העמים א[שר אתה ירא מפניהמה וגם את הצרעה]

[ישלח יהוה אלוהיכה] במה עד אבוד הנשא[רים והנסתרים מפניכה לוא תערוץ מפניהמה]

[כי יהוה אלוהיכה] בקרבכה אל גד[ול ונורא ונשל יהוה אלוהיכה את הגוים האל]

[מפניכה מעט מעט לוא ת]וכל לכלותמ[ה מהר פן תרבה עליכה חית השׂדה ונתנמה יהוה]

Mis à part les variantes orthographiques, ce fragment nous offre dans la partie conservée uniquement une variante: l'addition du *lamed* à l'infinitif *pi'el* כלתם du TM, dans notre manuscrit écrit לכלותמה. Cette variante, que nous retrouvons uniquement dans les Targumim sous l'influence de l'araméen, pourrait nous indiquer que la modernisation du manuscrit ne se limitait pas à l'orthographe, mais touchait aussi la syntaxe.

1.2 *4Q42 [4QDeut⁰]*

Parmi les manuscrits du Deutéronome encore inédits, 4Q42 est celui qui contient apparemment le plus grand nombre de fragments. Dans la planche PAM 43.055 on peut compter un total de 18 fragments, mais certains d'entre eux peuvent se raccorder à distance et nous les présentons donc ensemble. Trois autres fragments semblent appartenir à 4Q43 [4QDeutᵖ], malgré une écriture presque identique qui rend l'attribution à l'un ou à l'autre manuscrit très incertaine. On aurait donc en tout 15 fragments de ce manuscrit, dont deux n'ont pas été identifiés. Le fragment 1 provient de la partie finale d'une feuille de cuir et il garde encore dans toute sa longueur la marge intercolonnaire de gauche et les cordes d'attache à la feuille suivante. C'est le seul fragment dans lequel la réglure est encore visible dans les photographies. Le fragment 5 provient de la partie inférieure d'une colonne et a conservé aussi la marge intercolonnaire de gauche et le début d'un mot de la dernière ligne de la colonne suivante. Les fragments 2 et 12 par contre ont conservé la marge intercolonnaire de droite, mais il n'est pas sûr que les traces que l'on peut constater dans les marges proviennent de la fin de quelques mots des colonnes précédentes. L'écriture du fragment est du type hasmonéen que l'on peut dater aux environs de l'année 100 avant J.-C. L'orthographe du manuscrit est quelque peu plus pleine que celle du TM, mais sans que l'on puisse pour cela la classer comme orthographe du type qumrânien selon la typologie de Tov.

Transcription: PAM 43.055. Autres photographies: PAM 41.423, 41.42.003, 42.006, 42.712.

Frag. 1

[היך	]	1
ולא [	]	2
אשנים[	]	3
ולמקצה [	]	4
או הנשמע [	]	5
עת[	]	6

Frag. 2

כמן	1
אתה]	2
באתות]	3
ל[ ] לן	4

Frag. 3

[מה וביד]	]	1

Frag. 4

[ינו יהוה]	]	1
[היו הדברן	]	2

Frag. 5

[הוה	]	1
[ם	]	2
[כבך	]	3
[ביתך	]	4
Vacat [	]	5
[וליעקב	]	6
[לאת	]	7

Frag. 6

[תך בדרך ובן	]	1

Frag. 7

[יו לטטפות]	]	1
] Vacat [	]	2
[להיך אל]	]	3

Frag. 8

[בקול יהוה אן	]	1
[ללות האלה והשינ	]	2
[אדמתך שנר אלפין	]	3

Frag. 9

[אכל עם אשר]	]	1
[כן]הוה]	]	2

Frag. 10

[הוה אלהיך]	]	1
[בצמא ובערום]	]	2
[מרחוק מקן	]	3

Frag. 11

[בהן	]	1
[תרות צאנן	]	2
[בהן בכלן	]	3

Frag. 12

לא תשן	1
הזה את]	2
ונאמנים]	3
אשר לאן	4
הייתם]	5

Frag. 13

[בחמתו ואמרו כן	]	1
[אמרו על אשר עזבו]	]	2
[מארץ מצרים]	]	3

Frag. 14

[לא חן	]	1
[לן	]	2

Frag. 15

[ה אותרן	]	1
[ים ען	]	2

Reconstruction:

Frag. 1 + 2 + 3: Deut 4:30-34

[לך ומצאוך כל הדברים האלה באחרית הימים ושבת עד יהוה אל]היך

[ושמעת בקלו כי אל רחום יהוה אלהיך לא ירפך ולא ישחיתך] ולא

[ישכח את ברית אבתיך אשר נשבע להם כי שאל נא לימים ר]אשנים

[אשר היו לפניך למן היום אשר ברא אלהים אדם על הארץ] ולמקצה

[השמים ואד קצה השמים הנהיה כדבר הגדול הזה] או הנשמע

כמ[הו השמע עם קול אלהים מדבר מתוך האש כאשר שמ]עת

אתה [ויחי או הנסה אלהים לבוא לקחת לו גוי מקרב גוי במסות]

באתות [ובמופתים ובמלח]מה וביד [חזקה ובזרוע נטויה ובמוראים]

[גד]ל[י]ם ככל אשר עשה לכם יהוה אלהיכם במצרים לעיניך אתה הראת]

Les quelques mots conservés correspondent exactement au TM, avec comme seule variante orthographique l'écriture pleine de באתות dans le frag. 2.

Frag. 4 + 5 + 6 + 7 Deut 6:5-11

[   ] Vacat שמע ישראל יהוה אלה]ינו יהוה [אחד ואהבת את י]הוה

[אלהיך בכל לבבך ובכל נפשך ובכל מאדך ו]היו הדבר]ים האלה אשר אנכי מצוך היו]ם

[על לבבך ושננתם לבניך ודברת בם בשבתך ביתך ובלכ]תך בדרך ובש]כבך

[ובקומך וקשרתם לאות על ידך וה]יו לטטפות [בין עיניך וכתבתם על מזוזת] ביתך

[ובשעריך   ] Vacat [Vacat

[והיה כי יביאך יהוה א]להיך אל [הארץ אשר נשבע לאבתיך לאברהם ליצחק] וליעקב

[לתת לך ערים גדלת וטבת אשר לא בנית ובתים מלאים כל טוב אשר לא מ]לאת

Dans cet ensemble il n'y a qu'une seule variante orthographique par rapport au TM, l'écriture pleine de לטטפות dans la première ligne du frag. 7. En plus, tant le frag. 5 que le frag. 7 ont un ample *vacat* qui correspond à la *parašah setumah* dans le TM, faisant ainsi la correspondance encore plus complète. Ce qui justifie la reconstruction d'un *vacat* aussi à la ligne 1, correspondant à la *parašah petuḥah* du TM, *vacat* exigé d'ailleurs par l'espacement imposé par les mots conservés dans le frag. 4 de lecture certaine dans PAM 42.712.

Frag. 8 Deut 28:15-19

[והיה אם לא תשמע] בקול יהוה א]להיך לשמר לעשות את כל מצוותיו וחקתיו אשר אנכי מצוך היום]

[ובאו עליך כל הק]ללות האלה והשיגן]וך ארור אתה בעיר וארור אתה בשדה ארור טנאך ומשארתך]

[ארור פרי בטנך ופרי] אדמתך שגר אלפי]ך ועשתרות צאנך ארור אתה בבאך וארור אתה בצאתך]

Les mots préservés s'accordent complètement avec le TM, y compris l'omission de ופרי בהמתך que l'on trouve dans le PS et dans le même

TM à Deut 18:4. L'espacement régulier des lignes reconstruites nous assure aussi qu'en Deut 28:15 notre manuscrit contenait les mots omis par le PS.

Dans le reste des fragments nous rencontrons uniquement une variante orthographique, la lecture ובערום dans le frag. 10, 2 (avec la même graphie du PS) au lieu de בעירם du TM.

Frag. 9 Deut 28:33-35

[וכל יניאך י]אכל עם אשר [לא ידעת והיית רק עשוק ורצוץ כל הימים והיית משגע ממראה]

[עיניך אשר תראה י]כ[כ]ה י]הוה [בשחין רע על הברכים ועל השקים אשר לא תוכל להרפא מכף]

Frag. 10 + 11 Deut 28:47-52

[תחת אשר לא עבדת את י]הוה אלהיך [בשמחה ובטוב לבב מרב כל ועבדת את איביך אשר]

[ישלחנו יהוה בך ברעב ו]בצמא ובערום [ובחסר כל ונתן על ברזל על צוארך עד השמידו]

[אתך ישא יהוה עליך גוי] מרחוק מק[צה הארץ כאשר ידאה הנשר גוי אשר לא תשמע לשנו]

[גוי עז פנים אשר לא ישא פנים לזקן ונער לא יחן ואכל פרי] בה[מתך ופרי אדמתך עד]

[השמדרך אשר לא ישאיר לך דגן תירוש ויצהר שגר אלפיך ועש]תרות צאנ[ך עד האבידו אתך]

[והצר לך בכל שעריך עד רדת חמתיך הגבהות והבצרות אשר אתה בטח] בהן בכל [ארצך והצר]

Frag. 12 Deut 28:58-62

לא תש[מר לעשות את כל דברי התורה הזאת הכתובים בספר הזה ליראה את השם הנכבד והנורא]

הזה את [יהוה אלהיך והפלא יהוה את מכתך ואת מכות זרעך מכות גדלות ונאמנות וחלים רעים]

ונאמנים [והשיב בך את כל מדוה מצרים אשר ינרת מפניהם ודבקו בך גם כל חלי וכל מכה]

אשר לא [כתוב בספר התורה הזאת יעלם יהוה עליך עד השמדרך ונשארתם במתי מעט תחת אשר]

הייתם [ככוכבי השמים לרב כי לא שמעת בקול יהוה אלהיך והיה כאשר שש יהוה עליכם להיטב]

Frag. 13 Deut 29:22-25

[אדמה וצבויים אשר הפך יהוה באפו ו]בחמתו ואמרו כ[ל הגוים על מה עשה יהוה ככה]

[לארץ הזאת מה חרי האף הגדול הזה ו]אמרו על אשר עזבו [את ברית יהוה אלהי]

[אבתם אשר כרת עמם בהוציאו אתם] מארץ מצרים [וילכו ויעבדו אלהים אחרים וישתחוו]

L'identification des fragments 14 et 15 reste incertaine.

1.3 *4Q43 (4QDeut^p)*

Dans la même planche du PAM (43.063) dans laquelle sont reproduits les fragments de 4Q34 (4QDeut^g), un manuscrit dernièrement publié par S.A. White,[20] se trouve un petit fragment avec des restes de 5

---

[20] S.A. White, "Three Deuteronomic Manuscripts from Cave 4, Qumran", *JBL* 112 (1993), 23-42.

lignes et la marge intercolonnaire droite. Apparemment ce fragment et les trois fragments de la partie inférieure droite de PAM 43.055 sont les restes d'une autre copie de Deut encore inédite, 4Q43 ou 4QDeut^p. Ce frag. (frag. 4) est en réalité formé de trois petits fragments aux joints sûrs, mais dont le joint au niveau de la ligne 3 se trouve légèrement décalé dans la photographie. La graphie de ce manuscrit est très similaire à celle du manuscrit précédent, bien qu'avec un ductus un peu plus grossier, et devrait être datée vers la même époque.

Transcription: PAM 43. 055 et 43.063. Autres photographies: PAM 42.632, 42.172, 42.732.

Frag. 1

[הם שמעו/תן]	]	1
[כם היום ולמ]	]	2
[רית בחרב לא]	]	3
[אנחנו אלה פה ה]	]	4
[כי עמד]	]	5
[יראתם]	]	6

Frag. 3

[מתחת]	]	1
[י אנכי יהו]	]	2
]Vacat [	]	3

Frag. 2

] Vacat	1
[ואשר במים]	2
] ל[]	3

Frag. 4

[ל ערב] מין]	]	1
[ ]ינהו ואת הכוס ואת ה]		2
והאנפה למינה ואת ה]		3
[ ] כל עוף טהור ת]		4
[ ]לה או מכר לנכ]		5

Reconstruction:

Frag. 1 Deut 5:1-5

[(?) [Vacat] ויקרא משה אל כל ישראל ויאמר אל]הם שמעו/תן]
[את החקים ואת המשפטים אשר אנוכי דבר באזני]כם היום ולמ[דתם]
[אתם ושמרתם לעשתם יהוה אלהינו כרת עמנו ב]רית בחרב לא [את]
[אבתינו כרת יהוה את הברית הזאת כי אתנו] אנחנו אלה פה ה[יום]
[כלנו חיים פנים בפנים דבר יהוה עמכם בהר מתוך האש אנ]כי עמד
[בין יהוה וביניכם בעת ההוא להגיד לכם את דבר יהוה כי] יראתם

Le texte préservé dans le fragment s'accorde parfaitement avec le TM, sauf dans une variante unique à la ligne 1. La lecture de la deuxième personne du singulier de l'impératif du TM et de tous les autres témoins (שמע ישראל), est certainement exclue dans notre manuscrit. Le 'ayin est suivie d'une autre lettre avec laquelle elle est liée. Cette lettre n'est pas entièrement conservée et peut être lue comme un waw sans tête ou comme la hampe droite d'un taw. Dans les deux cas, on aboutit à la lecture du verbe au pluriel, qui pourrait s'expliquer par un désir d'harmonisation avec les verbes suivants ou comme une erreur du copiste. Si on lit l'impératif pluriel, il faudrait reconstruire quelque chose comme בני ישראל comme sujet; si l'on préfère lire le *taw*, il faudrait compléter שמעתם en parallèle avec les verbes suivants et ajouter le pronom אתם comme sujet afin de remplir l'espace jusqu'à la marge (supposée) de la colonne.

Frag. 2 + 3 Deut 5:8-9

Vacat ‬[לא תעשה לך פסל כל תמונה אשר בשמים ממעל ואשר בארץ] מתחת

ואשר במים [מתחת לארץ לא תשתחוה להם ולא תעבדם כ]י אנכי יהו[ה]

[אלהיך א]ל [קנא פקד עון אבות על בנים ועל שלשים ועל רבעים]

La correspondance des deux petits fragments avec Deut 5:8-9 semble assurée, mais le raccord à distance ne se fait pas sans problèmes, dûs aux espaces vides que l'on trouve dans les deux fragments et au double emploi du mot מתחת dans Deut 5:8. Le frag. 2 provient apparemment de la partie droite d'une colonne et les mots préservés contiennent sans doute le début de la ligne; la partie supérieure est vide, ce qui pourrait indiquer que nous avons à faire avec le début d'un colonne ou avec un *vacat* dans la ligne précédente. Le frag. 3, pour sa part, a conservé une partie de cuir non écrit en-dessous de sa deuxième ligne. La seule manière de respecter ces données me semble celle de considérer le frag. 3 comme provenant de la fin de la colonne, et de postuler que le mot יהוה a été écrit mordant dans la marge intercolonnaire et qu'au début de la ligne 1 du frag. 2 se trouvait un *vacat* non attesté dans le TM, correspondant au début de Deut 5:8. L'alternative de considérer le frag. 3 comme le début d'une colonne et de relier directement les deux fragments donne une colonne d'à peine la moitié de l'extension des autres colonnes du manuscrit, et oblige à postuler un *vacat* au milieu d'une phrase. Pour le reste, les deux fragments ne contiennent pas de variantes par rapport au TM.

Frag. 4: Deut 14:14-21

[למינה ואת כ]ל ערב [ל]מי[נו ואת בת היענה ואת התחמס ואת השחף ואת הנץ]

[למ]ינהו ואת הכוס ואת ה[ינשוף והתנשמת והקאת ואת הרחמה ואת השלך והחסידה]

והאנפה למינה ואת ה[דוכיפת והעטלף וכל שרץ העוף טמא הוא לכם לא תאכלו]

[מהם] כל עוף טהור ת[אכלו לא תאכלו כל נבלה לגר אשר בשעריך תתננה]

[ואכ]לה או מכר לנכ[רי כי עם קדוש אתה ליהוה אלהיך לא תבשל גדי בחלב]

Malgré le peu de texte préservé, le fragment pourrait avoir un certain intérêt pour la critique textuelle, bien qu'il soit très difficile de tirer des conclusions sûres. Dans le texte réellement conservé dans le fragment, on peut signaler uniquement deux variantes par rapport au TM: le *waw* dans ואת הכוס (avec tous les autres témoins et Lev 11:17) et le ואת qui précède הדוכיפת (?) (avec PS, qui lit le nom comme הדנפת, et Lev 11:19). Il est bien connu que les variantes du PS dans cette péricope sont de trois types divers: le PS fait précéder chaque sorte d'oiseau de l'indicatif d'objet ואת, il change l'ordre dans lequel certains oiseaux sont nommés dans la série, et il change l'expression לא יאכלו du TM 14:19 en לא תאכלו מהם. L'addition de ואת à la ligne 3 pourrait nous indiquer que notre manuscrit représente un texte semblable au PS, mais on ne peut pas exclure que cette variante, comme celle de la ligne 2, soit due au désir d'harmoniser le texte avec celui du Lev. La transposition de את הנץ avec למינהו (PS למינו) ne se trouvait certainement pas dans notre manuscrit, qui fait suivre למינהו de ואת הכוס (sur la transposition de ואת השלך on ne peut rien savoir à cause de la lacune). Quant à la variante du troisième type, sa présence dans notre manuscrit peut être raisonnablement déduite: - le manuscrit conserve la marge droite dans les lignes 2 et 3; l'alignement avec cette marge dans la ligne 4 montre que uniquement trois lettres manquent en début de ligne et ne permet pas de reconstruire יאכלו avant le כל préservé (comparer avec ואכ[לה] de la ligne 5), mais permet aisément la reconstruction de מהם du PS et de la LXX; - en plus sans une addition comme celle du PS et de la LXX l'extension de la ligne 3 reste bien au-dessous de la moyenne des lettres que l'on peut calculer pour les autres lignes. Je crois donc très vraisemblable la présence de cette variante dans 4Q**43**.

1.4 *MasDeut (Masada 1043, Mas1c)*

Parmi les manuscrits bibliques provenant de Masada se trouve aussi une copie du Deutéronome, apparemment encore inédite (planches 302367 et 302372 de *The Dead Sea Scrolls on Microfiche*) et qui sera publiée avec les autres manuscrits de Masada par le Professeur S. Talmon. Quatre fragments ont été préservés. Le fragment 1, assez grand et avec des restes de la marge supérieure et de la marge intercolonnaire, peut se raccorder à distance avec le frag. 2, mais l'état abrasé du cuir ne permet pas un joint matériel. Par contre les fragments 3 et 4 offrent un joint direct au niveau de la déchirure qui coupe les lignes 5 et 6. Les quatre fragments proviennent de la dernière colonne du rouleau, et le fragment 2 se trouve encore attaché à une très ample feuille de cuir destinée à protéger le rouleau. La belle graphie avec laquelle a été copié le manuscrit pourrait être désignée, avec Cross, comme "late Herodian formal hand", et être datée aux environs des années 50 du premier siècle.

Transcription: IAA 302367. Autre photographie IAA 302372.

Frag. 1 col. i

4 ‏ר[‏

5 ‏]כר‏

Frag. 1 col. ii

marge

1 ‏[שה] וְהם רבבות אפרים והם אל[ן‏

2 ‏[שמח זבולן בצאתך ויששכר באהלין‏

3 ‏שם יזבחו זבחי צדק כי‏

4 ‏טמוני חול ולנד אמרן‏

5 ‏שכן וטרף זרוע אף קן‏

6 ‏חלקת מחקק ספון ון‏

7 ‏עשה ומן‏

Frag. 2			Frag. 3 + 4		
‏[‏	]	1	‏[את כל]‏	]	1
‏[הר יקרא]‏	]	2	‏[ארץ יהודן‏	]	2
‏[שפני‏	]	3	‏[קעת]‏	]	3
‏[ ] [‏	]	4	‏[לן]ו זאת]‏	]	4
‏[ ] ראשית [ ] שם‏	]	5	‏[יצן]ק וליעקן] לאמןר‏	]	5
‏[ם צדן] יהוה‏	]	6	‏[מה לא תעבר וימת שמן‏	]	6
‏[ר דן גור‏	]	7	‏[וה ויקבר]‏	]	7
‏[פתלן] שבע‏	]	8	‏[יש]‏	]	8
‏[מר‏	]	9			

L'élément le plus notable de ces fragments est que, dans les parties préservées, ils n'offrent *aucune* variante, même pas orthographique, par rapport au TM. L'accord avec TM s'étend aussi, pour autant qu'il soit possible de le vérifier, aux divisions du texte. Un ample espace laissé en blanc à la ligne 4 du frag. 1 correspond à une *parašah setumah* dans le TM, et la distribution des mots dans les lignes 1, 7 et 9 du texte reconstruit permet aussi la reconstruction des autres *parašot setumot* du TM. Ce qui, en supposant la même régularité dans les parties perdues, permet une reconstruction aisée de la colonne. Vu que la partie supérieure de la colonne suivante (la feuille de garde) a été préservée avec le frag. 2, on peut en conclure que la fin du Deutéronome se trouvait intégralement dans cette colonne. Comme l'écriture est assez régulière et chaque ligne contient environ 40-43 espaces en moyenne, on peut calculer que dix lignes manquent entre les deux ensembles conservés, et encore quelques dix autres lignes pour compléter le reste. Le total de 38 lignes est assez élevé par rapport à d'autres manuscrits procédant de Masada,[21] mais ne semble pas exagéré outre mesure (S. Talmon estime à 44 les lignes par colonne du MasPs[b]).[22] Avec la même méthode on pourrait, peut-être, identifier les quelques lettres qui restent de la col. i; mais les éléments hypothétiques sont trop grands pour autoriser un tel exercice.

Reconstruction

Frags. 1 + 2 (Deut 33:17-24) + frags. 3 + 4 (Deut 34:2-6)

margin

1	ולזבולן אמר] [והם רבבות אפרים והם אל[פי מנ]שה
2	שמח זבולן בצאתך ויששכר באה[ליך עמים] הר יקרא[ו]
3	שם יזבחו זבחי צדק כ]י שפע ימים יינקו ו[שפני
4	טמוני חול ולגד אמר] ברוך מרחיב גד כלביא[
5	שכן וטרף זרוע אף ק[דקד וירא] ראשית [לו כי] שם
6	חלקת מחקק ספון ו[יתא ראשי ע]ם צד[קת] יהוה
7	עשה ומ[שפטיו עם ישראל ולדן אמ]ר דן גור
8	[אריה יזנק מן הבשן ולנפתלי אמר נ[פתל]י שבע
9	[רצון ומלא ברכת יהוה ים ודרום ירשה ולאשר א]מר
11	[ברוך מבנים אשר יהי רצוי אחיו וטבל בשמן רגלו]
12	[ברזל ונחשת מנעליך וכימיך דבאך אין כאל ישרון]
13	[רכב שמים בעזרך ובגאותו שחקים מענה אלהי קדם]
14	[ומתחת זרעת עולם וינרש מפניך איב ויאמר השמד]
15	[וישכן ישראל בטח בדד עין יעקב אל ארץ דגן ותירוש]
16	[אף שמיו יערפו טל אשריך ישראל מי כמוך עם]
17	[נושע ביהוה מגן עזרך ואשר חרב גאותך ויכחשו]
18	[איביך לך ואתה על במותימו תדרך ויעל משה]
19	[מערבת מואב אל הר נבו ראש הפסגה אשר על]
20	[פני ירחו ויראהו יהוה את כל הארץ את הגלעד]
21	[עד דן ו]את כל [נפתלי ואת ארץ אפרים ומנשה]
22	[ואת כל] ארץ יהוד[ה עד הים האחרון ואת הנגב]
23	[ואת הככר ב]קעת [ירחו עיר התמרים עד צער ויאמר]

---

[21] Par exemple, le rouleau de Ben Sira contient 25 lignes par colonne (Y. Yadin, *The Ben Sira Scroll from Masada* [Jerusalem, 1965]), le manuscrit MasShirShab a 26 lignes (C. Newsom - Y. Yadin, "The Masada Fragment of the Qumran Songs of the Sabbath Sacrifice", *IEJ* 34 [1984], 77-88) et un des rouleaux des Psaumes de Masada, MasPs[a], ne compte pas moins de 28 lignes (G.W. Nebe, "Die Masada-Psalmen-Handschrift M1039-160 nach einem jüngst veröffentlichten Photo mit Text von Psalm 81,2-85,6", *RevQ* 53 [1989], 89-97).

[22] S. Talmon, "Fragments of a Psalms Scroll from Masada, MPs[b] (Masada 1103-1742)", M. Brettler - M. Fishbane, *Minhah le-Nahum. Biblical and other Studies Presented to Nahum M. Sarna in Honour of his 70th Birthday* (JSOTS 154; Sheffield, 1993), 318-327.

24 ‏[יהוה א]ל[י]ו זאת [הארץ אשר נשבעתי לאברהם]

25 ‏[ל]יצ[ח]ק וליעק[ב] לאמ[ר לזראך אתננה הראיתיך בעיניך]

26 ‏[וש]מה לא תעבר וימת שם [משה עבד יהוה בערץ מואב]

27 ‏[אל פי יה]וה ויקבר [אתו בני בארץ מואב מול בית]

28 ‏[פעור ולא ידע א]יש [את קברתו עד היום הזה ומשה]

1.5 X̣Hev/Se3 (H̱evDeut)

Parmi les matériaux provenant du Naḥal Ḥever ou du Wadi Seiyal se
trouve aussi un petit fragment, avec des restes de deux colonnes (dont
la première présente une marge gauche assez irrégulière), d'un manuscrit du Deutéronome. L'écriture pourrait se placer entre la "late Herodian formal script" de 4Q85 et la "post-Herodian Biblical hand" de
XHev/Se4 de la typologie de Cross, et être datée dans la deuxième
moitié du premier siècle. Les quelques lignes conservées nous offrent
un texte identique au TM, sans aucune variante.

Transcription: PAM 42.187

	Col. ii	Col. i	
		‏ה[	] 1
2 [	‏וא[ן	‏[שר לבבך	] 2
3 [	‏ובמס[ן	‏[הגוים	] 3
4 [	‏יהו[ן	‏[ך ולמען	] 4
5 [	‏על[ן	‏[אבתיך	] 5
		‏[בצדקתך	] 6
		‏[זות	] 7
		‏ל[	] 8

Reconstruction

Col. i Deut 9:4-6

1 ‏[את הארץ הזות וברשעת הגוים האלה יהו]ה

2 ‏[מורישם מפניך לא בצדקתך ובי]שר לבבך

3 ‏[אתה בא לרשת את ארצם כי ברשעת]הגוים

4 ‏[האלה יהוה אלהיך מורישם מפני]ך ולמען

5 ‏[הקים את הדבר אשר נשבע יהוה ל]אבתיך

6 ‏[לאברהם ליצחק וליעקב וידעת כי לא]בצדקתך

7 ‏[יהוה אלהיך נתן לך את הארץ הטובה ה]זות

8 ‏[לרשתה כי עם קשה ערף אתה   זכר א]ל

Col. ii Deut 9:21-23

2 וא[שלך את עפרו אל הנחל הירד מן ההר ובתבערה]
3 ובמס[ה ובקברת התאוה מקצפים הייתם את]
4 יהו[ה ובשלח יהוה אתכם מקדש ברנע לאמר]
5 על[ו ורשו את הארץ אשר נתתי לכם ותמרו]

2. *Liste des références*

La publication des textes encore inédits nous permet de dresser un inventaire *exhaustif* de toutes les références du Deutéronome trouvées dans les textes *bibliques* de la Mer Morte, et de compléter ainsi les listes publiées auparavant par J.A. Fitzmyer,[23] García Martínez,[24] et A.S. van der Woude,[25] et celle encore sous presse de U. Gleßmer.[26] Ne sont incluses dans cette liste, ni les références au Deutéronome des Tefillin et Mezuzot, ni les citations de Deutéronome dans des manuscrits non bibliques, ni les références dans des compositions comme les "paraphrases" dont le caractère biblique n'a pas été déterminé.

Il est vrai que le caractère biblique ou non biblique de certains des 32 manuscrits classés comme bibliques est encore discuté. Duncan[27] considère 4QDeut^j comme un texte avec des extraits du Deutéronome plutôt qu'un manuscrit biblique; White[28] fait la même chose avec

[23] J.A. Fitzmyer, *The Dead Sea Scrolls. Major Publications and Tools for Study* (SBL Sources for Biblical Study 8; Missoula, 1975), 156-157; Revised Edition (Atlanta, 1990), 213-217.
[24] F. García Martínez, "Lista de MSS procedentes de Qumrán", *Henoch* 11 (1989), 149-232.
[25] A.S. van der Woude, "Fünfzehn Jahre Qumranforschung (1974-1988)" (Fortsetzung), *TRu* 55 (1990), 284-287.
[26] Uwe Gleßmer, "Liste der Biblischen Texte aus Qumran", *RevQ* 15/62 (1993) (sous presse)
[27] J.A. Duncan, "Considerations of 4QDt^j in Light of the 'All Souls Deuteronomy' and Cave 4 Phylactery Texts", J. Trebolle Barrera - L. Vegas Montaner (eds.), *The Madrid Qumran Congress* (STDJ XI,1; Leiden-Madrid, 1992), 199-215, pl. 2-7.
[28] S.A. White, "The All Souls Deuteronomy and the Decalogue", *JBL* 109 (1991), 193-206, et "4QDt^n: Biblical Manuscript or Excerpted Text?", H. Attridge - J.J. Collins - T.H. Tobin (eds.), *Of Scribes and Scrolls. Studies on the Hebrew Bible, Intertestamental Judaism, and Christian Origins.* Presented to John Strugnell on the occasion of his sixtieth birthday (College Theology Society Resources in Religion 5; Lanham, 1990), 13-20, et déjà H. Stegemann, "Weitere Stücke von 4QpPsalm 37, von 4QPatriarchal Blessings und Hinweis auf eine unedierte Handschrift aus Höhle 4Q mit Exzerpten aus dem Deuteronomium", *RevQ* 6 (1967), 193-227.

4QDeut[n]; Brooke[29] propose la même interprétation pour 4QDeut[k1], et considère 4QDeut[k2] comme un manuscrit non biblique sur la base de l'emploi du *tetragrammaton* en caractères paléo-hébraïques. Mais dans l'attente d'une clarification définitive, et puisque dans l'édition officielle de *DJD* ils seront inclus parmi les manuscrits bibliques, nous les incluons ici dans cette liste.[30]

1,1-17	4Q35 1	5,29-6,3	4Q37 6-7
1,4-5	11Q3	6,4-6	4Q43
1,7-9	2Q10	6,5-11	4Q42 4-5-6-7
1,8 ?	4Q45 1	6,8-10	4Q43
1,9-13	1Q5 1	7,2-5	4Q45 2
1,22-23	4Q35 2	7,3-4	4Q30 4
1,22-25	1Q4 1	7,6-7	4Q45 3-4
1,29-32	4Q35 3	7,12-16	4Q32 2 i
1,33-39	4Q35 4	7,15-24	5Q1 1 i
1,41	4Q35 5	7,16-21	4Q45 5-6
1,43-2,6	4Q35 6	7,18-22	4Q40 3
2,24-36	4Q31 i	7,21-25	4Q45 7-8-9-10
2,28-30	4Q35 7	7,21-8,4	4Q32 2 ii + 3 i + 4
3,14-4,1	4Q31 ii	7,22-26	4Q33 2-3
3,18-22	4Q40 1	8,1-5	4Q30 5
3,24	4Q32 1	8,2-14	4Q33 4-5-6
3,25-26	4Q30 1	8,5-7	4Q32 5
4,13-17	4Q30 2 + 3 i	8,5-10	4Q37 8
4,23-26	4Q33 1	8,5-10	4Q41 i
4,30-34	4Q43 1-2-3	8,5-9,2	5Q1 1 ii
4,31-32	4Q30 3 ii	8,8-9	1Q5 2
4,31-34	4Q35 N	8,11.15-16	4Q32 3 ii
4,32-34	4Q40 2	8,18-19	1Q4 3-4
4,47-49	1Q4 2	9,4-6	XHev/Se3 i
5,1-5	4Q43 1	9,6-7	4Q33 7
5,1-6	4Q41 ii	9,10	1Q5 3
5,1-11	4Q37 1	9,11-12	4Q30 6
5,6-14	4Q41 iii	9,12-14	4Q34 1
5,8-9	4Q43 2-3	9,17-19	4Q30 7-8
5,13-15	4Q37 2	9,21-23	XHev/Se3 ii
5,14-21	4Q41 iv	9,27-28	1Q4 5
5,21	4Q37 3	9,29-10,2	4Q30 9
5,21-28	4Q41 v	10,1-3	Mur2 1 i
5,22-27	4Q37 4	10,5-8	4Q30 10
5,28	4Q37 5	10,8-12	2Q12
5,28-32	4Q38a 1	10,11-12	4Q45 11
5,28-6,1	4Q41 vi	10,12	4Q39 1

---

[29] G. Brooke, "Torah in the Qumran Scrolls", in: H. Merklein - H.Müller - G. Stemberger (eds.), *Bibel in jüdischer und christlicher Tradition*. Festschrift für Johann Maier zum 60. Geburtstag (BBB 88; Bonn, 1993), 97-120.

[30] Les versets indiqués sont ceux qui ont laissé des traces de lettres réellement visibles dans le manuscrit.

10,14	4Q**39** 2
11,2-3	Mur**2** 1 ii
11,3	4Q**30** 11
11,4	4Q**122** 1
11,6-10	4Q**37** 9
11,6-13	4Q**38a** 2
11,9-13	4Q**30** 12-13-14
11,12-13	4Q**37** 10
11,18	4Q**30** 15
11,21	
+ Exod 12,43	4Q**37** 11
11,27-30	1Q**4** 6
11,28	4Q**45** 12
11,30-31	1Q**5** 4
11,30-12,1	4Q**45** 13-14
12,2-5	4Q**45** 15-16
12,11-12	4Q**45** 17
12,18-19	4Q**30** 16-17
12,22	4Q**45** 18
12,25-26	Mur**2** 2 i
12,26	4Q**30** 18
12,30-31	4Q**30** 19
13,1-4	1Q**4** 7-8
13,4-6	1Q**4** 9
13,5	4Q**30** 20
13,7	4Q**30** 21-22
13,11-12	4Q**30** 23
13,13-14	1Q**4** 10
13,16	4Q**30** 24 ii
13,19-14,1	4Q**45** 19
14,2-4	4Q**45** 20
14,15-21	4Q**43** 4
14,19-22	4Q**45** 21 i + 22
14,21	1Q**4** 11
14,24-25	1Q**4** 12
14,26-29	4Q**45** 23-24
15,1-4	4Q**30** 25
15,2	Mur**2** 3
15,5-6	4Q**45** 25
15,8-10	4Q**45** 21 ii
15,14-15	1Q**5** 5
15,15-19	4Q**30** 26-27-28
16,2-3	4Q**30** 29
16,4	1Q**4** 13
16,6-7	1Q**4** 14
16,6-11	4Q**30** 30 i + 31
16,20-17,5	4Q**30** 30 ii + 32
17,7	4Q**30** 33
17,12-15	2Q**11**
17,15-18,1	4Q**30** 34-39
17,16	1Q**5** 6
17,17-18	4Q**33** 8

18,6-10	4Q**33** 9
18,18-22	4Q**33** 10-11-12
19,2-3	4Q**45** 26
19,8-16	4Q**38b** 3
19,17-20,3	4Q**33** 13-14-15
19,21	4Q**35** 8
20,4-6	4Q**33** 16
20,6-15	4Q**38b** 4
20,9-13	4Q**36** 1 + 2 i
20,16-19	4Q**38b** 5
21,4-12	4Q**33** 17-18-19
21,8-9	1Q**5** 7
21,23-22,9	4Q**36** 3 i + 4 + 5 i
22,3-6	4Q**45** 27-28=29
22,12-19	4Q**33** 20-21-22-23
22,21-26	3Q**33** 24-25
23,6-8	
+ 23,12-16	4Q**36** 3 ii + 5 ii
23,7	4Q**45** 30
23,12-15	4Q**45** 31-32
23,18-20	4Q**34** 2
23,18-20	4Q**43**
23,22-24,3	4Q**38b** 6
23,23-24,1	4Q**36** 6
23,26-24,8	4Q**28**
24,2-7	4Q**33** 26-27-28
24,10-16	1Q**5** 8 ii
24,16-22	4Q**34** 3
25,1-5	4Q**34** 4-5
25,4-9	4Q**33** 29-30-31
25,13-18	1Q**5** 9
25,14-19	4Q**34** 6-7-8
25,19-26,5	4Q**38b** 7
26,2-5	4Q**34** 9
26,14-15	4Q**46**
26,18-19	4Q**38b** 8
26,18-27,10	4Q**33** 32-33-34-35
26,19-27,1	4Q**30** 40
26,19	6Q**3**
27,24-28,7	4Q**30** 41-42-43 i
28,8-11	4Q**30** 44-45
28,12-13	4Q**30** 46
28,15-18	4Q**42** 8
28,15-18.20	4Q**45** 33
28,18-20	4Q**30** 47
28,21-24	4Q**34** 10
28,22-25	4Q**30** 43 ii
28,27-29	4Q**34** 11
28,29-30	4Q**30** 48
28,33-35	4Q**42** 9
28,44-48	1Q**5** 10
28,47-52	4Q**42** 10-11

28,48-50	4Q30 49	32,7-8	4Q37 14
28,58-62	4Q42 12	32,10-11	4Q45 36-37
28,61	4Q30 50	32,13-14	4Q45 38-39-40
28,67-68	4Q39 3	32,17-18	4Q38a 9
29,2-5	4Q39 4	32,17-21	1Q5 16
29,9-11	1Q5 11	32,21-29	1Q5 17-18-19
29,12-20	1Q5 12-13 i	32,22-23	4Q38a 10
29,17-19	4Q30 51	32,25-27	4Q38a 11
29,22-24	4Q42 13	32,27-43	4Q44 1-2-3-4 i
29,24-27	4Q29 1		+ 4 ii
30,3-14	4Q29 2 i + 3	32,33-35	4Q45 41
30,19-31,6	1Q5 13 ii	33,1-2	4Q39 6
31,7-10	1Q5 14	33,2-8	4Q45 42-43
31,9-11	4Q45 9	33,8-22	4Q35 10-11-12-13
31,9-17	4Q29 2 ii + 4	33,12-14.16-17	1Q5 20
31,12	4Q39 5	33,17-24	Mas1c 1 ii + 2
31,12-13	1Q5 15	33,18-19	1Q5 21
31,16-19	4Q30 52-53	33,21-23	1Q5 22
31,17	4Q42	33,29-34,1	4Q45 44
31,24-32,3	4Q29 5	34,2-6	Mas1c 3-4
31,29	4Q45 34	34,4-6	4Q39 7
32,6-8	4Q45 35	34,8	4Q39 8

DEUTERONOMY'S MONOTHEISM AND THE CHRISTIANS THE CASE OF DEUT 6:13 AND 10:20

A. HILHORST

Rijksuniversiteit Groningen

The service of the one God is one of the great ideas of Deuteronomy. Moses in his discourses surrounding the law code never tires of inculcating the lesson. "Yahweh is God indeed, in heaven above as on earth beneath, he and no other" (4:39). "Listen, Israel: Yahweh is our God, Yahweh alone" (6:4). "You must fear Yahweh your God, you must serve him, by his name you must swear" (6:13). "See now that I, I am He, and there is no other god. It is I who deal death and life; when I have struck it is I who heal and none can deliver from my hand" (32:39).[1] Although we have to do here with the concept of the incomparability of Yahweh rather than with a strict monotheism,[2] we may expect the monotheistic religions of late antiquity, Judaism and Christianity, to exploit these statements to underpin their argument. The material ready for checking this, however, is huge. In the following I will therefore concentrate on some uses of Deuteronomy 6:13 and 10:20, especially their first two clauses, in early Christian literature. Before, however, embarking on our exploration, some basic information should be provided.

Textual matters

The passages in question, 6:13 and 10:20, and especially their first two clauses, can be studied together. The reason for that is simple: the first two clauses of 6:13 are virtually identical with the first two of 10:20, the only difference being the absence in 10:20 of the conjunction w^e

---

[1] The translations from Scripture in this article are those of the Jerusalem Bible.

[2] As has been well worked out by Cas Labuschagne, to whom I dedicate this essay in memory of long-standing friendly relations in general and an unforgettable journey to Egypt and Jordan in particular. The study I hinted at is of course his Pretoria thesis *Die Onvergelyklikheid van Jahwè in die Ou Testament*, of which *The Incomparability of Yahweh in the Old Testament* (POS 5; Leiden, 1966) is a revision and translation.

introducing the second clause.[3] Also the respective contexts are similar: both passages occur in the first part of Moses' second discourse in which he introduces the Deuteronomic Code and stresses its animating principle: to love Yahweh is the essence of the Law.

In the Septuagint the first two clauses of Deut 6:13 are identical with those of 10:20. In the close rendering of the Hebrew parent text which we read in the fourth century uncial MSS. codex Vaticanus and codex Sinaiticus they run as follows:

κύριον τὸν θεόν σου φοβηθήσῃ καὶ αὐτῷ λατρεύσεις.[4]

There are, however, textual variants in the Greek; usually those of 6:13 correspond to those of 10:20. Two of these variants play an important part in patristic literature: προσκυνήσεις replacing φοβηθήσῃ and μόνῳ reinforcing αὐτῷ, so that in Christian texts the usual form of the text is:

κύριον τὸν θεόν σου προσκυνήσεις καὶ αὐτῷ μόνῳ λατρεύσεις

Yet we should not think both variants to be inseparable: μόνῳ has imposed itself much more absolutely than προσκυνήσεις.[5]

New Testament

The first two clauses of Deut 6:13 and 10:20[6] are quoted in the New Testament. In the pericope of Jesus' temptation (Matt 4:1-11; Luke 4:1-13) the devil tries to seduce Jesus to worship him, whereupon

---

[3] In the MT. It is, however, present in a good number of mediaeval MSS., in the versions (including Tg Jonathan), in a Tefillin (4Q138) and in a Mezuzah from Qumran. In the biblical MSS. from Qumran Deut 6:13 and 10:20 have not been preserved.

[4] As we shall see in a moment, this is also the form found in the New Testament. It has even be claimed that the variants in the LXX were derived from the New Testament, but T. Holtz, *Untersuchungen über die alttestamentlichen Zitate bei Lukas* (Texte und Untersuchungen 104; Berlin, 1968) 61-63, who studied the question in detail, rejects that.

[5] For the witnesses to the several variants the critical apparatus of the edition by J.W. Wevers (Göttingen, 1977), should be consulted. - There are also other passages which tend to attract the addition of μόνος to θεός, e.g. Deut 1:17 as quoted by Philo *Somn.* 2,24; Josh 24:14 as quoted in Macarius Magnes *Apocr.* 4,23. Judges 10:16 codex Vaticanus. The expression "to serve Yahweh alone" occurs elsewhere in the Hebrew Bible, e.g. 1 Sam 7:3-4; cf. also Exod 22:20; 2 Kings 19:15.19. The reading φοβηθήσῃ, which is in the only place where Philo cites the clause, *Migr.* 132, is found consistently in the *Pseudo-Clementine Homilies* and in the one occurrence of our text in Julian (fr. 67 Masaracchia); it occasionally occurs in Clement of Alexandria (*Strom.* 4,170,4), Origen (*Cels.* 7,64; *Chain on Job* PG 17,104A), Tertullian (*Adv. Marc.* 2,13,5) and the *Pseudo-Clementine Recognitions* (5,13,3).

[6] For easy reference I shall mention only 6:13 in the following, taking for granted that 10:20 is included in it.

Jesus replies with the very words of Deut 6:13, identically quoted in both Gospels: in Matt 4:10 ὕπαγε, σατανᾶ· γέγραπται γάρ· κύριον τὸν θεόν σου προσκυνήσεις καὶ αὐτῷ μόνῳ λατρεύσεις, and in Luke 4:8 γέγραπται· κύριον τὸν θεόν σου προσκυνήσεις καὶ αὐτῷ μόνῳ λατρεύσεις. So we have here an Old Testament verse cited in the New Testament. When studying its history in patristic texts we should be aware of that. An author may refer to the Old or the New Testament context; accordingly we have to do with the direct or indirect history of the Deuteronomy saying. Often no hint to the context is given at all.

Now we can proceed to review the patristic evidence.[7] First we will consider some features of a general purport, then discuss some contexts in which the saying from Deuteronomy found application.

Combination of verses

The commandment contained in the first two clauses of Deut 6:13 and in Matt 4:10 and Luke 4:8 is sometimes welded together with other Deuteronomic statements. Justin *1 Apol.* 16,6 makes one sentence out of Deut 6:13 and 6:5. Likewise Clement of Alexandria *Strom.* 5,14,11-5, 5 combines 6:13 with 6:4, and Irenaeus *Adv.Haer.* 5,22,1 with both of them. One cannot always determine whether these combinations were known as such or whether they were units in the minds of their users. Most authors, however, can be shown to be well aware of their composite character. Thus several of them list quite a number of "monotheistic" statements from Deuteronomy. To quote some examples: Cyprian in his treatise *Ad Fortunatum* ch. 2 under the caption *Quod deus solus colendus est* mentions Deut 5:7 and 32:39 in addition to 6:13. He is surpassed, however, by the author of the *Pseudo-Clementine Homilies*. In the sixteenth *Homily* (16,7) Peter and Simon hold a public debate on the question whether there is one God or there are many gods besides Him. Peter, who takes the first view, cites no less

---

[7] The vast majority of relevant passages is mentioned in J. Allenbach *et al.* (eds.), *Biblia Patristica. Index des citations et allusions bibliques dans la littérature patristique* (Paris, 1975ff.), which is, however, still unfinished. For Augustine we have A.-M. La Bonnardière, *Biblia Augustiniana. A. T. Le Deutéronome* (Paris, 1967), with an interesting introduction. For the patristic exegesis of Jesus' temptation see K.-P. Köppen, *Die Auslegung der Versuchungsgeschichte unter besonderer Berücksichtigung der Alten Kirche* (Beiträge zur Geschichte der biblischen Exegese 4; Tübingen, 1961); M. Steiner, *La temptation de Jésus dans l'interprétation patristique de saint Justin à Origène* (Études Bibliques; Paris, 1962); V. Kesich, "Empire-Church Relations and the Third Temptation", *Studia Patristica* 4,2 (Texte und Untersuchungen 79; Berlin, 1961), 465-471; id., "The Antiocheans and the Temptation Story", *Studia Patristica* 7,1 (Texte und Untersuchungen 92; Berlin, 1966), 496-502.

than six passages from Deuteronomy including 6:13 and a text composed out of Isaiah 49:18; 45:21, and 44:6. The same thing occurs in Julian's *Against the Galileans* fr. 64 Masaracchia, where, however, Deut 6:13 is lacking.

Comments on words

Some authors go into the meaning of the verbs used in the commandment. As we saw, the reading προσκυνήσεις was much more popular than φοβηθήσῃ. To this the circumstance that worshipping is more specific in relation to God than fearing may have contributed. At the same time it spared an explanation of the problem why God, who "is love" (1 John 4:8.16), should be feared. Finally, and most importantly, this was the reading in Matthew and Luke. Nevertheless there are authors who know, and discuss, the reading φοβηθήσῃ. To Tertullian, in his argument against Marcion, it is of great importance to show that the one God is both just and merciful. The reason for this he sums up in a few words (*Adv. Marc.* 2,13,5): *Ideo lex utrumque definit: diliges deum, et: timebis deum. Aliud obsecutori proposuit, aliud exorbitatori,* combining in a catching way Deut 6:5 and 6:13. *Pseudo-Clementine Homily* 10,5 stresses the profitable effect of fearing God, which frees man from many hurtful fears. In the same vein Origen comments on Job 41:5, "Terror is round about his teeth" (PG 17,104A): ἀλλ' ἐὰν ἔχῃς τὸν Χριστὸν ἐν σεαυτῷ, μὴ φρόντιζε τούτου τοῦ φόβου. κύριον γὰρ τὸν θεόν σου φοβηθήσῃ καὶ πλὴν αὐτοῦ μὴ φοβοῦ τὸν ἄλλον.

Most authors, however, have the reading προσκυνήσεις, which also asks for elucidation. The question is here, whether the act of προσκυνεῖν is a worship due to God alone. For the author of the texts preserved in Armenian under Irenaeus' name this is clearly the case, on the basis of just our verse. To quote the relevant statement in Jordan's German translation: "»*Da trat hin zu ihm die Mutter der Söhne Zebedaei mit ihren Söhnen, betete an.*« Und dies nicht umsonst. Da sie nicht hinzugetreten war zu irgendeinem gerechten und weisen Menschen, und nicht zu einem Propheten, sondern als [einen] Gott betete sie an. Denn Angebetetwerden ist eigentümlich Gott. »*Den Herrn deinen Gott sollst du anbeten und ihn allein ehren*«".[8] Augustine, however, denies this on several occasions. According to him, only the verb of the second clause, λατρεύειν, denotes a service of God alone. As this is not sufficiently clear in the Latin version, he takes the trouble to discuss the Greek. Thus in his *Quaestiones in Heptateuchum*,

---

[8] H. Jordan, *Armenische Irenaeusfragmente mit deutscher Übersetzung* (Texte und Untersuchungen 3,6,3 = 36,3; Leipzig, 1913), 182.

when dealing with Gen 18:21, *Et a semine tuo non dabis seruire principi*, he argues that *seruire* here denotes "worship as God" (*Quaest. Hept.* 3,66; PL 34,706): *Non enim ait* δουλεύειν, *sed* λατρεύειν *in Graeco, quod Latinus non solet interpretari nisi ut dicat seruire, plurimum autem distat. Nam seruire hominibus sicut serui seruiunt, quod non est* λατρεύειν, *sed* δουλεύειν, *scriptura non prohibet, seruire autem secundum id quod est* λατρεύειν *non iubetur hominibus nisi uni uero deo, sicut scriptum est: dominum deum tuum adorabis et illi soli seruies.*[9]

Martyrdom

One might expect to find the precept of serving the one God regularly used by Christians being tried by pagan judges and urged to pay honour to the gods of the empire. In fact the surviving authentic acts of the martyrs offer only two cases of this, and in the form of an allusion rather than a quotation. The first of these is *Martyrdom of Pionius* 3,3, in which the Christian Pionius, when reminded οἴδατε πάντως τὸ διάταγμα τοῦ αὐτοκράτορος, ὡς κελεύει ὑμᾶς ἐπιθύειν τοῖς θεοῖς, replies by saying οἴδαμεν τὰ προστάγματα τοῦ θεοῦ ἐν οἷς κελεύει ἡμᾶς αὐτῷ μόνῳ προσκυνεῖν. The first two clauses of our saying have been condensed into one: αὐτῷ μόνῳ προσκυνεῖν.[10] Pionius was martyred under the persecution of Decius, A.D. 250 and so comes after Apollonius, who died a martyr ca. 184 A.D. The account of the latter's martyrdom, however, dates only from the fifth or sixth century and seems to have suffered several modifications; so we discuss it in the second place, using it, as Musurillo urges us, with caution.[11] The situation is roughly the same as with Pionius: Apollonius, invited by his judge to προσκυνεῖν τοὺς θεούς, declines worshipping the idols; instead he professes: θεῷ δὲ τῷ ἐν οὐρανοῖς λατρεύω καὶ αὐτῷ μόνῳ προσκυνῶ (*Martyrdom of Apollonius* 15). Again a free rendering of the Bible text; there are two clauses but the verb of the second one is that of the first one in the Bible and vice versa. This results in using the verb προσκυνεῖν in combination with αὐτῷ μόνῳ, just as in the *Martyr-*

---

[9] For the other passages in Augustine see La Bonnardière (n. 6) 21-22. For λατρεύειν as a term for the service of God see A. Hilhorst, "'Servir Dieu' dans la terminologie du judaïsme hellénistique et des premières générations chrétiennes de langue grecque", *Fructus Centesimus. Mélanges ... Bartelink* (Instrumenta Patristica 19; Steenbrugis-Dordrecht, 1989), 177-192.

[10] The verb προσκυνεῖν could replace λατρεύειν all the easier because since the Greek Bible and Josephus it was often construed with a dative instead of an accusative.

[11] H. Musurillo, *The Acts of the Christian Martyrs* (Oxford, 1972), xxv.

dom of Pionius. Is this a variant proper to martyrdom texts? We lack the evidence to determine this.

To these anonymous texts we can add the testimony of a Church Father who knew persecution from personal experience, namely Cyprian. In chapter 7 of his treatise *De lapsis*, where he complains the big number of backsliders among the brethren, he reminds of the numerous exhortations in Scripture which should have prepared the faithful to hold their own: *Nonne fidem nostram semper armans et dei seruos caelesti uoce corroborans dicit scriptura diuina: dominum deum tuum adorabis et illi soli seruies?*

None of these passages makes clear whether the context of Deuteronomy or of the Gospels is in the writers' mind. In the acts of the martyrs we have no clue whatsoever. Cyprian's *semper* suggests both the Old and the New Testament. There is, however, a passage referring in so many words to the temptation scene, and that is the ending of Tertullian's *Scorpiace*, written against the Gnostics' denial of the value of martyrdom. He evokes the passage in the Acts of the Apostles, ch. 21, where Paul shows himself ready to die for the name of the Lord Jesus, and imagines Gnostics like Prodicus and Valentinus attending the scene (*Scorp.* 15,6): *Quodsi iam tunc Prodicus aut Valentinus adsisteret suggerens non in terris esse confitendum apud homines, ... statim audisset a seruo dei quod audierat diabolus a domino: recede, satana, scandalum mihi es. Scriptum est: dominum deum tuum adorabis et illi soli seruies.* Here the temptation to worship the idols and so to spare oneself the martyr's death is associated with Jesus' temptation to worship the devil.

Moral exhortation

The application of our saying to the situation of martyrdom was not, however, the normal one. Especially the temptation story offered itself as a biblical example to be followed. Irenaeus uses the story when demonstrating against the Gnostics that the Creator God is identical with God the Father, but finds room for a moral application (*Adv. Haer.* 5,22,2): Christ teaches us ὑπὸ πλούτου τε καὶ κοσμικῆς δόξης καὶ παρούσης φαντασίας μὴ ἁρπάζεσθαι, εἰδέναι δὲ ὅτι κύριον τὸν θεὸν δεῖ προσκυνεῖν καὶ αὐτῷ μόνῳ λατρεύειν καὶ μὴ πιστεύειν τῷ ψευδῶς ὑπ-ισχνουμένῳ τὰ μὴ ἴδια, λέγοντι· ταῦτά σοι πάντα δώσω, ἐὰν πεσὼν προσκυνήσῃς μοι. Augustine, who brings up the temptation scene several times, when commenting on the First Letter of John points out that Jesus did nothing extraordinary by defeating the devil. In reality he spoke as he did to instruct us how to act in a similar case: *Quid magnum, a domino diabolum uinci? Quid ergo respondit diabolo, nisi quod te docuit ut respondeas? Scriptum est: dominum deum tuum adorabis et illi soli seruies (In Io. ep. tr. 2,14).*

Polemics

A further field for application of our verse were the theological debates in which the Christians engaged, especially with various sorts of dissenters. Mention has already been made of Irenaeus' fight against the Gnostics, but he is by no means the sole theologian to make a stand against them. Thus in his commentary on the Gospel of John Origen observes that "the heterodox" regard Jesus' saying in John 8:19, "You do not know me, nor do you know my Father", as evidence to the effect that the Creator God of the Jews cannot be the Father of Christ. He refutes this claim with a reference to biblical usage (*Comm. Joh.* 19,3): ταῦτα δὲ λέγουσιν ἅτε μὴ ἀνεγνωκότες τὰς θείας γραφάς, μηδὲ τὴν συνήθειαν τῆς ἐν αὐταῖς λέξεως τετηρηκότες· κἂν γὰρ διεξοδεύειν τις δύνηται τὰ περὶ θεοῦ ἐκ πατέρων μεμαθηκὼς ὅτι τούτῳ λατρεύειν μόνῳ δεῖ, μὴ βιοῖ δὲ καλῶς, τοῦτόν φασιν οὐκ ἔχειν γνῶσιν θεοῦ. The Deuteronomy verse is explained as ordering a virtuous life.

As time went on, other adversaries were assailed with the aid of the same text. Epiphanius, who attacked every heresy known to him in his *Panarion*, polemicises against the opinion of the Arians that God created his Son and asked mankind to adore him. This cannot be true, he continues (*Pan.* 69,36,2-3): μωρὸν γὰρ τὸ κτίσιν θεολογεῖν, ἀθετεῖν δὲ πρώτην ἐντολὴν τὴν λέγουσαν· κύριον τὸν θεόν σου προσκυνήσεις καὶ αὐτῷ μόνῳ λατρεύσεις. διὸ ἡ ἁγία τοῦ θεοῦ ἐκκλησία οὐ κτίσμα προσκυνεῖ, ἀλλὰ υἱὸν γεννητόν, πατέρα ἐν υἱῷ, υἱὸν ἐν πατρί, σὺν ἁγίῳ πνεύματι. So the Gnostics are foolish in a double way: by calling God what is in their own opinion a creature, they adore two divine beings and so disobey the commandment of Deut 6:13. Also Augustine joins battle with the Gnostics, once more by using the Deuteronomy text. Thus in a writing against the Arian bishop Maximinus he censures the idea of the son as a minor god (*Contra Maxim.* 2,13,1): *Non enim dictum est: dominum deum tuum patrem adorabis et illi plus seruies, ut seruire permitteremur et filio, plus tamen patri tanquam maiori, minus autem filio tanquam minori deo, sed dictum est: dominum deum tuum adorabis et illi soli seruies, soli scilicet omnipotenti, soli sapienti deo, ut uos repelleremini, qui nolentes accipere unum solum deum patrem et filium et spiritum sanctum et dicentes unum dominum deum, cui soli seruiendum est, non esse nisi deum patrem et tamen etiam filium deum et dominum confitentes, apertissime duos deos et dominos, maiorem unum, minorem alterum dicitis.*

Epiphanius uses the Deuteronomy verse in still another polemic, namely the controversy about the icons. The veneration of images, he argues, is incompatible with the commandment to serve only the Lord God (*Imag.* 21; p. 70-71 Ostrogorsky): Ὁ θεὸς γὰρ ἐν πάσῃ τῇ παλαιᾷ καὶ καινῇ ταῦτα ἀναιρεῖ, ἀκριβῶς λέγων· κύριον τὸν θεόν σου προσκυνήσεις καὶ αὐτῷ μόνῳ λατρεύσεις, λέγων· ζῶ ἐγώ, λέγει κύριος, καὶ ἐμοὶ κάμψει πᾶν γόνυ. οὐ δυνάμεθα οὖν δυσὶ κυρίοις δουλεύειν, ζῶντι καὶ νεκρῷ.

Attacks from the outside

In his treatise *On the Holy Spirit* Gregory of Nyssa argues that adoring the Father necessarily implies adoring the Son and the Holy Spirit, because they are an indivisible unity (Gregorii Nysseni Opera 3,1, p. 110): σὺ δὲ πεπεισμένος οἴων καὶ ὅσων παρεκτικόν ἐστι τὸ πνεῦμα τὸ ἅγιον ὑπερορᾷς τῆς αἰτήσεως καὶ καταφεύγεις ἐπὶ τὸν νόμον τὸν κελεύοντα κύριον τὸν θεὸν προσκυνεῖν καὶ αὐτῷ μόνῳ λατρεύειν; πῶς οὖν αὐτῷ μόνῳ λατρεύσεις, εἰπέ μοι, ἀποσχίσας αὐτὸν τῆς πρὸς τὸν μονογενῆ καὶ τὸ πνεῦμα ἑαυτοῦ συναφείας; Excluding the Son and the Spirit, he continues, amounts to a Jewish adoration: ἀλλ᾽ αὕτη Ἰουδαϊκὴ ἡ προσκύνησις. It is not clear whether this is just a theoretical conclusion of Gregory or whether he thinks of actual Jewish positions. Is there evidence that the Jews confronted the Christians with the prescript of Deut 6:13? Indeed they did so with other monotheistic statements from Deuteronomy and other books.[12] The texts under discussion, however, were not used, at least not in rabbinic literature; neither do patristic texts mention examples of Jews polemicising with these verses against Jesus and the Spirit as divine persons.

Nevertheless it must have been tempting for an outsider to quote the verses in view of the startling Christian conception of three divine persons. Indeed this has been done by someone who had become an outsider by choice, Julian "the Apostate". His work *Against the Galileans* does not survive in its original form, but much of it can be recovered from Cyril of Alexandria's refutation of it. In a passage on the Old Testament concept "son(s) of God" he writes (fr. 67 Masaracchia): ὁ οὖν Μωσῆς πολλὰ τοιαῦτα καὶ πανταχοῦ λέγει· κύριον τὸν θεόν σου φοβηθήσῃ καὶ αὐτῷ μόνῳ λατρεύσεις. πῶς οὖν ὁ Ἰησοῦς ἐν τοῖς εὐαγγελίοις παραδέδοται προστάττων· πορευθέντες μαθητεύσατε πάντα τὰ ἔθνη, βαπτίζοντες αὐτοὺς εἰς τὸ ὄνομα τοῦ πατρὸς καὶ τοῦ υἱοῦ καὶ τοῦ ἁγίου

---

[12] Cf. the essay of J.T.A.G.M. van Ruiten in this volume, and H. Schreckenberg, *Die christlichen Adversus-Judaeos-Texte und ihr literarisches und historisches Umfeld (1.-11. Jh.)* (Europäische Hochschulschriften 23,172; Frankfurt a.M.-Bern, 1990²), 161-168 (the passages marked by "(2)").

πνεύματος, εἴπερ καὶ αὐτῷ μόνῳ λατρεύειν ἔμελλον; ἀκόλουθα δὲ τούτοις καὶ ὑμεῖς διανοούμενοι μετὰ τοῦ πατρὸς θεολογεῖτε τὸν υἱόν[13]. Julian is well aware of the fact that Matt 28:19, to which he opposes the Deuteronomic precept of serving God alone, is one of the New Testament passages the Christians cited in support of the doctrine of Trinity.

Conclusion

In early Christian literature the commandment of Deut 6:13 and 10:20 was one of the stock texts of the service of the one God. As such it could be used to add force to the call to live according to the will of God. Just as much, however, it was employed as a weapon against adversaries who were supposed to worship more than one God: not only the Roman authorities who urged the Christians to sacrifice to the gods of the Empire, but also Gnostics and Marcionites who distinguished the Creator God of the Old Testament from the Most High God, Arians who split the Father from the Son, and worshippers of images. On the other hand, the Christians were themselves confronted with this text in view of their doctrine of three divine persons by the Emperor Julian the Apostate, who was himself a Christian by birth.

Since the text was used in the story of Jesus' temptation by the devil in Matthew 4 and Luke 4, Christian allusions to the text often refer to that story and concern the original Deuteronomy context only indirectly. This reflects itself in the text form: although the Hebrew text reads "You must fear Yahweh your God, you must serve him" and a literal Greek translation of this was available, the New Testament has, with part of the Septuagint MSS., "You must *worship* the Lord your God, and serve him *alone*". This is also the usual text form among the Church Fathers.[14]

---

[13] On this passage cf. the bibliography mentioned in G. Rinaldi, *Biblia Gentium* (Roma, 1989), 293.

[14] I am grateful to Harry Gaylord for correcting my English.

THE ENDING OF THE SONG OF MOSES:
ON THE PRE-MASORETIC VERSION OF DEUT 32:43

ARIE VAN DER KOOIJ
Rijksuniversiteit Leiden

The Hebrew text of the Song of Moses (Deut 32:1-43) has undergone, presumably in the Hellenistic era, remarkable changes in verses 8 and 43. As attested by Qumran witnesses and the Septuagint (LXX), the primary version of verse 8 reads (in translation):

> he laid down the boundaries of every people according to the number of the sons of *God*

but its ending was changed into the following text:

> ... according to the number of the sons of *Israel*.

And as to verse 43 the beginning of its primary version reads (in translation):

> Rejoice *you heavens, with Him ...*

but it was changed into:

> Rejoice you *nations, about His people ....*

Because of the nature of these shifts (sons of God > sons of Israel; heavens > nations; with Him > His people) R. Meyer has made the interesting suggestion that these changes point to a demythologisation of the ancient Song.[1]

These two verses, in particular verse 8, have been dealt with in several publications.[2] Our contribution in honour of Cas Labuschagne

---

[1] R. Meyer, "Die Bedeutung von Deuteronomium 32, 8f.43 (4Q) für die Auslegung des Moseliedes", in: A. Kuschke (ed.) *Verbannung und Heimkehr. W. Rudolph zum 70. Geburtstage* (Tübingen, 1961), 197-209, 205.

[2] For verse 8 see e.g. C. McCarthy, *The Tiqqune Sopherim and Other Theological Corrections in the Masoretic Text of the Old Testament* (OBO 36; Freiburg-Göttingen, 1981), 211-214; M. Lana, "Deuteronomio e angelologia alla luce di una variante qumranica (4QDt 32,8)", *Henoch* 5 (1983), 179-207; E. Tov, *Textual Criticism of the Hebrew Bible* (Minneapolis-Assen, 1992), 269, and for verse 43 see now P.M. Bogaert, "Les trois rédactions conservées et la forme originale de l'envoi du Cantique de Moïse (Dt 32,43)", in: N. Lohfink (ed.), *Das Deuteronomium,*

will be devoted to verse 43, with particular attention to the question of the number of cola of the earlier, 'premasoretic' version of the text.

II

In his article on the Song of Moses, Labuschagne typifies verse 43 as "the poet's exhortation for praise".[3] He then remarks, "the poet returns to where he started (verse 1, vdK) and addresses the heavens, calling on all heavenly beings to rejoice and bow down before Yahweh" (ibid.). However, the literary correspondence between verse 1 and verse 43, which is assumed here, is not to be found in the masoretic version (MT). It presupposes an earlier version of verse 43: "This verse should be reconstructed on the basis of the LXX and the new fragments from Qumran to read as translated in the New English Bible" (ibid.).

The text of verse 43 in the New English Bible to which Labuschagne refers, reads as follows:

Rejoice with him, you heavens,
bow down, all you gods, before him,
for he will avenge the blood of his sons
and take vengeance on his adversaries;
he will punish those who hate him
and make expiation for his people's land.

This text differs markedly from MT which reads in translation as follows:

Rejoice you nations about his people,
for he will avenge the blood of his servants,
and will take vengeance on his adversaries,
and make expiation for his land (and) his people.

The translation of the NEngB reflects a version of verse 43 which does not only contain some variant readings, but differs also in the number of cola: six over against four in MT. Especially as to this second element it will be seen whether the decision of the NEngB is justified in the light of the available data.

Entstehung, Gestalt und Botschaft (BETL 68; Leuven, 1985), 329-340. As to verse 8 the fully attested reading in Qumran is known from 4QDeut[j] (בני אלוהים; cf. LXX υἱῶν θεοῦ); the reading of 4QDeut[q] is only partly legible (בני אל[).

[3] C.J. Labuschagne, "The Song of Moses", in: I.H. Eybers *et al.* (eds.), *De fructu oris sui. Essays in Honour of Adrianus van Selms* (POS 9; Leiden, 1971), 85-98, 98.

III

The relevant textual data of this case read as follows:

MT: הרנינו גוים עמו
כי דם־עבדיו יקום
ונקם ישיב לצריו
וכפר אדמתו עמו

4QDeut^{q:4}   הרנינו שמים עמו
והשתחוו לו כל אלהים
כי דם בניו יקום
ונקם ישיב לצריו
ולמשנאיו ישלם
ויכפר אדמת עמו

LXX: εὐφράνθητε, οὐρανοί, ἅμα αὐτῷ,
καὶ προσκυνησάτωσαν αὐτῷ πάντες υἱοὶ θεοῦ·
εὐφράνθητε, ἔθνη, μετὰ τοῦ λαοῦ αὐτοῦ,
καὶ ἐνισχυσάτωσαν αὐτῷ πάντες ἄγγελοι θεοῦ·
ὅτι τὸ αἷμα τῶν υἱῶν αὐτοῦ ἐκδικεῖται,
καὶ ἐκδικήσει καὶ ἀνταποδώσει δίκην τοῖς ἐχθροῖς,
καὶ τοῖς μισοῦσιν ἀνταποδώσει
καὶ ἐκκαθαριεῖ κύριος τὴν γῆν τοῦ λαοῦ αὐτοῦ.

First, the following variant readings are to be noted:

MT גוים] שמים Q, cf. LXX
עבדיו] בניו Q, cf. LXX
כפר] יכפר Q, cf. LXX (?)
אדמתו] אדמת Q, cf. LXX.

The Samaritan Pentateuch (SP) supports the readings of MT except in the case of אדמתו; here SP goes with the text of Q.

Further, beside these variant readings Q, together with LXX, presents two cola which are not found in MT (and in SP as well):

⁴ For the photo of this fragment see P.W. Skehan, "A Fragment of the 'Song of Moses' (Deut 32) from Qumran", *BASOR* 136 (1954), 13, and E. Würthwein, *Der Text des Alten Testaments. Eine Einführung in die Biblia Hebraica* (Stuttgart, 1988⁵), 153. See now esp. E. Tov with the collaboration of S.J. Pfann (eds.), *The Dead Sea Scrolls on Microfiche. A Comprehensive Facsimile Edition of the Texts from the Judean Desert* (Leiden, 1993), nr 41.209.

והשתחוו לו כל אלהים
ולמשנאיו ישלם

Finally, LXX has two cola not attested by Q:

εὐφράνθητε, ἔθνη, μετὰ τοῦ λαοῦ αὐτοῦ,
καὶ ἐνισχυσάτωσαν αὐτῷ πάντες ἄγγελοι θεοῦ.

Interestingly, the first one of these two cola shows agreement with the
first colon of MT, whereas the second is without any parallel in Deut
32:43 (MT,Q, SP).

As far as the number of cola is concerned it is clear that MT attests a
text with four, Q with six, and LXX even with eight cola. The NEngB
to which Labuschagne refers appears to reflect the idea that the text of
Q (4QDeut^q), with six cola, is to be seen as the earlier, pre-masoretic
version of Deut 32:43. This assumption has been argued for by R.
Meyer in 1961 (see note 1), but it has been disputed most recently by
P.M. Bogaert (see note 2). He is of the opinion that the primary
version of verse 43 did not consist of the text of Q with six cola, but
with four of them (i.e. without both cola [the second and fifth] which
have no parallel in MT). In discussing this question we concentrate
mainly on MT and Q, since there are good reasons to believe that the
text of LXX represents in its third and fourth colon an expanded and
contaminated text, partly based on the (proto)masoretic version of
verse 43.[5]

IV

MT and Q have four cola which, be it with variant readings, run
parallel:

	MT (Ketib)		Q
a	הרנינו גוים עמו		הרנינו שמים עמו
b			(...)
c	כי דם עבדיו יקום		כי דם בניו יקום
d	ונקם ישיב לצריו		ונקם ישיב לצריו
e			(...)
f	וכפר אדמתו עמו		ויכפר אדמת עמו

---

[5] See Meyer (note 1), 200, Lana (note 2), 187, and Bogaert (note 2), 336.

It is agreed upon by scholars as Meyer, Bogaert and others, that the variant readings of Q, with the support of LXX, attest an earlier version of verse 43. It may well be that this does not apply to the reading ויכפר, which, in my view, represents a linguistic adaptation to later, post-biblical Hebrew usage of which examples are known from 1QIsaᵃ.[6]

As to colon *a* Bogaert argues that the reading שמים is to be regarded as secondary. He assumes that originally אלהים was written in this place. "Il me paraît plus logique que l'expression mythologique qui faisait le plus difficulté se soit trouvée dès le début dans le texte" (333). His idea is that the reading אלהים would have caused more trouble than the (attested) reading שמים. However, as I see it, there are no clear indications or strong arguments in support of the view of Bogaert. On the contrary, the fact that the most ancient witnesses, Q and LXX, both attest the reading שמים, and the observation of the literary link between verse 1 and verse 43 (Q), as has been noted by Labuschagne (see above), do support the assumption that the reading of Q can be seen as being the primary one.[7]

Though not so much a matter of text, but more of interpretation it may be appropriate to discuss also the view of Bogaert on the meaning of דם בניו in colon *c*. He suggests that this expression is not to be taken in the sense of "the blood of his sons", but of "the blood shed by his sons", by arguing that in the Song the sons of God (Israel) are depicted as being rebellious and inobedient. The problem with this view is that, in the Song of Moses, the sons of God are never accused of having shed innocent blood, as are the enemies of Israel (verse 25); instead, the sins of the sons of God, Israel, have only to do with the worship of other gods.

As has become clear from the textual data the text of Q contains two cola (*b* and *e*) which are not found in MT. They read as follows:

b   והשתחוו לו כל אלהים

e   ולמשנאיו ישלם

If the earliest version of verse 43, for which there is evidence, did include these two cola, one has to assume that the scribe-redactor,

---

[6] See E.Y. Kutscher, *The Language and Linguistic Background of the Isaiah Scroll (1 Q Isaᵃ)* (STDJ 6; Leiden, 1974), 357f. ("MT perfect + *waw* conversive = Scr. imperf + *waw*").

[7] In LXX the rendering of שמים in verse 1 and 43 shows an interesting variation: οὐρανέ and οὐρανοί respectively. Compare for this variation also LXX Isa 1:2 and 40:23.

responsible for the proto-masoretic text, left them out. Bogaert has his doubts about such a possibility. "... l'histoire de la rédaction révèle que, pour la Tora, l'addition reste possible alors même que la suppression ne l'est plus" (330). I do not think that this general argument is strong enough to rule out the possibility of a shortening of the text, even in the case of the Law. For we know of a deletion of several words in the book of Genesis, 46:20 where, as has been pointed out by D. Barthélemy,[8] part of the text has been left out in order to reach the number of seventy sons of Israel (instead of the number of seventy-five in the pre-masoretic version; see also Gen 46:27, and Exod 1:5). It is possible, therefore, that the pre-masoretic text of Deut 32:43 constituted a longer text than the one attested by MT.

However, one may doubt on other grounds that cola b and e were part of the earlier text. The point is that colon b constitutes an exact parallel to Ps 97:7 (ending), whereas the text of colon e is also found in verse 41 of the Song of Moses. One could imagine that, at some later stage of the transmission of the text, b was added from Ps 97, and e from verse 41.

Yet there are some considerations which favour the view that the pre-masoretic version of verse 43 consisted of six cola. First, it is also possible that the last part of Ps 97:7 has been borrowed from Deut 32, or that both texts have a common background. Second, as to colon e it is to be noted that this colon is not the only one with a parallel in verse 41b: the same applies to colon d. Third, and more importantly, the poetic structure of the verse has to be taken into account. Without colon b the first line of verse 43 (cola a + c) would not display the poetic structure which is characteristic of the Song of Moses as a whole, viz. the parallelism of each pair of cola (bicolon). For stylistic reasons the 'extra' colon b is needed in order to create the first line of verse 43: הרנינו שמים עמו והשתחוו לו כל אלהים. The 'heavens' run parallel to 'gods', and the same applies to 'with him' and 'to him'. For a parallelism between heavens and heavenly beings, see also Job 38:7: 'when the morning stars sang together, and all the sons of God shouted for joy'.[9]

Arguments of style and structure apply also to the rest of verse 43. Colon e is needed in order to get a nice structural balance in this part of the verse:

---

[8] D. Barthélemy, *Etudes d'histoire du texte de l'Ancien Testament* (OBO 21; Fribourg-Göttingen, 1978), 106f.

[9] See C. Houtman, *De hemel in het Oude Testament* (Franeker, 1974), 117f.

כי דם בניו יקום   ונקם ישיב לצריו
ולמשנאיו ישלם   ויכפר אדמת עמו

Beside elements of parallelism within the two lines (נקם // יקום; יכפר
// ישלם) this part of the verse is structured chiastically: 'the blood of
his sons' is related to the last colon, about the expiation for the land of
his people, and the vengeance on his adversaries is clearly parallel to
the colon about the punishment of those who hate him (cf. verse 41).
As for the contents of the verse, namely the relationship between
bloodshed, impurity of the land, and the importance of vengeance, one
is reminded of Num 35:33: "You shall not defile your land by bloodshed. Blood defiles the land, and expiation cannot be made on behalf
of the land for blood shed on it except by the blood of the man that
shed it." (NEngB)[10]

To conclude, in the light of these considerations and stylistic
observations it is very likely indeed that the primary, pre-masoretic
version of Deut 32:43, as attested by 4QDeutq, consisted of six cola.[11]
Thus the decision of the NEngB is fully justified.

Though we have left aside LXX so far some comments on colon
b in the LXX are in order here because of the following difference
between LXX and Q:

כל אלהים ... - ... πάντες υἱοὶ θεοῦ

The question arises whether this part of LXX reflects a Vorlage
different from Q, namely כל בני אלהים. Bogaert argues that, since there
are no other cases where אלהים has been rendered by the Greek υἱοὶ
θεοῦ (336), the underlying Hebrew text must have read בני אלהים. It is
true that the Greek rendering υἱοὶ θεοῦ for Hebrew אלהים has no
parallel in LXX (compared with MT), but in this particular case the
following considerations may have led to this translation of Hebrew
אלהים (= Q):

(a) the rendering πάντες θεοί (without υἱοί) would be inappropriate
in the light of verses 17, 31, and 37, where θεοί is used in a negative
sense;

(b) the rendering with υἱοὶ (θεοῦ) is likely to be seen as an
assimilation to LXX verse 8: ... κατὰ ἀριθμὸν υἱῶν θεοῦ.[12]

---

[10] For the notion of expiation in verse 43 see further B. Janowski, *Sühne als
Heilsgeschehen* (WMANT 55; Göttingen, 1982), 129-131.

[11] For the views of P.W. Skehan and F.M. Cross see the critical remarks of
Bogaert (note 2), 330f.

[12] For this reading see LXX *Deuteronomy*, ed. J.W. Wevers.

V

Whatever the historical background, the scribal milieu, and the motives behind the remarkable changes in verse 43 (and in verse 8 as well) of the Song of Moses may have been,[13] the conclusion that the (proto-) masoretic version of verse 43 results from a shortening of an earlier text, has an interesting effect on the poem as a whole. (It is to be noted that the new, shorter text of verse 43 displays a new parallelism in the first line: 'his people'//'his servants', a parallelism also found in [and presumably inspired by] verse 36. The second verse line, however, lacks a parallel structure.)

In its pre-masoretic form the poem as a whole counts 142 cola, or 71 verse-lines, but due to the shortening of verse 43 the (proto-)maso-retic version of the Song of Moses has 140 cola, or 70 verse lines.[14] This last number (70) is also the one referred to by "the number of the sons of Israel" in verse 8. As stated above, Barthélemy has pointed out that the change in this verse is related to textual corrections in Gen 46:20.27 and in Exod 1:5: all these corrections, or *tiqqunim* as Barthé-lemy puts it, show a great interest in the number of the seventy sons of Israel (instead of the number of seventy-five of the earlier tradition [Gen 46:20.27 and Exod 1:5]).

The changes of Deut 32:43 are closely connected with the change of verse 8: the corrections of both verses reflect a great interest in the significance of "the sons of Israel", the people of Israel, for the nations (cf. verse 8b: "he laid down the boundaries of *every people* according to the number of *the sons of Israel*", and verse 43: "Rejoice you *nations*, about *His people* ..."). Deut 32:43 apparently belongs to the same group of corrected texts as verse 8 does. This means that the shortening of verse 43, with the effect that the Song of Moses has 70 verse-lines, was likely meant to bring the composition of the poem in line with "the number of the sons of Israel", being at the same time the number of all the nations.

---

[13] For suggestions see Meyer (note 1), 205, Barthélemy (note 8), 109, and Lana (note 2), 188ff.

[14] For this number as attested in the masoretic tradition (in Masseket Soferim) see D. Barthélemy, "Les ruines de la tradition des soferim dans le manuscrit d'Alep: la gageure de Shelomoh ben Buya'a", *RB* 99 (1992), 14.

ANALYSE FORMELLE ET NUMÉRIQUE
DE 2 SAMUEL 7:1-17

François Langlamet

EBAF - Jérusalem

Encore 2 Sam 7 ? Les questions posées et les "observations" formulées par G. Hentschel[1] exigent-elles un complément quelques mois à peine après la parution de son livre ?

L'aimable invitation du Comité de rédaction de la *Festschrift Labuschagne* n'est pas étrangère à la genèse du présent article. Elle n'explique pourtant pas le choix de 2 Sam 7. C'est bien l'ouvrage de Hentschel qui est à l'origine de cette étude. Il faut souligner qu'elle le présuppose, car il a semblé inutile de répéter ici des références bibliographiques, d'ailleurs connues, que le lecteur retrouvera facilement chez Hentschel. Cet article est né — ou plutôt rené — de circonstances imprévues. La lettre du Comité m'a décidé à interrompre la rédaction, presque achevée, d'un article-recension à propos du livre de Hentschel. Le début de l'article projeté paraîtra comme compte rendu dans le bulletin de la *Revue Biblique*. La suite, à peine modifiée, est offerte en hommage à C.J. Labuschagne. Le dédicataire et G. Hentschel voudront bien excuser ce partage: il exprime à la fois l'estime et l'amitié.

Hommage de recenseur pris au dépourvu, le présent article est en outre un travail de profane, qui n'a jamais pratiqué qu'à son insu l'"analyse logotechnique". Non initié à cette méthode,[2] il doit néan-

---

[1] G. Hentschel, *Gott, König und Tempel. Beobachtungen zu 2 Sam 7, 1-17* (ETS 22; Leipzig, 1992), avec bibliographie (pp. ix-xiii).

[2] Ce n'est pas par hasard que l'"Arithmétique des scribes ..." (*RB* 97 [1990], 380, n. 1) se réfère à un article synthétique de C.J. Labuschagne (*NTT* 41 [1987], 1-16) sans citer C. Schedl, *Baupläne des Wortes. Einführung in die biblische Logotechnik* (Wien, 1974). La "logotechnique" m'avait paru incertaine: "il y a quelque chose, mais ..." (mais quel texte choisir, à partir de quelle époque, et quel intérêt pour l'analyse des textes anciens?). C'est en cherchant à préciser numériquement les résultats d'une analyse formelle qui s'inspirait de la *Formkritik* de W. Richter que j'ai fait mes premiers pas en "analyse numérique". W. Richter, *Exegese als Literaturwissenschaft. Entwurf einer alttestamentlichen Literaturtheorie und Methodologie* (Göttingen, 1971), n'avait même pas mentionné Schedl, dont les articles des années soixante (cités dans Schedl, *Baupläne*, 30-1) avaient irrité plutôt que convaincu la majorité des exégètes. Il faut avouer qu'à première vue la méthodologie de Richter et l'analyse logotechnique de Schedl semblent incompatibles. Les deux méthodes sont certainement différentes et Schedl, *Baupläne*, 19, avait noté lui-même les

moins reconnaître que l'analyse logotechnique et son analyse "numérique" aboutissent à des résultats comparables. Doit-il pour autant modi-
fier sa méthode archaïque? Ce serait manquer l'occasion de mettre en
lumière la convergence de voies d'accès différentes. Mieux vaut rejoindre Labuschagne et la voie royale de la logotechnique par des sentiers
perdus qui menaient jadis au même but.

L'analyse formelle et numérique qui constitue l'essentiel de l'article
restera donc fidèle à la "syntaxe des scribes",[3] sans écarter pourtant les
questions que se posent les critiques: elles paraissent d'autant plus
légitimes qu'une étude synchronique du récit et de sa structure formelle
oblige en quelque sorte le lecteur à les formuler. Éluder ces problèmes
sous prétexte de rigueur méthodologique, ce serait se priver des
services qu'un examen de la structure formelle peut rendre à l'exégèse
critique (en particulier à l'histoire de la rédaction), laisser inexploitées
les données mises au jour par une *étude synchronique* du texte, dont la
Literarkritik a fait trop longtemps l'économie. Hentschel l'a bien senti,

---

points de désaccord. En lisant aujourd'hui cette page, je constate qu'en appliquant
l'analyse formelle au *texte actuel* (avant toute *Literarkritik*), je me suis rapproché
sans le savoir de la méthode de Schedl. Mais l'analyse formelle n'était à mes yeux
qu'un point de départ, un travail préparatoire au service de la critique, qui doit
partir du texte actuel et le retrouver au terme du voyage. "Vaste programme", peut-
être irréalisable, qui du moins permet à l'exégèse d'éviter de s'engager sur de
fausses pistes dès le début de son travail, d'aborder les 'aspects de la méthodologie'
avec toutes les données que peut fournir une étude synchronique du texte - ou,
mieux encore, du texte et des versions - et, une fois achevée l'étude critique,
d'essayer de rejoindre le récit actuel en repérant quelques jalons d'une histoire dont
le cours exact nous échappera toujours.
[3] "Syntaxe des scribes", en ce sens qu'elle est sûrement attestée dans le texte
consonantique de nombreux récits en prose. Mais la "syntaxe des scribes" était déjà
celle des rédacteurs, voire des auteurs (ou de réviseurs adaptant le texte à l'usage
des "écoles"). Pour mettre au jour la "syntaxe des scribes", l'analyse syntaxique
doit être précisée et complétée par des données numériques (nombre des mots dans
chaque proposition), par un examen de l'"équilibre" des propositions, etc. (cf.
infra). J'ai exposé les principes de cette syntaxe "archaïque", dans une recension de:
W. Richter, *Grundlagen einer althebräischen Grammatik. B. Die Beschreibungsebe-
nen. III. Der Satz (Satztheorie)* (ATS 13; St. Ottilien, 1980), cf. *RB* 90 (1983), 100-
48 (surtout 103-10). A cette occasion, j'avais noté quelques divergences, apparentes
ou réelles, entre la "syntaxe des scribes" et celle de Richter (*ibid.*, 107-10), tout en
soulignant en conclusion qu'on pouvait parler d'*accord global* (p. 110). W. Richter,
Biblia Hebraica transcripta BH[t]. 1. *Genesis* (ATS 33. 1; St. Ottilien, 1991), en
ajoutant des sigles aux lettres qui, pour chaque verset, indiquent la division en
propositions, a résolu presque tous les problèmes (cfr. *infra*, n. 7). Il ne reste qu'un
point litigieux: le cas des propositions substantives, désignées par une lettre propre,
donc séparées de la proposition principale (cf. Gen 1:4b. 10d. 12c. 18b. 21c. 25c;
2:19c; 3:5b. 6bc. 7c. 11c, etc.). Pourquoi ne pas conserver la lettre assignée à la
proposition principale en la faisant suivre, ici encore, d'un sigle (cf. aI pour
l'infinitif, aR pour la proposition relative, etc.)?

qui consacre au récit actuel la moitié de son livre. Ses lecteurs regrette-
ront seulement que les cinq pages où il leur présente les propositions et
les sections de 2 Sam 7:1-17 (Hentschel, 7-11) soient trop rapides,
contestables sur certains points et peu utilisées par la suite. Pour ouvrir
l'exégèse à de nouvelles méthodes, il ne suffit pas de juxtaposer "nova
et vetera", il faut tenter d'intégrer. Née de ce souci d'intégration, la
présente étude est néanmoins synchronique, mais son orientation est
bien diachronique.

   Sur un point particulier, important pour les traducteurs, il semble que
l'analyse formelle et numérique apporte un nouvel argument à la
solution adoptée par Hentschel à propos de la syntaxe de 2 Sam 7:9c-
11b: dans ces versets, nous aurions bien cinq w^{e}qatal, à traduire au
passé et non pas au futur (Hentschel, 9, 22-3; cf. 35-6, 87-9). Sans
reprendre en détail cette question controversée, le dernier paragraphe
l'abordera sous son aspect "numérique" (*infra*, § 6).

1. *2 Sam 7:1-17: cinquante-neuf ou quarante-neuf propositions ?*

Si l'on compare le paragraphe suivant (§ 2) à l'analyse de Hentschel
(7-10), on constatera des divergences. En voici la liste (avec références
aux versets tels que les divise Hentschel):

- 1a *wyhy ky yšb hmlk bbytw*
- 3b *kl 'šr blbbk* / 3c *lk* / 3d *'šh*
- 7a *bkl 'šr hthlkty bkl bny yśr'l* / 7b *hdbr dbrty 't 'hd šbṭy yśr'l* / 7c *'šr ṣwyty lr'wt 't 'my 't yśr'l l'mr*
- 8a *w'th* / 8b *kh t'mr l'bdy ldwd*
- 9a *w'hyh 'mk* / 9b *bkl 'šr hlkt*
- 9d *w'śty lk šm gdwl kšm hgdlym* / 9e *'šr b'rṣ*
- 10e *wl' ysypw bny 'wlh l'nwtw k'šr br'šwnh* / 11a *wlmn hywm 'šr ṣwyty špṭym 'l 'my yśr'l*
- 11c *whgyd lk YHWH* / 11d *ky byt y'śh lk YHWH*
- 12c *whqymty 't zr'k 'ḥryk* / 12d *'šr yṣ' mm'yk*
- 14b *whw' yhyh ly lbn* / 14c *'šr bh'wtw* / 14d *whkhtyw bšbṭ 'nšym wbng'y bny 'dm*
- 15b *k'šr hsrty m'm š'wl* / 15c *'šr hsrty mlpnyk*
- 16a *wn'mn bytk* / 16b *wmmlktk 'd 'wlm lpnyk*

D'un point de vue linguistique, l'analyse proposée par Hentschel est en
général acceptable. Néanmoins, si l'on veut s'en tenir à la "syntaxe des
scribes" telle qu'on peut la retrouver et la vérifier dans de multiples
récits bibliques, on devra renoncer aux divisions trop abstraites: "Diviser ce qui est divisible; se contenter d'analyser ce qui résiste à la
division" (*RB* 90 [1983], 105).

   Par définition, les propositions *relatives* sont dénuées du minimum d'indépendance qui permettrait de les isoler des propositions principales. Dans le texte analysé par Hentschel, les exemples les plus clairs apparaissent aux vv. 7c, 9e, 12d, 15c, auxquels il faut ajouter 7a (*bkl 'šr hthlkty*) et 9b (*bkl 'šr hlkt*), l'un et l'autre simples compléments de lieu (9b sûrement; 7a très probablement, encore qu'on puisse y voir un complément de temps).

Le cas du v. 3 est plus délicat: 3b est le complément d'objet de 3d. Hentschel a opté pour une division tripartie: 3b *kl 'šr blbbk* / 3c *lk* / 3d *'śh*. Il serait plus logique de ne pas diviser du tout: "tout ce que tu as l'intention de faire, va le faire" (TOB). Mais notre "logique" n'est pas celle des rédacteurs et des scribes, qui reconnaissaient à chaque impératif une certaine indépendance. Si étrange qu'elle puisse paraître, la solution conforme à la "syntaxe des scribes" ne peut être ici que: *kl 'šr blbbk lk* / *'śh*.

En 10e, 11a, la division traditionnelle des versets - déjà relativisée par Rashi[4] - a sans doute influencé Hentschel. Elle ne justifie pourtant pas l'analyse qu'il propose, surtout si l'on admet que le *waw* du début du v. 11 est explicatif (Hentschel, 16, n. 85-6, et 25, n. 147). Hentschel aurait pu tout au plus, conformément à sa pratique habituelle, isoler au v. 11a la proposition relative *'šr ṣwyty* ..., ce que la "syntaxe des scribes" nous interdit de faire. Le § 2 (*infra*) traitera *k'šr br'šwnh* (fin du "10e" de Hentschel) et le v. 11a comme une seule proposition dont le verbe, sous-entendu, est le piel de *'nh*, explicite en "10e".

Au v. 14c, la traduction de Hentschel (9: "Wenn er sich verfehlt") semble indiquer qu'il reconnaît ici à la conjonction relative *'šr* un sens temporel/conditionnel. Si l'on en juge par les traductions des commentateurs, cette interprétation est commune (cf. Calmet, Smith, Gressmann, Schulz, Leimbach, Bible du Centenaire, Médebielle, Rehm, de Vaux, van den Born, Bressan, Ackroyd, Alonso-Schökel, Stolz, Anderson). Au sens temporel/conditionnel on peut néanmoins préférer un sens consécutif (avec Keil, Kittel, Nowack, Hertzberg): dans le texte actuel, 14b et 14c sont étroitement liés[5] (cf. les pronoms-suffixes, qui se réfèrent à *bn*) et la traduction de *'šr* par "de sorte que" a l'avantage d'exprimer cette corrélation.[6] Ce n'est pas dans *'šr* qu'on cherchera ici

---

[4] Sur 2 Sam 7:11: *wlmn hywm 'šr ṣwyty. mhwbr 'l h'lywn wl' ywsypw l'nwtw k'šr br'šwnh qwdm hšwptym wk'šr 'św mymy hšwptym 'd k'n.* Cf. Rabbenu Yeshaya, qui par ailleurs estime le *waw* superflu.

[5] F. de Hummelauer, *ad loc.*: "Haec per 'šr praecedentibus intime copulata ostendunt agi de severitate *paterna.*" Le lien existe, en tout cas dans le texte actuel, et l'interprétation proposée peut certainement s'en réclamer.

[6] Sur 'šr au sens consécutif, cf., outre les dictionnaires, GK, § 166b; Joüon, § 169f. Voir aussi C. Gaensle, *The Hebrew Particle* 'šr (Chicago, 1915), § 116.

la nuance temporelle/conditionnelle, mais bien dans *bh'wtw* (*b*-inf.): "so dass, wenn sie sich verfehlt" (Kittel). Mais, s'il en est ainsi, pourquoi ne pas considérer 14c tout simplement comme une proposition relative? Les traductions les plus fidèles au texte sont probablement celles de Klostermann ("den ich, wenn er Unrecht begeht..."), Schloegl ("den ich, wenn er Unrecht thut...") et Dhorme ("un fils, que je châtierai - s'il vient à faire le mal").

En "syntaxe des scribes", *'šr bh'wtw* (14c), proposition relative infinitive, ne semble pas, à première vue, séparable de l'antécédent *bn*. Faudrait-il donc réintégrer en 14b ces deux premiers mots de 14c ? Ce serait oublier la suite de 14 (*whkhtyw* ...) où le *w*ᵉqataltí et le pronom rétrospectif indiquent nettement que la proposition relative infinitive est en *casus pendens* par rapport à "14d". La place logique de ce *casus pendens* est en "14d" plutôt qu'en 14b. En conséquence, l'analyse proposée ci-dessous (§ 2) maintiendra la division entre 14d et 14c (avec Hentschel, 9), mais elle supprimera le "14d" de Hentschel (10) en l'intégrant à 14c. Cette solution respecte la "syntaxe des scribes", qui ne sépare du contexte ni les propositions relatives, ni les "propositions" infinitives, mais reconnaissons qu'il s'agit ici d'un cas limite, dont la difficulté trahit probablement l'intervention d'un rédacteur (addition du v. 14c).

Les propositions *substantives*, quelle que soit leur fonction (sujet ou objet), ne peuvent être séparées du verbe principal. Le v. 11d de Hentschel est en réalité le complément de 11c. Il faut donc supprimer 11d et rattacher à 11c la proposition substantive, objet de *whgyd*.

Au v. 16a, Hentschel découvre deux propositions. La présence de *lpnyk* semble favoriser cette analyse, qui pourrait d'ailleurs se recommander de la *New English Bible* commentée par Ackroyd (CBC). L'interprétation habituelle reste pourtant la plus vraisemblable: "maison" et "royauté" sont difficilement séparables dans le contexte du v. 16, si unies même qu'on pourrait considérer "maison et royauté" comme un hendiadys (cf. Kittel: "dein Königshaus"). Le paragraphe suivant traitera le v. 16a comme une unique proposition.

La fonction déictique de *w'th* ne transforme pas cet adverbe en proposition ("8a"). Inversement, *wyhy*, "Text-Deiktikon", doit être néanmoins considéré comme une proposition verbale.[7] En conséquen-

---

[7] M. Lambert, *Traité de grammaire hébraïque* (Paris, 1938), p. 459, § 1329, avait noté "la force verbale de *wyhy* ou *whyh*", tout en reconnaissant que "parfois le sens de *hyy* s'affaiblit". W. Richter, *Grundlagen* (*cit. supra*, n. 3), n'a pas tort de parler, à propos de *wyhy*, de "Desemantisierung" (p. 25, n.79, et p. 60): employé comme incipit de récit ou de scène, *wyhy* est avant tout un mot-signal, d'ailleurs plus important ou tout aussi important dans la narration que l'est *w'th* dans les

ce, le v. 1a de Hentschel deviendra ci-dessous 1a et 1b, tandis que 8a et 8b seront regroupés sous 8a.

Bref, les *divergences* entre l'analyse de Hentschel et celle du § 2 portent sur les onze versets suivants, où

au lieu de:	nous lirons:
1a	1a.b (*wyhy* / prop. temp)
3b.c.d.	3b.c (objet anticipé + impér. / impér.)
7a.b.c.	7a (compl. de lieu + prop. interr. + prop. rel.)
8a.b	8a (*w'th kh t'mr...*)
9a.b.	9a (prop. princ. + compl. de lieu)
9d.e.	9c (prop. princ. + prop. rel.)
10e, 11a	10e [10f + 11a] (prop. verb. / prop. compar. verbe sous-entendu)
11c.d.	11c (w^{e}qatal + prop. subst. objet)
12c.d.	12c (prop. princ. + prop. rel.)
14c.d.	14c (prop. rel. en *casus pendens* + w^{e}qaltí avec pron. rétr.)
15b.c.	15b (prop. compar. + prop. rel.)
16a.b.	16a (*bytk wmmlktk* proche de l'hendiadys).

2. Les quarante-neuf propositions et leur équilibre

Dans ce paragraphe et les suivants, l'"analyse formelle et numérique" sera surtout *numérique*: ce sont en effet les nombres et les mesures qui révèlent le mieux l'architecture de l'édifice actuel, qui intègre en l'agrandissant — nous l'entreverrons plus d'une fois — un édifice antérieur. L'analyse syntaxique elle-même indiquera donc, après chaque proposition, le total des mots calculé à partir du début du récit et, à rebours, à partir de la fin (ce dernier chiffre visant, bien entendu, le premier mot de la proposition).

---

discours (en 2 Sam 7, il est donc illogique de lier, au v. 1, *wyhy* à la proposition suivante et d'isoler *w'th* au v. 8a, comme le fait Hentschel, pp. 7-8). Dans BH^t (*cit. supra*. n. 3), Richter a certainement raison de considérer comme une proposition *wyhy*, seul (Gen 6:1a; 12:11a; 15:12a.17a; 20:13a, etc.) ou suivi d'une indication des circonstances (ordinairement temporelles, cf. GK, § 111g) de l'événement que va relater le récit (Gen 4:3a.8b; 7:10a; 8:6a.13a; 11:2a; 12:14a; 14:1; 19:17a.29a. 34a; 21:22a; 22:1a.20a, etc.). On notera que Richter assigne une ligne propre, mais non point une lettre différente, aux "propositions" infinitives (I), ce qui a le double avantage de les présenter clairement sans pourtant les séparer de leur contexte (cf. Gen 4:8bI; 11:2aI; 12:14aI; 19:17aI.29aI). Même procédé pour les propositions relatives (voir, par exemple, Gen 1:7bR1.7bR2), parfois aussi, mais sans sigle spécial, pour *w'th* (Gen 3:22c; 12:19d; 24:49a; 27:8a.43a; 44:30a). - Sur *w'th*, bibliographie dans *THAT II* (1976), col. 379 (Jenni) ou *TWAT VI* (1989), col. 475 (Kronholm).

2 Sam 7:1-17: les quarante-neuf propositions

1	1a *wyhy*	001.	256
2	1b *ky yšb hmlk bbytw*	005.	255
3	1c *wYHWH hnyḥ lw msbyb mkl 'ybyw*	**011.**	251
4	2a *wy'mr hmlk 'l ntn hnby'* :	**016.**	245
5	2b *r'h n'*	018.	240
6	2c *'nky ywšb bbyt 'rzym*	**022.**	238
7	2d *w'rwn H'LHYM yšb btwk hyry'ḥ.*	027.	234
8	3a *wy'mr ntn 'l hmlk* :	031.	229
9	3b *kl 'šr blbbk lk*	035.	225
10	3c *'śh*	036.	221
11	3d *ky YHWH 'mk*	039.	220
12	4a *wyhy blylh hhw'*	042.	217
13	4b *wyhy dbr YHWH 'l ntn l'mr* :	048.	214
14	5a *lk*	**049.**	208
15	5b *w'mrt 'l 'bdy 'l dwd* :	054.	207
16	5c *kh 'mr YHWH* :	057.	202
17	5d *h'th tbnh ly byt lšbty*	**062.**	199
18	6a *ky l' yšbty bbyt lmywm h'lty 't bny yśr'l mmṣrym w'd hywm hzh*	**075.**	194
19	6b *w'hyh mthlk b'hl wbmškn.*	079.	181
20	7a *bkl 'šr hthlkty bkl bny yśr'l hdbr dbrty 't 'ḥd šbty yśr'l 'šr ṣwyty lr'wt 't 'my 't yśr'l l'mr*	099.	177
21	7b *lmh l' bnytm ly byt 'rzym.*	**105.**	157
22	8a *w'th kh t'mr l'bdy ldwd* :	110.	151
23	8b *kh 'mr YHWH ṣb'wt* :	114.	146
24	8c *'ny lqḥtyk mn hnwh m'ḥr hṣ'n lhywt ngyd 'l 'my 'l yśr'l*	126.	142
25	9a *w'hyh 'mk bkl 'šr hlkt*	131.	130
26	9b *w'krth 't kl 'ybyk mpnyk*	136.	125
27	9c *w'śty lk šm gdwl kšm hgdlym 'šr b'rṣ.*	144.	120
28	10a *wśmty mqwm l'my lyśr'l*	148.	112
29	10b *wnt'tyw*	149.	108
30	10c *wškn thtyw*	151.	107
31	10d *wl' yrgz 'wd*	154.	**105**
32	10e *wl' ysypw bny 'wlh l'nwtw*	159.	102
33	10f *k'šr br'šwnh* 11a *wlmn hywm 'šr ṣwyty špṭym 'l 'my yśr'l*	169.	097
34	11b *whnyḥty lk mkl 'ybyk.*	173.	087
35	11c *whgyd lk YHWH ky byt y'śh lk YHWH* :	181.	083
36	12a *ky yml'w ymyk*	184.	**075**
37	12b *wškbt 't 'btyk*	187.	072
38	12c *whqymty 't zr'k 'ḥryk 'šr yṣ' mm'yk*	194.	069
39	12d *whkynty 't mmlktw*	197.	**062**
40	13a *hw' ybnh byt lšmy*	201.	059
41	13b *wknnty 't ks' mmlktw 'd 'wlm*	207.	055
42	14a *'ny 'hyh lw l'b*	211.	**049**
43	14b *whw' yhyh ly lbn*	215.	045

44	14c 'šr bh'wtw whkhtyw bšbṭ 'nšym wbng'y bny 'dm	223. 041
45	15a whsdy l' yswr mmnw	227. 033
46	15b k'šr hsrty m'm š'wl 'šr hsrty mlpnyk	234. 029
47	16a wn'mn bytk wmmlktk 'd 'wlm lpnyk	240. 022
48	16b ks'k yhyh nkwn 'd 'wlm.	245. 016
49	17 kkl hdbrym h'lh wkkl hḥzywn hzh kn dbr ntn 'l dwd.	256. 011

En parcourant les chiffres de droite (total des mots), on constate
d'emblée que le rédacteur-éditeur du récit actuel a cherché à équilibrer
son texte:

Propositions 1-3	= proposition 49	= 11 mots
Propositions 1-4	= propositions 48-49	= 16 mots
Propositions 1-6	= propositions 47-49	= 22 mots
Propositions 1-14	= propositions 42-49	= 49 mots
Propositions 1-17	= propositions 39-49	= 62 mots
Propositions 1-18	= propositions 36-49	= 75 mots
Propositions 1-21	= propositions 31-49	= 105 mots

Au point où nous en sommes, l'équilibre est encore imparfait: les 19
dernières propositions (n°s 31-49) ont le même nombre de mots que les
21 premières (105 mots). Si l'on veut centrer l'ensemble du texte
(propositions et mots) sur la 25e proposition (5 mots) qui contient les
deux mots médians ('mk bkl: "avec toi partout"), une correction s'impose, d'autant plus nécessaire que les 3 propositions n°s 22-24 ont un
total de 21 mots. Les 46 mots des 9 propositions du centre vont donc
être répartis de la manière suivante:

22	5 mots	25 5 mots	26 5 mots
23	4		27 8
24	12		28 4
			29 1
			30 2
	21 mots / 3 prop.	5 mots / 1 prop.	20 mots / 5 prop.

Il est frappant de constater que ce sont précisément les vv. 9c-10c
(prop. 27-30), dont la traduction est discutée, qui assurent l'équilibre
du système. Par ailleurs, on notera que le v. 10 concerne, non le roi,
mais le peuple d'Israël. Ce v. 10 révélerait-il un des soucis majeurs du
rédacteur final ? A cette question le total général des mots (256) ne
permet pas de répondre: 256 n'est peut-être que le résultat d'une série
d'additions (1 + 1 = 2; 2 + 2 = 4; 4 + 4 = 8; 8 + 8 = 16; 16 + 16 =
32; 32 + 32 = 64; 64 + 64 = 128; 128 + 128 = 256). Mais regardons
de plus près l'équilibre numérique des 49 propositions.

2 Sam 7:1-17: Équilibre des quarante-neuf propositions

Prop.Mots.   Prop.Mots.   Total des mots.

1.	1	49.	11	12	12	256		
2.	4	48.	5	9	21	244		
3.	6	47.	6	12	33	235		
4.	5	46.	7	12	45	223		
5.	2	45.	4	6	51	211		
6.	4	44.	8	12	63	205		
7.	5	43.	4	9	**72**	193		
8.	4	42.	4	8	80	184	8	112
9.	4	41.	6	10	90	176	18	104
10.	1	40.	4	5	95	166	23	94
11.	3	39.	3	6	101	161	29	89
12.	3	38.	7	10	111	155	39	83
13.	6	37.	3	9	120	145	48	73
14.	1	36.	3	4	124	136	52	64
15.	5	35.	8	13	137	132	65	60
16.	3	34.	4	7	**144**	119	**72**	47
17.	5	33.	10	15	159	112	87	**40**
18.	13	32.	5	18	177	97	105	25
19.	4	31.	3	7	184	79	112	7
20.	20	30.	2	22	206	**72**		
21.	6	29.	1	7	213	50		
22.	5	28.	4	9	222	43		
23.	4	27.	8	12	234	34		
24.	12	26.	5	17	251	22		
25.	5			5	256	5		

Les 14 propositions des extrêmes (nos 1-7 + 43-49) ont au total 72 mots; les 11 propositions centrales (nos 20-30) ont également 72 mots. Entre les extrêmes et le centre 24 propositions symétriques (112 mots au total) se subdivisent en deux groupes: nos 8-16 + 34-42: 18 propositions / 72 mots; nos 17-19 + 31-33: 6 propositions / 40 mots. Le système d'équilibre joue sur le nombre 4 (les 256 mots de l'ensemble = 4 x 4 x 4 x 4; les 40 mots du groupe de 6 propositions = 4 x 10), mais plus encore sur le nombre 12 (72 = 12 x 6): sur les 49 propositions de l'ensemble, 43 (les 3 groupes de 72 mots) sont fondées sur 12 et les 32 propositions des extrêmes ont au total 144 mots (12 x 12). Le rédacteur final, préoccupé du "peuple d'Israël" (nos 28-33 / vv. 10-11a), déjà mentionné, semble-t-il, dans son texte de base (nos 20, 24 / vv. 7a, 8c), identifie ce peuple aux "douze tribus".

Mais n'est-il pas prématuré de parler de "rédacteur final" ? Précisée numériquement, l'analyse syntaxique du récit nous oriente bien vers le

rédacteur-éditeur responsable de la fixation définitive du texte consonantique conservé dans le TM. Une vérification s'impose néanmoins,
car, si le texte est "canonisé", il doit comporter sa clé numérique
comme ailleurs dans le livre de Samuel. Les deux mots médians et leur
contexte immédiat ne fournissent aucune "grille". Faut-il chercher la
grille des *lettres* du texte ? J'aurai recours une fois de plus (cf. *RB* 97
[1990], 381-3) à la ligne de 43 lettres, sans pourtant imposer au lecteur
l'examen d'un texte en *scriptio continua*.

3. *Les neuf cent soixante-dix-huit lettres et leurs grilles*

Transcrit sur des lignes de 43 lettres, 2 Sam 7:1-17 (978 lettres)
occupe 22 lignes complètes et une 23ᵉ ligne de 32 lettres seulement:

1.	wyhy ky yšb hmlk bbytw wYHWH hnyh lw msbyb mkl 'ybyw w-	43
2.	y'mr hmlk 'l ntn hnby' r'h n' 'nky ywšb bbyt 'rzym w'r-	86
3.	wn h'lhym yšb btwk hyry'h wy'mr ntn 'l hmlk kl 'šr blb-	129
4.	bk lk 'śh ky YHWH 'mk wyhy blylh hhw' wyhy dbr YHWH 'l n-	172
5.	tn l'mr lk w'mrt 'l 'bdy 'l dwd kh 'mr YHWH h'th tbnh ly	215
6.	byt lšbty ky l' yšbty bbyt lmywm h'lty 't bny yśr'l mm-	258
7.	srym w'd hywm hzh w'hyh mthlk b'hl wbmškn bkl 'šr hth-	301
8.	lkty bkl bny yśr'l hdbr dbrty 't 'hd šbty yśr'l 'šr sw-	344
9.	yty lr'wt 't 'my 't yśr'l l'mr lmh l' bnytm ly byt 'rzy-	387
10.	m w'th kh t'mr l'bdy ldwd kh 'mr YHWH sb'wt 'ny lqhtyk	430
11.	mn hnwh m'hr hs'n lhywt ngyd 'l 'my 'l yśr'l w'hyh 'mk	473
12.	bkl 'šr hlkt w'krth 't kl 'ybyk mpnyk w'śty lk šm gdwl	516
13.	kšm hgdlym 'šr b'rṣ wśmty mqwm l'my lyśr'l wnt'tyw w-	559
14.	škn thtyw wl' yrgz 'wd wl' ysypw bny 'wlh l'nwtw k'šr	602
15.	br'šwnh wlmn hywm 'šr swyty špṭym 'l 'my yśr'l whnyh-	645
16.	ty lk mkl 'ybyk whgyd lk YHWH ky byt y'śh lk YHWH ky yml-	688
17.	'w ymyk wškbt 't 'btyk whqymty 't zr'k 'hryk 'šr ys' m-	731
18.	m'yk whkynty 't mmlktw hw' ybnh byt lšmy wknnty 't ks-	774
19.	' mmlktw 'd 'wlm 'ny 'hyh lw l'b whw' yhyh ly lbn 'šr bh-	817
20	'wtw whkhtyw bšbṭ 'nšym wbng'y bny 'dm whsdy l' yswr	860
21.	mmnw k'šr hsrty m'm š'wl 'šr hsrty mlpnyk wn'mn bytk	903
22.	wmmlktk 'd 'wlm lpnyk ks'k yhyh nkwn 'd 'wlm kkl hdbr-	946
23.	ym h'lh wkkl hhzywn hzh kn dbr ntn 'l dwd	978

Les trois lignes médianes en *scriptio continua* (A = 'alef; C = 'ayin)

```
        1234567890123456789012345678901234567890123
11. MNHNWHMAHRHSANLHYWTNGYDCLCMYCLYŚRALWAHYHCMK        473
12. BKLAŠRHLKTWAKRTHATKLAYBYKMPNYKWCŚTYLKŠMGDWL        516
13. KŠMHGDLYMAŠRBARSWŚMTYMQWMLCMYLYŚRALWNTCTYWW        559
```

La grille des lettres est à chercher comme à l'ordinaire dans les lettres
médianes et leurs voisines des trois lignes médianes. Ce texte de 978
lettres a deux lettres médianes: les 489ᵉ et 490ᵉ. La lettre 489 est le *hé*
final de *w'krth*; la lettre 490, le *'alef* initial de *'t* (ligne 12). Les mots

les plus proches sont, à la ligne 11, *ḥṣ'n lḥywt*; à la ligne 13, *b'rṣ*. Deux combinaisons sont possibles: la première intègre le *ṣadé* de *ṣ'n* et omet le *ṣadé* de *'rṣ*; la seconde commence au *'alef* de *ṣ'n* et maintient le *ṣadé* de *'rṣ*. Si, en additionnant successivement les lettres de la grille, on se reporte aux lettres du texte qui correspondent au total obtenu, on constate que la grille 2 est de beaucoup la plus intéressante: elle attire l'attention sur le début des promesses divines (v. 12a).

Voici ces deux grilles, avec les **lettres** (et les mots) qui correspondent aux sommes successives:

	Grille 1				Grille 2	
Lettre.	Total.	Mot correspondant.	Lettre.	Total.	Mot correspondant	
442^e	S	90	HALHYM (1. 3)	443e A	1	WYHY (1. 1)
443	A	91	HALHYM (1. 3)	444 N	51	HMLK (1. 2)
444	N	141	YHWH (1. 4)	445 L	81	ARZYM (1. 2)
445	L	171	AL (1. 4)	487 R	281	MTHLK (1. 7)
487	R	371	LMH (1. 9)	488 T	681	YHWH (1.16)
488	T	771	AT (1.18)	489 H	686	YMLAW (1.16)
489	H	776	MMLKTW (1.19)	490 A	687	YMLAW (1.16)
490	A	777	MMLKTW (1.19)	530 A	688	YMLAW (1.16)
530	A	778	MMLKTW (1.19)	531 R	888	HSRTY (1.21)
531	R	978	DWD (1.23)	532 Ṣ	978	DWD (1.23)

Les promesses de Yhwh (de la ligne 16, lettre 658, à la ligne 22, lettre 939 = vv. 11c-16b) ont été rédigées avec un soin tout particulier; l'ensemble comprend 14 propositions, 72 mots, 282 lettres; la formule d'introduction (v. 11c / prop. 35), 8 mots, 26 lettres; la prophétie proprement dite (v. 12-16 / prop. 36-48), 64 mots (= 4 x 4 x 4), 256 lettres (= 4 x 4 x 4 x 4). Le rédacteur-éditeur a donc ménagé une correspondance entre la prophétie (256 lettres) et l'ensemble du récit (256 mots). Mais il y a beaucoup d'autres calculs, sur lesquels le § 5 nous donnera plus de détails. Pour découvrir et situer ces détails, nous devons examiner la structure du récit plus attentivement que ne l'a fait Hentschel (10-1).

4. *La structure du récit: les deux scènes et leurs subdivisions*

La *première scène* (vv. 1-3) est un *dialogue* très simple:

- narration (vv. 1a-2a): 4 propositions, 16 mots, 61 lettres;
- discours de David (v. 2b-d): 3 propositions, 11 mots, 46 lettres;
- narration (v. 3a): 1 proposition, 4 mots, 14 lettres;
- réponse de Natan (v. 3b-d): 3 propositions, 8 mots, 24 lettres.

Soit, au total, dans la narration: 5 propositions, 20 mots, 75 lettres; dans le dialogue: 6 propositions, 19 mots, 70 lettres.

La *seconde scène* (vv. 4-17), introduction (v. 4ab) et conclusion (v. 17) mises à part, n'est qu'un *discours* de Yhwh à Natan, qui commence par un *ordre* (v. 5ab), dont la conclusion narrative relatera l'*exécution* (v. 17). On notera au passage que la présence du schéma "ordre-exécution" n'invite guère à considérer le v. 17 en bloc comme une simple notice secondaire (contre Hentschel, 55, 92). L'ordre de mission (v. 5a) est précisé par une "dictée" du message, plus exactement par deux "dictées", dont la seconde semble découler de la première:

- v. 5b: *w'mrt 'l 'bdy 'l dwd* (qatal-x)
- v. 8a: *w'th*
     kh t'mr l'bdy ldwd (x-yiqtol).

Les deux discours à transmettre sont introduits par la "formule du messager" (ici: oraculaire):

- v. 5c: *kh 'mr YHWH*
- v. 8a: *kh 'mr YHWH ṣb'wt.*

Le second discours est interrompu au v. 11c, où, après l'oracle de Yhwh, le prophète reprend la parole pour annoncer à David que Yhwh lui "fera une maison"; puis, de nouveau, c'est Yhwh qui s'adresse à David et formule des promesses qui, dans le texte actuel, semblent viser principalement Salomon.

La seconde scène a donc la structure suivante:

(1) Introduction narrative (v. 4ab)
    (2) Ordre de mission et annonce du contenu du message (v. 5ab)
        (3) Formule oraculaire (v. 5c)
            (4) Premier oracle (vv. 5d-7b)
    (5) Suite "logique" de l'annonce du contenu du message (v. 8a)
        (6) Formule oraculaire (v. 8b)
            (7) Deuxième oracle (vv. 8c-11b)
    (8) Annonce par le prophète d'une promesse divine (v. 11c)
        (9) Promesses divines (vv. 12a-16b)
(10) Conclusion narrative: relation de l'exécution de l'ordre (v. 17).

5. La structure "numérique" de 2 Sam 7:4-17

Sections	(1)	(2)	(3)	(4)	(5)	(6)	(7)	(8)	(9)	(10)
Propositions:	2	2	1	**5**	1	1	**11**	1	**13**	1
1°					38					
2°				23				15		
3°	2				35					1
4°	2			21				14		1
5°	2		8				27			1
6°	1	2		6	1		12	14		1
Mots:	9	6	3	**48**	5	4	**59**	8	**64**	11
1°					217					
2°				134				83		
3°	9				197					11
4°	9			125				72		11
5°	9		57				140			11
6°	9	6		51	5		63	72		11
Lettres:	33	18	9	**183**	19	14	**236**	26	**256**	39
1°					833					
2°				512				321		
3°	33				761					39
4°	33			479				282		39
5°	33		210				551			39
6°	33	18		192	19		250	282		39
Sections	(1)	(2)	(3)	(4)	(5)	(6)	(7)	(8)	(9)	(10)

1°) L'ensemble de la scène 2 (narration et discours) comprend: 38 propositions (= 19 x 2), 217 mots (= 31 x 7), 833 lettres (= 17 x 7 x 7). On notera que 31 est un nombre alphabétique: *l'* / *'l*.

2°) Les sections (1)-(7) ont 512 lettres, le double des lettres de la section (9), 256 lettres, 64 mots, où la moyenne exacte est de 4 lettres par mot (pour l'ensemble de la scène et du récit, la moyenne approximative est de 3,8 lettres par mot). Nous entrevoyons ici la main du rédacteur-éditeur, d'autant plus sûrement que la moyenne exacte de 4 lettres par mot était déjà respectée à la section (7), 236 lettres, 59 mots. Mais — nous le pressentions (cf. *supra*, § 3) — ce sont les promesses divines de la section (9), rédigées en 256 lettres, qui constituent le sommet, la quintessence, du récit dans son ensemble (256 mots). Le décompte des lettres des sections (1)-(7) révèle quelle importance avait la section (9) aux yeux de l'éditeur: elle lui sert de base de calcul (256 x 2 = 512). Ces 512 lettres semblent indiquer également que, pour le rédateur-éditeur, le 2ᵉ oracle (7) était lié au 1ᵉʳ oracle (4) encore plus étroitement (mais cf. *infra*, 5°) qu'au discours de promesses (9). Aussi

bien, *w'th* (v. 8a) présente le 2ᵉ oracle comme la suite logique du 1ᵉʳ
(cf. *supra*, § 4). De ce point de vue, la disposition adoptée ci-dessus (§
4), où les sections (3), (6) et (8) se correspondent, ne rend compte que
d'une partie des données: il est vrai qu'en (2) et (5), c'est *Yhwh* qui
parle à Natan, tandis qu'en (3), (6) et (8), c'est *Natan* qui s'adresse à
David, mais à certains égards, la section (8) marque une division plus
nette que la section (5). Celle-ci en effet (v. 8a) est une transition
plutôt qu'une division. Celle-là (v. 11c) est bel et bien une division. En
revenant au v. 11b sur le thème du "repos", de la paix relatée dès le
début du récit (v. 1c), le rédacteur *conclut* pour mieux marquer que le
v. 11c est une introduction. Les 512 lettres des sections (1)-(7), qui
nous invitent à considérer comme un tout les sept premières sections
de la scène 2, permettent donc de corriger et de compléter le plan du §
4, établi en fonction de la narration et du discours et, dans le discours
lui-même, des changements de locuteur ou de destinataire.

3° Les sections narratives (1) et (10) ont au total 3 propositions, 20
mots, 72 lettres. Ce dernier chiffre (12 x 6) montre que le rédacteur-
éditeur distinguait fort bien la narration du discours. Celui-ci, pris dans
son ensemble, comporte 35 propositions (7 x 5), 197 mots, 761 lettres.

4° Ici comme en 2°, mais cette fois pour les propositions et les mots et
non plus pour les lettres, nous retrouvons groupées les sections (2)-(7),
21 propositions, 125 lettres (5 x 5 x 5), d'une part, les sections (8)-(9),
14 propositions, 72 mots, d'autre part. L'arithmétique du rédacteur-
éditeur met en lumière une interprétation du discours dont il faudra
tenir compte dans l'examen des vv. 9c-11b (*infra* § 6).

5° En 2° et 4°, nous avions constaté qu'il existe un lien étroit entre les
deux premiers oracles. Néanmoins, le contenu des deux oracles est
différent: le 1ᵉʳ, argumentant contre la construction du Temple (par
David), se réfère à l'histoire d'Israël; le 2ᵉ, à l'histoire personnelle de
David (à ce que Yhwh a déjà fait en sa faveur) et encore au peuple
d'Israël (passé ou futur?). Comme le 2ᵉ oracle, les promesses concer-
nent David: l'avenir de sa dynastie. Les 140 mots des sections (5)-(9)
illustrent à leur manière cet aspect davidique: *dwd* x 10. 5° nous
permet ainsi de nuancer 2° et 4°.

6° Les chiffres parlent d'eux-mêmes, y compris 192 (= 12 x 4 x 4) et
282, somme de 26 (chiffre du Tétragramme) et de 256 (= 4⁴). La
structure "numérique" correspond bien à la structure du récit (narration
et discours). Le plan proposé au § 4 paraît donc confirmé. Il ne dit pas

tout, mais il est exact.

6. *Les versets 9c-10c, 11b: "analepses" ou "prolepses" temporelles ?*

En s'inspirant de G. Genette,[8] Hentschel (22-8) a établi une *Zeittafel*
(28) des vv. 6-16 qui plaide graphiquement, de manière assez probante,
en faveur d'une traduction au passé des vv. 9c-10c, 11b. Déjà proposée
par quelques exégètes — et non des moindres (cf. Hentschel, 23, n.
135) — , cette traduction au passé se heurte à la tradition textuelle et
exégétique: elle aura donc du mal à s'imposer. C'est une raison de plus
pour lui donner toutes ses chances, car, si Hentschel l'a défendue avec
de bons arguments (22-3, cf. 35-6, 87-9), il n'a pas su tirer parti de son
examen de la "structure formelle" du récit (tout juste rappelée, page
28). L'analyse proposée ci-dessus pourrait-elle apporter un argument de
plus à l'*opinion minoritaire*,[9] qui semble solidement fondée après les
"observations" de Hentschel ?

Si l'on compare à la *Zeittafel* de Hentschel le plan de la seconde
scène établi au § 4 (*supra*), on constatera que les analepses temporelles
(vv. 6-11 + 1b [= 1c]) figurent dans les deux premiers oracles / sections (4) et (7); les prolepses temporelles (vv. 12-16 + 11d [= 11c])
dans le troisième oracle / promesses divines de la section (9). Signa-
lons toutefois quelques exceptions: l'analepse du v. 1c ("1b" de Hent-

---

[8] G. Genette, *Figures III* (Poétique; Paris, 1972). Voir en particulier, dans
"Discours du récit. Essai de méthode" (65-282), le chap. 1er intitulé: "Ordre" (77-
121), où Genette désigne "par *prolepse* toute manœuvre narrative consistant à
raconter ou évoquer d'avance un événement ultérieur, et par *analepse* toute
évocation après coup d'un événement antérieur au point de l'histoire où l'on se
trouve" et réserve "le terne général d'*anachronie* pour désigner toutes les formes de
discordance entre les deux ordres temporels" (82), c'est-à-dire entre "l'*ordre*
temporel de succession des événements dans la diégèse et l'ordre pseudo-temporel
de leur disposition dans le récit" (78). Les notions de "portée" et d'"amplitude", qui
sont à la base de la *Zeittafel* de Hentschel (28), sont ainsi définies par Genette:
"Une anachronie peut se porter, dans le passé ou dans l'avenir, plus ou moins loin
du moment 'présent', c'est-à-dire du moment de l'histoire où le récit s'est interrompu pour lui faire place: nous appellerons *portée* de l'anachronie cette distance
temporelle. Elle peut aussi couvrir elle-même une durée d'histoire plus ou moins
longue: c'est ce que nous appellerons son *amplitude*" (89). Sur les "analepses", voir
pp. 90-105; sur les "prolepses", pp. 105-15.
[9] A.A. Anderson, *2 Samuel* (WBC 11; Dallas, Texas, 1989), 120. Mais Anderson est "inclined to follow the minority view" (*ibid.*). De fait, il opte pour la
traduction au passé (110). Parmi les commentateurs (mais cf. Hentschel, 23, n. 135),
les prédécesseurs d'Anderson sont faciles à énumérer. A ma connaissance: Keil,
Caspari, Goslinga (Hertzberg traduit au présent, cf. *infra*, n. 13). Curieusement, la
traduction au passé est attestée, au xixe siècle, dans les bibles françaises de Darby,
Segond, Crampon et même dans la Bible du Rabbinat (qui pouvait, il est vrai, se
recommander de Gersonide).

schel), d'autant plus intéressante que nous la retrouverons au v. 11b
(thème du "repos"), et celle du v. 15b (non signalée par Hentschel,
page 28); les vv. 10d et 10e, qui viseraient, selon Hentschel (24-5), le
présent ou un futur vague. Quoi qu'il en soit de ces exceptions, dont
nous devrons tenir compte, la correspondance, presque parfaite, entre la
Zeittafel de Hentschel et les sections (4), (7) et (9), mises au jour au §
4 et "mesurées" au § 5, nous invite à examiner les trois oracles pour
eux-mêmes, en concentrant notre attention sur les formes des verbes et
le temps qu'elles indiquent ou peuvent indiquer. Aux vv. 9c-10c, 11b,
le texte consonantique ne permet pas de trancher entre wᵉqataltí (qatal-
x, futur) et wᵉqatal (passé): le verbe hébreu sera donc reproduit tel
quel. Tous les autres verbes seront remplacés par yiqtol-x / x-qatal
(passé) et par qatal-x / x-yiqtol (futur), sans précisions sur les "x", qui
n'apporteraient presque rien à la solution de notre problème. Ainsi
réduit aux verbes des propositions isolables (sinon "indépendantes"), le
texte des trois oracles — (4) vv. 5d-7b; (7) vv. 8c-11b; (9) vv. 12a-16b
— se présente de la manière suivante:

vv.	Passé	?	Futur .	Prop.	Mots	Lettres	
5d			x-yiqtol	17.	5	18	1.
6a	x-qatal			18.	13	49	2.
6b	yiqtol-x			19.	4	20	3.
7a	x-qatal			20.	20	76	4.
7b	x-qatal			21.	6	20	5.
8c	x-qatal			24.	12	44	6.
9a	yiqtol-x			25.	5	18	7.
9b	yiqtol-x			26.	5	20	8.
9c		w'śty		27.	8	29	9.
10a		wśmty		28.	4	19	10.
10b		wnt'tyw		29.	1	7	11.
10c		wškn		30.	2	9	12.
10d			x-yiqtol	31.	3	10	13.
10e			x-yiqtol	32.	5	21	14.
10f+11a (verbe ss-entendu)				33.	10	42	15.
11b		whnyḥty		34.	4	17	16.
12a			x-yiqtol	36.	3	11	17.
12b		qatal-x		37.	3	12	18.
12c		qatal-x		38.	7	29	19.
12d		qatal-x		39.	3	15	20.
13a			x-yiqtol	40.	4	14	21.
13b		qatal-x		41.	6	23	22.
14a			x-yiqtol	42.	4	12	23.
14b			x-yiqtol	43.	4	13	24.
14c		qatal-x		44.	8	37	25.
15a			x-yiqtol	45.	4	15	26.

15b	x-qatal		46.	7	30	27.
16a		qatal-x	47.	6	27	28.
16b		x-yiqtol	48.	5	18	29.
				―――	―――	
Total:				171	675	

Schématisé, le premier oracle est clair. Introduit par une proposition interrogative au *futur* (v. 5d), il développe une argumentation fondée sur une "rétrospection" et entièrement formulée au *passé* (vv. 6a-7b). Le troisième oracle, consacré aux promesses (vv. 12a-16b), est naturellement au *futur* (exception faite de l'analepse temporelle du v. 15b). Restent le deuxième oracle (vv. 8c-11b) et les versets litigieux 10a-c, 11b.

Nous avons noté ci-dessus (§ 2) que les vv. 9b-10c assurent l'équilibre du système des 49 propositions, attesté dans le texte consonantique, donc émanant probablement du dernier rédacteur-éditeur. Cet équilibre numérique, qui joue sur 72, le chiffre des douze tribus, avait attiré notre attention sur le v. 10, où le discours divin passe sans transition de David au peuple d'Israël (déjà mentionné, il est vrai, aux vv. 7a, 8c) avant de revenir à David au v. 11b (cf. par. 1c).

Au § 5, nous avons vu avec quel soin le rédacteur-éditeur avait repris, mesuré, calculé (donc probablement complété) les propositions, les mots et les lettres de la scène 2, en particulier des sections (4), (7) et (9), "citation" des paroles mêmes de Yhwh que Natan devait transmettre à David. Le tableau ci-dessus confirme ces observations: les trois oracles divins ont au total 171 mots (= 19 x 9) et 675 lettres (= 15 x 15 x 3); les 22 premières propositions de cet ensemble (prop. 17-21, 24-34 et 36-41) ont 133 mots (= 19 x 7) et les 7 dernières (prop. 42-48), 38 mots (= 19 x 2). Le 133e mot est à la fin du v. 13 (relatif à Salomon, constructeur du Temple), ce qui montre quelle importance notre calculateur reconnaissait à ce verset "salomonien" (à supposer qu'il n'en soit pas l'auteur).

Cette dernière remarque nous invite à ne pas négliger le v. 5d (prop. 17). La première phrase du premier oracle (*h'th tbnh ly byt lšbty*), proposition interrogative au futur, appelle une réponse négative, non formulée explicitement. Cette "question rhétorique" (Hentschel, 12, cf. 31-2, 62, 72-3, 76) est limpide, du moins dans le texte actuel: ce n'est pas David qui bâtira le Temple (v. 5d), c'est Salomon (v. 13a). Synchroniquement, on ne peut dissocier le v. 5d du v. 13. Nous devrons donc intégrer le v. 5d à la liste des propositions rédigées au futur.

Il faut en dire autant des vv. 10d et 10e (prop. 31 et 32), même si l'on reconnaît à ces deux propositions une nuance consécutive. Ainsi, c'est toute la colonne "Futur" du Tableau précédent que nous devons maintenant étudier, 15 propositions au total (prop. 17, 31-32, 36-45 et 47-48).

Prop.		vv.	Mots.	Total des mots.		Lettres.	Total des lettres.	
1	(17)	5d	5	5	70	18	18	275
2	(31)	10d	3	8	65	10	28	257
3	(32)	10e	5	**13**	62	21	49	247
4	(36)	12a	3	16	57	11	60	226
5	(37)	12b	3	19	54	12	72	215
6	(38)	12c	7	**26**	51	29	101	203
7	(39)	12d	3	29	44	15	116	174
8	(40)	13a	4	33	41	14	130	159
9	(41)	13b	6	**39**	37	23	153	145
10	(42)	14a	4	43	31	12	165	122
11	(43)	14b	4	47	27	13	178	110
12	(44)	14c	8	55	23	37	215	97
13	(45)	15a	4	59	15	15	230	60
14	(47)	16a	6	**65**	11	27	257	45
15	(48)	16b	5	70	5	18	275	18

1	5d	"Est-ce toi qui me bâtiras une Maison pour que j'y réside ?
2	10d	Il [Israël] ne tremblera plus
3	10e	et point ne recommenceront les fils d'iniquité à l'opprimer.
4	12a	Quand seront accomplis tes jours
5	12b	et que tu seras couché avec tes pères,
6	12c	j'élèverai ton rejeton après toi, qui sortira de tes entrailles,
7	12d	et j'établirai fermement sa royauté.
8	13a	C'est lui qui bâtira une Maison à mon nom
9	13b	et j'établirai fermement son trône royal, à jamais.
10	14a	Moi, je serai pour lui un père,
11	14b	et lui, il sera pour moi un fils,
12	14c	que, s'il agit mal, eh bien, je le corrigerai, avec le bâton des hommes et par les coups des fils d'homme,
13	15a	mais ma fidélité ne s'écartera point de lui.
14	16a	Stable sera ta maison royale à jamais devant toi.
15	16b	Ton trône sera ferme à jamais."

Les promesses, on le voit, ont bien leur *structure* propre:

1	5d	"Est-ce *toi* qui me bâtiras une *Maison* pour que j'y réside?
8	13a	C'est *lui* qui bâtira une *Maison* à mon nom
9	13b	et j'établirai fermement son *trône royal*, à jamais.
14	16a	Stable sera ta *maison royale* à jamais devant toi.
15	16b	Ton *trône* sera ferme à jamais.

Ces cinq propositions clés, réparties entre les extrêmes et le centre du système du futur, ont au total: 5 + 4 + 6 + 6 + 5 = 26 mots; 18 + 14 + 23 + 27 + 18 = 100 lettres.

Nous retrouvons 26, chiffre du Tétragramme,[10] et plus générale-
ment les multiples de 13, dans les sommes successives des *mots* des
propositions. Le nombre 13 et ses multiples jalonnent, de trois en trois,
les neuf premières propositions: prop. 3 (total: 13), prop. 6 (total: 26),
prop. 9 (total: 39). Vingt-six mots de plus et nous arrivons au dernier
mot de la 14e proposition (total: 65). Enfin, les cinq mots de la 15e
proposition donnent un total général de 70. Rédigées en soixante-dix
mots,[11] les promesses de Yhwh à David ont la perfection qu'on pouvait attendre de leur Auteur. Elles garantissent à jamais la fermeté du
trône de David.

Que conclure de ces observations? S'il existe bien un "système" du
futur — et les remarques qui précèdent semblent l'indiquer clairement
—, l'auteur de ce système considérait les événements relatés aux vv.
9c-10c, 11b comme appartenant au passé. S'il n'est pas l'auteur de ces
versets, ils existaient avant lui: 10d et 10e, qui font partie du système
du futur, présupposent le début du v. 10. Aussi bien, tout porte à croire
que le système du futur est inséparable du système d'ensemble, œuvre
du rédacteur-éditeur qui a fixé — "canonisé" — le texte consonantique. Les vv. 9c-11b, essentiels à l'équilibre du texte (cf. *supra*, § 2),
émanent probablement de lui. Il a écrit dans sa langue, qui n'était déjà
plus classique, et continué en w^{e}qatal les wayyiqtol corrects[12] du v. 9

---

[10] Cf. *supra*, § 5, 6°. Le nombre 26 est bien le chiffre du Tétragramme: Y + H +
W + H = 10 + 5 + 6 + 5 = 26, fort utilisé en "arithmétique des scribes". Les scribes
jouent également sur 15 = Y + H = 10 + 5. Le nombre 26, multiple de 13, commu-
nique en quelque sorte sa "sainteté" à tous les multiples de 13: 39, 52, 65, etc. Que
YHWH 'HD = 26 + 13 = 39 (Schedl, *Baupläne*, 245, cf. 121-4), c'est arithmétiquement incontestable. S'ensuit-il que les scribes aient pensé à ce "chiffre" chaque fois
qu'ils ont utilisé le nombre 39? Le chiffre 17, "JHWH, nach kleiner Zählung"
(Schedl, 245), relève déjà ici de la cabale. En arithmétique alphabétique, 17 = 10 + 7,
comme 19 = 12 + 7 (!). Le lecteur de Schedl apprend avec quelque gêne que "*Sefär
jesîrah* sich als guter Führer für die Logotechnik erwies" (245, cf. 240-1). En
étudiant l'arithmétique alphabétique des scribes, je me suis interdit tout recours à la
cabale. Celle-ci avait, il est vrai, un fondement numérique dans le texte fixé
arithmétiquement, mais les anciens scribes s'en tenaient au *texte*, aux lettres du
texte et à leur valeur numérique stricte. Ils soulignaient tout au plus, à l'usage des
initiés, les passages qui leur semblaient les plus importants, soit théologiquement,
soit professionnellement (les "grilles" aide-mémoire par exemple).

[11] Les 275 lettres des 70 mots semblent calculées sur la base de 11 (275 = 11 x
5 x 5), procédé courant en arithmétique alphabétique. Je ne sais si Schedl aurait
rattaché 275 au "Tetraktys-Modell" (cf. *Baupläne*, 49, 242): 275 = 55 x 5. Le
nombre 11 fournit une explication à la fois plus simple et plus vraisemblable.

[12] Au v. 9b, on peut attribuer au rédacteur-éditeur le choix de la forme
wā'akritāh (avec -*āh* final): nous avons vu (§ 3) que le *hé* final est la première des
deux lettres médianes du texte. Tardive ou non, cette forme est bien attestée, cf.
GK, § 49e; E. König, *Historisch-comparative Syntax der hebräischen Sprache.
Schlusstheil des historisch-critischen Lehrgebäudes des Hebräischen* (Leipzig,

(d'où la méprise des massorètes, des traducteurs et des commentateurs, anciens et modernes). Il entendait bien parler du *passé*.[13] La présence des vv. 1c et 11b dans le texte établi par ses soins en est le meilleur indice. Rashi lui-même avait senti la difficulté du TM. Il l'escamote en

---

1897), § 200 (93). 1 Chron 17:8 lit: *wā'akrît*.

[13] Mais alors, le récit se réfère d'abord à la carrière de David (vv. 8c-9c), ensuite seulement à la *conquête* (cf. Gelston, *ZAW* 84 [1972], 93) ? Non, si l'on en croit Hentschel (25): "Erst durch die Heilstaten des Herrn in der Zeit Davids hat das Volk in Kanaan sicheren Lebensraum erhalten; erst jetzt ist es wirklich eingepflanzt worden." Le *māqôm* du v. 10a, traduit par "Raum" page 9, serait donc un *Lebensraum* ? Le sens exact de *māqôm* au v. 10a reste une *crux interpretum* (Anderson, *op. cit.*, 121). D.F. Murray, "*mqwm* and the Future of Israel in 2 Samuel vii 10" *VT* 40 (1990), 298-320, a critiqué Gelston (et McCarter qui adopte son hypothèse) de manière si convaincante que le débat semble clos depuis 1990. Touchant le v. 10a (mais non 10b-e), j'avais été séduit par l'interprétation de Gelston: *māqôm* désignerait le Temple (cf. *RB* 83 [1976], 130). Indépendamment de Murray, mais en se référant à K. Seybold, Hentschel affirme que "in V 10 weder vom König noch vom Tempel die Rede ist" (Hentschel, 52, avec n. 296). Il faut donner raison à Murray: *māqôm* ne désigne pas le Temple et la formulation du v. 10 ne correspond pas à celle du Deutéronome. La traduction au passé du v. 10a-c fournit d'ailleurs un argument supplémentaire à l'opinion de Murray: le Temple n'est évidemment pas construit quand Yhwh charge Natan de dire à David que ce n'est pas lui, David (v. 5d), mais bien Salomon (v. 13a), qui bâtira le Temple. Pourtant, le dernier mot n'est pas dit. Si l'on admet avec Hentschel (88-9) que les vv. 10a-11a sont l'œuvre d'un deutéronomiste tardif (l'analyse ci-dessus nous inviterait même à le considérer comme le dernier rédacteur), on doit supposer que ce rédacteur avait déjà sous les yeux 2 Sam 6:17 et 7:2. Il prend l'histoire *après* l'installation de l'Arche "en son lieu" (6:17), "au milieu de la Tente" (6:17; cf, 7:2). Que Yhwh ait déjà "établi un lieu pour Israël" au moment où Natan transmet à David l'oracle divin, c'est certain: Israël a maintenant son "Lebensraum", où, après la destruction des ennemis de David (v. 9b, cf. 11b), il n'a plus rien à craindre de ses oppresseurs d'autrefois (vv. 10d-11a). Mais Israël n'a-t-il pas aussi un lieu de culte: la Tente, où l'Arche est installée "en son lieu" (6:17)? Ce n'est peut-être pas encore *le* Lieu choisi par Yhwh dont nous parle le Deutéronome (cf. Murray, 307), mais c'est bien un lieu de culte provisoire, en attendant la Maison dont Salomon sera le bâtisseur (v. 13a). Si l'on admet ce double sens de *māqôm* — ou plutôt le sens obvie doublé d'une allusion discrète —, on sera tenté d'aller plus loin. Au retour de l'Exil, après le rétablissement du culte (Esdr 3), avant la construction du second Temple, Israël avait retrouvé, à Jérusalem, une place au soleil et un lieu de culte provisoire. Israël avait enfin repris racine dans le Pays. Il espérait y demeurer, libéré de la peur et de l'oppression des "fils d'iniquité". Qui sait si le v. 10 n'a pas été rédigé à cette époque? L'histoire recommençait, comme au temps de David. Le rédacteur attendait la restauration du Temple, mais, à défaut du Lieu, Israël avait déjà un lieu. Beaucoup plus tard, interprété comme une promesse, le v. 10 fera vivre d'espérance le Peuple à nouveau dispersé. Ici nous rejoignons le commentaire de Hertzberg, qui justifie largement sa traduction au présent (cf. *supra*, n. 9): "So wird Vergangenes gemeint sein (vgl. Rost S. 59f.). Vielleicht ist das absichtlich in der Schwebe gehalten worden, weil erwartet wird, das, was der Herr bisher getan hat, werde auch weiterhin in Kraft bleiben" (H.W. Hertzberg, *Die Samuelbücher* [ATD 10; Göttingen, 1956], 229).

glosant le v. 11: *"Je te donnerai du repos.*[14] De plus en plus, jusqu'à ce que tu te reposes de tous tes ennemis.*"* Il n'y a pas de difficulté si l'on traduit le texte au passé. L'analyse formelle et numérique du texte consonantique recommande cette traduction. Mais la tradition s'explique, elle peut encore revendiquer ses droits: compréhensible et compris comme une annonce prophétique, le v. 10 était encourageant et personne, même aujourd'hui, n'oserait dire qu'il est pleinement réalisé.

Conclusion

L'objet de cet article n'était ni de présenter, ni de discuter les "observations" de G. Hentschel sur 2 Sam 7:1-17 (cf. *supra*, n. 1), mais simplement de développer, en rectifiant quelques détails, les cinq pages où l'auteur étudie la "structure formelle" du récit (Hentschel, 7-11). Au lieu de subdiviser le texte en cinquante-neuf propositions, dont plusieurs relatives (Hentschel), l'analyse ci-dessus le divise en quarante-neuf propositions (§ 1). Ces quarante-neuf propositions forment un véritable édifice, harmonieusement construit, parfaitement équilibré. Le v. 9a ("j'ai été *avec toi partout* où tu es allé", résumé théologique de l'"ascension de David") en constitue la clé de voûte: il contient les deux mots médians (*'mk bkl*), 128e et 129e, de ce texte de 256 mots (§ 2). Les lettres centrales apparaissent au v. 9b: dernière lettre de *w'krth* et première lettre de *'t* (489e et 490e lettres). Disposées sur 22 lignes de 43 lettres et une dernière ligne de 32 lettres, les 978 lettres du texte ont deux "grilles" médianes qui attirent spécialement l'attention sur les *promesses* faites à David (§ 3). Le récit comprend bien deux scènes (cf. Hentschel), mais on peut subdiviser la première (vv. 1-3) en quatre sections et la seconde (vv. 4-17) en dix sections (§ 4). Ces subdivisions permettront d'étudier pour elle-même la structure "numérique" de la seconde scène: elle révèle elle aussi l'importance des vv. 12-16 (promesses). Aux yeux du rédacteur-éditeur, le *futur*, l'avenir, les promesses constituent l'essentiel du récit (§ 5). Que penser alors des vv. 9c-10c, 11b? Faut-il les traduire au futur ou au parfait? Les trois oracles proprement dits — les paroles mêmes que YHWH adresse à David — intègrent un "système" du futur (70 mots au total) dont les vv. 9c-10c, 11b ne font pas partie. C'est un argument de plus en faveur de la traduction au passé, défendue par Hentschel (§ 6).

Le résumé qui précède n'est pas une vraie conclusion, et pour cause: considérée comme un travail préparatoire, l'analyse formelle et numéri-

---

[14] *whnyḥwty lk. ywtr wywtr 'd štnwh mkl 'wybyk.* — Remarquer *tnwh* où l'on voit que Rashi interprétait comme un futur *whnḥty lk* (v. 11b). Le ton mile'el peut s'expliquer par une nesîgah (le cas d'Ex 33:14 est encore plus clair).

que doit bien se garder de conclure. Si elle fournit à l'exégèse quelques données utilisables, sa tâche est achevée. Il reste tout à faire. Dans le cas présent, où tout a été dit, il suffirait, espérons-le, mais c'est déjà tout un programme, de relire les auteurs et de confronter les résultats.

OF BARLEY, BULLS, LAND AND LEVIRATE

J.A. LOADER

Unisa, Pretoria

I

It has become customary for introductions to papers on what is perceived to be legal problems in the Book of Ruth to suggest that other
papers on the subject testify to the complexity of the difficulties of
relating these to legal passages in the Pentateuch, especially the levirate
law of Deuteronomy 25:5-10 and the law of redemption in Leviticus
25:25-28.[1] The issue has even been called a "Pandora's box of legal
problems",[2] and it is generally assumed that this is an unsatisfactory
state of affairs (Pandora's box having contained, as everyone knows,
all sorts of nasty things which made life miserable). Agreement
between scholars is presented as something positive, while the lack of
it is taken to be a call for searching in other directions. The implication
is that this is expected to lead to consensus which, it seems to be assumed, would amount to the resolution of the problems in Pandora's
box.[3]

In this paper I would like to question the seemingly self-evident
desirability of consensus in matters such as these, and I propose to use
the "legal problems" of the Book of Ruth for the purpose. Only when
one desires consensus does a variety of opinions seem confusing. But
why should we want consensus? To me this desire seems self-destructi-
ve. For, if we were to reach the logical consequence of the desire and
its concomitant effort, we would have nothing left in Old Testament

---

[1] Cf. D.R.G. Beattie, "The Book of Ruth as evidence for Israelite legal practice",
VT 24 (1974), 251; J.M. Sasson, "The issue of *gᵉ'ullâ* in *Ruth*", *JSOT* 5 (1978), 52;
B.A. Levine, "In praise of the Israelite *mišpāhâ*: Legal themes in the Book of
Ruth", in: H.B. Huffmon *et al.* (eds.), *The quest for the kingdom of God: Studies in
honor of George E. Mendenhall* (Winona Lake, 1983), 95; H.-F. Richter, "Zum
Levirat im Buch Ruth", *ZAW* 95 (1983), 123.

[2] S. Niditsch, "Legends of wise heroes and heroines", in D.A. Knight & G.M.
Tucker eds., *The Hebrew Bible and its modern interpreters* (Philadelphia, 1985),
452.

[3] This is not an unknown feature of the introduction to doctors' dissertations,
enabling as it does candidates to justify their choice of theme. Cf. R.F. West, *Ruth:
A retelling of Genesis 38?* Dissertation submitted to the Southern Baptist Theological Seminary, 1987, 19-20.

scholarship to achieve. We would, as Wellhausen is reputed to have claimed in the previous century, have to look for other fields of research—until nothing at all is left for us to do. The opening sentence of H.H. Rowley's famous study of the problems surrounding the marriage of Ruth,[4] is a serene statement that for many of these difficulties "no final solution can ever be reached". Indeed. Having said this, Rowley goes on happily to argue the case for *his* view on the matters involved. Acceptance that such lost solutions are irretrievable does not imply inactiveness. On the contrary, by not chasing after the ideal of a static general agreement, it avoids precisely that. We may still make *proposals*, that is, we may still offer readings in which possibilities of coping with such problems are suggested. Finality is not necessary for meaningful work. This goes not only for so-called "literary" readings of stories, but also for the "historical-critical" readings which are blamed for the "impasse" in which the study of, among other things, the legal aspects of the Book of Ruth is said to find itself.

The question with which we must begin, is "whether it is valid to derive any conclusions as to legal procedure from a text of the nature of Ruth, which is essentially a short story and by no means a treatise on jurisprudence".[5] Let us start by considering this question with reference to a well-known text concerning clan loyalty resulting in a marriage, the involvement of a clanleader in the matter, the issue of dire social difficulties that can be solved by such a marriage, the arrangements for it to take place, and the legalities involved. I refer to Gaetano Donizetti's opera, *Lucia di Lammermoor* composed to the libretto by Salvatore Cammarano and based on Sir Walter Scott's novel, *The bride of Lammermoor*. Let us use the operatic version for our purpose. It is a dramatic story and not at all a legal treatise. A historical-critical argument can be put forward that Scott modelled his novel on the historical vicissitudes of the Scottish Stair family and that this is also reflected in Cammarano's libretto. Whether the argument is correct or not, we are still confronted by the question: If we have no or few legal documents available from which to determine what relevant Scottish law of the seventeenth century stipulated, would we be able to derive conclusions from *Lucia* as to the law and custom of seventeenth century Scottish society? I submit we would.

We would be able to derive the following information on law and

---

[4] "The marriage of Ruth" (dating from 1946), in *The Servant of the Lord and other essays on the Old Testament* (Oxford, [2]1965), 171-194.

[5] Beattie, "The Book of Ruth as evidence for Israelite legal practice", *VT* 24 (1974), 251.

custom from listening to the opera: In seventeenth century Scotland (the date is indicated by the mentioning in Lord Enrico Ashton's lines of the names of royalty) family leaders had great power over their kin; a carefully arranged marriage could have beneficial effects for a family in dire straights; marriages were sealed by the signing of a contract; a marriage seems to have needed the blessing of a Presbyterian minister (Raimondo counsels Lucia that a *ministro*, not a *sacerdote*, needs to solemnise marriage); since her signature, and thus her consent, was necessary, a woman was a free agent to choose whom she wanted to marry (in Act II Scene 2, after the signing of the documents, Enrico's sigh of relief emphasises that his sister could have chosen *not* to marry the man of his choice); the power of the family head could render the woman's freedom practically worthless (Enrico overrules his sister's legal freedom); clan loyalty was an extremely strong force (Lucia agrees to marry Lord Arturo Bucklaw as a result of Enrico's frequent appeals to her loyalty).

Since the opera is a dramatic story, it is not about laws; it is about a human tragedy. However, in order to be an artistic success it has to be authentic and must therefore reflect the historical reality of the human world in which it is set. The legal motifs are part of this historical reality and as such stand in the service of the plot. So they are important in the work of art only in as far as they undergird the story. Nevertheless, they are there and they do refer to the historical world of humans living in seventeenth century Scotland.

Lucia's story leaves us with several questions: Was her marriage to Arturo legal? She only signed the contract after having been pressurised and having been given false information about her lover, Edgardo of Ravenswood. Was a contract valid if it had been signed under coercion? Neither Sir Walter Scott nor Donizetti and Cammarano may have intended it and the story does not depend on it, but they have suggested the question. Other such suggestions are: What took precedence, the interests of the family or the individual? Was a marriage only legal if a Presbyterian minister blessed it, or is this motif a projection by Sir Walter Scott or Cammarano from the nineteenth into the seventeenth century? Was it perhaps an earlier law that had already become obsolete by the late seventeenth century? We cannot be quite sure, but the setting of the opera on the whole seems to yield a historically authentic picture. Differing genres like law codes, history books and operas display differing degrees of historical accuracy, but we may suspect that we are not too far off the mark with our inferences about legal matters.

Having written the above paragraph, I went in search of evidence with the help of a legal historian. The picture gleaned from listening to the opera is confirmed in several respects: a woman was a free agent who could choose whom she wanted to marry[6] and a marriage contract was necessary.[7] Several of the questions suggested to us by the opera are also answered: the contract, and thus the marriage, was not valid if consent was induced by coercion or fear;[8] a minister of the Church of Scotland[9] could solemnise the marriage, although since pre-Tridentine times no religious ceremony was necessary.[10] The relevant Scottish legalities, then, can to a great extent be inferred from the opera. Of course we may compare *Lucia* to the legal texts in question. We may pose historical questions, such as whether the law could adequately provide for a situation as the one depicted in the opera or whether it was practical in the light of the clan system and social pressure, because the plot of the opera *could* have happened. All of which would be a legitimate questioning of the text, and none of which would imply that we are misreading the opera by testing it on issues foreign to its artistic scope.

This is the kind of thing that historical-critical readers of the Book of Ruth have been doing in order to understand the marriage of Ruth and Boaz and the legalities with which it is associated in the text. Ruth is a childless widow with no brother-in-law. She marries a kinsman because he is the redeemer (*go'el*; 2:20; 3:9.12). The kinsman, Boaz, redeems family property said to belong to Ruth's mother-in-law, Naomi (4:3.9). The proceedings of marriage and redemption are linked (4:5, where a textual problem is present into the bargain, 4:9-10). Is the marriage a levirate marriage if it is not a union between the widow and her brother-in-law as required by Deuteronomy 25? If so, does the information in the story contribute to our knowledge of the character and purpose of the levirate? How should we explain the relationship between the situation depicted and the legal text on levirate marriages found in Deuteronomy 25:5-10? What is the relationship between this marriage and the redemption of Naomi's field and between this situation and the legal stipulations of Leviticus 25:25-28? Could widows inherit from their late husbands? Very interesting answers have been given to questions such as these. Leaving aside the commentaries in order to concentrate on contributions specifically concerned with this

---

[6] D.M. Walker, *Principles of Scottish Private Law* Vol. I (Oxford, ³1982), 223, 227f.
[7] *Ibid.*, 227-228.
[8] *Ibid.*, 228.
[9] *Ibid.*, 230.
[10] *Ibid.*, 228.

issue, let us briefly survey some of them. Some of the scholars cited below will receive more detailed attention than others. This does not necessarily imply that they carry more weight than the others, but their contributions are highlighted for the purpose of my argument.[11]

II

J.A. Bewer[12] connects the institutions of levirate and redemption and reconciles the tensions between the relevant texts by suggesting a historical development: In the first stage the redeemer must marry the sonless widow even if he is not the brother of the deceased, which is the situation in Ruth, and which means that this kind of marriage originated in the practice of g^e'ullâ or redemption; in the next stage the levirate duty is restricted to the actual brothers of the dead man; then a further restriction is introduced, notably that the duty only applies to brothers who live together, which is what we find in Deuteronomy; finally, no man may have his brother's wife, which may reflect the interests expressed in the incest law of Leviticus 18:16.

J. Morgenstern[13] has it partially the other way round: In the earliest stage only brothers have the levirate duty (cf. Gen 38); next, the duty is limited to brothers living together (Deut 25:5-6); then the rights of the widow are introduced (Deut 25:7-9); the fourth stage is concerned with property even more than with offspring (cf. Ruth 4:9); finally, the son born of the levirate is no longer regarded as the son of the deceased (cf. Ruth 4:12).

In a series of influential papers M. Burrows[14] claims that, in the early stage, there was no levirate, but a "redemption-marriage[15] as an affair of the whole clan", followed by a transitional stage to be seen in the Book of Ruth, and a final stage of the levirate marriage proper "as an affair of the immediate family" as represented by the law of Deuteronomy 25.

A.R. Johnson[16] thinks that the concepts of redemption and levirate

---

[11] The study by D.A. Leggett, *The levirate and go'el institutions in the Old Testament with special attention to the Book of Ruth* (Cherry Hill, 1974), was not available to me.

[12] "The ge'ullah in the Book of Ruth", *AJSL* 19 (1902-03), 143-148.

[13] "The Book of the Covenant, Part II", *HUCA* 7 (1930), 163-183.

[14] "Levirate marriage in Israel", *JBL* 59 (1940), 23; "The marriage of Boaz and Ruth", *JBL* 59 (1940), 453-454.

[15] The idea of a *go'el*-marriage as something separate from the levirate proper seems to have been mooted for the first time by A. Geiger, "Die Leviratsehe, ihre Entstehung und Entwicklung", *Jüdische Zeitschrift* 1 (1862), 32. Cf. H.-F. Richter, "Zum Levirat im Buch Ruth", *ZAW* 95 (1983), 123.

[16] "The primary meaning of *g'l*", *SVT* 1 (1953), 70.

are so narrowly related that they presuppose one another. The levirate, as much as the institution of redemption, originates in the intertwining of the idea of soil, that is, the economic aspect of society, with the idea of biological offspring. Although we need not agree with Johnson's argument, much can be said in support of his result, viz. that these two institutions were naturally interrelated, because situations were probable in which this would become necessary.

H.H. Rowley[17] regards the marriage of Ruth as "not strictly a case of levirate marriage, since Boaz is not a brother-in-law". However, it seems to reflect a primary stage of the custom that was later codified in the law of Deuteronomy 25, since complex customs tend to become restricted in law. An example, according to Rowley, is the fact that the Deuteronomic law says nothing of any property complications because they would, in his opinion, probably not arise. However, this is precisely the moot point and cannot be ignored by only surmising that the property issue would "probably" not arise. By "combining" the two the Book of Ruth demonstrates the opposite.

These scholars present us with historical-critical readings of the Ruth story in which attempts are made to explain the tensions between its references to matters legal and the laws known to us as they are formulated in the Books of Deuteronomy and Leviticus.[18] They proceed from the assumption that material contained in stories (not only Ruth, but the thematically related story of Judah and Tamar in Gen 38 as well) can and should indeed be compared to legal texts. They also work on the assumption that conclusions drawn from such comparisons are valid. Without any indication of reflection on whether this kind of procedure would be as applicable and as called for in the reading of or listening to texts such as those of Sir Walter Scott, Donizetti and Cammarano, they accept the procedure as standard for working with ancient texts.

III

The theses summarised so far often differ thoroughly on various points, but they all[19] accept that the levirate and redemption are linked in some way. However, among the scholars who have more recently investigated the issue of the legal motifs in the Book of Ruth and in

---

[17] "The marriage of Ruth", 171, 175-180.

[18] In principle this holds good for Johnson also, despite the fact that his is a paper concerned with philological arguments concerning the root *g'l*, and that he has a wider range of interest than the legal problems of the Book of Ruth.

[19] Even Rowley; cf. "The marriage of Ruth", 184-185.

legal texts, there are several who dissent.

R. Gordis[20] claims that the Ruth story tells of the custom of redemption of land, but not of the levirate. In his opinion there are too many discrepancies between the story and Deuteronomy 25, and the picture drawn by the story-teller cannot be fitted into any stage of the development of the levirate in Israel. The title of Gordis's paper is significant, for it clearly supposes that evidence for determining what a legal situation was, can be derived from what he calls "a moving story of a distant and idealized past". Which is exactly what Gordis does. He arrives at his denial of the presence of the levirate by doing the same thing that those do who affirm it, viz. by relating his readings of respectively the narrative and the legal texts. Why I cannot agree with his result, will become apparent in the discussion below of Sasson (who shares Gordis's denial) and Levine (who does not).

J.M. Sasson[21] argues that Ruth's marriage has nothing to do with the institution of redemption. Moreover, he denies that the marriage itself is an instance of the levirate, since Ruth is regarded by Boaz "to be a free agent when it came to remarriage" (Ruth 3:10). He thinks that the redemption issue concerned only Naomi and that even this differs markedly from the legal picture gained from Leviticus 25:26-28 since, in his opinion, Naomi was not an impoverished landowner. Several criticisms can be made of Sasson's view, for instance that Ruth and Naomi have to make use of the pauper law on gleaning (cf. Deut 24:19) in order to stay alive and that their destitute situation does make Naomi an "impoverished landowner". However, when we think of Lucia who was a "free agent" when it came to marriage but who nevertheless married because of the pressure of *hesed* towards the family, we may begin to wonder whether this is such a strong argument as Sasson claims. I am not saying that Ruth had no sincere affection for Boaz or that she did not *want* to marry him, but the freedom of Ruth was directed and even dictated by the requirements of her situation, which were the need to be provided for and the need for an heir to the family estate, in other words, the needs addressed by the levirate. Further, in Sasson's proof text Ruth is blessed for not "going after" younger men. This expression does not mean "to marry"; in fact,

---

[20] "Love, marriage, and business in the Book of Ruth: A chapter in Hebrew customary law", in: H.N. Bream *e.a.* (eds.), *A light unto my path. Old Testament studies in honor of Jacob M. Myers* (Philadelphia, 1974), 241-264.

[21] "The issue of g^e'ullāh in Ruth", *JSOT* 5 (1978), 52-64; *Ruth. A new translation with a philological commentary and a formalist-folklorist interpretation* (Baltimore, 1979), 128-129.

in both sexual (cf. Prov 7:22) and religious (cf. Num 15:39)[22] contexts it has a distinctly negative connotation. So Boaz only praises
Ruth for not flirting around, which does not necessarily imply her "free
agency" in matters matrimonial.

H.-F. Richter[23] reviews his earlier opinion, that Ruth's marriage to
Boaz was not a "real levirate marriage", and now claims that it was,
which becomes a viable interpretation for him because of a number of
textual emendations to the text of the story.

The contribution by B.A. Levine[24] is singularly interesting. He
develops the argument "that the author of Ruth entertained a meta-legal
attitude". Applying G.E. Mendenhall's idea of "policy" as reflected in
law, he argues that the story-teller regarded law as a set of policies and
that, in his story, he transposed *laws* into *legal themes*. Therefore, in
Levine's opinion, we need not endeavour to painstakingly reconcile the
differences between the legal texts of the Pentateuch and the Book of
Ruth, since the author of the latter used the legalities of the system in
order to "extol the spirit, rather than the letter of Israelite law". The
author construes his plot in such a way that, what in terms of the
Deuteronomic law could not be a levirate union, becomes just that in
the story. In this way the story can "work" and display the virtue of
hesed in Israelite law. Some questions may be posed about this thesis.

In the first place, it is only tenable on the assumption that the Book
of Ruth is younger than the laws of Deuteronomy and Leviticus. This
is a moot point, and it may be that Levine's late dating of Ruth is done
under pressure of his thesis.

Without pressing this point, it seems to me, moreover, that Levine's
thesis that the Ruth story extols the spirit of the law overlooks an
important *critical* aspect in the narrative. As far as the law of redemption (Lev 25:25f.) is concerned, Levine argues that it is a departure
from the classic redemption pattern reflected in Jeremiah 32, since the
redeemer is required to *restore* what he redeems to the impoverished
owner without himself gaining title to the land. Now the author of the
Ruth story, by making so many deaths occur in quick succession,
creates "an ideal situation for applying the law of inheritance, not for
invoking the duty of redemption".[25] At the deaths of Mahlon and
Kilyon, the childless heirs of Elimelech, the law of Numbers 27:8-11

---

[22] Cf. G. Sauer, in *THAT* I, col. 490-491, *s.v. hlk.*
[23] "Zum Levirat im Buch Ruth", *ZAW* 95 (1983), 123-126.
[24] "In praise of the Israelite *mišpāḥâ*: Legal themes in the Book of Ruth", in:
H.B. Huffmon *et al.* (eds.), *The quest for the kingdom of God: Studies in honor of
George E. Mendenhall* (Winona Lake, 1983), 95-106.
[25] *Ibid.*, 102.

applies, which requires property to be inherited by the nearest relatives if there are no children or brothers. So the primary redeemer and Boaz (Ruth 4:4) were in line anyway for inheriting the property in question. Therefore there was no room for their redeeming function. In my opinion the author, by invoking in this situation of his own making the legalities of *redemption*, not of inheritance, has not only praised "the laudable motivations and purposes of that system".[26] He has also created a situation in which redemption, according to him, *ought* to work. That would amount to a critical stance, for he would be making a statement: Here is a situation in which the inheritance law applies technically, while actually not the rights of clansmen to inheritance, but the plight of widows in need should be of primary concern.

The same can be said of the levirate motif in the story. According to Levine,[27] the author has created a situation in which the law of Deuteronomy 25:5-10 cannot apply. There are no brothers left to perform the levir's duty, yet the author, by a subtle use of words found in Deuteronomy 25:6,7 (*yāqûm 'al šēm 'aḥîw hammēt* and *lᵉhāqîm lᵉ'āḥîw šēm* become *lᵉhāqîm šēm hammēt 'al naḥᵃlātô*), does invoke the levirate motif. Having created this situation himself, and having made a marriage take place that fulfills the basic function for which the levirate law[28] is there, the story-teller is making a statement: Here is a completely credible situation in which the levirate law does not apply, but in which it *should* apply. If Levine's late dating of Ruth is correct (and I do not think it is), this critical stance is the more topical, since it would concern Deuteronomy 25:5-10 directly. If Ruth should be dated earlier, my argument remains valid, since in that case the critical aspect would address the earlier law/custom concerning levirate responsibilities. In either case, this non-Deuteronomic type of levirate was topical and may therefore actually have occurred.

So, Levine may be quite right that the narrator extols the virtue of the spirit lying *behind* the law, but then the narrator is also criticising the law itself for not making adequate provision for thoroughly thinkable cases (or at least he is showing how the law should be interpreted and applied, which would qualify for being called a constructive "critical" stance). The author may be propounding a "meta-legal" attitude, but it is manifested in a concern for down-to-earth legal realities. He is showing that the spirit of *ḥesed* is needed, but, like Sir Walter Scott,

---

[26] Levine, *ibid.*, 103.
[27] *Ibid.*, 104-106.
[28] In my view the levirate law was formulated only later in the form we have it. However, the relative dating of Ruth and Deuteronomy is not central for the argument I am developing here.

Donizetti and Cammarano, he is also, by the very authenticity of the
legal *casus* conjured up in his story, evoking a legitimate perspective
on practical jurisprudence.

Another important contribution to our topic is that by D.R.G.
Beattie.[29] He declares "that a text such as Ruth may be used for the
study of law and legal procedure". His argument is that a story-teller
will not knowingly sacrifice credibility with his audience by creating a
legal situation which is impossible.[30] This is qualified by the statement that a work of fiction should not be required to have the preci-
sion of statement of a legal textbook. Beattie shows sensitivity to the
fact that the major passage relevant to legal problems, Ruth 4, "has
been created by the author purely to provide a dramatic climax to his
story",[31] a sensitivity, in other words, for the literary character of the
book. The legal processes of inheritance, redemption and the levirate
are considered. Beattie concludes that Naomi's possession of property
(Ruth 4:3) proves that this was possible in Israel despite the fact that
the Pentateuchal inheritance laws contain no provision covering the
case. The substantiation for this is the principle that the author would
not have created an impossible situation, and that the practice had
become obsolete by the time that the laws were written. In this way
Beattie combines respect for the literary character of the text and for
its historicity and historical relevance.

However, objecting to an association of the two institutions by other
scholars (including the tenth century Qaraite commentator, Salmon ben
Yehoram, who said of the levirate and redemption: "Every levir is a
redeemer but not every redeemer is a levir"),[32] Beattie denies that the
Book of Ruth presents us with an instance of the levirate. His argument focuses on 4:5-6, where a crucial textual problem occurs (Kethib
"I acquire" and Qere "you acquire"). He thinks that Boaz confronts the
primary redeemer with the declaration that Boaz (the Kethib reading)
will acquire Ruth when the other man acquires the field which is to be
redeemed. However, this does not take into account the *literary* aspect
of the passage. The author is making the primary redeemer accept a
formulated offer in which no mention is made of a marriage to Ruth.
Why should he not go for it? There is a chance that he may get away
with it and acquire the field without the complications that would set
in if he had to marry Ruth, sire an heir for her deceased husband and

---

[29] "The Book of Ruth as evidence for Israelite legal practice", *VT* 24 (1974),
251-267.
[30] *Ibid.*, 252.
[31] *Ibid.*, 265.
[32] *Ibid.*, 259.

therefore lose the field again when the as yet unborn child takes
possession of it. But when Boaz adds that a son needs to be sired for
the sake of keeping the name of the dead alive on that "inheritance"
(i.e. the field), the offer is formulated differently. Now it ceases to
sound like a bargain, for the man will have to pay with means making
up part of his present estate, thereby diminishing it (Ruth 4:6). This
brings the element of tension into the scene. The offer is formulated
once without the complication to enable the primary redeemer to
accept and thereby heighten the tension that has been building up since
the previous chapter, and once with the complicating factor to afford
the author a credible way of removing the tension so that the happy
ending can be prepared.

Moreover, Beattie himself closely associates the levirate institution
with the preservation of family property within that family. This
preservation, according to him, is the *raison d'être* of levirate marriage.[33] But it is also the *raison d'être* of redemption, in fact, in
circumstances of financial destitution it is what redemption *is* (cf. Lev
25:25). While denying the presence of the levirate motif in the story,
Beattie nevertheless concludes that the economic aspect of the levirate
is fundamental to its existence. Now, since both institutions are the
responsibility of the family in question, there must have arisen overlap-
ping. Even on the assumption that the only real levirate union was
where an actual brother of the deceased was involved (the situation
described in Deut 25:5-10), this would still have been the case, since
brothers can also be redeemers. The fact that a complex of possible
permutations existed as to who is responsible or can shoulder the
responsibilities in question, becomes the more obvious when we consider that, as envisaged by Salmon ben Yehoram, the two sets of legal
obligations can occur together. A childless widow can be expected to
be destitute (widows as such were regarded as among the most helpless
in society, cf. Deut 24:17-22, where the law on gleaning, so central in
the Book of Ruth, is included). Therefore such widows are to be
expected to stand in need of the benefits of both the levirate and
g^e'ullâ. It would, therefore, be more natural to expect the two institutions to be intertwined than disentangled (to borrow a word from
Sasson's argument cited above). Accordingly, the onus of proof on
those like Beattie and Sasson who would deny this is greater than on
those who would affirm it.

I submit that the author of Ruth has painted into his canvas this kind
of situation. The laws of Deuteronomy 25 and Leviticus 25 are not so

---

[33] *Ibid.*, 265, 267.

formulated that these situations are covered by what they say. Even though they may have been put in their present form much later than the Ruth story, the legal tradition in which they stand probably mentioned only what they contain, that is, the basic and normal situation for which the law is intended. The author of Ruth, then, created a story in which a natural and thoroughly credible legal situation is posited. Therefore the story prompts the reader to consider that the spirit of the law (as Levine would say) and the practical application of the law ought to operate in this way. Even if we choose not to call it criticism of the law, it can be read as a constructive representation of how the law should be applied. Seen in the context of the story's insistence on ḥesed, it would mean that the legal dimension of the Ruth story is not merely part of its backdrop or decor, but it is one of the themes[34] integrated in the story's overarching theme of ḥesed: this is how ḥesed should work in the sphere of the law.

An attempt at addressing the historical dimension of reading Ruth while respecting the literary character of the story has already been offered in 1968 by Thomas and Dorothy Thompson.[35] Proceeding from what they call "the unique interrelationship" between g^e'ullâ and the levirate, they observe that both institutions are "essentially connected to the ownership of land". As far as the levirate is concerned, the perceived contradictions between the stories of Ruth and of Judah and Tamar (Gen 38) on the one hand and the law of Deuteronomy 25:5-10 on the other hand are, according to them, "not contradictions at all, but only differences in the forms of the texts". They then state that these narratives should not be interpreted on the basis of the legal texts, but that the narratives should rather be given "the greater weight" since they contain concrete examples of how the custom was actually practiced. I would not be inclined to speak of the one as deserving "greater weight" than the other, for that would imply that the one is more authentic than the other, while actually they are all authentic expressions of a common concern, but in different "forms of texts" (as the Thompsons themselves would say) and different spheres of life (the courtroom and social gathering - to permit myself an anachronism).

In the case of the levirate, they explain what they call "the subtle mixture of the customs of the levirate and the ge'ulah" as the author's literary device to hide the outcome of the plot. This is the result of their healthy respect for attention to the literary quality of the story. As

---

[34] Together with those of the openness to other nations, the openness to other religions, the complementarity of divine and human responsibility for what happens in life, the royal theme etc.

[35] "Some legal problems in the Book of Ruth", *VT* 18 (1968), 79-99.

I have intimated above, I do not think we should speak of a "mixture". To be sure, the author has construed a literary creation, but he has also put before us a completely thinkable legal situation. This was necessary because a story must be credible in order to be a literary success.[36] Therefore, the author needed to involve the law.

The Thompsons proceed to criticise the way in which Deuteronomy 25 has usually been interpreted, notably as if it prescribed "all, and only, the situations and limitations under which the custom is to be effected".[37] They, instead, think that the Deuteronomic law only provides the typical situation in which the law would normally be used. Whether this is right or not, my suggestion made above, that the author of the Ruth story is depicting possible and realistic situations in which the law ought to apply, is not affected. At most the critical mentality with which I have credited him would be tuned down somewhat.

The levirate, they think, is borne by two fundamental principles, viz. support and protection of the widow on the one hand and maintenance of the family property within the family on the other hand. Ruth's dependence on the estate renders not only the institution of redemption necessary, but also marriage (so that she can be cared for), and this marriage must automatically provide an heir for her deceased husband. Therefore, if the intention of what became the Deuteronomic law on the levirate is to be respected, all of these issues are to be catered for in terms of it.

IV

The final contribution we are to consider is something completely different, that of C.M. Carmichael.[38] One can call his contribution "adventurous", which is what H.D. Preuss[39] says of his work on Deuteronomy in general, but it is engaging all the same. Carmichael argues that the levirate law of Deuteronomy 25 is thoroughly indebted to the Judah-Tamar story in Genesis 38. In his view the Deuteronomic method is to constantly survey the traditions available to him and to draw from them, in accordance with his strict moral views, material for

---

[36] On the necessity of a "degree of conformity with familiar elements of the readers' social world" in stories, specifically the story of Ruth, cf. J.L. Berquist, "Role dedifferentiation in the Book of Ruth", *JSOT* 57 (1993), 23-24.

[37] *Ibid.*, 89.

[38] "A ceremonial crux: removing a man's sandal as a female gesture of contempt", *JBL* 96 (1977), 321-336; "'Treading' in the Book of Ruth", *ZAW* 92 (1980), 248-266; cf. *The laws of Deuteronomy* (Ithaca, 1974), 232-240.

[39] *Deuteronomium* (Darmstadt, 1982), 109-110.

his ideal programme of law. Among his examples of this procedure are
Deuteronomy 23:1, which narrows down the situation encountered in
Genesis 35:22 (Reuben's intercourse with his father's wife), Deuteronomy 23:16-17, which formulates into a law the picture of Jacob the
fleeing "slave" (Gen 32:5, 33:5.14), and others.

In the first of his cited studies he argues that the sandal ceremony in
Deuteronomy 25 prescribes a symbolic punishment for a brother who
is not willing to fulfill his levirate duty to his dead brother. In the
Judah-Tamar story Onan is punished by God for spilling his seed on
the ground in order not to sire an heir for his brother so that he himself
may gain from a greater part of the inheritance. In the law the unwilling brother is punished symbolically because a punishment such as that
of Onan in the narrative was not enforceable. The woman spits in the
unwilling man's face, symbolising the spilled seed, and takes off his
sandal. Citing, among others, Arabic evidence, Carmichael contends
that the sandal is the symbol of the female sexual organ and the foot
the symbol of the male organ. By taking off his sandal the woman
emphasises both his Onan-like passivity and withholds sexual intercourse with him. His house bears his shame too, because he was
unwilling to build the house of his brother (Deut 25:10). This has
implications for our understanding of the last chapter of the Book of
Ruth. Having uncovered Boaz's "feet" (Ruth 3:7), Ruth has prepared
the audience for the sexual aspect of the sandal ceremony, which they
would readily understand. However, there is another, distinct, symbolic
use of the sandal involved as well. It could also be the symbol of
ratification of a transaction - treading on land would mean to take
possession of it, which in time was symbolised by the sandal with
which one treads. The primary redeemer actively takes off his shoe
(Ruth 4) to symbolise his transference of the right to the land. This
second symbolic meaning could not be understood so readily, which is
why the author explains its commercial reference (Ruth 4:7).

In another article[40] Carmichael proceeds even more boldly to claim
that treading has a double meaning in the Book of Ruth: threshing of
grain (the story focuses on barley), which makes available not only
food, but also seed for further agricultural fertility, and the treading of
a woman, that is, sexual intercourse. Here Carmichael goes much too

---

[40] "'Treading' in the Book of Ruth", ZAW 92 (1980), 248-266. In this study he
cites C.J. Labuschagne, "The crux in Ruth iv 11", ZAW 79 (1967), 364-367, in
support of his view that there was an "association of human fertility and Ephrathah"
(cf. ZAW 92, 254, 263). However, this stretches Labuschagne's argument (that *hyl*
in Ruth 4:11 means "procreative power") beyond what the latter could be held
accountable for.

far, since he uncritically uses all kinds of words for movement (like *hlk, drk, p'm* and *s'd*) as evidence in support of his thesis. It could also be remarked that, if "treading" in the sense of threshing barley is so prominent in the story, it is quite surprising that this activity is not mentioned in the book. Not only does the verb *dwš* not occur in the story, but we do encounter the activities of reaping and winnowing the barley harvest, while the agricultural activity that takes place between them is absent. If it were such a central idea, one would have expected threshing to be at least mentioned. Further, Carmichael almost exclusively looks upon the barley harvest as the gathering of "seed". Even when Ruth goes gleaning, she does not seem to go in search of food, sustenance for her and her mother-in-law, but for seed in order to symbolise the procreative aspect. This double meaning is also apparent in the sandal ceremony (cf. above), where Boaz receives the right to "tread" on the land (meaning no. 1: agricultural) and to "tread" Ruth (meaning no. 2: sexual).

Quite intriguing is Carmichael's idea that the law immediately preceding the Deuteronomic levirate law, that prohibiting the muzzling of an ox that is threshing (Deut 25:4), should be linked to the levirate law. Since it seems to stand all on its own, this verse is to be taken as "proverbial law". Carmichael regards it impracticable to try to keep an unmuzzled ox treading away at its threshing task, so he reads it symbolically. When an ox, symbol of an Israelite, treads, seed "is produced at both the agricultural and the human level".[41] Carmichael does not pause to consider whether the word *šôr* used here, indeed means "ox" as he and, as far as I am aware, all commentators suppose. The Hebrew word can refer to a bull or to an ox, but oxen, and not bulls, are universally used for threshing where mechanical means are not available. It would have been to his advantage if he had investigated this, since of all animals an ox is the very last to be considered suitable for sexual symbolism. Still, Carmichael's two aspects (procreation and food) are what the levirate law and the transaction in Ruth 4 are about.

Although his thesis may be criticised on several counts, Carmichael has captured the essence of the whole issue of the interrelatedness of begetting a child (the sexual aspect) and of providing for a livelihood (the economic aspect), which constitutes the fundamentals of both the levirate law and the redemption law. Therefore his reading of the story of Ruth and his relating it to the law as well as to ancient Near Eastern comparative material have made salutary contributions to the topic, not

---

[41] *Ibid.*, 250-252.

to speak of the fun of working through and questioning his thesis.

V

Having given my responses to various theses as we went along, I may now draw together some of the threads:

* Since they need to be credible, narratives such as the Book of Ruth may be compared with and related to legal texts to the advantage of those who wish to understand either.

* The levirate and $g^{e'}ull\hat{a}$ have closely related objectives, notably the maintenance of family property in the family.

* The author of the Ruth story, though earlier than the laws of Deuteronomy and Leviticus, presents authentic situations in which such laws ought to apply, and in the process shows what the spirit of the law should be: *hesed.*

Let us now return to the beginning of this paper and ask ourselves whether we have been occupying ourselves with a Pandora's box. Have the readings of the Book of Ruth, of Deuteronomy and other narrative and legal passages which we have surveyed, confronted us with nasty experiences? Have they made us despair of the doldrums into which Old Testament scholarship has sunk? I think not. I have not experienced the sensation of bewilderment at the many differing and opposing views (and I have surveyed only a few). On the contrary, I think that the older as well as the more recent contributions testify to a vibrant and fascinating occupation with narratives and laws and their interrelationships. All of the scholars we have consulted accept that stories and laws have a bearing on one another, but they do not need this agreement among themselves to salvage some meaning from their different approaches, historical reconstructions, literary appreciations and theses. I would submit, therefore, that not only "literary" or "esthetic" readings of a story such as the Book of Ruth have the right, somewhat like a production of *Lucia di Lammermoor*, to be called "creative". The historical-critical and the literary alike present us with so many perspectives, none of which is "right" and none of which is "wrong". Of course their various exponents may be criticised (even the famous Callas *Lucia* was criticised), but there is no ultimate state of consensus. Therefore we should not strive for it.

MOAB ODER SICHEM — WO WURDE DTN 28 NACH DER FABEL DES DEUTERONOMIUMS PROKLAMIERT?

NORBERT LOHFINK

Sankt Georgen - Frankfurt am Main

Selten hat jemand so auf dem gegebenen Text insistiert wie Casper J. Labuschagne. Das ist die Stärke seiner Arbeit am Deuteronomium. In der Festgabe zu seinem 65. Geburtstag möchte ich deshalb eine Frage behandeln, die auf den Sinn des endgültigen Textes des Deuteronomiums zielt. Sie gehört, literaturwissenschaftlich gesprochen, zur Frage nach der "Fabel": Welche objektive Handlungsabfolge impliziert das Deuteronomium in seiner Endgestalt?[1] Konkret ist es die Frage, ob Mose die in Dtn 28 enthaltenen Segen- und Fluchtexte im Lande Moab am Tag der Deuteronomiumsproklamation über Israel ausgerufen oder ob er zu diesem Zeitpunkt nur ihre spätere Proklamation im eroberten Lande angeordnet habe. Die übliche Deutung geht auf die erste Möglichkeit. Sie ist vielleicht sogar vorzuziehen, zumindest kann man sie nicht einfach für falsch erklären.[2] Aber da in dieser Sache kaum ein Problembewußtsein besteht, möchte ich die Frage gern reflex nach beiden Seiten hin diskutieren und vor allem die Gründe für die unübliche Deutung herausstellen.

Zur Forschungslage

Die weit verbreitete und zweifellos auch richtige Überzeugung, daß Dtn 27 Zusätze enthält, die relativ spät und ohne Rücksichtnahme auf das ursprüngliche Konzept des Buches Deuteronomium dort eingeschoben worden sind,[3] scheint so mächtig zu sein, daß man für diesen

---

[1] Vgl. Lohfink, Fabel Dtn 30-31; ders., Fabel.

[2] In Lohfink, Dtn 28,69, 45f, habe ich die zweite Deutungsmöglichkeit offen vertreten und als Argument eingesetzt. In dieser Untersuchung werde ich etwas zurückhaltender urteilen. Doch bin ich nicht der Meinung, daß damit meine Gesamtargumentation gegen van Rooy in Frage gestellt wäre.

[3] Natürlich wird auch immer wieder einmal die ursprüngliche Einheit von Dtn 27 vertreten. So bei Craigie, der das ganze Deuteronomium auf Mose oder Josua zurückführt, oder zuletzt bei Hill, Ebal Ceremony. Die Begründung läuft dafür seit einiger Zeit stets über die Analogie altorientalischer Verträge, die zweifellos vorhanden ist, aber nicht so, daß sie solche Annahmen tragen könnte. Craigie geht bei dem Vergleich wenig ins wirkliche Detail, und auch bei Hill handelt es sich um hoch

Bereich des Buches fast nur noch diachrone Fragen erörtert. Die Frage,
ob durch die Einbauten sich vielleicht etwas an der Fabel des Deuteronomiums geändert habe, wird nicht aufgeworfen.[4]
Auch Peter C.
Craigie, der in Dtn 27 keinen späteren Einschub an-
nimmt, beurteilt zwar 27:11-26 als Anweisungen "for the ceremony of
blessing and cursing which would take place at the renewal of the
covenant to be held in the vicinity of Shechem",[5] aber mit 28:1 "the
focus in the address of Moses returns to the present moment". Dtn 28
sei eine in Moab selbst vorgetragene Ermahnung, "based upon the
blessings and curses pronounced during the renewal of the covenant on
the plains of Moab".[6]

In der Tat sprechen sowohl Nachrichten über Joschija[7] als auch
formgeschichtliche Überlegungen—im Blick auf altorientalische
Gesetze ebenso wie im Blick auf Staatsverträge[8]—dafür, daß zu den
deuteronomischen Gesetzen recht früh auch Segen und Fluch, zumindest jedoch ein Fluchtext gehört hat. Auch traditionsgeschichtliche[9]

über dem Text schwebende pseudo-formkritische Spekulation. - Bei Annahme von
Schichtung rechnet mit den Sichem-Passagen als ältester Textschicht Weinfeld,
Deuteronomy 1-11, 10 (alt: 27:1-8.11-26; jünger: 26:16-19; 27:9f; auf der dann
folgenden Seite stehen etwas unterschiedliche Angaben). Ob er das durch Text-
analyse plausibel machen kann, bleibt abzuwarten, da der betreffende Teil des Kom-
mentars noch nicht erschienen ist.
[4] Die einzige Ausnahme in der jüngeren Kommentarliteratur, die mir bekannt ist,
findet sich bei Braulik, 199. Georg Braulik und ich haben den Gegenstand seit
längerer Zeit miteinander diskutiert, und ich möchte Georg Braulik für seine kritischen Fragen und viele Anregungen herzlich danken. Ferner danke ich Hans Ulrich
Steymans für einen gründlichen Briefwechsel zum Thema, der mich dazu gebracht
hat, alles noch einmal zu überdenken.
[5] Craigie, 330. Er spricht nicht nur vom Fluch, sondern auch vom Segen und
meint doch eindeutig nur 27:15-26. Das Fehlen von Segenssprüchen läßt er als
Rätsel stehen: "There is no mention in the chapter of the subsequent declaration of
the blessings, and the reason for this omission is uncertain ... It is not unlikely,
however, that the twelve blessings, which are not mentioned here, would have been
the exact reverse of the twelve curses that are stated" (331).
[6] Craigie, 335. Ich muß hier nicht auf die spezielle Theorie eingehen, die eigent-
lichen Segens- und Fluchtexte würden nur in 28:3-6 und 16-19 aufgenommen, und
der Rest des Kapitels sei so etwas wie eine Predigt über diese beiden Themen.
Denn auf jeden Fall ist Dtn 28 nach Craigie von Mose in Moab zu Israel aktuell
ermahnend gesprochen. Vgl. auch die Übersicht ebd. 212. In seiner speziellen
Theorie zur Gattung von Dtn 28 scheint Craigie vor allem durch Lewy, Puzzle,
inspiriert zu sein.
[7] Vgl. 2 Kön 22:16. Zu meiner eigenen Auffassung zu Schichtung, Alter und
historischer Zuverlässigkeit des Textes vgl. Lohfink, Kultreform.
[8] Knappe Information zu beidem bei Braulik, 6-8.
[9] Lange Zeit sehr einflußreich war der Rückschluß G. von Rads aus dem Aufbau
des Deuteronomiums, wie er ihn sah, auf den Ablauf eines von ihm angenommenen
israelitischen Bundesfestes: vgl. ders., Formgeschichtliches Problem, 24f.

und exegetische Beobachtungen[10] legen das nah. Man kann schließlich leicht einen älteren Textzustand rekonstruieren, in dem 28:1 unmittelbar oder nur durch einige Brückenverse vermittelt[11] an 26:19 an-
schloß. Auf dieser Textstufe proklamierte Mose (allein oder zusammen
mit den Priestern) ohne jeden Zweifel das Segen- und Fluchformular
von Dtn 28[12] innerhalb der Rede von Dtn 5-28 im Land Moab.

Aber das alles bewegt sich im Bereich diachroner Vorstadienrekon-
struktion und dispensiert nicht von der Frage, was der jetzige Text
meine. Damit komme ich zur Darstellung des kritischen Sachverhalts
und seiner Analyse.

Das Problem

Die Segen- und Fluchtexte von 28:1-68 stehen *jetzt* unter der Redeeinleitung von 27:11:

ויצו משה את העם ביום ההוא לאמר
An diesem Tag befahl Mose dem Volk

Es gibt zwischen ihr und 28:1 keine weitere Redeeinleitung. Diese
Einleitung könnte auch schon in einem Stadium, in dem der Abschnitt
27:12-26 noch nicht vorhanden war, den Text von Dtn 28 eingeführt
haben. Sie könnte notwendig gewesen sein, falls vorher mehrere
Sprecher gesprochen hatten, Dtn 28 aber allein von Mose proklamiert
werden sollte. Für die vorangehende Mehrheit von Sprechern kommen
in Frage Mose und die Ältesten von 27:1, Mose und die Priester von
27:9f. Wenn Dtn 28 von Mose allein proklamiert werden sollte, mußte
der Bucherzähler durch eine neue Redeeinleitung auf Mose allein
zurückschalten.

Allerdings fällt das Prädikat ויצו auf. Ist צוה das rechte Verb, um
eine Proklamation von Segen und Fluch einzuführen?[13] Wenn 27:9f
schon im Text stand - könnten die Priester in einem Textvorstadium

---

[10] Vgl. den Vorverweis in 11:26-28 und die metasprachlichen Aussagen in
28:61; 29:18.19.20.26; 30:1.7.19.

[11] Weithin rechnet man mit 27:9-10, manchmal wird 27:11 hinzugenommen. Mir
scheint, auch 27:1 gehörte noch dazu. Für Einzelheiten vgl. Lohfink, Älteste Israels.

[12] Auf Fragen innerer Wachstumsschichten in diesen Texten muß hier nicht ein-
gegangen werden.

[13] Die Fälle von Lev 25:21; Dtn 28:8; Ps 133:3 sind anderer Art. Da spricht
Gott nicht Fluch oder Segen, sondern ordnet ihre Realisierung an. Nah 1:14 ist eher
ein Gerichtsurteil als ein Fluch. Zu Redeeinleitungen durch צוה vgl. Meier, Speaking, 197-201. Er diskutiert unseren Fall allerdings nicht, ja er notiert ihn falsch als
27:9 (198, Anm. 2). Seiner Analyse der Belege ist eigentlich nur zu entnehmen, daß
צוה selbst da, wo man es erwartet, oft nicht steht.

ohne 27:12-26 nicht mit Mose zusammen den ganzen Segen- und Fluchtext von Dtn 28 proklamiert haben? Daß in Dtn 28 ein singularisches "Ich" als Subjekt hervortritt, muß nicht dagegen sprechen—auch 27:1b und 10 formulieren im singularischen "Ich", obwohl mehrere Personen sprechen.[14] Bei dieser Annahme wäre 27:11 erst mit dem Block von 27:12-26, der Anweisungen für später enthält, oder mit dessen erstem Schub in den Text gekommen. Das erklärt das Verb ויצו zweifellos besser. So ist diese Annahme vielleicht vorzuziehen. Die Folge für den Endtext ist allerdings, daß in ihm auch Dtn 28 durch ויצו eingeleitet wird.

In 27:12-26 bestimmt Mose, was geschehen soll בעברכם את־הירדן "wenn ihr über den Jordan gezogen seid" (27:12). Er gibt Anweisungen für eine große Segen- und Fluchzeremonie an Garizim und Ebal (27:12f). Und er diktiert von 27:14 an einen dort zu rezitierenden Text.

Das dadurch entstehende Zitat einer zukünftigen Proklamation erstreckt sich zunächst einmal zweifellos bis 27:26. Doch muß man, da keine neue Redeeinleitung folgt und die letzte das Verb ויצו gebraucht hat, fragen, ob dieses Zitat nicht weiter reicht.[15]

Lösung I: Auch die Proklamation von Dtn 28:1-68 wird für Sichem befohlen

Ich möchte zugunsten dieser Annahme auf zwei Eigentümlichkeiten der in 27:12 beginnenden Anweisungen aufmerksam machen.

1. Am Anfang werden je 6 Stämme an beiden Hängen des Tales aufgestellt: die eine Gruppe für den Segen, die andere für den Fluch. Es erscheint mir unwahrscheinlich, daß auch gesagt sei, die beiden Volks-

---

[14] Im Deuteronomium sind wörtliche Reden von mehreren Personen selten. Trotzdem scheint es mehrere Fälle zu geben, und zwar offenbar stets solche irgendwie ritueller Art, wo die betreffende Mehrzahl dann im "Ich" der Einzahl spricht. Neben den im Text genannten Stellen vgl. noch 26:13-15, das offenbar als eine Deklaration im Namen Israels gedacht ist, nicht etwa als Gebet des einzelnen Hausvaters (26:12 "in deinen Toren"), und 29:18, der geheime Gegensegen, der nicht nur einzelnen Männern und Frauen, sondern auch Sippen oder Stämmen zugetraut wird (29:17). Das Phänomen könnte zum Numeruswechsel in der Anrede Israels komplementär sein.

[15] Die Abschnittseinteilung des masoretischen Textes durch Setuma und Petucha ist für die hier entwickelte Fragestellung höchstens indirekt aufschlußreich. Sie weist vor jedem ארור ein ס auf, und dann vor 28:1 ein פ. Ihr Zweck ist es offenbar, jedes einzelne Gebot (das in einem ארור-Satz ja impliziert ist), als solches abzugrenzen und dann Kapitel 28 als Text anderer Art und anderen Inhalts zu kennzeichnen. Eine Abgrenzung von Reden scheint auch mit פ in diesem Kontext nicht beabsichtigt zu sein, vgl. die benachbarten Fälle vor 26:1 und 29:1.9; 30:11. Höchstens den Fall von 29:1 könnte man entsprechend interpretieren.

hälften sollten Segen und Fluch in einer Art Sprechchor rezitieren. Das ist eher eine Überinterpretation des Textes.[16] Aber auf jeden Fall folgen in 27:15-26 nur Verfluchungen.[17] Die Leviten sollen sie sprechen. Das Volk soll jeweils mit "Amen" antworten. Erst Dtn 28 enthält eine Segen-Fluch-Komposition, die dem in 27:13f gezeichneten symmetrischen Bild der Stämme mit ihrer Zuordnung zu Segen und Fluch entspricht. So scheint ein Zusammenhang zwischen dem Anfang von Moses Anweisung für die Zeremonie in Sichem in 27:12f und Dtn 28 zu bestehen.[18]

2. In 27:15-26 gibt Mose nach jeder Verfluchung—insgesamt sind es zwölf—die Regieanweisung:

ואמר כל העם אמן

Und das ganze Volk soll sagen: Amen!

Niemals gibt Mose jedoch nach dem "Amen" des Volks eine dem parallele Anweisung, die Leviten sollten dann den nächsten Fluch aus-

---

[16] Gewöhnlich wird 27:12 יעמדו לברך את־העם so interpretiert. Doch die Parallelformulierung für den Fluch in 27:13 ist anders: יעמדו על־הקללה. Meint das wirklich: Sie sollen die קללה vortragen? In der Parallelstelle 11:29 soll Israel Segen und Fluch "auf" die beiden Berge "geben" (על ... ונתתה)—was immer das heißt. Die den Text auslegende Ausführungserzählung in Jos 8:33f kennt zwar die Aufstellung der beiden Gruppen, aber Segen und Fluch werden von *Josua* im Rahmen des Vortrags der gesamten Tora gesprochen. Dort kann in 8:33 לברך את־העם ישראל infolgedessen unmöglich eine Proklamation durch die Stämme meinen. Außerdem müßten dann alle, nicht nur 6 Stämme—gegen die Vorlage in Dtn 27—den Segen proklamieren (oder, falls Euphemismus vorliegt, den Fluch). Natürlich könnten Jos 8:33f die Vorlage aus Dtn 27 uminterpretieren. Aber könnten Jos 8:33f nicht auch den Sinn des Textes wiedergeben (und auf Josua hin konkretisieren), der in Dtn 27 vor der (im Josuabuch offensichtlich nie stattgehabten) Überschwemmung des Deuteronomiums (und dabei auch von 27:14) mit Levitennennungen gegeben war? Da im Hebräischen bei Infinitivanschlüssen das Subjekt des Infinitivs nicht mit der Notwendigkeit, die in unseren europäischen Sprachen herrscht, die zuletzt genannte Person sein muß, würde ich in 27:12 eher vorsichtig übersetzen: "sie sollen (dort) stehen zur Segnung des Volkes". Das ließe offen, wer den Segen sprechen soll.

[17] Weinfeld, Deuteronomy 1-11, 11, subsumiert schon 27:11-13 unter dem Titel "blessing and curses" und betrachtet dann den Text von 27:14-26 als ein zusätzliches Ritual: "In addition, we find there curses for transgressors who perpetrate crimes clandestinely." Doch ist damit der Textsinn umgebogen. 27:12f handelt nur von der Aufstellung der Stämme zu Segen und Fluch, nicht von Segen und Fluch selbst. Ferner ist dort nicht gesagt, daß es sich beim Fluch nicht um Flüche über geheime Übertreter handeln könne. Der weqātal-Einsatz von 27:14 kann nur so gelesen werden, daß jetzt die Proklamation jener Flüche vorgeschrieben wird, zu deren Ausrufung die Stämme nach 27:12f sich aufstellen sollen.

[18] Vgl. Preuss, Deuteronomium, 151: Was in 27:12f vorbereitet wird, "findet in Kap. 27 nirgend statt! So schaut V.12 bereits auf 28,3ff. voraus."

sprechen. Wir würden hier an sich jedesmal, wenn auch vielleicht
etwas gekürzt, Formulierungen erwarten, die der einleitenden Anweisung in 27:14 analog wären:

וענו הלוים ואמרו אל־כל־איש ישראל קול רם

Die Leviten sollen über alle Männer Israels mit lauter Stimme ausrufen

So etwas fehlt aber ganz. Den Fluchtext zitiert Mose jeweils ohne eine
neue Redeeinleitung weiter, während er die liturgischen Reaktionen des
Volks stets einführt. Die Kontinuität des proklamierten Textes wird
dem Leser als Selbstverständlichkeit insinuiert, während die Akkla-
mationen des Volkes metasprachlich abgesetzt werden.
   Das ist eine hochinteressante Darstellungsweise für einen Ritualtext.
Mit abkürzender Schreiberroutine von späteren Kopisten wird man
nicht rechnen können, da von ihnen natürlich auch die Einführungen zu
den Antworten des Volkes hätten verkürzt oder ausgelassen werden
können. Vermutlich soll stilistisch unterstrichen werden, daß das Volk
für jeden der Fälle wirklich die Verantwortung auf sich nimmt.[19]
   Doch in unserem Fragezusammenhang kommt es auf etwas anderes
an: Am Ende von Dtn 27 ist der Leser des Deuteronomiums durch
diese Darstellungsweise darauf eingestimmt, daß nach jedem Amen des
Volks der in Sichem durch die Leviten zu rezitierende Text weiterläuft,
ohne daß ihn eine eigene Regiebemerkung von neuem einleiten würde.
Diese Erwartung muß dann natürlich auch das Leserverständnis bei
28:1 bestimmen. Auch für 28:1-68 gilt dann noch die Anweisung: "Die
Leviten sollen über alle Männer Israels mit lauter Stimme ausrufen."
Man kann 28:1-68 nicht ohne weiteres aus dem Text herauslösen, der
nach Moses Anweisung in Sichem proklamiert werden soll.
   Natürlich setzt in 28:1 Neues ein. Die ארור-Sätze laufen nicht
weiter. Der letzte (27:26) hatte, da er nach lauter konkreten Einzelaus-
sagen auf ein generalisierendes Niveau aufsteigt, auch ein Gefühl von
nahendem Abschluß erzeugen können. Doch war es der Abschluß aller
befohlenen Texte überhaupt, oder nur der Abschluß dieser Zwölferreihe? In 28:1 springt die Sprache aus der 3. Person in die Anrede. Ein
singularisches "Ich" redet jetzt. Der mosaische Promulgationssatz aus
der Paränese und der Gesetzesverkündigung früherer Kapitel erklingt
zumindest am Anfang und beim Übergang vom Segen zum Fluch

---

[19] Eine etwas andere, diachrone Erklärung gibt Meier, Speaking, 30f, der auf die
textkritischen Differenzen zwischen verschiedenen Textzeugen in Jos 24:22 und Ps
145 verweist. Er qualifiziert das Phänomen in unserem Text als "unevenness, which
is unique in the Hebrew Bible" (30).

mehrfach.[20] Rhetorische Reihen und langgestreckte Perioden stellen sich ein. Es geht nicht mehr um einzelne Taten einzelner, sondern ums Ganze des Verhaltens Israels. Dazu hin hatte sich allerdings in 27:26 die Zwölferreihe selbst schon bewegt. Zunächst wird auch der Segen zum Thema, erst später kommt der Fluch wieder zurück—vor der Folie des Segens umso gewaltiger.

Kapitel 28 läßt also auf vielfache Weise neue Töne erklingen. Es bringt zweifellos ein Anschwellen und eine Steigerung. Aber, wie schon das einleitende והיה klarstellt: Es ist zugleich Fortsetzung.

Denkbare Signale dafür, daß Moses Anweisung für die Proklamation der Leviten in Sichem nicht weiterlaufe, bleiben aus. Keine Überleitungsaussage durch Mose selbst, erst recht keine neue Redeeinleitung des Bucherzählers sagt dem Leser, mit והיה höre Mose auf, die zukünftigen sichemitischen Proklamationen der Leviten anzuordnen, er schalte vielmehr ohne Rücksicht auf das in 27:11 und 14 als Charakterisierung des folgenden Textes Gesagte darauf um, über das jetzt in Moab vor ihm versammelte Israel performativ Segen und Fluch auszurufen.

Als einzige Gegeninstanz läßt sich anführen, daß in 28:1 (und dann wieder in 28:13-15) der Promulgationssatz ("seine Gebote, auf die *ich* dich *heute* verpflichte") genau jenen Redestil aufnimmt, der in früheren Kapiteln Mose als in Moab aktuell Redenden in Erinnerung brachte. Doch nach Jos 8:34f hat Josua in Sichem die ganze Tora, also auch die Paränese und Gesetze, wörtlich vorgelesen. Daß also ein im "Ich" des Mose formulierter Text auch nach Moses Tod ohne Ausmerzung seiner mosaischen Ich-Merkmale vorgetragen werden konnte, ist zumindest nach Jos 8 kein Problem.

Die Konsequenz für die Fabel liegt auf der Hand: Mose teilt Dtn 28 in Moab dem Volk Israel zwar als Text mit, da er den Wortlaut des sichemitischen Segens und Fluches ja öffentlich vorschreibt. Aber diesen Text proklamiert Mose in diesem Augenblick nicht formell über Israel. Mose befiehlt nur die Proklamation dieses Textes für eine spätere Zeremonie in Sichem. Wie er in Dtn 1-3:5 und 9f zurückgeblickt hatte, so blickt er nicht nur in Dtn 27, sondern auch in Dtn 28 voraus.

Das heißt nicht, daß im Endtext des Deuteronomiums Dtn 28:1-68 deshalb nicht mehr zum ספר התורה gehöre. Auch dieser vorausweisende Text ist von Mose in den ספר eingetragen. In Dtn 28 selbst ebenso wie in Dtn 29-30 gibt es selbstreferentielle Aussagen über Flüche, die im ספר התורה aufgezeichnet seien (28:61; 29:18.19.20.26; 30:10). Damit müssen Texte aus Dtn 28 gemeint sein.

---

[20] Dtn 28:1.13.14.15. Anders 28:45.58.61.

Wichtig ist für die hier gewonnene Deutung nur eines: In der Fabel des Deuteronomiums werden Segen und Fluch von Dtn 28 nicht in Moab, sondern erst später in Sichem formell proklamiert. Der Bundesschluß in Moab kommt gewissermaßen erst nach der Landnahme in seine volle Form.[21] In Moab selbst werden Segen und Fluch nur vorformuliert und bekanntgegeben, und ihr ritueller Vollzug nach der Landnahme wird befohlen.

In Moab werden sie offenbar nur in kurzen Segen- und Fluchformeln innerhalb der Hauptgebotsparänese sowie in dem knappen Segen-Fluch-Formular von Dtn 30:15-20 angedeutet.[22] Außerdem verweisen die Paränesen in 29:15-27 schon auf die Flüche der Tora zurück. Das ist möglich, da der ספר התורה in der Fabel des Deuteronomiums dann, wenn die beiden Versammlungen von Dtn 5-28 und 29-31 stattfinden, schon von Mose niedergeschrieben ist und Mose sie in Händen hält.[23]

Doch nun zur Begründung der anderen Deutungsmöglichkeit, die normalerweise vorgetragen wird, ohne daß sie je explizit begründet worden wäre.

Lösung II: Die Proklamation von Dtn 28,1-68 geschieht schon in Moab

Diese Deutung legt sich spontan nah, weil man damit rechnet, die ursprüngliche Struktur des Bundesschlusses, zu der der Text von Dtn 28 nun einmal gehört, halte sich auch in der definitiven Fassung durch. Doch das ist eine Art interpretativer Vorentwurf, der einer genauen Analyse standhalten müßte.

Auf analytischer Ebene läßt sich zu seinen Gunsten jedoch eine stilistische Eigentümlichkeit der deuteronomischen Mo0sereden anführen, die von den Kommentatoren vielleicht nicht reflex erfaßt, vermutlich aber intuitiv gespürt wird.[24]

Es gibt nämlich in den Mosereden normalerweise keine formelle Zitatbeendigung durch den redenden Mose. Mose bringt in seinen ei-

---

[21] Vgl. die Formulierung bei Weinfeld, Deuteronomy 1-11, 10: "the establishment of the people at the plains of Moab cannot be dissociated from the foundation ceremony at Mount Ebal. Moses' farewell address in Deuteronomy is a kind of preparation for the ceremony at Gerizim and Ebal." Dies scheint mir sehr gut gesehen, auch wenn ich die diachronen Annahmen von Weinfeld nicht teile.

[22] Hierzu vgl. Lohfink, Dtn 28,69.

[23] Hierzu Lohfink, Fabel Dtn 31-32.

[24] Vermutlich partizipiert der deuteronomische Stil hier einfach am generellen narrativen und gesetzgeberischen Stil Israels, ja vielleicht der meisten semitischen Literaturen. Vgl. Meier, Speaking, 50-57 ("Post-Positioned DD Markers")—eine allerdings vielleicht den Gegenstand nicht erschöpfende Ausführung. Ich beschränke mich im folgenden auf die Mosereden des Deuteronomiums, und selbst da gehe ich selektiv voran.

genen Reden ja häufig Zitate. In mehreren Fällen ist seine Rede nichts
als eine Komposition referierter Reden, selbst eigener, die er früher
einmal gehalten hatte. Die verschiedenen dabei verwendeten Möglichkeiten zumeist indirekter Zitatbeendigung seien am Beispiel von
Dtn 1 kurz vorgeführt.

Dort finden sich innerhalb der ab 1:6 laufenden Moserede insgesamt
13 Zitate.[25] Eine formelle Aussage, jemand habe aufgehört zu reden,[26] steht nirgends. Eine sofort folgende formelle Referenz auf das
vorangehende Zitat, die natürlich dessen Ende voraussetzt, findet sich
einmal, in 1:32 ("trotz dieses Wortes"[27] - aber vgl. unten). Ein indirekter Hinweis auf das vorangehende Zitat durch כם und ein Wort für
Zorn (התאנף - vgl. vorher in 1:34 ויקצף) stehen in 1:37 - das setzt
natürlich das Ende des Zitats voraus. In fünf Fällen folgt sofort eine
neue Redeeinleitung und klärt die Lage: 1:9.14.37.41.42. In 1:18 zeigt
eine neue Zeitangabe (בעת ההוא), daß wieder die Stimme Moses, des
Erzählers, spricht. In allen anderen Fällen können nur Umsprünge in
Person, Numerus, Subjekt und Verbkonjugation den Leser einen
Stimmenwechsel vermuten lassen, und der Inhalt des Gesagten ent-
scheidet dann, ob das Zitat noch weitergeht oder wieder die Erzäh-
lerstimme spricht.

Dabei kann es durchaus unklare Sachverhalte geben. Innerhalb von
Dtn 1 dürfte das bei 1:31 der Fall sein. Dieser Satz könnte noch zum
Selbstzitat Moses gehören, das in 1:29b beginnt. Er könnte aber auch
eine vom Erzähler Mose angehängte paränetische Erweiterung seiner
damaligen Aussage sein.[28] Für letzteres spräche der Numeruswechsel
in der Anrede vom Plural zum Singular in 1:31a. Für ersteres dagegen
die referentielle Bezugnahme auf das Zitat, die erst in 1:32 kommt.
Vom Inhalt her läßt sich in diesem Fall kaum etwas entscheiden.[29]
Wie unklar an dieser Stelle das Zitatende ist, zeigt die Tatsache, daß
Moshe Weinfeld in seiner Kommentar-Übersetzung sogar noch die

---

[25] Ich sehe von Zitaten in Zitaten ab.

[26] Als Beispiel hierfür vgl. 5:22 - beim Dekalog.

[27] Falls man בדבר הזה auf die Rede und nicht auf den in ihr hervorgehobenen
Sachverhalt bezieht. So etwa Wijngaards, 43: "Niettegenstaande deze woorden".
Doch üblich ist die andere Interpretation. Für sie vgl. zuletzt Perlitt, 82: "Doch
(selbst) auf das (alles) hin".

[28] Es geht hier nur um den synchronen Befund. Die diachrone Möglichkeit, daß
diese Unklarheiten durch eine sekundäre Erweiterung entstanden sind, kann hier
nicht erörtert werden. Sie wird oft angenommen.

[29] Labuschagne, Deuteronomium IA, 120-126, rechnet 1:31 noch zur zitierten
Rede. Zur vom Numeruswechsel her vergleichbaren Situation in 2:7 vgl. Lohfink,
Stimmen, 213 Anm. 14. Dort votiere ich bezüglich 2:7 für die Mose-Erzähler-
stimme. Doch ist dort die Lage noch komplizierter als in 1:31, da im vorausgehen-
den Zitat ein weiteres Zitat eingebettet ist und dessen Ende ebenfalls nicht klar ist.

Verse 1:32f durch Anführungszeichen in das Zitat einschließt.[30]

Die Analyse der Zitatbeendigungen in Dtn 1 sollte stellvertretend sein. Ich wende mich nun dem Großkontext von Dtn 28 zu, der "zweiten Moserede" von Dtn 5-28. Ich möchte hier nicht alle Zitate untersuchen. Da es sich bei unserem Problem am Anfang von Dtn 28 um die Frage handelt, wann eine für die Zukunft vorgeschriebene Rede, die Mose wörtlich zitiert, zuende ist, sollen im folgenden nur für die Zukunft vorgeschriebene Reden innerhalb von Dtn 5-28 untersucht werden. Wie wird ihr Ende signalisiert?

Die erste derartige Vorschrift steht in 6:21-25. Die dem Familienvater vorgeschriebene Sohnesbelehrung ist als ganze vom "wir" der 1. Person Plural dominiert—in pluralischer Rednerselbstidentifikation und in Selbstreferenz durch pluralische Suffixe. In 7:1 beginnt, mit Jahwe als grammatischem Subjekt, wieder die für die Mose-Paränese typische Du-Anrede. Die bald als solche erkennbare historisierende Gebotseinleitung setzt wieder die Redesituation Moses vor der Landeroberung voraus: "Wenn Jahwe, dein Gott, dich in das Land führt...". Das ist inhaltlich ein Umsprung gegenüber der im Zitat der Hausvaterrede vorausgesetzten Situation nach der Landeroberung.

In 20:3aβ-4.5aβ-7.8aββb schreibt Mose drei Ansprachen vor, die in Zukunft vor einem Krieg bei der Musterung gehalten werden sollen. Das Ende der ersten und zweiten Ansprache ist durch die Redeeinleitung zur je folgenden Ansprache signalisiert, das Ende der dritten durch einen Temporalsatz, der die Beendigung der Reden der שׁטרים konstatiert (20:9: והיה ככלת השטרים לדבר אל־העם).

In 21:7b-8a schreibt Mose das Gebet vor, das die Stadtältesten im Falle eines Mordes durch Unbekannt sprechen müssen. In 21:8b folgt eine Nifal-Aussage bezüglich dieser Ältesten (ונכפר להם הדם). Sie kann nicht mehr zu deren Gebet gehören. Vom Inhalt her ist klar, daß wieder Mose spricht.

Ähnlich ist es bei der Erklärung der Eltern eines störrischen und widerspenstigen Sohnes vor den Stadtältesten in 21:20aβ.b.

Bei der Erklärung der Frau, der die Leviratsehe verweigert wurde, bleibt unklar, ob sie nur aus 25:9bβ besteht oder ob auch 25:10 zu ihr gehört. Es ist kein Signal zu erkennen, das 25:10 ausschlösse. Inhalt-

---

[30] Weinfeld, Deuteronomy 1-11, 145. In seinen "Notes" setzt er inkonsistenterweise allerdings voraus, daß schon in 1:31 wieder Mose-Erzählertext vorliegt. Denn er bezieht 1:31 המקום הזה auf Bet-Pegor, wo Mose jetzt redet, nicht auf Kadesch, wo er die zitierte Rede gehalten hat (ebd., 149). Anders wieder im "Comment" (153).

lich sind beide Möglichkeiten denkbar.[31] Erst der Anfang eines neuen Gesetzes in 25:11 zeigt eindeutig, daß zumindest jetzt das Zitat nicht mehr weiterläuft.

Im Gesetz über die Darbringung der Erstlingsfrüchte 26:1-11 werden zwei Erklärungen vorgeschrieben. Die erste (26:3bβ) wird durch eine Ritualvorschrift fortgesetzt, in der der Sprecher der Erklärung im Suffix von מידך erscheint. Also kann er nicht mehr der Redende sein. Auch nach der zweiten Erklärung (26:5aβ-10a) zeigt die dann folgende, als solche erkennbare weitere Ritualvorschrift das Ende der Erklärung an.

Mit der Erklärung, die im Gesetz über die Ablieferung des Armen-Zehnten 26:12-15 vorgeschrieben wird (26:13aβ-15), schließt das Gesetz selbst, ja darüber hinaus das ganze Gesetzeskorpus. Das wird daran erkennbar, daß in 26:16 mit היום הזה eine deklarativ-performative Verpflichtungserklärung einsetzt, die die mosaische Du-Anrede an Israel wieder aufnimmt.

In den untersuchten Fällen aus dem Bereich von Dtn 5-26 gibt es also nur einen einzigen mit einer formellen Zitatbeendigung: 20:8aβ.b. Sonst wecken syntaktische Signale die Aufmerksamkeit, und der Inhalt, der nicht mehr zu dem bisherigen Zitat paßt, sich aber wieder als Moserede empfiehlt, gibt den Ausschlag dafür, das Zitat als beendet zu betrachten. In einem Fall war die Lage so unklar, daß keine eindeutige Entscheidung gefällt werden konnte.

Angesichts dieser literarischen Technik, die dem Leser des Deuteronomiums, wenn er bei Dtn 28 angekommen ist, in ihrer Eigenart vertraut ist, muß er damit rechnen, daß auch das in 27:15 begonnene Zukunfts-Zitat irgendwann ohne formelle Zitatbeendigung aufhören kann und nur kleine syntaktische Änderungen, zusammen mit inhaltlichen Signalen, ihm zeigen, daß Moses rituelle Vorschrift für die Sichemzeremonie zuende ist und Mose dann wieder in Moab ganz formell zu seinen Zuhörern redet. Die oben schon aufgezählten Änderungen, die Dtn 28:1-68 gegenüber 27:15-26 aufweist, können in diesem Sinne interpretiert werden—vor allem die in 28:1 einsetzende Du-Anrede und die Promulgationsformeln im Mose-Ich in 28:1 und 13-15. Sie würden zeigen, daß Mose nun nicht mehr eine Vorschrift für

---

[31] Labuschagne, Deuteronomium II, 269, spricht für 25:10 vom "Deuteronomisten". Das dürfte Rückkehr zur Mosestimme bedeuten. Diese Meinung wird in fast allen neueren Kommentaren vertreten, wenn auch ohne Diskussion. Ausnahmen sind nur: Hummelauer, 419; Junker, HSAT, 104; ders., EB, 517. Sie votieren für die Fortsetzung der Rede der Frau in 25:10. Hummelauer nennt ältere Exegeten. Einleitend stellt er fest: "Vix attingunt interpretes quaestionem, sintne v. 10 verba mulieris legisve decretum."

die Zeremonie in Sichem gibt, sondern direkt zu dem vor ihm in Moab
stehenden Israel spricht. Segen und Fluch von Dtn 28:1-68 würden in
Moab selbst von Mose formell über Israel ausgerufen.

Dann bliebé natürlich die Aufstellung der Stämme in Sichem für
Segen und Fluch ein totes Motiv—denn in 27:14-26 würde nur eine
Fluchzeremonie vorgeschrieben. Ferner wäre die Redeeinleitung mit
ויצו unsauber. Sie gälte im strengen Wortsinn nur für 27:12-26, nicht
mehr für den auch an ihr hängenden Text von 28:1-68. Doch ließe sich
hier auf eine andere Redeeinleitung in den deuteronomischen Mosereden hinweisen, die ebenfalls inhaltlich unsauber ist: In Dtn 1:6-4:40
spricht Mose in Moab zu "ganz Israel" (1:1). Die Anrede ist fast
durchgehend pluralisch. In 3:18 leitet er ein Selbstzitat folgendermaßen
ein: "Damals habe ich *euch*[32] befohlen (ואצו)." Wie dann in 3:18-20
der Inhalt des Zitats klar zeigt, sind die Angeredeten jedoch nicht
"ganz Israel", sondern nur die ostjordanischen Stämme.[33] Hier wird
vom Leser also erwartet, daß er allein vom Inhalt des Zitats her die
umfassendere Angabe der Redeeinleitung einschränkt. In Erinnerung an
eine solche Ungenauigkeit könnte sich der Leser in 28:1 berechtigt
fühlen, die Aussage der Redeeinleitung mit ויצו in 27:11 wegen des
nun beginnenden andersartigen Inhalts großzügig zu interpretieren.

Man sieht, auch für das übliche Verständnis der Fabel im Blick auf
Dtn 28 läßt sich durchaus plausibel argumentieren. Gerade der dem
deuteronomischen Stil eigene Mangel an Formalität in der Zitatbeendigung macht dieses Verständnis möglich. Welche Deutung ist nun die
wahrscheinlichere?

Abwägung und Schlußüberlegungen

Ich neige dazu, Dtn 28 noch als Fortsetzung des Zitats für die Zeremonie in Sichem anzusehen. Doch ist das fast schon eine Gefühlsent-
scheidung. Vielleicht hilft hier die Unterscheidung zwischen dem der
synchronen Lektüre gegebenen reinen Textsinn und der historischen
Intention des Redaktors oder Ergänzers, der die Sichem-Texte in Dtn
27 eingebaut hat. Es könnte nämlich sein, daß die "letzte Hand" die

---

[32] Daß אתכם eine Verschreibung aus אתם sei (Bertholet, Steuernagel), ist zumindest nicht durch Handschriften oder alte Übersetzungen abstützbar. Smith, 53, betrachtet אתכם als "a symptom of the want of absolute preciseness in the writer's
style". Das Phänomen scheint mir zu einmalig zu sein, als daß man es als "Symptom" nehmen dürfte.

[33] So auch Labuschagne, 204: "Dat Mozes zich nu specifiek tot de oostjordaanse
stammen richt, wordt niet expliciet aangegeven, maar uit de context blijkt dat duide-
lijk, als over de andere stammen gesproken wordt als ʾuw broeders, de Israëlie-
tenʾ."

formelle Proklamation von Dtn 28 durchaus nach Sichem verlegen
wollte. Da sie aber bei der Ergänzung des Textes konservativ vorgehen
mußte, durfte sie an den vorhandenen Text in Dtn 28 nicht rühren.
Dessen ursprüngliche Zuordnung hätte dann vom sonstigen deuteronomischen Stil her doch ein solches Eigengewicht behalten, daß die
Intention der "letzten Hand" zwar erkennbar wäre, sich aber nicht voll
durchgesetzt hätte.

Man kann noch die Frage stellen, ob nicht die doppelte Ankün-
digung von Dtn 27-28 in 11:26-29[34] zur Klärung beiträgt. Wird hier
nicht zwischen dem Segen und dem Fluch, die Mose "heute", also am
Tag des Moabbundes, Israel "vorlegt" (11:26: אנכי נתן לפניכם היום),
und Segen und Fluch, die Israel nach der Landeroberung (11:29 ...
כי יביאך יהוה אלהיך אל-הארץ) auf die beiden Berge bei Sichem
"geben" soll (11:29: נתן על), unterschieden? Die Doppelung der
Aussage spricht für zwei Proklamationen, wobei die eindeutig chiastische Anordnung gegenüber Dtn 27-28 die Proklamation von Dtn 28
nach Moab, die des Fluchtextes von Dtn 27 und eines dort allerdings
fehlenden Segentextes nach Sichem verlegen würde. Doch die verschiedenen Wendungen mit dem Verb נתן (נתן לפני und נתן על) könnten auch auf verschiedenen juristischen Charakter der angekündigten
Aktionen schließen lassen. Es könnte gerade die Unterscheidung von
Kenntnisnahme zwecks Entscheidung und formeller Auferlegung vor-
liegen. In diesem Fall wäre das Fehlen eines Segentextes in Dtn 27
unproblematischer. Ich kann in diesem Aufsatz die Lösung dieser
Frage nicht mehr versuchen.

Setzt man die von mir zögernd bevorzugte Lösung voraus und
betrachtet sie als Ergebnis einer bewußten textgestaltenden Handlung,
so kann man fragen, warum in einer Spätphase der Buchgeschichte die
formelle Proklamation von Segen und Fluch von Moab nach Sichem
verlagert worden ist.

Vielleicht leitete der Gedanke, daß Segen und Fluch so sehr mit der
Existenz im Land und mit dem möglichen Verlust des Landes verbunden sind, daß sie eigentlich erst im Land formell in Kraft gesetzt
werden können. Deshalb werden sie Israel nach 11:26 und 30:15.19 in
Moab "vorgelegt" (נתן לפני), nach 11:29 dagegen sollen sie nach der
Landeseroberung auf die Berge Garizim und Ebal "daraufgelegt"
werden (נתן על). Segen wie Fluch wären fast substanzhaft vorgestellt.

---

[34] Vgl. Lohfink, Hauptgebot, 232-234; Wijngaards, 105. Ähnlich, erst von 11:31
ab etwas anders, Craigie, 212; Christensen, 222f. Für eine andere Sicht, die auch
11:26-28 auf die Sichemzeremonie zu beziehen scheint und keinen Bezug zu Dtn 28
sieht, vgl. Weinfeld, 450-455. Auch Labuschagne, Deuteronomium IB, scheint
keinen Bezug von 11:26-28 zu Dtn 28 zu notieren.

Vielleicht wird es auch dadurch erst systematisch durchdenkbar, daß in Dtn 4:29-31 und 30:1-10 nach eingetretenem Fluch und damit auch nach dem Verlust des Landes neue Segenszuwendung Gottes verheißen wird. Gerade deshalb mußte vor allem der Fluch vielleicht so sehr an das Land gebunden werden.

Literaturverzeichnis

(Kommentare sind im Text nur mit Autornamen angegeben, Bücher und Artikel mit Autornamen und Stichwort)

Bertholet, A., *Deuteronomium* (KHC 5; Freiburg, 1899).

Braulik, G., *Deuteronomium 1-16,17* (NEB; Würzburg, 1986).

—, *Deuteronomium II: 16,18-34,12* (NEB; Würzburg, 1992) [die Seitenzählung der 1. Lieferung läuft mit S. 121 weiter].

Christensen, D. L., *Deuteronomy 1-11* (WBC 6A; Dallas, 1991).

Craigie, P. C., *The Book of Deuteronomy* (NICOT; Grand Rapids, 1976).

Hill, A. E., "The Ebal Ceremony as Hebrew Land Grant?" *JETS* 31 (1988), 399-406.

Hummelauer, F. de, *Commentarius in Deuteronomium* (CSS 3,2; Paris, 1901).

Junker, H., *Das Buch Deuteronomium* (HSAT 2,2; Bonn, 1933).

—, "Das Buch Deuteronomium," in: *Die Heilige Schrift in deutscher Übersetzung* I (EB; Würzburg, 1955), 443-549.

Labuschagne, C. J., *Deuteronomium: Deel IA* (POT; Nijkerk, 1987).

—, *Deuteronomium: Deel II* (POT; Nijkerk, 1990)

Lewy, I., "The Puzzle of Dt. xxvii: Blessings Announced, but Curses Noted," *VT* 12 (1962), 207-211.

Lohfink, N., *Das Hauptgebot: Eine Untersuchung literarischer Einleitungsfragen zu Dtn 5-11* (AnBib 20; Rom, 1963).

—, "Die Kultreform Joschijas von Juda: 2 Kön 22-23 als religionsgeschichtliche Quelle," in: ders., *Studien zum Deuteronomium und zur deuteronomistischen Literatur II* (SBAB 12; Stuttgart, 1991), 209-227 [= deutsche Fassung von ders., "The Cult Reform of Josiah of Judah: 2 Kings 22-23 as a Source for the History of Israelite Religion," in: P.D. Miller *et al.* (eds.), *Ancient Israelite Religion* (FS F. M. Cross; Philadelphia, 1987), 459-475].

—, "Dtn 28,69 - Überschrift oder Kolophon?," *BN* 64 (1992), 40-52.

—, "Zur Fabel in Dtn 31-32," in: R. Bartelmus *et al.* (eds.), *Konsequente Traditionsgeschichte: Festschrift für Klaus Baltzer zum 65. Geburtstag* (OBO 126; Freiburg-Göttingen, 1993), 255-279.

—, "Die Ältesten Israels und der Bund: Zum Zusammenhang von Dtn 5,23; 26,17-19; 27,1.9f und 31,9," *BN* 67 (1993), 26-42.

—, "Die Stimmen in Deuteronomium 2" *BZ* 37 (1993), 209-235.

—, "Zur Fabel des Deuteronomiums" [im Druck].

Meier, S. A., *Speaking of Speaking: Marking Direct Discourse in the Hebrew Bible* (SVT 46; Leiden, 1992).

Perlitt, Lothar, *Deuteronomium* (BK V,1-2; Neukirchen, 1990 und 1991).

Preuss, H. D., *Deuteronomium* (EdF 164; Darmstadt, 1982).

Rad, G. von, *Das formgeschichtliche Problem des Hexateuch* (BWANT 4.26; Stuttgart, 1938); Abdruck in: ders., *Gesammelte Studien zum Alten Testament* (TB 8; München, 1958), 9-86.

Smith, G. A., *The Book of Deuteronomy* (Cambridge Bible; Cambridge, 1918).

Steuernagel, C., *Das Deuteronomium* (HKAT I,3.1; Göttingen, [2]1923).

Weinfeld, M., *Deuteronomy 1-11* (AB 5; New York, 1991).

Wijngaards, J., *Deuteronomium* (De Boeken van het Oude Testament 2,3; Roermond, 1971).

FOR I LIFT UP MY HAND TO HEAVEN AND SWEAR: DEUT 32:40

J. LUST

Leuven

Deuteronomy 32:40 uses the expression נשא יד with the Lord as subject. The same phrase occurs repeatedly in Ezekiel. It is usually understood as an oath formula having exactly the same meaning as the *niphal* form of the verb שבע "to swear".[1]

It is our thesis that the usual translation of נשא יד is interpretative and probably unfounded. Literally the expression simply means: "(the Lord) lift up (his) hand".[2] This lifting up of the hand is to be seen as a sign introducing an action. See Ez 20:6: I lifted up my hand to them to bring them out of the land of Egypt". In the present contribution we will first deal with the case presented in Deut 32:40, and then compare it briefly with the other attestations of the expression.[3]

---

[1] See recently S. Kreuzer, *Der lebendige Gott* (BWANT 116: Stuttgart, 1983), 163; B.E. Freedman-Willoughby, נשא, *TWAT* V, 640; T. Römer, *Israels Väter. Untersuchungen zur Väterthematik im Deuteronomium und in der deuteronomistischen Tradition* (OBO, 99; Freiburg-Göttingen, 1990), 504-506; compare P. Ackroyd, יד, *TWAT* III, 453.

[2] See J. Lust, *Traditie, Redactie en Kerygma bij Ezechiël. Een analyse van Ez 26,1-26* (Brussel, 1969), 154-167; "Une Parodie de l'histoire religieuse d'Israël", *ETL* 43 (1967), 160-166; G. Bettenzoli, *Der Geist der Heiligkeit* (Quaderni di Semitistica 8; Firenze, 1979), 201.

[3] S. Carillo Alday, "Genéro literario de Cántico de Moisés (Dt 32)", *Estudios Bíblicos* 26 (1967), 69-75; "El Cántico de Moisés (Dt 32)", *Estudios Bíblicos* 26 (1979), 143-185. 227-248. 327-352. 383-393; *El Cántico de Moisés (Dt 32)* (Madrid, 1970); C.J. Labuschagne, "The Song of Moses: Its Framework and Structure", in: I.H. Eybers *et al.* (eds.), *De Fructu Oris Sui*, FS van Selms (POS 9; Leiden), 85-98; J. Luyten, "Primeval and Eschatological Overtones in the Song of Moses (Dt 32,1-45)", in: N. Lohfink (ed.), *Das Deuteronomium; Entstehung, Gestalt und Botschaft* (BETL, 68; Leuven, 1985), 341-347; further bibliographical information can be found in: H.D. Preuss, *Deuteronomium* (EdF; Darmstadt, 1982), 240-241; among the newer commentaries, special mention should be made of G. Braulik, *Deuteronomium II* (NEB; Würzburg, 1992), 226-235.

1. *A Special Case: Deut 32:40*

a. *The Poem*

Deut 32 is a didactic poem, taking the form of a farewell address.[4] After an introduction (1-3.4-6), the poet describes the initiative of the Lord which has brought Israel safely through the wilderness, and planted it in a land blessed with fertility (7-14). He continues with a description of Israel's infidelity (15-18). Then the Lord, in his first speech, announces his threatening punishment (19-26) and his decision to change his plans because the nations might misunderstand the punishment, and themselves take credit of destroying Israel (27). This speech is followed by the poet's comment (28-31). A second speech of the Lord brings the announcement of judgment upon the ennemies (32-35). In his comment the poet explains that this is how the Lord will vindicate his people (36). In his third speech the Lord solemnly confirms that he is the only true God triumphing over the so-called other gods and their nations (37-42). The poet concludes the composition with an exhortation to praise (43). The expression נשא יד (40) occurs in the third speech of the Lord (37-42).

b. *Verses 39 and 40 in the MT*

The Hebrew text of the third speech is composed of lines each containing two parallel cola with two or three accents.[5] The last part of verse 39 seems to be an exception. It ends with a mono-colon. It is often assumed that this final colon is a later addition, interrupting the rhythm of the poem.[6] A literal translation of verses 39-41 may illustrate this:[7]

39 (See now that:) I, I am he   and there is no god beside me
I kill and make alive   I wound and I heal
and none delivers from my hand
40 for I lift up my hand to heaven   (And I say:) As I live for ever
41 When I whet my glittering sword   and my hand takes hold on judgment
I will take vengeance on my enemies   and requite those who hate me

However, the printing of the verse lines in BHK and BHS, as well as the classical numbering of the verses may be misleading. It is possible, and even likely, that 40a should be read as the parallel colon to the last

---

[4] See Labuschagne 1971, 93-98.
[5] See S. Carillo Alday 1967, 338.
[6] Thus e.g., S. Carillo Alday 1967, 346.
[7] We put in between brackets the first words of v. 39 and the first word of v. 40b which may be prosaic interruptions.

colon of v.39. In that case it functions as a causal י‍ב‍-clause substanti-
ating the foregoing sentence. The text should then be printed as follows:

39 (See now that:) I, I am he	and there is no god beside me
I kill and make alive	I wound and I heal
and none delivers from my hand	40 for I lift up my hand to heaven
	(And I say:) As I live for ever
41 When I whet my glittering sword	and my hand takes hold on judgment
I will take vengeance on my enemies	and requite those who hate me

The problem with this reading is that it leaves the oath in v. 40 as an
exceptional mono-colon. At this point it may be useful to have a look
at the Greek.

c. *Verses 39 and 40 in the Greek Version*

In the Greek translation the exception disappears. The first part of
verse 40 ("for I will lift up my right hand to heaven") is a parallel to
the final colon of verse 39 ("and none delivers from my hand"). So far
the Septuagint confirms our reconstruction of the Hebrew. The next
colon of the Greek text "and I swear by my right hand" has no coun-
terpart in the MT, and forms a good parallel with the oath in the
following colon:[8] "and I say: As I live forever". Again, a literal translation may offer a visual aid:

39 See, see that I am	and there is no god beside me
I kill and make alive	I slay and I heal
and none delivers from my hand	40 for I lift up my hand to heaven
and I swear with my right hand	and say: As I live for ever
41 When I whet my sword like light-	and my hand takes hold of judgment
ning	
I will take vengeance on my enemies	and requite those who hate me

Both the Hebrew and the Greek affirm that none can deliver from the
Lord's hand. In the Greek, more clearly than in the Hebrew, this
affirmation receives a further substantiation. The lifting up of the hand
to heaven is understood as an act making it impossible to be delivered
out of that hand. The gesture of the raised hand has no direct relation

---

[8] C. Dogniez & M. Harl, *Le Deutéronome* (La Bible d'Alexandrie 5; Paris,
1992), 339 note the "plus" in the LXX and opine that it was inserted by the
translator in order to create a parallelism. Implicitly the suggestion is that the
parallelism is with the lifting of the hand in the foregoing colon. In this view,
however, not only the last colon of verse 39 (and none delivers from my hand), but
also the last colon of 40 (and I say "as I live for ever"), are left without parallel
colon.

with the Lord's oath. In the Greek the oath is introduced by a "plus": καὶ ὀμοῦμαι τὴν δεξιάν μου[9] "and I swear with my right hand".

d. *The Qumran text*

The parallel setting of the last colon of v. 39 and the first of v. 40 may also be attested in Qumran. 4QDeut[q] contains important fragments of Deut 32:37-43 in a stichometric arrangement. Its preliminary edition has been taken care of by P.W. Skehan.[10] In this edition verse 43 is fully preserved and contains 6 cola whereas the MT has 4 and the LXX 8. Its text stands closer to that of the LXX than to that of the MT.[11] It forms the lower part of a page containing one column of 11 lines, beginning with 41d and ending with 43. The column is written one colon to the line.

For our concern, verses 39-40 are more important. They belong to the immediately preceding leaf which presumedly had also 11 lines. Unfortunately, the three fragments containing traces of 39-40 are in a badly damaged state. The bottom of the first fragment shows the following characters of 39a:

39　　　... ...] כי אני [...
　　　　see, see] that I am [?

The top of the second and third fragments display respectively two *alephs* and a final *yod* pertaining to 40a. The third fragment, with the *yod*, is still connected to the column containing most of 40d-43:

40　　　כי אש[א א]ל שמים יד[י　　　　　　　　　| 43c
　　　　for I lift u]p t[o heaven the hand of m]e　|

Two years later Skehan announced that another piece of the song had been found.[12] In his short statement no picture or transcript is given. The fragment is said to be very small, but, according to Skehan, it suffices to make it clear that lines 5-8 and 11 each had two cola. For the reader it is not unambiguously clear what the contents are of these

---

[9] Thus Wevers in the Göttingen edition. Var.: τῃ δεξια μου adopted by Rahlfs.

[10] P. Skehan, "A Fragment of the 'Song of Moses' (Deut 32) from Qumran", *BASOR* 136 (1954) 12-15.

[11] See P.-M. Bogaert, "Les trois rédactions conservées et la forme originale de l'envoi du Cantique de Moïse (Dt 32,43)", in: N. Lohfink (ed.), *Das Deuteronomium*, 329-340, with further bibliography.

[12] See SVT 4 (1957) 150, note 1. When the final draft of the present article was completed the photographs of 4QDeut[q] were made available to me in *The Dead Sea Scrolls on Microfiche*, ed. E. Tov (Leiden, 1993), Nr 42, 164. I will discuss these new data in a contribution to be published in *Textus* 18.

lines. On the basis of the photograph given in the earlier article verses 39a and 40a appear to pertain respectively to lines 6 and 7, or to lines 6 and 8. In both cases, each one of these two cola appears to have been combined with a parallel colon on the same line. Since 40a figures on the strip that shows the left margin, connected to the following leaf, its characters must have belonged to the second colon of the line. Most likely then the first colon of the line must have been 39d, as in the Septuagint.

e. *Possible Objections*

Two objections may be discussed here. One might be inclined to say that the MT version of v. 40 is the more plausible one since it seems to combine two cola that belong together as an oath-gesture and an oath-formula: "For (כי) I lift up my hand to heaven and I say: As I live for ever". This objection can be answered as follows: The gesture of the raised hand may be related to an oath in our culture. The same, however, was not necessarily the case in the culture in which the poem originated. We will briefly return to that topic in the second part of this contribution. For the time being it may suffice to note that the said combination is unusual in the Bible. Ezekiel is the only biblical book in which both the gesture of the raised hand (נשא יד), and the solemn formula "as I live" (חי אני), occur with some frequency.[13] The two formulae, however, are nowhere combined directly one with another.[14] The phrase חי אני is most often put in the mouth of the Lord, and is frequently connected with the expression נאם יהוה, which is the equivalent of ואמרתי in Deut 32:40b.

One might also object that the odd final colon of v. 39 does not ask for a parallel member. A comparison with Is 43:13; Hos 2:12; 5:14; Job 10:7; Tob 13:2; Wis 16:15 might seem to plead in that direction. In all these instances the phrase expressing that none can deliver from God's hand does not seem to be completed with a כי-clause. It should, however, be noted that the question of a possible deliverance, expressed with the *hiphil* of נצל, is repeatedly combined with a כי-sentence: Jgs 18:28; Is 44:17; Ez 44:18; Ps 22:9; 143:7; 2 Chr 32:14.

---

[13] Both expressions also occur in Num 14, in v. 21 and in v. 30 respectively. They are not directly related to each other. The context recalls Ezekiel.

[14] One may refer to Dan 12:7 where the raising of the hand is explicitly followed by an oath. According to several authors the MT of Deut 32:40 may have influenced Dan 12:7. The differences, however, are numerous. In Dan 12:7 an angel (not the Lord) lifts his hands (not *a* hand) and swears "by him who lives for ever". Note that the verb rendered by "to lift" is רום and not נשא.

The tentative conclusion is that, in the original text of Deut 32:40, the expression: "for I lift up my hand to heaven" was most likely connected to the preceding colon: "none delivers from my hand". The metre of the MT points in that direction, as well as the Greek version, and probably also the Hebrew text found at Qumran. The phrase had no relation with an oath of the Lord but rather with his active intervention against Israel's enemies.

2. *The Sign of the Raised Hand*

Our interpretation of the expression ‏נשׂא יד‎ in Deut 32:40 asks for some further background information. Several questions arise which can hardly be discussed here in detail: Was the sign of the raised hand related to swearing in Israel's cultural environment? How is the expression ‏נשׂא יד‎ used elsewhere in the Bible? What about the passages, mostly dealing with the promise of the land, in which the phrases ‏נשׂא יד‎ and ‏נשׁבע‎ (to swear) seem to be interchangeable? For the first question we limit ourselves to some general remarks. In the texts and pictures of the Ancient Near East the sign of the raised hand is by no means exclusively related to swearing. As a rule the sign appears to express either prayer, or blessing, or active intervention for or against somebody, or protection of somebody. Interesting data confirming this, especially in as far as the Egyptian pictorial materials are concerned, can be found in the studies of O. Keel.[15] Here we will confine ourselves to the biblical data.

a. ‏נשׂא יד‎ *with Man as Subject*

Before we examine the contexts in which the Lord is said to lift up his hand, it may be relevant to analyse the passages in which one finds a human subject. If the expression ‏נשׂא יד‎ had been used in the description of the Lord's swearing, then one should certainly expect to find it in the context of human oaths. A brief investigation of the relevant texts demonstrates that this is not the case.

Men lift up their hands (‏נשׂא ידים‎) to pray: Ps 28:2; 63:5; 134:2, or to bless Lev 9:22. In these contexts the object is plural: "hands". Compare Hab 3:10.

In two texts only is it said that men raise (‏נשׂא‎) "the" or "a" hand. Rebels raise their hand to attack David (2 Sm 18:28; 20:21). The same aggressive action can be indicated with alternative expressions: ‏שׁלח יד‎

[15] See e.g., *Wirkungsmächtige Siegeszeichen im AT* (OBO 5), 95 and pictures 36.37: one raised hand of the deity (situated behind the pharaoh) seems to suggest "support". For other non-biblical parallels see Lust 1969, 155-157.

or רום יד (1 Sm 24:7.11; 1 Kgs 11:26.27). In all these cases the indirect object is introduced with the prefix ב.

Nowhere it is told that men lift up their hand to swear. If נשא יד had been an oath formula it should have been attested at least in some of the numerous descriptions of human oaths in the Bible. The usual verb in these passages appears to be שבע.[16]

b. נשא יד with God as Subject

With the Lord as subject, the expression can also adopt different meanings. In general it appears to point in the direction of an active intervention by the Lord. The instances in which the formula נשא יד seems to replace the verb נשבע deserve a special treatment. We will first treat the other cases.

- Ps 10:12 is most significant. The Lord is urged to "stand up and raise his hand" in order to intervene in favor of the oppressed. It is obvious that in this context the raising of the hand does not have any connotation of an oath. The prayer clearly asks for an active intervention.

- In Is 49:22 נשא יד is explained by the parallel expression רום נס (to raise a signal). The raising of the hand is a sign given by the Lord. This signal causes the return of Israel.

- In two passages in Ezekiel, 36:7 and 44:12, the Lord lifts up his punishing hand: against the Levites, and against Israel's enemies respectively. In 44:12 a parallel sentence announces the Lord's punishment: "they shall bear their guilt (נשא עון)". The formula נשא יד, which precedes, may have been chosen in a play on words with נשא און. A similar sentence occurs in 36:7: "they shall bear their reproach (נשא כלמה)". Here the threatening punishment is phrased as an oath introduced by the particle אם־לא. This is exceptional. Nowhere else is the expression נשא יד followed by the combined particles אם־לא. On the other hand, נשא יד is frequently followed by the particle אל, or על, or ל, indicating the indirect object, i.e., those towards or against whom the hand is raised. Examples can be found, e.g., in Is 49:22; Ez 44:12 and 20:5.6.15. This leads to the following hypothesis. The manuscripts of Ez 36:7 originally read אל. A copyist, who understood the נשא יד-formula as an oath-gesture, interpreted this as an abbreviation of the introductory oath formula: א׳ ל׳. The Septuagint read ἐπί which presupposes Hebrew אל.[17]

---

[16] See e.g. Gen 24:3ff.; 26:28ff.; Num 5:19.
[17] Compare Zimmerli 1969, 855, whose reasoning goes the other way round.

The conclusion is that the expression נשא יד, in this first series of sentences with the Lord as subject, does not appear to be connected with an oath.

c. נשא יד *as an Alternative for* נשבע

The expression נשא יד is often found in passages dealing with the delivery out of Egypt and with the gift of the land: Ez 20:5.6.15.23.28. 43; 47:14; Ex 6:8; Num 14:30; Ps 106:26; Neh 9:15. All of these verses may be attributed to priestly traditions. In a similar context other literary sources or layers, especially Deuteronomy and the deuteronomistic writings, use the verb נשבע which unambiguously means "to swear": e.g. Deut 1:8.35; 2:14; 4:31; 6:10.18.23.

The parallel use of נשא יד and נשבע leads to the precarious assumption that both expressions have the same meaning, implying that the first is to be identified with the second. The following arguments plead against this presumption.

First, we saw that in other contexts the raising of the hand referred to an active intervention rather than to an oath. Second, it is by no means sure that the priestly writers used נשא יד simply as a synonym of נשבע. When they replaced נשבע by נשא יד, they probably did so because of theological reasons. They could not accept the Lord as the subject of an oath. Indeed, in the ancient near east an oath had to be taken with God, or gods, as witnesses. In Israelite priestly circles Yahweh could not be envisaged as calling upon other gods. This explains why the priestly texts used the verb נשבע with man, but not with the Lord, as subject. In the contexts where Deuteronomy or the deuteronomist report that the Lord swears (נשבע) to give the land, they replace the notion of swearing by a notion expressing action. The Lord does not swear to give the land, he raises his hand to give it effectively. This leads us to a third argument against a simple identification of the two expressions. The verb נשבע is often used when the Lord promises to (ל) the fathers to (ל) give the land to their children. The context is that of a promise for future generations (see e.g. Ex 13:5; Deut 6:10.23; 7:13). This is never the case with the נשא יד expression. The Lord never lifts up his hand to the fathers to give the land to their sons. He does do so to the fathers to give the land to them. See e.g. Ex 6:8: "And I will bring you in the land concerning which I lifted up my hand to give it to ...". In other words, unlike נשבע, the phrase נשא יד does not necessarily include a promise for future times.

d. *The Greek Version of the Expression* נשא יד

We already discussed the Greek translation in Deut 32:40. What about the other passages? Most often the Greek translates literally: (ἐξ)αίρω τὴν χεῖρα (e.g. Ez 20:15; 36:7). In no instance does the translator clearly recognize in the Hebrew expression the characteristics of an oath. Occasionally he unambiguously interprets the raised hand as an sign of an active intervention.

- The Greek renderings of the expression in Ez 20:5.6 are most relevant: ἀντελαβόμην τῇ χειρί μου αὐτῶν: "I helped them with my hand (to bring them out of the land of Egypt...)". In the Bible, the verb ἀντιλαμβάνομαι usually means "to help" (for Ezekiel see 12:14: 16:49), never "to swear".

- In Ez 44:12 the Greek has a "minus" at the end of the verse. After the expression "I lifted up my hand against them, says the Lord" the Hebrew continues with "and they shall bear their guilt". Not so the Greek. There the sign of the risen hand ends the verse, which makes it even more difficult to interpret it as an oath, since the object of the oath, which is supposed to be formulated, is omitted by the LXX.

- In Ps 10:12 the Greek has a passive form: "let your hand be lifted up". Again this translation seems to plead against the usual interpretation of the Hebrew formula.

- Ex 6:8 reads: "And I will bring you into the land *where* (or) *about which* (אשר) I lifted up my hand to give it to" or "... *which* (אשר) I swore to give it to". The Greek translated literally. However, the rendition of אשר forced the translator to chose between different possibilities: "And I will bring you into the land *towards which* (εἰς ἥν) I stretched out my hand to make you dwell upon it". If the translator had understood the Hebrew as an oath, he most likely would have used another translation of the particle אשר, e.g., "... the land *concerning which* (ἐφ' ᾗ) I lifted up ...".[18]

Concluding Remarks

1. The "raising of the hand" is certainly not the most typical gesture of an oath (see Gen 24:9). When it does as such occur (Dan 12:7), the expression נשא יד is not used, and God is the witness rather than the subject.

---

[18] Compare Ez 47:14; Nm 14:30.

2. The "hand" is often a metaphor for power, especially in theological contexts. The powerful activity of God is repeatedly expressed by the use of יד in associations with forms of the root חזק. A common expression is ביד חזקה ובזרוע נטויה, mostly used in the context of the delivery from the captivity in Egypt ("with mighty hand and out-stretched arm" Deut 26:8; Ez 20:33.34).

3. The "raising of the hand" (נשא יד) with God as subject often occurs in similar contexts. The Lord lifts up his hand to intervene for or against somebody. This happens almost exclusively in priestly and late texts. These traditions avoid the mention of a divine oath, for the simple reason that in their philosophy, the Lord cannot be said to swear with the "gods" as witnesses.

4. The earliest Greek translation appears to have understood the phrase in a similar way.

5. Our interpretation of the sign of the raised hand in Deut 32:40, understanding it as a reference to an active intervention and not to an oath, is in agreement with the general meaning of the sign and of the expression. According to our proposal the first colon of verse 40 is to be read as a parallel to the last colon of verse 39:

39e *And none delivers from my hand*   40a *for I lift up my hand to heaven.*

DEUTERONOMY 14 AND THE DEUTERONOMIC
WORLD VIEW

A.D.H. Mayes

Dublin

The purpose of this paper is to discuss the nature and purpose of Deuteronomy in general, to examine at least one aspect of the relationship between the world view it reflects and the society out of which it came, and, finally, to discuss the place of the dietary regulations of Deut 14 within the framework of Deuteronomy as a whole, from the point of view of the understanding of Israel which is presupposed.

I

In reaction against what he perceives as an over-emphasis on the literary and homiletical character of Deuteronomy, S.D. McBride has argued for an interpretation which gives due weight to its immediate social and political significance. Deuteronomy is, for McBride, more than a sermon, more than mere advice. To confine it to these categories diminishes its normative and prescriptive force. The demands of Deuteronomy are real social and political demands, backed up by sanctions; all Israelites, including the king, are addressed by its laws, and on their diligent obedience depends the fate of the whole people.[1] This is not a new view of Deuteronomy, for, McBride argues, it is just such an understanding that Josephus held, and, indeed, Deuteronomy itself projects this as its own self-understanding.

If this is so, then the demands of the dietary laws in Deut 14 must have a quite specific role. They are the means by which the people of Yahweh are to demonstrate their separateness from the peoples and cultures of their environment. This is "a people holy to the Lord [their] God", whom "the Lord has chosen ... to be a people for his own possession, out of all the peoples that are on the face of the earth". Israel's dietary code is a set of laws to be obeyed; whatever their background and origin, whatever the purpose they may originally have served, their role in the framework of Deuteronomy understood as a social and political constitution must, then, be the very concrete one of marking out the individuality and peculiarity of Israel from its environment. Just

---

[1] S.D. McBride, "Polity of the Covenant People. The Book of Deuteronomy", *Int* 41 (1987), 232-233.

as with the rest of the laws of Deuteronomy, so these too must be real demands, intended to be explicitly observed in the daily life of Israel; they are not just teaching or "sage advice offered in the name of Moses to guide the faithful along a divinely charted path of life"; rather, these laws, with the rest of the deuteronomic legislation, constitute "the divinely authorized social order that Israel must implement to secure its collective political existence as the people of God".[2]

It is precisely in this immediate relationship to the concrete conditions of life that the particular theological significance of Deuteronomy is believed, by McBride, to lie. This is not a call out of and away from the political, social and economic conditions of life into a world-rejecting relationship with Yahweh which somehow transcends history and society. It is, rather, a world-affirming attitude in which faithfulness to Yahweh is realized in the observance of a particular form of social, political and economic existence. Israel's very existence in these terms depends upon her obedience to all the law of Deuteronomy, including the dietary prescriptions of Deut 14.

I have already found reason to note that this is a perception of the role and purpose of Deuteronomy which comes out of a quite specific theological and philosophical tradition.[3] Biblical scholars have become increasingly aware, largely through the work of H.-G. Gadamer, of the fact that the interpretation of texts is no innocently objective activity, but rather proceeds from a relationship of dialogue between the interpreter and the text; the meaning of the text is established in an encounter to which the interpreter brings his or her own particular world of understanding, a world which yields the questions, the pre-understandings, the anticipations of meaning, on the basis of which the dialogue with the text, leading ultimately to its understanding, is first established. Insofar as the text is the Bible and the interpreter one who is at least rooted in the tradition to which the Bible also belongs, the process of interpretation is a matter of the rearticulation of the text within the tradition; the anticipations of meaning which the interpreter brings first to the text are not simply the particular pre-understandings of the interpreter's individual life context, but rather the pre-understandings which are yielded by the tradition of which the Bible itself is a part.[4]

The implications of this for our present context are these: McBride's understanding of the purpose of Deuteronomy represents the rearticula-

---

[2] McBride, op.cit., 233, refers to the deuteronomic law in general rather than the dietary laws in particular.

[3] Cf. A.D.H. Mayes, "On Describing the Purpose of Deuteronomy", JSOT 58 (1993), 13-33.

[4] H.-G. Gadamer, Truth and Method (London, 2nd ed. 1979), 261.

tion of the meaning of Deuteronomy within the context of the particular theological and philosophical tradition to which McBride belongs. At this stage there is no point in simply debating the truth of that understanding; rather, it is in the first instance a question of trying to perceive the nature of the tradition which forms the context within which that understanding has recommended itself. The tradition in question is fairly clear. It is one characterized by the empirical and positivist approaches which continue to be dominant within American and British biblical scholarship. For this tradition truth is an objective phenomenon of the real world, which is more or less adequately reflected in literary texts. So the significance of Deuteronomy, and its theological importance, lie in its immediate relationship to the actual institutions and laws by which Israel ordered its life in the world. It is not in ideas or in beliefs in themselves that theological significance is to be found, but rather in their correlation with the events and institutions of Israel's life in the physical world.

It is important to note that such an approach to Deuteronomy, or indeed to the Bible as a whole, does not represent simply the imposition of a modern positivistic philosophical outlook quite alien to the text which is interpreted in this way. Rather, it is an interpretation which is strongly rooted in the Bible itself. In general, the Bible locates the revelatory acts and words of God very firmly in history and not simply in the beliefs of individuals or of Israel as a whole; in particular, Deuteronomy certainly presents itself as a written constitution for Israel, a book of law from which both king and people may learn to fear Yahweh "by keeping all the words of this law and these statutes, and doing them" (Deut 17:19). In this way, Israel will secure her life in the land. Deuteronomy, therefore, including the dietary laws of Deut 14, is not simply teaching, but commandment, the means by which Israel should secure its political and social existence in concrete and real terms.

II

This is a clear and powerful argument, persuasive on the basis of its inherent reasonableness and its evident link with Deuteronomy's own self-understanding. Moreover, there can be no doubt but that at least in time the biblical laws, including the dietary prescriptions, came to function in the way that McBride describes. It must be noted, however, that whatever about how Deuteronomy came eventually to be understood, this is an interpretation which is at some variance with an equally strong approach to Deuteronomy, represented especially by Noth and von Rad. Here, considerable care is taken to ensure that

Deuteronomy's independence from the state and its legal requirements is maintained. So Noth argued that it goes against the "obvious intention" of Deuteronomy to represent it as a compilation designed to be introduced as state legislation, and that Josiah, by making the elders of Judah and Jerusalem, who were the spokesmen of the people of his kingdom, a party to the covenant with God, did indeed treat Deuteronomy as state law, as a foundation for political measures, but in doing so went quite against its purpose.[5] The framework of reference of Deuteronomy is not the state; it is not Israel as a political and social entity whose life is here governed. Rather, Deuteronomy's reference is the people of Yahweh which, since the pre-monarchic period, existed in the form of a sacral confederacy. This confederacy had been weakened through the monarchic period, but it still existed. Deuteronomy's purpose in this regard was "to give a new vitalized life, adapted to the changed historical circumstances, to the association of Israelite tribes as party to Yahweh's covenant".[6]

This way of viewing Deuteronomy is given even stronger expression by von Rad. The commandments, in von Rad's view, are not addressed to the state or any other form of secular community, but rather to the community of Yahweh. In fact, Deuteronomy can be seen as something like "a last stand against the beginning of legislation";[7] it has no intention of presenting itself as civil law, but is rather addressed to Israel as a sacral community, the holy people of Yahweh.[8] With Noth, there seems perhaps to be a certain ambiguity about the nature of this sacral community, for in his use of the amphictyony analogy the way was open for understanding it in at least quasi-political terms. In von Rad's presentation, however, this option is closed off: Israel is a faith community, and the law is a "saving ordinance", not "a dictate which imperiously called into being its own community".[9] The background of the book of Deuteronomy is "an obviously intensive preaching activity", and the book itself is "simply and solely an artistic mosaic made up of many sermons on a great variety of subjects ... here is gathered the total expression of an obviously extensive preaching activity". The intention of the book is "something like a totality of teaching. You shall not add to this, nor take from it". The 'torah' which it constitutes is not law; rather, "the Deuteronomic term 'torah'

[5] M. Noth, "The Laws in the Pentateuch. Their Assumptions and Meaning", *The Laws in the Pentateuch and Other Essays* (Edinburgh, 1965), 42-43, 46-47.
[6] Noth, *op.cit.*, 48.
[7] G. von Rad, *Old Testament Theology* I (Edinburgh, 1962), 201.
[8] von Rad, *op.cit.*, 228-229.
[9] von Rad, *op.cit.*, 201.

means the whole of the bestowals of Jahweh's saving will".[10]

Again, it should be noted, this remarkable and persuasive interpretation of the book does not represent an alien imposition of a theological perspective which is quite foreign to the time and place of Deuteronomy's origin. For here too an interpretation is offered which stands in a line of tradition which reaches back to the Old Testament itself, and it is from that tradition that the anticipation of meaning which leads eventually to this interpretation has been taken. As Barton has noted, this "is an interpretation of data that are really there in the text. The Old Testament very plainly *is* a book of faith, expressing a conscious decision to take history as manifesting a certain divine plan, whatever the odds".[11] The community of the Old Testament is a faith community, and it is in the faith of that community that the Old Testament places theological significance. Israel the people of Yahweh is not simply the group which Yahweh led out of Egypt and into the land, but rather is that group which can adopt for itself the confession "the Lord brought us out of Egypt with a mighty hand and an outstretched arm, with great terror, with signs and wonders; and he brought us into this place and gave us this land, a land flowing with milk and honey" (Deut 26:8-9). Empirical Israel with its secular institutions is not the concern of this law.

III

The validity of these different approaches by no means justifies a total relativism, the view that any interpretation is justified as long as it makes sense for the person or group which proposes it. Certain limits exist: in each case the interpretation offered is, in fact, solidly rooted in the Bible itself. Yet there is clear diversity here, and in each case the claim is being made for an understanding of the intention of Deuteronomy in its origin. Is then one to rest with a moderately relativistic position, such as that maintained by some historians: history is not necessarily a fiction, but there is no such thing as an objectively valid history; history is an account of the past which is meaningful for a particular group, a particular time.[12] It is clear that a major issue here is to do with the validity of the presuppositions or pre-understandings

---

[10] von Rad, *op.cit.*, 221-222.

[11] Cf. R. Morgan with J. Barton, *Biblical Interpretation* (Oxford, 1988), 103.

[12] See the papers collected in *The Philosophy of History in our Time*, ed. H. Meyerhoff (New York, 1959); also M. Mandelbaum, *The Anatomy of Historical Knowledge* (Baltimore, 1977), and A. Momigliamo, *Essays in Ancient and Modern Historiography* (Oxford, 1977).

or anticipations of meaning which one brings to the text being interpreted or the past being reconstructed. All interpretation involves
pre-understandings, all historical reconstruction involves generalizations, whether these are explicit or not. The nature and status of these
pre-understandings and generalizations are the issues of direct significance: if they are necessarily bound by time and context then the
interpretations and reconstructions which issue from them are also only
provisional and relative; if they can be demonstrated to have a validity
which is not so limited, then the interpretations and reconstructions
have to that degree a stronger claim to objective validity. Is there the
possibility of agreed and objectively founded pre-understandings, which
may be held to transcend the particularisms of time and context, and
which might lead to a more widely accepted and more objectively
based interpretation or reconstruction?

It is to Norman Gottwald that Old Testament scholarship owes most
in the discussion of these basic theoretical questions, for it was with
his *Tribes of Yahweh* that the methodological issues involved in the
understanding of Israelite history and religion first received extensive
and fruitful discussion. Much has been written in this area since that
study, and much even of its fundamental argument has been shown to
be faulty,[13] but the questions which it raised, and raised for the first
time over such a comprehensive range of issues, are still there, and no
study of ancient Israel can now ignore them. For our present context,
the significance of Gottwald's work is very much increased by the fact
that he made very extensive use of the approach of an anthropologist,
Marvin Harris, who has also made effective contributions to the study
of the dietary laws. Both Harris and Gottwald have argued for a
particular form of Marxist historical materialism as an objectively valid
generalization, a generally justifiable presupposition, on the basis of
which history and ideology may be reliably reconstructed and understood.

Gottwald, following Harris, understands Marxist theory in terms of
the so-called pyramid of culture: at the base lies the environment, as
the fundamental determinant of history and culture; on its foundation
economic and social relationships come into existence as people act on
the environment; on the foundation of these two levels there then exists
human ideological thinking, including religious thinking. So, "at the
root of all social organization and mental ideation, including religion,
is the way human beings within nature act upon nature to produce their

[13] Cf. the discussion in A.D.H. Mayes, *The Old Testament in Sociological
Perspective* (London, 1989), 89-96, 106-113.

means of subsistence and thereby fashion their own social nature".[14] Marx is quoted as providing the basic insight: "Morality, religion, metaphysics, all the rest of ideology and their corresponding forms of consciousness ... no longer retain the semblance of independence. They have no history, no development; but men, developing their material production and their material intercourse, alter, along with this their real existence, their thinking and the products of their thinking. Life is not determined by consciousness, but consciousness by life". For Gottwald this means that "changes in the form of production ... lead correlatively to changes in social and political forms and to changes in ideas, including religious ideas". Modes of production change with developing technology; these bring about new social structures, and these in turn introduce new ideas. This, argues Gottwald, is Marxism "minus rhetorical flourishes".[15]

Harris, too, sees all human institutions and ideas as the direct result of material circumstances. So the dietary regulations of any people are a consequence of economic and ecological circumstances.[16] The cow is a sacred animal in India, not for theological reasons but for its economic value: they are essential as draught animals in the agricultural context, and too expensive simply to use for food. In Israel it is the general conditions of the Near East which mean that cud chewing animals, reckoned in Israel as clean, are those economically most suited for food: they can feed on grass and other plant foods for which humans have no use, and by converting them into meat supply a food resource which, in economic terms, provides an ideal return. On the other hand, it is for the same kind of environmental and economic reasons that the pig is regarded as an unclean animal prohibited for food: "Pastoral nomads never rear pigs because pigs cannot be herded over long distances in arid grasslands: pigs can't live on grass and can't swim across rivers. Seminomadic groups, who in more humid zones can rear pigs, would be especially likely to develop strong explicit sacred prohibitions against both eating and handling pigs, as would settled farmers in regions that had undergone deforestation, erosion, and desiccation. Both kinds of groups would find it tempting to rear the pig for short-time benefits, but the practice would become extremely costly and maladaptive as it intensified. Total interdiction by

---

[14] N.K. Gottwald, *The Tribes of Yahweh. A Sociology of the Religion of Liberated Israel*, 1250-1050 B.C.E. (London, 1980), 631.

[15] Gottwald, *op.cit.*, 633-634, 638.

[16] A full discussion of Harris may be found in: W. Houston, *Purity and Monotheism. Clean and Unclean Animals in Biblical Law* (JSOTS 140; Sheffield, 1993), 83-93.

appeal to sacred sanctions is a predictable outcome in situations where
the immediate temptations are great, but the ultimate costs are high,
and where the calculation of cost-benefits by individuals may lead to
ambiguous conclusions".[17] The pig is a creature of woods and river-
banks, where it feeds naturally on roots and fruits. But with the deforestation of Palestine it lost its natural habitat and could be raised only
by feeding on grain. This made the pig a direct competitor with human
beings for food, and so economically costly for the community. The
prohibition of the pig has, therefore, a direct economic and environmental foundation: its breeding was attractive in terms of its providing
an immediate food resource for the individual, but in the longer term it
was economically prohibitive for the community.

The same kind of argument can be applied to other animal prohibitions: the camel, as well as horses and donkeys, were animals kept for
transport, a primary function which would have been adversely
affected by the use of them for food. Clearly, however, not every
prohibited animal, as, for example, the unclean birds, can be accounted
for in the same way, and in such cases Harris is prepared to admit that
priestly speculation is at work: the lists of unclean animals reflect the
codifiers' attempt to prove a special knowledge of the natural and
supernatural worlds. Again, Harris is ready to acknowledge that rather
than that food taboos always arise from ecological conditions, it may
occasionally be the case that the food taboos are primary, being a mark
of religious conversion, and as such may react back upon the economic
and ecological conditions.[18] In exactly the same way, Gottwald also
argues that religious ideas constitute an effective "servo-mechanism"
which react back upon society in order to inhibit its development.[19]
But in both cases, the primary, causative element is the ecological and
environmental: the independent action of religious ideas upon social
and economic institutions is a secondary action which ultimately is to
be understood and explained in terms of the origin of these ideas in
these social and economic institutions.

IV

The detailed problems which considerably weaken this materialistic
interpretation of religious thinking in general and the dietary regula-

---

[17] M. Harris, *Cultural Materialism. The Struggle for a Science of Culture* (New York, 1980), 193.
[18] Harris, *op.cit.*, 82, 86.
[19] Gottwald, *op.cit.*, 642-643.

tions in particular need not be considered at this point[20]. Rather, it is the general principles, the pre-understandings, which inform the reconstructions of Harris and Gottwald that are of importance. That there is a relationship between (religious) ideas and the social and economic contexts of those who hold them is not in question; the nature of that relationship does, however, have some importance for our overall theme.

Both Harris and Gottwald express a materialistic interpretation which they identify as Marxist: changes in the economic base lead to new social structures, and then new ideas emerge as the deposit and reflection of those changes and developments. This is, however, a very crude and mechanistic version of Marxism, and scarcely one that can claim Marx himself as an authority. Marx did not in general promote a pyramid of culture view of society. Indeed, it is true that at one point he argued that "The production of ideas, of conceptions, of consciousness, is at first directly interwoven with the material activity and the material intercourse of men, the language of real life. Conceiving, thinking, the mental intercourse of men, appear at this stage as the direct efflux of their material behaviour".[21] But this view relates to the Marxist theory that a pre-class stage of society was characterized by lack of differentiation and by common ownership of property, in which consciousness was the direct reflection of social and economic circumstances. The determinist view of human thinking thus related to pre-state societies. With the development of private property and the state, class conflict emerged and both history and society were from then on the conscious result of the struggle between different classes.[22]

The theory of a pre-state classless society, in which thinking is the direct efflux of society, has no anthropological support: the proposed reconstruction of a pre-state classless society is built on a series of antitheses to a class society rather than on any reliable evidence of this as a demonstrable stage of social evolution. In any case, Marxist theory is by no means exclusively identified with this (in terms of its use as a productive form of analysis) fruitless aspect of its overall approach; rather, it is Marx as a conflict theorist who still provides an analytic approach which remains useful for historical reconstruction. For this dialectical stage of Marxism, consciousness originates in the interaction

---

[20] On the former, cf. Mayes, *The Old Testament in Sociological Perspective*, 23-27, 95-6, 108-113; for the latter, cf. Houston, *op.cit.* 83-93.
[21] Cf. K. Marx, *Selected Writings,* ed. D. McLellan (Oxford, 1977), 164.
[22] Cf. A. Giddens, *Capitalism and Modern Social Theory. An Analysis of the Writings of Marx, Durkheim and Max Weber* (Cambridge, 1971), 208-209.

of men together in history with the environment; consciousness is a social and historical product through which the world is apprehended and in terms of which it is changed; consciousness is a product of the history of people evolving in material circumstances. The attempt to maintain a genuine dialectic here is not to be disregarded as a 'rhetorical flourish' which can be ignored in favour of a strict and one-way determinism.

The most persuasive attempt to re-state a Marxist view of social development, and one which, moreover, makes a vital contribution to our understanding of Deuteronomy, has come from J. Habermas.[23] In order to maintain the integrity of the Marxist dialectic, Habermas has emphasized the irreducible nature of both forms and relations of production. This means that the forms of production, human action on the environment, on the one hand, do not determine the relations of production, the forms of social interaction and integration, on the other. Forms of production are based on technical knowledge; relations of production are based on communicative knowledge; and there is no simple causal relationship between them. Changes and developments in the forms of production indeed prompt changes in the relations of production, but the latter take place only on the basis of developments in communicative knowledge. For example, a tribal society whose organization is based on the kinship principle would be put under pressure to change by developments in technical skills dealing with water supply and agriculture, which required wider and more complex forms of social interaction and co-operation than kinship permitted; but the new forms of social integration which would cope with those technical advances depend upon developments in communicative knowledge, a resource which is not the product of advances in technical knowledge but rather results from the developing learning capacities of individuals in society.

Cognitive developmental psychology provides the model by which the development of communicative knowledge in society may be understood. As the individual progresses from a self-centered acceptance of the given to a relativistic self-understanding in which the self is marked out from the environment and capable of reflection from a universalist perspective, so societies develop in terms of their world view from a mythological fusion of social and natural phenomena, in which the tribal group has not yet formed "a distinct consciousness of the normative reality of a society standing apart from objectivated

---

[23] Cf. Mayes, "On Describing the Purpose of Deuteronomy", *JSOT* 58 (1993), 13-33.

nature",[24] through the stage in which the social structure of the state is legitimated by a mythological world view, to that point where mythological thought is replaced by a universalism in which philosophical and theological reflection and argument take the place of any naive traditionalism or acceptance of given dogma.

A theoretical model of social development of this nature is a very suitable framework within which to situate Israelite social development and Israelite social learning processes. The mythological legitimation of social structures may be perceived particularly in work, such as that of the Yahwist or source material used by the deuteronomistic historian, from the monarchic period: divine promises to Abraham, the covenant between Yahweh and David, still reflect the stage of moral development analogous to that of the child who "cannot perceive, understand and judge situations independently of its own standpoint".[25] This self-centered mythological world view could not be contained in the face of the competing world views to which Israel was exposed in the monarchic period through increasingly close contact with the world powers of her day. It was, however, prophetic preaching which explicitly destroyed the egocentrism of this traditional Israelite world view, and introduced the possibility of a more reflective universalism that had broken with the older mythological concern to legitimate Israelite social structures. The deuteronomic doctrine of the election of Israel, which presupposes the universalist perception that Yahweh could have chosen another people, stands in direct descent from the prophetic breakthrough to the perception expressed in Amos 9:17 "Are you not like the Ethiopians to me, O people of Israel, says the Lord".

This fundamental transformation of Israelite self-understanding, a process extending over the whole monarchic period, is the essential presupposition for the emergence of Deuteronomy. Deuteronomy expresses a reflective universalism which attempts to transform and revitalize traditional Israelite belief for an age which presented a serious threat to that belief. It is a good example of the operation of learning processes in which forms and ideas, existing hitherto only as possibilities, are developed in a systematic way to meet a threat posed to traditional Yahwism by dominant Assyrian culture.[26] This is a development which takes place not simply as the product of social and

---

[24] Cf. J. Habermas, *Communication and the Evolution of Society* (London, 1979), 104.
[25] Habermas, *op.cit.*, 101.
[26] For this see especially N. Lohfink, "Culture Shock and Theology", *BTB* 7 (1977), 15-19.

economic conditions, so as to provide a kind of validation of those conditions, but very much as the result of more comprehensive social, historical and political experience which necessitates a new expression of belief within the framework of which new forms of life may be worked out. Deuteronomy is an expression of religion as a cultural system giving meaning to human experience.[27]

V

Deuteronomy is thus to be understood primarily as the expression of a world view: it is a theological statement, representing a breakthrough to a perception of Israel in its relation to Yahweh, which both depends on tradition and proclaims a new understanding designed to supplant alternatives. It is both teaching and constitution; more than wise advice in that it offers not simply a possible way of living but rather the only way of living; less than prescriptive law in that it cannot be directly related to the actual implementation of law in Israel. This is so with both Deuteronomy as a whole and with Deut 14 in particular. In both cases, the material is to be understood in terms of world view; that it is the same world view in each case, is, however, a different issue. In fact, there is much to suggest that the perception of Israel in its relationship to Yahweh in Deut 14 is strikingly different from that which characterizes the remainder of the book.

In a recent article, L. Stulman[28] has argued that Deuteronomy exhibits a concern for group survival which sits uneasily with a lack of clarity in the definition of the group. That is to say, the attitude which Deuteronomy requires 'Israel' to take towards those who do not belong to the people may be fairly clearly delineated; but the nature of the membership of this 'Israel' is ambiguous and obscure. So, when Israel enters the land all centres of foreign worship are to be destroyed, and no intermarriage with the Canaanites is permitted (Deut 7); Israel is to be holy to Yahweh and separated from the outsiders. On the other hand, while Ammonites and Moabites are excluded from membership in "the assembly of the Lord", this is not so with Edomites who, in the third generation, may be accepted (Deut 23:4-9; EV 3-8); or again, marriage with a foreign woman taken captive in war is permitted (Deut 21:10-14); or, even more strikingly, Israelites should care for the *ger*

---

[27] The description is that of C. Geertz, *The Interpretation of Cultures* (New York, 1973), 87ff.; it is Lohfink, *op.cit.*, who supplies the historical framework essential for Deuteronomy in particular.

[28] L. Stuhlman, "Encroachment in Deuteronomy. An Analysis of the Social World of the D Code", *JBL* 109 (1990), 613-632.

(Deut 14:29; 16:11,14 etc.), the foreigner living in her midst, a category which, given the motivation referring to Israel being *gerim* in Egypt, must include true foreigners and not simply Israelites temporarily away from their own homes.[29]

It is clear that, as Stulman argues, there is a lack of consistency in Deuteronomy, which may be defined in terms of an incongruity between ideology and social reality: the ideology, which defines the true people of Yahweh, is one of clear distinction and separation; the social reality, of Israel in the world, is one where the boundaries are blurred. Through an examination especially of those laws which provide capital punishment for violators of their norms, Stulman is able to show that the reason for this is that the 'outsiders' or 'foreigners' against whose practices Israel is warned are in fact, in social terms, groups who are encountered regularly and threaten the integrity of Israel because they live *within* the community. Those forces which threaten to undermine Israel are deviants involved in religious and cultic practices which are not distinctively Israelite, or deviants who do not acknowledge the authority structures in the community. These are not simply foreigners, but rather insiders, and particularly leaders in the civil hierarchy, who act as foreigners: they must be purged *from the midst* of Israel (Deut 13:6 [EV 5]; 17:7 etc.), in order to achieve an internal coherence in which ideology and social reality will correspond. This is, as Alt[30] recognized, a programme for the future, the programme of a restoration movement which, through preaching and exhortation, commends a revitalized tradition in the hope of persuading faithful Israelites to separate themselves from those faithless Israelites who threaten her with internal disintegration. The programme certainly aims for a conformity of ideology with social reality; that is, there is an intention here to create a social community congruent with the demands which Deuteronomy makes. Yet there is a clear recognition that social reality in the present does not conform with the requirements of the Yahwistic ideology; the new reality requires a response to the call which Deuteronomy makes.

That the dietary regulations of Deut 14 can be adequately understood within this framework is unlikely. Our concern here is not with the

---

[29] Cf. A.D.H. Mayes, *Deuteronomy* (NCBC; London, 1979), 124-125; idem, "Deuteronomy 29, Joshua 9, and the Place of the Gibeonites in Israel", in: N. Lohfink (ed.), *Das Deuteronomium: Entstehung, Gestalt und Botschaft* (BETL 68; Leuven, 1985), 321-325.

[30] A. Alt, "Die Heimat des Deuteronomiums", *Kleine Schriften zur Geschichte des Volkes Israel* II (Münich, 1953), 250-275.

origins and background of these regulations,[31] but rather with the understanding of Israel in the world that they presuppose and which they bring to expression. In terms of general world view, much of value has been provided by Douglas and Soler. Both have indicated the close relationship between the dietary regulations and the Israelite understanding of creation: clean animals are those that conform to the plan of creation, that is, they are herbivorous and they clearly belong to an appropriate element in creation: earth, sky or water; unclean animals are those that transgress boundaries, particularly through exhibiting means of locomotion which fit them to more than one element, and those which exhibit any blemish.[32]

This treatment does, however, leave the dietary regulations very much in the realm of speculation, for the acknowledged link between the dietary laws and perception of the world is by no means satisfactorily understood simply through an indication of the connections between these dietary regulations and the creation story. Indeed, apart from other relevant observations, the fact that there is considerable difference between the dietary regulations of Lev 11 and those of Deut 14, and these differences relate in large measure to the relationship between the regulations and Gen 1, is sufficient to indicate that the world view reflected in the dietary regulations is not completely accounted for by Gen 1.[33] Gen 1 is itself the expression of a world view which must be given more comprehensive description in terms of its relationship to Israelite life and experience. Soler indeed acknowledged this in general terms by pointing out that "dietary prohibitions are ... a means of setting a people off from others", and that they

---

[31] For the most recent comprehensive treatment, cf. Houston, op.cit.

[32] There are certainly problems with the detail of this, particularly with regard to the classification of birds (see the discussion in E. Firmage, "The Biblical Dietary Laws and the Concept of Holiness", ed. J.A. Emerton, Studies in the Pentateuch, [SVT 41; Leiden, 1990], 178-80), but in general terms the approach is undoubtedly correct.

[33] M. Douglas takes Deut 14 and Lev 11 together, and writes of the Israelites' having "absorbed freely from their neighbours, but not quite freely. Some elements of foreign culture were incompatible with the principles of patterning on which they were constructing their universe; others were compatible", Purity and Danger. An Analysis of the Concepts of Pollution and Taboo (London, 1966), 49. On the relationship of Lev 11 and Deut 14 see the differing views of J. Milgrom, Leviticus 1-16 (AB 3; New York, 1991), 698-704 (Deut 14 is an abbreviation of Lev 11), and W.L. Moran, "The Literary Connections between Lv 11,13-19 and Dt 14,12-18-", CBQ 28 (1966), 271-7 (Lev 11 is later than Deut 14). H. Eilberg-Schwartz, The Savage in Judaism: An Anthropology of Israelite Religion and Ancient Judaism (Bloomington, 1990), 219, argues persuasively that the dietary regulations of Lev 11 represent a supplementing and modification of those of Deut.14 in order to make them compatible with Gen 1.

constitute a "social sign" which "cannot be understood in isolation. It must be placed into the context of the signs in the same area of life; together they constitute a system; and this system in turn must be seen in relation to the systems in other areas, for the interaction of all these systems constitutes the sociocultural system of a people. The constant features of these systems should yield the fundamental structures of the Hebrew civilization". Moreover, Soler also realized that "Christianity could only be born by breaking with the structures that separated the Hebrews from the other peoples" and that "one of the decisive ruptures concerned the dietary prescriptions".[34]

In her later writings on the subject, Mary Douglas recognized that her own earlier views had failed to relate the classifications of animals to a context of social relations. Classification reflects and strengthens social roles, especially those to do with marriage and residence.[35] Thus the dietary regulations are not to be seen as relics of tradition, but are learned compositions of the late pre-exilic and exilic periods, which derive from a people who abhorred anomalies and accepted no obligation to exchange womenfolk beyond narrowly defined kindred.[36] They strongly reinforce the perception of self as separate, marking out boundaries which distinguish Israel from other peoples. This social function of the dietary regulations is unquestionably true and significant, but that function also has another and quite distinctive aspect. Dietary regulations perform a role not only with respect to marking out one group from another, but also with respect to the internal self-understanding of the group. They give expression to a particular self-understanding of the group in its experience of its world, and it is here that fundamental differences between the dietary regulations of Deut 14 and the remainder of the deuteronomic law appear.

Eilberg-Schwartz has argued that there is a correspondence between religious symbolism and whether status in society is ascribed or achieved. Ascription means that status depends on qualities such as age, sex and kinship ties, while achieved status is based on success in achieving certain goals. In societies in which status is ascribed individuals have little control over their lives; the world is experienced objectively as a given; impurity is the essential objective property of a

---

[34] J. Soler, "The Dietary Prohibitions of the Hebrews", *New York Review of Books* 26/10, 1979, 25, 30.

[35] M. Douglas, *Implicit Meanings* (London, 1975), 261ff., 296. Douglas is here explicitly following Durkheim's view that classification systems derive from and are properties of the social systems in which they are used. Cf. also Milgrom, *op.cit.*, 719-726.

[36] Douglas, *Implicit Meanings*, 307ff.

thing. In societies in which status is achieved, on the other hand, the world is not experienced objectively; impurity and pollution are not objective qualities, but rather are the consequence of what one does; impurity derives from subjective action, the internal organs of the body being treated as its source.

In practice it will, of course, be found that status in society may be both achieved and ascribed, in which case then there is a parallel ambivalence with regard to the understanding of impurity. These two forms do, nevertheless, serve as very useful models[37] by means of which the essential nature of any given society may be better understood. In particular, Eilberg-Schwartz has used these categories to draw attention to an essential difference between the priestly community and the early Christian community: in the former, membership of the community is determined by genealogical descent, and so status in the community is clearly ascribed; in the latter genealogical descent is replaced by commitment to belief, so that status is achieved. Correspondingly, impurity for the priestly community, expressed in part through its dietary regulations, is an intrinsic quality of certain kinds of objects, whereas in the Christian community that form of objective impurity is replaced by an understanding of pollution as deriving from the conscious acts of individuals.[38]

It would seem that in a number of very fundamental respects the nature of the community presupposed by the dietary regulations in Deut 14 is not the same as that presupposed in the remainder of Deuteronomy. The dietary regulations presuppose a community which is separate and intolerant of marriage relationships with outsiders; the deuteronomic laws presuppose the eventual acceptance of some outsiders, the ongoing membership of the 'stranger', and the possibility of marriage with a foreigner taken captive in war. The dietary regulations presuppose a community in which status is ascribed by birth; for the deuteronomic laws in general, membership of the people of Yahweh is not determined by birth, insofar as it is clear that there are those within who behave as outsiders and so must be purged from the midst of the people of Yahweh. Membership of the community of Yahweh for the

---

[37] On models or ideal types, cf. Mayes, *The Old Testament in Sociological Perspective*, 38f. It is in such terms that status ascribed and status achieved societies are best understood.

[38] Eilberg-Schwartz, *op.cit.*, 206ff., has found ambivalent perceptions in Qumran and the Mishnah. Acceptable genealogical descent and a mastery of scripture are both necessary for membership of the community; so, impurity is to be found not only as an intrinsic quality of certain objects but also in the individual's violation of communal norms.

deuteronomic laws is achieved through response to the call to obey the law of Yahweh.[39]

VI

The conclusion to which we are pointed is that the dietary regulations of Deut 14 are not an original part of the deuteronomic lawcode. This does not necessarily mean that the practice which these regulations require is later than the lawcode, for undoubtedly in many respects, as, for example, in the avoidance of the pig and the consumption of domestic animals, this is traditional practice which reaches back to the earliest days of Israel. The creation of a dietary system, however, is a work of the priestly school, in which traditional practice has been elaborated into a theoretical system by which external manifestation might be given to a society perceived on other grounds as a closed system.[40] The deuteronomic law might be a step along the road towards the creation of such a social system, insofar as it fosters the idea of a separate people chosen by Yahweh, which is to be realized in history through the purging out of unfaithful elements of Israel. It has not, however, yet reached the stage of presupposing, as the dietary regulations do, that a society of the type reflected in the work of the priestly writers of the post-exilic period, may actually be prescribed for. The dietary regulations of Deut 14 represent, therefore, a post-exilic priestly insertion in the deuteronomic law, made with the aim of bringing to expression a much more rigidly clear understanding of the nature of Israel than the deuteronomic law had envisaged.

---

[39] Cf. also M. Weinfeld, *Deuteronomy and the Deuteronomic School* (Oxford, 1972), 215, who, in contrasting Deut 15:19 and Lev 27:26, concludes that "In the deuteronomic view, sanctity is not a taboo that inheres in things which by nature belong to the divine realm but is rather a consequence of the religious intentions of the person who consecrates it". This would hold true for the general tenor of the deuteronomic laws, although it must be noted that in certain isolated instances, relating, for example, to the laws on Moabites and Ammonites and to physical imperfection (Deut 23:2ff.; EV 1ff.), these laws carry with them ideas of ascribed rather than achieved status.

[40] Cf. also Firmage, *op.cit.*, 185, for the dietary laws as a priestly transformation of a socio-economic reality in order to give effect to Israel's separateness. For a criticism of some aspects of Firmage's approach, cf. Houston, *op.cit.*, 117-120.

POETIC FRAGMENTS IN DEUTERONOMY AND THE DEUTERONOMISTIC HISTORY

JOHANNES C. DE MOOR

Kampen - The Netherlands

1. *Introduction*

The poems incorporated into Deuteronomy and the Deuteronomistic History of Israel[1] constitute a well-known problem to O.T. scholarship. The best known examples of such poems are Jacob's Blessing (Gen 49), the Song of the Sea (Ex 15), the Blessings and Curses of Deut 27-28, the Song of Moses (Deut 32), the Blessing of Moses (Deut 33), the Song of Deborah (Judg 5), the Song of Hannah (1 Sam 2), David's Lament (2 Sam 1:17-27) and Thanksgiving (2 Sam 22). However, there are many more smaller passages in verse,[2] like the oath of Lamech (Gen 4:23-24), various poetic fragments in Exodus,[3] the adhortation of the ark (Num 10:35f.), the victory song of Heshbon (Num 21:27-30), Balaam's oracles (Num 22-24), Jotham's fable (Judg 9:7-15),[4] the victory song for David (1 Sam 18:7), David's testament (2 Sam 23:1-7), various passages in Kings,[5] etcetera.

---

[1] We agree with those who hold the Deuteronomistic School largely responsible for the composition of the historical account from Genesis to 2 Kings 25, cf. e.g. C.J. Labuschagne, *Gods oude plakboek: Visie op het Oude Testament* ('s-Gravenhage, 1979²), 106-119; C. Houtman, *Inleiding in de Pentateuch* (Kampen, 1980), 247; M.A. O'Brien, *The Deuteronomistic History Hypothesis: A Reassessment* (OBO, 92; Freiburg, 1989), esp. 288: "The nature of DtrH as a combination of source and redaction shows that DTR was heir to a lively tradition of Israelite literary activity and thought. Nevertheless one may justifiably describe DtrH as a new and unique contribution to this tradition".
Probably we have to assume integration of this work into a priestly composition which was subsequently further edited by later redactors, cf. E. Blum, *Studien zur Komposition des Pentateuch* (BZAW, 189; Berlin, 1990).
[2] Cf. C.F. Pfeiffer, "Epic Elements in Biblical History", *Journal of Hebraic Studies* 1,2 (1970), 1-15.
[3] R. Althann, "Unrecognized Poetic Fragments in Exodus", *JNSL* 11 (1983), 9-27; J.C. de Moor, *The Rise of Yahwism: The Roots of Israelite Monotheism* (BETL, 91; Leuven, 1990), 164-68 on Ex 19:3-6.
[4] De Moor, *The Rise of Yahwism*, 182-196.
[5] W.T. Koopmans, "The Testament of David in 1 Kings ii 1-10", *VT* 41 (1991), 429-49; W.T.W. Cloete, "Distinguishing Prose and Verse in 2 Ki. 19:14-19", in: J.C. de Moor - W.G.E. Watson (eds.), *Verse in Ancient Near Eastern Prose*

The amount of verse in Deuteronomy and the Deuteronomistic History becomes even larger if we include what has been described as "narrative poetry", poetry in which external parallelism is more prominent than "normal" internal parallelism within the verse.[6] Here the borderline between prose and poetry tends to become blurred. Perhaps this should be ascribed to a prosaic redaction of earlier epic material.[7] But it is just as well possible to simply assume a different genre of verse which coexisted next to lyrical poetry from the beginning. For this too, parallels exist in the Ancient Near East.[8]

The origin and function of this poetic material require an explanation. To that end we shall start with a description of a number of significant characteristics of these inset poems. These characteristics will provide us with a key to their function. Subsequently we shall formulate a hypothesis concerning the origin of the poems.

2. Characteristics

2.1 Date

Recent investigations refer to parallels from the ancient world to explain the juxtaposition of a prose narrative to a lyrical account of the same events in verse, or to narratives leading up to a poem.[9] Mostly a

---

(AOAT, 42; Neukirchen-Vluyn, 1993), 31-40.

[6] The promising research in this area is still in its infancy. Many poetic passages have been identified by J.P. Fokkelman, *Narrative Art and Poetry in the Books of Samuel* I-III (Assen 1981-1990). See furthermore e.g. D.L. Christensen, "Prose and Poetry in the Bible: The Narrative Poetics of Deuteronomy 1:9-18", *ZAW* 97 (1985), 179-189; W.T. Koopmans, "The Poetic Prose of Joshua 23", in: W. van der Meer, J.C. de Moor (eds.), *The Structural Analysis of Biblical and Canaanite Poetry* (JSOTS 74; Sheffield, 1988), 83-118; Idem, *Joshua 24 as Poetic Narrative* (JSOTS 93; Sheffield, 1990); J. Kim, *The Structure of the Samson Cycle* (Kampen, 1993); P. Auffret, "A Poem in Prose: The Burning Bush Passage—Structural Analysis of Ex 3:2-6", in: De Moor - Watson, *Verse in Ancient Near Eastern Prose*, 1-12; L. Roersma, "The First-Born of Abraham: An Analysis of the Poetic Structure of Gen 16", *ibid.*, 219-41.; D.T. Tsumura, "The Poetic Nature of Hebrew Narrative Prose in 1 Sam 2:2-17", *ibid.*, 293-304.

[7] Usually this theory is attributed to the Albright School, but even more important were the early contributions of U. Cassuto. See especially his "The Israelite Epic", in: U. Cassuto, *Biblical and Oriental Studies* II, transl. I. Abrahams, (Jerusalem, 1975), 69-109, an article which appeared in Hebrew as early as 1943.

[8] See the literature cited in: J.C. de Moor, "The Poetry of the Book of Ruth (Part I)", *Or* 53 (1986), 262-71; Idem, "Narrative Poetry in Canaan", *UF* 20 (1988), 149-71; De Moor - Watson, *Verse in Ancient Near Eastern Prose*, ix-xviii.

[9] K.L. Younger, Jr., "Heads! Tails! Or the Whole Coin?!: Contextual Method and Intertextual Analysis: Judges 4 and 5", in: K.L. Younger, Jr.- W.W. Hallo - B.F. Batto (eds.), *The Biblical Canon in Comparative Perspective* (Scripture in

contemporaneous origin may be assumed for both the prose and the poetry in these authentic ancient documents. It is tempting to conclude from these parallels that also in the O.T. the poems may have been contemporaneous to their context. However, such a conclusion would be premature. There has always been a great deal of uncertainty among scholars accepting the Documentary Hypothesis as to where to situate these poems within the sources.[10] It appears to be impossible to attribute them to one or the other of the traditional sources with any amount of certainty. In many cases the inset poems contain archaic obsolete terms and grammatical constructions which have been cleared up only with the help of Ugaritic and other ancient Canaanite languages.[11] From a philological point of view, the nature of these phenomena renders deliberate archaizing very improbable. Mostly the Hebrew tradition did not recognize their meaning anymore, as is testified by the Septuagint and other ancient witnesses.

Moreover, these poems contain religious concepts which are surprisingly close to those of the early Canaanites and patently foreign to the theology of Deuteronomy and the Deuteronomistic School.[12] As a result the scribes who incorporated the poems into their grand history of Israel often felt obliged to censor them.[13] In a few cases the concept needing correction was apparently discovered so late that textual evidence of the emendation made is still available.[14] In other cases,

---

Context IV; New York, 1991), 109-35; J.W. Watts, *Psalm and Story: Inset Hymns in Hebrew Narrative* (JSOTS 139; Sheffield, 1992); Idem, "'This Song': Conspicuous Poetry in Hebrew Prose", in: De Moor - Watson (eds.), *Verse in Ancient Near Eastern Prose*, 345-58.

[10] For a survey see J.A. Soggin, "Ancient Israelite Poetry and Ancient 'Codes' of Law, and the Sources 'J' and 'E' of the Pentateuch", *Congress Volume Edinburg 1976* (SVT 28; Leiden, 1975), 185-195.

[11] Unfortunately a complete survey and critical evaluation of the numerous proposals that have been made is lacking. For some information see e.g. E.R. Martínez, *Hebrew-Ugaritic Index to the Writings of M.J. Dahood* I (Rome, 1967); II (Rome, 1981); D.A. Robertson, *Linguistic Evidence in Dating Early Hebrew Poetry* (Missoula, 1972); Y. Avishur, *Stylistic Studies of Word—Pairs in Biblical and Ancient Semitic Literatures* (AOAT 210; Neukirchen-Vluyn, 1984), 669-71; O. Loretz, *Ugarit und die Bibel* (Darmstadt, 1990), 31-38.

[12] See M.C.A. Korpel, *A Rift in the Clouds: Ugaritic and Hebrew Descriptions of the Divine* (UBL 8; Münster, 1990), 622-624.

[13] M. Weinfeld, *Deuteronomy and the Deuteronomic School* (Oxford, 1972), 10 rightly observes, "The author of Deuteronomy, however, has found these old poems unsatisfactory." For some examples of such censoring see De Moor, *The Rise of Yahwism*, 162f. (Deut 33:2-5); Korpel, *A Rift in the Clouds*, 532f. (Gen 49:22-26), 535 (Num 23:24).

[14] For example Deut 32:8, see e.g. P.W. Skehan, "A Fragment of the 'Song of Moses' (Deut 32) from Qumran", *BASOR* 136 (1954), 12-15; R. Meyer, "Die Bedeutung von Deuteronomium 32,8f.43 (4Q) für die Auslegung des Moseliedes",

like the Song of Deborah, it can be demonstrated that they were heavily edited already at a much earlier date to accommodate them to the changed political realities of the divided kingdom. Yet the Song still contains many elements pointing to its origin in pre-monarchical times.[15] Probably other poems, like Gen 49, Deut 32, Deut 33, have a similar complicated pre-deuteronomic history behind them.

Of course it was much easier to adapt passages written as 'narrative poetry' to the needs of the Deuteronomic/Deuteronomistic movement because their structure was less rigid than that of lyrics. Yet in these cases too intrinsic evidence often suggests a fairly early date for the original narrative. One might point to the stone of witness in Josh. 24:26 as an example.[16] Or to the early monarchical date which is generally assigned to Joshua 2.[17]

All these observations tend to support the conclusion that generally speaking these inset poems pre-date the Deuteronomic/Deuteronomistic corpus. Yet they do not belong to J or E. Somehow the Deuteronomists must have been the first to gain access to these old poems. They used them at strategic points in the account of Israel's history. Apparently the venerable age of the songs lended authority to their work.

2.2 *Priestly Circles*

However, not only the Deuteronomistic chroniclers of the history of Israel had access to these poetic fragments. The same is true of circles directly connected with the cult. The easiest example is David's

---

in: A. Kuschke (ed.), *Verbannung und Heimkehr. Fs. W. Rudolph* (Tübingen, 1961), 197-209; M. Lana, "Deuteronomio e Angelologia alla Luce di una Variante Qumranica (4Q Dt 32,8)", *Henoch* 5 (1983), 179-205.

[15] J.C. de Moor, "The Twelve Tribes in the Song of Deborah," forthcoming in *VT* 43 (1993).

[16] Koopmans, *Joshua 24*, 404f.

[17] M. Noth, *Das Buch Josua* (HAT 7/3; Tübingen, 1971), 24, 29f.; J. Gray, *Joshua, Judges and Ruth* (London, 1967), 53, 56; J.A. Soggin, *Le livre de Josué* (CAT Va; Neuchatel, 1970), 35; G.M. Tucker, "The Rahab Saga (Joshua 2): Some Form-Critical and Traditio-Historical Observations", in: J.M. Efird (ed.), *The Use of the Old Testament in the New and Other Essays: Studies in Honor of W.F. Stinespring* (Durham, 1972), 66-86; E. Otto, *Das Mazzotfest in Gilgal* (Stuttgart, 1975), 88; R.G. Boling, *Joshua* (AB 6; Garden City, 1982), 143, 150; M. Ottoson, "Rahab and the Spies", in: H. Behrens *et al.* (eds.), DUMU-E₂-DUB-BA-A: *Studies in Honor of Åke W. Sjöberg* (Philadelphia, 1989), 426f.; idem,   *Josuaboken: En programskrift för davidisk restauration* (Uppsala, 1991), 43-53.

In the radical dissection of J.P. Floss, *Kunden oder Kundschafter? Literaturwissenschaftliche Untersuchung zu Jos 2*, Bd. 1 (St. Ottilien, 1982), 79, 210f. only a few verses of the original narrative survive. In a separate structural analysis of the chapter the present writer hopes to demonstrate its basic unity.

Thanksgiving, a slightly different version of which was also adopted in the Book of Psalms (Ps 18). Other Psalms, like Ps 29[18] and Ps 68:2-25,[19] exhibit the same archaisms and 'Canaanite' concepts. They may well belong to the same corpus of archaic traditions.

The author of Habakkuk 3 heavily adapted an existing old song to the needs of the moment after the fall of Jerusalem.[20] His ample use of סלה identifies him as an anonymus Psalmist or cultic prophet.[21] Apparently he still had access to a *written* source of the ancient song he was actualizing.

It has long been observed that also the Priestly Code contains a number of poetic fragments which may go back to the same collection of old poems.[22] Because the centralization of the cult which is so prominent in Deuteronomy was also in the interest of the priests, it is a plausible hypothesis that the poetic fragments stem from a collection guarded in the temple.

2.3 Re-worked Poetry

What complicates the whole issue considerably is the later re-working of the old poetic material. In the cases we discussed up till now, the old poems were still recognizable, even though they were edited to bring them into line with the later prevailing theology. In other cases, however, the process of editing may well have gone further, all but obliterating the older song. Many passages in Deuteronomy and the Priestly Code have a poetic flavour which might go back to such adaptations of older poetic material which, however, cannot be extracted with confidence from the present text anymore.[23] Sometimes the later redactors used the old poems to create a completely new, well-balanced poem of their own liking. This is the case for example

---

[18] See, e.g., C.J.L. Kloos, *Yhwh's Combat with the Sea* (Leiden, 1986), 13-124; Y. Avishur, *Studies in Hebrew and Ugaritic Psalms* (Hebr.) (Jerusalem, 1989), 23-75.

[19] See, most recently, De Moor, *The Rise of Yahwism*, 118-28; Idem, "Ugarit and Israelite Origins", forthcoming in SVT.

[20] See, most recently, Avishur, *Studies in Hebrew and Ugaritic Psalms*, 76-137; De Moor, *The Rise of Yahwism*, 128-36. The date of 605-603 B.C. proposed by R.D. Haak, *Habakkuk* (SVT 44; Leiden, 1992), 111-154, would seem too high.

[21] For further arguments connecting Habakkuk with the cult see Haak, *Habakkuk*, 110f.

[22] J.S. Kselman, "The Recovery of Poetic Fragments from the Pentateuchal Priestly Source", *JBL* 97 (1978), 161-73; De Moor, *Rise of Yahwism*, 176f. (Num 27:16f., 21).

[23] Cf. M. Paran, *Forms of the Priestly Style in the Pentateuch: Patterns, Linguistic Changes, Syntactic Structures* (Hebr.) (Jerusalem, 1989), 98-136.

with the blessings and curses of Lev 26.[24] Apparently the author of
this chapter makes use of the same traditional material which the
Deuteronomic movement applied in Deut 27-28. Yet we are unable to
reconstruct the 'original' verses from the sources at our disposal.

Let me give another example. C.J. Labuschagne is doubtlessly right
in regarding the present text of Deut 26:5-11 as late, possibly exilic or
post-exilic.[25] In accordance with his spectacular logotechnical analysis
he discovers a superb compositional unity in 25:5-26:19 which renders
it impossible to extract an older "credo" from the present context.[26] In
the opinion of the present writer Deut 26:5b-10 is a new poem, exhibiting the main Deuteronomistic theologoumena. The poetic nature of the
piece is obvious from the many internal and external parallel pairs it
contains.

ארמי אבד אבי	5bA
וירד מצרימה	5bB
ויגר שם במתי מעט	5bC
ויהי־שם לגוי גדול	5cA
עצום ורב	5cB
וירעו אתנו המצרים ויענונו	6aA
ויתנו עלינו עבדה קשה	6aB
ונצעק אל־יהוה אלהי אבתינו	7aA
וישמע יהוה את־קלנו	7aB
וירא את־ענינו ואת־עמלנו ואת־לחצנו	7aC
ויוצאנו יהוה ממצרים	8aA
ביד חזקה ובזרע נטויה	8aB
ובמרא גדל ובאתות ובמפתים	8aC
ויבאנו אל־המקום הזה	9aA
ויתן־לנו את־הארץ הזאת	9aB
ארץ זבת חלב ודבש	9aC
ועתה הנה הבאתי	10aC
את־ראשית פרי האדמה	10aB
אשר־נתתה לי יהוה	10aC
והנחתו לפני יהוה אלהיך	10bA
והשתחוית לפני יהוה אלהיך	10bC

Certainly a well-composed poem, but in its present form the late

---

[24] Cf. M.C.A. Korpel, "The Epilogue to the Holiness Code", in: De Moor,
Watson (eds.), *Verse in Ancient Near Eastern Prose*, 123-50.
[25] C.J. Labuschagne, *Deuteronomium*, deel II (POT; Nijkerk, 1990), 279, with
bibliography.
[26] Labuschagne, *Deuteronomium*, deel II, 261-63, 278f.; see also the separate
table, 74f.

Deuteronomistic origin can hardly be doubted.[27] Yet Von Rad and others[28] may be right in so far it is likely the poem was based on an older liturgical text in verse.[29] The piece does not fit well into its context. In v. 4 it is the priest who puts the firstfruits before YHWH. In v. 10 it is the Israelite bringing the oblation. Especially the opening words are without parallel in the Deuteronomistic literature. Because of its derogatory nature it may be the only genuine remnant of the old poem which served the Deuteronomists as a source of inspiration.[30]

In other cases more of the original poem can be salvaged, provided we proceed in a clearly defined methodical way. Let us study an example of such a case, another creed in Deuteronomy. Apparently Deut 6:4-9 and Deut 11:18-21 are related passages. At certain points both exhibit parallelistic structures suggesting a common poetic 'Vorlage'. Labuschagne may be right in explaining the differences in the final form of the two passages as the outcome of the different numerical structures employed.[31] However, this has nothing to do with the earlier history of the text. With regard to Deut 6:4 Labuschagne himself observes:

---

[27] Cf. W. Richter, "Beobachtungen zur theologischen Systembildung in der alttestamentlichen Literatur anhand des 'kleinen geschichtlichen Credo'", in: *Wahrheit und Verkündigung*, Fs M. Schmaus (Paderborn, 1967), 175-212.

[28] See especially G. von Rad, *Das formgeschichtliche Problem des Hexateuch* (Stuttgart, 1938 [= Idem, *Gesammelte Studien zum Alten Testament* I, München, 1958], 1-15, 48-65, 90; M.A. Beek, "Das Problem des aramäischen Stammvaters (Deut. XXVI 5)", *OTS* 8 (1950), 193-219, esp. 207; N. Lohfink, *Unsere großen Wörter: Das Alte Testament zu Themen dieser Jahre* (Freiburg, 1977), 76-91, esp. 80-82; S. Kreuzer, *Die Frühgeschichte Israels in Bekenntnis und Verkündigung des Alten Testaments* (Berlin, 1989), 63-81, 153-80; D.R. Daniels, "The Creed of Deuteronomy XXVI Revisited" (SVT 41; Leiden, 1990), 231-42.
Lipiński's statement that the Aramaeans are not attested before 1000 B.C., repeated in E. Lipiński, "'Mon père était un araméen errant': L'histoire carrefour des sciences bibliques et orientales", *OLP* 20 (1989), 23-47, needs revision in the light of new evidence from Emar and Egypt. See my paper "Ugarit and the Origin of Job", to be published in the *AOAT*-proceedings of the 1992 Manchester symposium on Ugarit and the Bible.

[29] It is absolutely certain that liturgical texts in the form of verse existed in the Canaanite world. See e.g. J.C. de Moor - P. Sanders, "An Ugaritic Expiation Ritual and its Old Testament Parallels", *UF* 23 (1991), 283-300; D. Pardee, "Poetry in Ugaritic Ritual Texts", in: De Moor - Watson (eds.), *Verse in Ancient Near Eastern Prose*, 207-18.

[30] On the authenticity of the incipit see A.R. Millard, "A Wandering Aramean", *JNES* 39 (1980), 153-55.
Already the ancient versions took offense at the statement in Deut 26:5, cf. F. Dreyfus, "'L'Araméen voulait tuer mon père': L'actualisation de Dt 26,5 dans la tradition juive et la tradition chrétienne", in: M. Carrez et al. (eds.), *De la Tôrah au Messie: Mélanges H. Cazelles* (Paris, 1981), 147-61.

[31] C.J. Labuschagne, *Deuteronomium deel IB* (POT; Nijkerk, 1987), 75f., 268f.

De historische vraag betreffende de ouderdom van de belijdenis en haar vroegere *Sitz im Leben* is voor het verstaan van haar functie in de huidige context niet relevant. Het is mijns inziens niet uitgesloten dat ze ouder is dan haar tegenwoordige *Sitz in der Literatur* en dat ze afkomstig is uit de voordeuteronomische 'YHWH-alleen'- of 'YHWH-nummer-één' beweging uit de 9de en 8ste eeuw v.C., of dat z*é* zelfs nog ouder is en in essentie teruggaat op de ontstaantijd van het YHWH-geloof.

De eerste connotatie, 'YHWH is nummer één' veronderstelt een polytheïstische context, waarbij er meer goden erkend worden, maar aan YHWH voorkeur wordt gegeven. Deze zou best de oudste betekenis van de belijdenis kunnen vertegenwoordigen.[32]

The present writer wholeheartedly endorses Labuschagne's opinion.[33] As a matter of fact, Deut 6:4 is a unique statement, without parallel in the O.T. Therefore it can hardly be an invention of the Deuteronomic School itself. Significantly, Deut 11 omits this particular phrase. This alone indicates a certain uneasiness with a statement a little too obvious to the taste of the Deuteronomic/Deuteronomistic School.

From a methodological point of view we have to separate what is unique or evidently old from the Deuteronomic/Deuteronomistic expansions. The phrase following the creed (Deut 6:5) belongs to the customary Deuteronomic phraseology and may in part have been borrowed from Ancient Near Eastern treaty terminology.[34] Deut 6:6 runs והיו הדברים האלה אשר אנכי מצוך היום על־לבבך. This becomes ושמתם את־דברי אלה על־לבבכם in Deut 11:18. The phrase אשר אנכי מצוך of Deut 6:6 is clearly Deuteronomic[35] as is the expression שים על לב[36] in Deut 11:18. Usually the remaining היה על לבב of Deut 6:6 is interpreted in a figurative way. However, the expression occurs only once more in the entire O.T. and has a literal meaning then. In Ex

---

[32] Labuschagne, *Deuteronomium deel IB*, 77f. Translation of quotation: "The historical question regarding the antiquity of the creed and its earlier *Sitz im Leben* is irrelevant to the understanding of its function in the present context. In my opinion it is not beyond possibility that it is older than its actual *Sitz in der Literatur* and originated in the pre-deuteronomic 'YHWH-alone'- or 'YHWH-number-one' movement of the 9th and 8th century B.C., or is even older and goes back essentially to the time of origin of the faith in YHWH. The first connotation, 'YHWH is number one' presupposes a polytheistic context, in which more deities are recognized, but YHWH is preferred. This might well represent the oldest meaning of the creed".

[33] De Moor, *The Rise of Yahwism*, 172f. with parallels from the Late Bronze Age.

[34] R. Frankena, "The Vassal Treaties of Esarhaddon and the Dating of Deuteronomy", *OTS* 14 (1965), 140f.; Weinfeld, *Deuteronomy and the Deuteronomic School*, 333f.

[35] Weinfeld, *Deuteronomy and the Deuteronomic School*, 356.

[36] Weinfeld, *Deuteronomy and the Deuteronomic School*, 335.

28:30 it describes the wearing of the Urim and Tummim on the breast of Aaron.

In the following verse Deut 6:7 again has the more original text as compared to Deut 11:19. The unique ושננתם is replaced by the more common and prosaic ולמדתם אתם and the parallelistic ודברת בם is turned into prose too: לדבר בם. The infinitives of Deut 6:7b certainly belong to the old poem. Except for Deut 11:19 they occur in no other text of the O.T. and Deut 11:19 takes them over without replacing the singular suffixes, as the context required.

Yet Deut 11 preserves something more original than Deut 6. It is the positioning of the bicolon concerning the signs on the hand and between the eyes. Deut 6 places this bicolon after the tricolon containing the infinitives (Deut 6:8), whereas Deut 11:18b places it after the phrase about the words on the heart. In view of what we observed about the literal meaning of this expression in Ex 28:30 this is almost certainly the correct position.

Therefore we may now reconstruct the original poem as follows,

שמע ישראל	4aA
יהוה אלהינו	4bA
יהוה אחד	4bB
והיו הדברים האלה	6aA
על לבבך	6aB
וקשרתם לאות על־ידך	8aA
והיו לטטפת בין עיניך	8aB
וכתבתם על־מזוזת ביתך ובשעריך	9aC
ושננתם לבניך	7aA
ודברת בם	7aB
בשבתך בביתך	7bA
ובלכתך בדרך	7bB
ובשכבך ובקומך	7bC

One further example may suffice to demonstrate the usefulness of this kind of approach. If we compare Josh 1:3-4 to Deut 11:24 it is clear that the two passages contain the same traditional unit which was expanded in different ways. Deuteronomy would seem to have preserved the more original version:

1 לכם יהיה (Deut 11:24aC) is *lectio difficilior* as compared to נתתיו לכם (Josh 1:3aC).

2 The stopgap כאשר דברתי אל משה (Josh 1:3aD, cf. Ex 9:12. 35, etc.)
  is lacking in Deut 11:24.
3 The ill—founded הזה in Josh 1:4aA is apparently introduced on the
  basis of הירדן הזה in Josh 1:2.
4 ועד הנהר הגדול (Josh 1:4aB) is easier than מן הנהר (Deut 11:24). It
  was probably derived from Deut 1:7. The ἀπὸ τοῦ ποταμοῦ τοῦ
  μεγάλου of the LXX in Deut 11:24 betrays the same need for clarification.
5 The explanatory Deuteronomistic gloss כל ארץ החתים (Josh 1:4aC,
  cf. Judg 1:26) is lacking in Deut 11:24.
6 The circumstantial formula הים הגדול מבוא השמש (Josh 1:4aD) is
  evidently inferior to the terse הים האחרון of Deut 11:24. Although
  הים הגדול would be acceptable in itself, the rhyme with הלבנון
  clearly argues in favour of הים האחרון.

The explanatory and legendary נהר פרת is an intrusion in both versions
of the poetical fragment, paving the way for 1 Kgs 4:21. Finally we
expect מן הנהר והים האחרון to be balanced by a מן המדבר והלבנון
instead of מן הנהר ועד הים האחרון. That this is indeed the original
version of the verse appears from Josh 23:4 where we find another
reminiscence of the fragment: מן הירדן ... והים הגדול מבוא השמש.

The original fragment may now be reconstructed as follows:

כל המקום אשר תדרך	aA
כף רגלכם בו	aB
לכם יהיה	aC
מן המדבר והלבנון	bA
מן הנהר והים האחרון	bB
יהיה גבלכם	bC

The internal parallelism דרך ‖ רגל[37] and ‑כם ‖ ‑כם, as well as
המדבר ‖ הנהר[38] confirms the poetic nature of the verses. The tricola
are connected by external parallelism: יהיה ‑כם‑, ‑כם ‖ גבול,[39] מקום ‖
יהיה ‖ and the specification of the מקום in the second verse.
    The reconstruction of this little piece of narrative poetry yields some
interesting by-products. In the original version of the poem "the River"
was the river Jordan. It is certain, especially after the discovery of the

---

[37] Also attested in poetic internal parallelism in Hab 3:19.
[38] The pair is also attested in Isa 41:18; 43:19f.; 50:2; Ps 107:33. Cf. Koopmans,
Joshua 24, 230.
[39] The same pair occurs in external parallelism in Deut 12:20f.; Joel 4:6f.; Ps
104:3f.; Job 38:19f.

Balaam text of Deir 'Alla, that הנהר in Num 22:5 also designates the river Jordan. In other cases this is at least a possibility: 2 Sam 8:3 Ketib[40] Josh 24:8, 14f[41] and Ps 66:6. Just as נהר and ים formed a traditional parallel pair,[42] so ירדן and ים could form a pair.[43] The author of the original poem appears to have held the 'narrow' view of Cisjordan as the land of YHWH (Josh 22:19; Ez 47:15-20).[44] The Promised Land covered the area from the Negeb in the South, from the (Anti)-Lebanon in the North, from the river Jordan in the East, and from the Mediterranean Sea in the West.

The transformation of the ancient poetic material in the cases we discussed above appeared to be fairly radical. However, sometimes a poem happens to be taken over in a variant, yet integral form that suited the purposes of the Deuteronomic/Deuteronomistic composition better.[45] The *jus talionis*, for example, is taken over from the Book of the Covenant (Ex 21:23-25) in a shortened form (Deut 19:21), as it is in Lev 24:20. In such cases nothing essential was changed.

2.4 *Interrelations*

A topic deserving further investigation are the interrelations between the poems embedded in Deuteronomy and the Deuteronomistic literature. A few striking examples may suffice. The theophany descriptions incorporated in Judg 5, Hab 3, Deut 33 and Ps 68 apparently stem from the same tradition.[46] It is now also attested in an inscription from Kuntillet 'Ajrud.[47] The exhortation recited before the movements of the ark (Num 10:35f.) is clearly reflected in Ps 68:2, 18. The number of close parallels between Ps 68 and Judg 5 is most astonish-

---

[40] See for example P.R. Ackroyd, *The Second Book of Samuel* (CBC; Cambridge, 1977), 87f.; P. Kyle McCarter, Jr., *II Samuel* (AB; New York, 1974), 248.

[41] Cf. De Moor, *The Rise of Yahwism*, 177f.

[42] See, e.g., Avishur, *Stylistic Studies of Word-Pairs*, 369f.

[43] Cf. Num 13:29; Judg 5:17; Ps 114:3,5.

[44] Cf. M. Ottoson, *Gilead*, transl. J. Gray (Lund, 1969), 240f.; D. Jobling, *The Sense of Biblical Narrative* (Sheffield, 1986), 88f.

[45] It is the strength of Labuschagne's logotechnical work that it offers a plausible explanation for this kind of contractions or expansions. See for the law of poetic expansion and contraction in general the literature cited by Koopmans, *Joshua 24*, 100, n. 8.

[46] See, e.g., L.E. Axelsson, *The Lord Rose up from Seir: Studies in the History and Traditions of the Negev and Southern Judah* (Stockholm, 1987), and for some new data the study "Ugarit and Israelite Origins" referred to in note 19.

[47] M. Weinfeld, "Kuntillet 'Ajrud Inscriptions and their Significance", *SEL* 1 (1984), 126.

ing.[48] A rare old word מִשְׁפְּתַיִם "sheepfold" occurs in three pre-Deuteronomic poems (Gen 49:14; Judg 5:16; Ps 68:14).[49] The verb צָעַד describing God as a striding bull occurs in Judg 5:4, Hab 3:12, Ps 68:8 and perhaps Gen 49:22. It has Ugaritic antecedents.[50] Ps 29 presupposes Ex 15.[51] Clearly there is a link between Gen 49:9 and Num 24:9. The terminology of Num 24:3f., 15f. has its closest parallel in 2 Sam 23:1. Ex 19:4 seems to echo Deut 32:11. Judg 5:8 recalls Deut 32:17. Deut 32:39 and 1 Sam 2:6 employ similar terminology.

There is no need to pursue this path further. The examples given suffice to demonstrate a remarkable coherence of the inset poetic material. These poems were not totally unconnected fragments, they belonged to a corpus of theologically fairly homogenous literature which differed in many respects from the Deuteronomic and Deuteronomistic ideas.

3. A Hypothesis

If the poetic material embedded in Deuteronomy and the Deuteronomistic History was pre-deuteronomic and theologically coherent, this means it must have come from a religious collection or library belonging to a group of kindred spirits. The many parallels with early Canaanite concepts, as well as the circumstance that the poems had to be censored and edited by those who used these texts to bolster up the authority of their own writings, suggest a considerable time gap between Deuteronomy and these poetic writings. Since they were also available to priestly circles, the old collection was probably housed in the temple.

By and large the affinity of the poetic fragments with the early prophetic literature is low. Except for some rather general parallels with regard to sin and retribution in e.g. Deut 32 and 1 Sam 2, the theology of the prophets is as far removed from that of the poems as that of the Deuteronomic/Deuteronomistic movement. Hosea, for example, expressly rejects the bull imagery which was still common at

---

[48] Ps 68:5,33 ‖ Judg 5:3; Ps 68:13 ‖ Judg 5:22, 30; Ps 68:14 ‖ Judg 5:16; Ps 68:19 ‖ Judg 5:12; Ps 68:22, 24 ‖ Judg 5:26.

[49] It is certain that *mšptym* corresponds to Ugaritic *mtpdm* and primarily means 'donkey-pack'. Cf. J.C. de Moor, "Donkey-Packs and Geology", *UF* 13 (1982), 303f.; Idem, "Ugaritic Smalltalk", *UF* 17 (1986), 221. However, because the V-shape of the sheepfold resembled the shape of a donkey-pack, it was designated by the same word. Cf. O. Eissfeldt, *Kleine Schriften* III (Tübingen, 1966), 61-70.

[50] Korpel, *A Rift in the Clouds*, 532.

[51] S.I.L. Norin, *Er spaltete das Meer: Die Auszugsüberlieferung in Psalmen und Kult des Alten Israel* (Lund, 1977), 127, 151.

the time when these poems were composed.[52] If these poems had still been circulating at that time, one would expect more direct references to them in the prophetic literature. If they existed at all then, they were apparently inaccessible to the prophets and at least in part forgotten.

This suggests a connection between the discovery of the Book of the Law by the high priest Hilkiah (2 Kgs 22) and the collection of old poems. The discovery in connection with repairs in the temple has a beautiful parallel in the famous find of long forgotten Hebrew manuscripts in the so-called Cairo Geniza.[53] True, the text of 2 Kgs 22 speaks of *the* Book of the Law. Usually it is taken to be a scroll of Deuteronomy, or some predecessor of this book.[54] Only J.R. Lundbom has proposed to identify the find with Deut 32.[55] Both opinions have their specific difficulties which need not concern us here. For even if it was only one presumably old scroll which Hilkiah handed over to Shaphan, this does not preclude the possibility that more manuscripts have been found on the same occasion. Exactly if the Deuteronomistic School wanted to make use of these venerable old documents, but deemed it unwise to publish the lot without careful purging, one would expect them to keep silent about the extent of the find.

A close parallel may be found in the medieval sect of the Karaites who somehow laid hands on a number of Dead Sea Scrolls. Some of them, like the so-called Zadokite Documents, they copied out, others were used in their own writings to further their own purposes.[56]

If Hilkiah's find comprised some fragmentary manuscripts containing old poetry, this would tally with all the characteristics of the material we examined. Because Gen 49, Deut 33 and even Judgs[57] presuppose the division of the country, the manuscripts from this

---

[52] Korpel, *A Rift in the Clouds*, 532-41.

[53] Cf. P. Kahle, *The Cairo Geniza* (Oxford, 1959²), 3-13.

[54] For excellent reviews of the state of the question see H.-D. Hoffmann, *Reform und Reformen: Untersuchungen zu einem Grundthema der deuteronomistischen Geschichtsschreibung* (ATANT 66; Zürich, 1980), 190-203; N. Lohfink, "Zur neueren Diskussion über 2 Kön 22-23", in: N. Lohfink (ed.), *Das Deuteronomium. Entstehung, Gestalt und Botschaft* (BETL 86; Leuven, 1985), 24-48; M.J. Paul, *Het Archimedisch Punt van de Pentateuchkritiek: Een historisch en exegetisch onderzoek naar de verhouding van Deuteronomium en de reformatie van koning Josia (2 Kon 22-23)* ('s-Gravenhage, 1988).

[55] J.R. Lundbom, "The Lawbook of the Josianic Reform", *CBQ* 38 (1976), 293-302.

[56] Cf. N. Wieder, "The Doctrine of the Two Messiahs Among the Karaites", *JJS* 6 (1955), 14-25; Idem, "The Qumran Sectaries and the Karaites", *JQR* 47 (1956-57), 97-113, 269-92; Idem, *The Judean Scrolls and Karaism* (London, 1962).

[57] See note 15 above.

'geniza' were only a few hundred years old at the moment of their discovery, though some of them may have been subject to a long history of editing already at the time of their manufacture.

DAS KAPITULATIONSANGEBOT IM KRIEGSGESETZ DTN 20:10FF. UND IN DEN KRIEGSERZÄHLUNGEN

E. NOORT

Rijksuniversiteit Groningen

I

In der Disziplin "Theologie des Alten Testaments" nimmt das Buch Deuteronomium seit den Arbeiten Gerhard von Rads eine wichtige Stelle ein.[1] Von Siegfried Herrmann konnte es sogar als "die Mitte biblischer Theologie" bezeichnet werden.[2] Eine genauso wichtige Rolle spielt das Buch in der Einleitungswissenschaft. Es ist wohl nicht zufällig, daß in der rekonstruierten Deuteronomistik mit seinen vielen Siglen in unserem Fach über die Tradierung und Bearbeitungen dieses Buches munter gestritten wird, und daß es dann meistens um Fragen geht, die sowohl die methodischen Zugänge überhaupt als die Entstehung der Bücher Genesis bis 2 Könige betreffen.[3]

Bei diesem Sperrfeuer von Fragen erstaunt es nicht, daß in letzter Zeit von Seiten der gelehrten Zunft nur Kleinkommentare verfaßt wurden.[4] Der Großkommentar[5] ist eine seltene Erscheinung geworden.

---

[1] G. von Rad, *Das Gottesvolk im Deuteronomium* (BWANT 47; Stuttgart, 1929); Ders., *Das formgeschichtliche Problem des Hexateuch* (BWANT 65; Stuttgart, 1938); Ders., *Deuteronomium-Studien* (FRLANT 58; Göttingen, 1947); Ders., *Theologie des Alten Testaments* I. Die Theologie der geschichtlichen Überlieferungen Israels (München, 1957); Ders., *Das fünfte Buch Mose*. Deuteronomium, übersetzt und erklärt (ATD 8; Göttingen, 1964). Weitere Titel bei K. von Rabenau, "Bibliographie Gerhard von Rad", in: H.W. Wolff (Hrsg.), *Probleme biblischer Theologie*, Fs. G. von Rad (München, 1971), 665-681.

[2] S. Herrmann, "Die konstruktive Restauration. Das Deuteronomium als Mitte biblischer Theologie", in Wolff (Hrsg.), *Probleme*, 155-170.

[3] Einen Überblick über die Forschungslage bieten H.D. Preuß, *Deuteronomium* (EdF 164; Darmstadt, 1982); O. Kaiser, *Einleitung in das Alte Testament* (Gütersloh, 1984⁵), 122-138; Ders., *Grundriß der Einleitung in die kanonischen und deuterokanonischen Schriften des Alten Testaments* I. Die erzählenden Werke (Gütersloh, 1992), 85-99.

[4] A. Phillips, *Deuteronomy* (CBC; Cambridge, 1973); A.D.H. Mayes, *Deuteronomy* (NCBC; Grand Rapids, 1981); G. Braulik (NEB; Würzburg, 1986 [I], 1992 [II]). Eine ausgedehnte Liste bei Preuß 1982, 203f. und bei Labuschagne 1990, 309f.

[5] Von L. Perlitt liegt eine Reihe exzellenter Aufsätze zum Deuteronomium vor, seine Kommentierung im BKAT Neukirchen ist bis Dtn 2:7 gediehen: L. Perlitt,

In dieser Situation will ich meinen Groninger Kollegen Cas Labuschagne mit diesen Zeilen nicht nur zu seinem Geburtstag herzlich
grüßen, sondern ihm auch zu der Tatsache gratulieren, daß sein opus
magnum fast komplett ist.[6] In dem breit angelegten Kommentar bringt
Labuschagne mit seiner logotechnischen Analyse nicht nur eine eigene
Sicht ein, sondern er führt auch eine behutsame—dem Ziel des Kom-
mentars angemessene—theologische Auslegung vor. Eine solche
Exegese ist in vielen Fällen gar nicht einfach, wenn man sich nicht auf
die Bastion unbeteiligter Darstellung des "Damals" zurückziehen will.
Dies gilt vor allem, wenn es um die Fragen nach Israel und seinem
Land, Israel und dem Verhältnis zu den Nachbarvölkern und um die
Fragen nach Kriegsführung und Bann in der Deuteronomistik geht. In
der Großkomposition Dtn 19:1-21:9 weist Labuschagne auf die unter-
geordnete Rolle der Kriegsgesetze hin. Sie würden schon durch ihre
Stellung inmitten der Vorschriften über Tötung, Mord und Blutschuld
entschärft.[7] Das stufenweise Vorgehen bei einer Belagerung bedeute
bereits eine Eingrenzung des Bannes.[8] Die Verbindung zwischen der
Landnahme und dem Gott, der für Israel streite, beruhe letztendlich auf
der unaufgebbaren Erinnerung an das befreiende Handeln JHWHs beim
Auszug aus Ägypten.[9] Und über den deuteronomisch/deuteronomisti-
schen Gedanken der Absonderung Israels heißt es:

> Wat we ook al mogen denken van deze afzonderingstheologie, ze was niet
> gebaseerd op een superioriteitsgevoel noch op verachting voor medemensen,
> groepsegoïsme of vreemdelingenhaat. Ze berustte uitsluitend op een diepe
> bezorgdheid om de zuiverheid van het eigen geloof en de daarmee verbonden
> eigen identiteit. Geplaatst in de context van toen, kunnen we haar begrijpen.
> Ondanks het begrip dat we kunnen opbrengen voor de afzonderingstheologie in
> Deuteronomium, kan ze echter nooit het laatste woord over de relatie tussen
> Israël en de volkeren hebben.[10]

Deuteronomium (BKAT V/1; Neukirchen, 1990; V/2; Neukirchen, 1991).

[6] C.J. Labuschagne, *Deuteronomium* (POT; Nijkerk, 1987 [Ia+Ib = 1:1-11:32],
1990 [II = 12:1-26:19]).

[7] Labuschagne 1990, 165. Labuschagne geht damit schon in eine Richtung, die
später von Braulik entschieden vertreten wird. Braulik beschreibt die Disposition der
Endredaktion des deuteronomischen Gesetzeskorpus als Auslegung des Dekalogs.
Dabei wird die Komposition Dtn 19:1-21:23 als Auslegung des fünften Gebotes
verstanden: Leben bewahren. G. Braulik, *Die deuteronomischen Gesetze und der
Dekalog. Studien zum Aufbau von Deuteronomium 12-26* (SBS 145; Stuttgart,
1991).

[8] Labuschagne 1990, 164.

[9] Labuschagne Ia, 1987, 126-130.

[10] Labuschagne Ib, 1987, 113. Labuschagne weist schließlich darauf hin, daß für
den Deuteronomisten selbst dies auch nicht das letzte Wort sei und nennt 1 Kön
8:41ff.

Mit diesen Bemerkungen greift Labuschagne in eine Diskussion ein, die jenseits der literarhistorischen Debatte stattfindet. So, wie das "Auge um Auge, Zahn um Zahn" (Ex 21:24) einerseits als Beschränkung der Blutrache ausgelegt, aber andererseits als Exempel der Rachsüchtigkeit des Alten Testaments rezipiert wurde, so werden auch die Kriegsgesetze des Deuteronomiums einerseits als Einschränkung der gemeinorientalischen Kriegspraxis, andererseits in der Wirkungsgeschichte als Bausteine für das Bild des grausamen, kriegführenden Gottes Israels verstanden.

Mit dieser wirkungsgeschichtlichen Realität im Hinterkopf wollen wir uns in diesem Beitrag mit dem Kapitulationsangebot im Kriegsgesetz Dtn 20:10-18 beschäftigen. Wie realistisch oder wie idealistisch war diese Abstufung? Wie verhalten sich die Teile dieses Kriegsgesetzes zur israelitischen und gemeinorientalischen Kriegspraxis? Und wie ist die Verbindung zwischen V. 10-14 und 15-18[11] zu denken?

II

Im Kriegsgesetz Dtn 20:10ff. wird die Anwendung des *ḥrm* tatsächlich insoweit relativiert, als Israel einer einzunehmenden Stadt zuerst ein Kapitulationsangebot unterbreiten soll. Erst bei Verweigerung einer friedlichen Unterwerfung darf die Stadt belagert werden. Dann wird JHWH die Stadt in die Hand Israels geben, und Israel wird die kriegsfähigen Männer töten. Ehe es also zur Vernichtung kommt, erhält der Gegner eine Möglichkeit zur freiwilligen Unterwerfung. Wenn diese abgelehnt wird, betrifft der Bann nur die kriegsfähigen Männer. Diese Abstufung wird nun durch V. 15 mit der Erläuterung zunichte gemacht, diese Regel gelte nur den weit entfernten Städten des verheißenen Landes. Für den Kanon der vorisraelitischen Bevölkerung Palästinas, wie er V. 17 geboten wird, gilt die Relativierung nicht: weder das vorhergehende Kapitulationsangebot, noch die Einschränkung auf die kriegsfähigen Männer. Hier soll der Bann gelten, wonach alles Lebendige getötet wird.

Wenn wir uns nun die Erzählungen des Josuabuches ansehen, kann tatsächlich festgestellt werden, daß weder Jericho, noch Ai, noch den Städten aus Jos 10-11 ein solches Kapitulationsangebot gemacht wurde. Das einzige Mal, wo es zu einem Bund zwischen Israel und der gibeonitischen Tetrapolis kommt,[12] gilt der Friedensschluß als Frevel.

---

[11] Labuschagne 1990, 161 verteidigt auf Grund seiner logotechnischen Analyse die Einteilung 10-15, 16-18. Eine Aufgabe dieses Aufsatzes wird sein, diese Einteilung zu überprüfen.
[12] Jos 9:1-27.

Dies bedeutet, daß für die Endgestalt der Gibeonerzählung die Kombination von Dtn 20:10-14 und 15-18 vorausgesetzt wird.[13] Daß aber eine friedliche Einigung nicht unmöglich war, zeigt die Mühe, die der Verfasser von Jos 11:19ff darauf verwendet, zu erklären, daß Josua alle Städte mit Gewalt genommen hat. Denn JHWH hatte es gefügt, so der Erzähler, daß sie verstockt würden und den Kampf mit Israel aufnähmen. So kann erklärt werden, daß alle gebannt wurden. Der Erzähler läßt also theoretisch die Möglichkeit einer friedlichen Einigung offen für den Fall, daß die Verstockung nicht stattgefunden hätte. Hierfür gibt es zwei Erklärungen. Entweder ist das Gebiet, das in Jos 11 beschrieben wird, so abgelegen, daß es unter die entfernten Städte gerechnet werden könnte. In diesem Fall muß die Hilfskonstruktion mit der Verstockung es Israel ermöglichen, die Städte doch noch unter den Bann zu bringen. Oder die territoriale Einschränkung des Kriegsgesetzes muß auf dieser Ebene des Erzählens als noch nicht bekannt vorausgesetzt werden. Schon solche ersten Fingerübungen zeigen, daß der Zusammenhang zwischen den Kriegsgesetzen und den deuteronomistischen Kriegserzählungen nicht so glatt ist, wie es allgemein angenommen wird.

Ehe wir uns nun wieder den literarischen Fragen zuwenden, ist zu fragen, welche Erzählungen das Alte Testament selbst über eine Belagerung und deren Verlauf, sowie die dazugehörende Terminologie bietet. Wo wird im Alten Testament eine Stadt belagert und/oder eingenommen, wo wird verhandelt?

2.1

Die folgende Zusammenstellung nennt zuerst Text, Subjekt (S) und Objekt (O). Die arabischen Ziffern stehen für folgende Kategorien: 1) initiierende Aktion, Vorbereitung, 2) göttlicher Beistand/Siegeszusage, 3) Hindurch-/Hinaufziehen, 4) Verhandlung, Unterwerfungsangebot, 5) Schlagen, 6) Belagern, 7) Streiten, 8) (Ein)nehmen, 9) Verwüsten, 10) Töten, 11) Bann, 12) in Brand setzen, 13) Be-/Umnennen, 14) in die Verbannung führen.

Der manchmal abweichenden Reihenfolge wird nur in der Analyse, nicht aber in der Tabelle Rechnung getragen.

---

[13] Chr. Schäfer-Lichtenberger, "Das gibeonitische Bündnis im Licht deuteronomischer Kriegsgebote. Zum Verhältnis von Tradition und Interpretation in Jos 9", *BN* 34(1986), 58-81; E. Noort, "Zwischen Mythos und Rationalität. Das Kriegshandeln Yhwhs in Jos 10,1-11", in: H.H. Schmid (Hrsg.), *Mythos und Rationalität. Vorträge auf dem VI. Europäischen Theologischen Kongreß Wien 1987* (Gütersloh, 1988), 149-161.

1) Num 21:21ff. S: *yśr'l* O: *syhn mlk-h'mry* 3: *'br* (Frage) 4: ja.

2) Num 32:41 S: *y'yr* O: *hwt* 3: *hlk* 8: *lkd* 13: *qr'*.

3) Num 32:42 S: *nbh* O: *qnt* + *bnwt* 3: *hlk* 8: *lkd* 13: *qr'*.

4) Dtn 2:34f. // 1. S: (*yśr'l*) O: *'rym syhn* 2: *yhwh ntn lpnynw* 4: Bitte um freien Durchzug (V. 26). Verstockung durch JHWH 5: *nkh* hif. 8: *lkd* 11: *hrm* hif.

5) Dtn 3:4 (Strukturell // 4) S: (*yśr'l*) O: *'rym 'wg* 2: *yhwh ntn byd* 8: *lkd* 11: *hrm* hif.

6a) Dtn 20:10 S: Du (sg.) O: *'yr* 3: *qrb* 4: *qr' 'lyh lšlwm* 7: *lhm* nif.

6b) Dtn 20:12ff. S: Du (sg.) O: *'yr* 2: *yhwh ntn bydk* 4: *l' tšlym* 5: *'śh mlhmh* 6: *swr 'l* 10: *nkh lpy-hrb 't-kl-zkwrh* (Durch die Interpretation von V. 15 nur die wehrfähigen Männer aus den weit entfernten Städten) 11: *hrm* hif.+ inf. (Durch die Interpretation von V. 15 totaler Bann für die sechs Feindvölker).

7) Dtn 20:19 S: Du (sg.) O: *'yr* 6: *swr 'l/'l* 7: *lhm 'l* nif. 9: *tpš*.

8) Jos 6:20ff. S: *h'm* O: *yryhw* 1: *rw'* + *tq'* bšprwt 2: *yhwh ntn lkm 't-h'yr* (V. 16) 3: *'lh* 8: *lkd* 10: *lpy hrb* 11: *hrm* hif. 12: *śrp b'š*.

9) Jos 8:18f. S: *h'wrb* O: *h'y* 1: *nth bkydwn 'l h'yr* 2: (*yhwh*) *ntn bydk* (1. Pers.) 3: *qwm, rws, bw'* 8: *lkd* 12: *yst b'š*.

10) Jos 8:21ff. //9. S: *h'rb* (def.), *kl yśr'l, yhwš'* O: *h'y* 8: *lkd* 10: *hrg* + *lpy hrb* 11: *hrm* hif. 12: *śrp*.

11) Jos 10:5 S: *hmšt mlky h'mry* O: *gb'wn* 1: *'sp* 3: *'lh* 6: *hnh 'l* 7: *lhm* nif.

12) Jos 10:28 S: *yhwš'* O: *mqdh* 8: *lkd* 10: *nkh lpy hrb* 11: *hrm* hif.

13) Jos 10:29f. S: *yhwš'* + *kl-yśr'l* O: *lbnh* 2: *yhwh ntn byd yśr'l* 3: *'br* 7: *lhm* nif. 10: *nkh lpy hrb* 11: [*hrm* hif.].

14) Jos 10:31f. S: *yhwš'* + *kl-yśr'l* O: *lkyš* 2: *yhwh ntn byd yśr'l* 3: *'br* 6: *hnh 'l* 7: *lhm* nif. 8: *lkd* 10: *nkh lpy hrb* 11: [*hrm* hif.].

15) Jos 10:34f. S: *yhwš'* + *kl-yśr'l* O: *'gln* 3: *'br* 6: *hnh 'l* 7: *lhm* nif. 8: *lkd* 10: *nkh lpy hrb* 11: *hrm* hif.

16) Jos 10:36f. S: *yhwš'* + *kl-yśr'l* O: *hbrwn* 3: *'lh* 7: *lhm* nif. 8: *lkd* 10: *nkh lpy hrb* 11: *hrm* hif.

17) Jos 10:38f. S: *yhwš'* + *kl-yśr'l* O: *dbr* 3: *šwb* 7: *lhm* nif. 8: *lkd* 10: *nkh lpy hrb* 11: *hrm* hif.

18) Jos 11:10f. S: *yhwš'* O: *hswr* 3: *šwb* 8: *lkd* 10: *nkh lpy hrb* 11: *hrm* hif. 12: *śrp* (V. 13).

19) Jos 11:12 S: *yhwš'* O: *kl-'ry hmlkym-h'lh* 8: *lkd* 10: *nkh lpy hrb* 11: *hrm* hif.

20) Jos 11:13 S: *yśr'l* O: *kl-h'rym h'mdwt 'l-tlm* 12: *l'-śrp* (!).

21) Jos 11:19f. // 6. S: *'yr* O: *bny-yśr'l* 2: *hzq* (pi.) *lb* 4: *šlm* hif. (nicht) 8: *lqh bmlhmh* 11: *hrm* hif.

22) Ri 1:8 S: *bny yhwdh* O: [*yrwšlm*] 7: *lhm* nif. 8: *lkd* 10: *nkh lpy hrb* 12: *šlh* (pi.) *b'š*.

23) Ri 1:12f. S: Wer? O: *qryt-spr* (Debir) 5: *nkh* 8: *lkd*.

24) Ri 1:13 S: *tny'l* O: *qryt-spr* 8: *lkd*.

25A) Ri 9:45 S: *'bymlk* O: *h'yr* (= Sichem) 7: *lhm* nif. 8: *lkd* 9: *nts* + *zr' mlh* 10: *hrg 't h'm 'śr-bh*.

25B) Ri 9:46ff. S: *'bymlk* O: *mgdl-škm* + *sryh byt 'l bryt* 12: *jst* (hif.) *b'š*.

26A) Ri 9:50 S: *'bymlk* O: *tbs* 3: *hlk 'l* 6: *hnh* 8: *lkd*.

26B) Ri 9:51ff. S: *'bymlk* O: *mgdl-tbs* 3: *bw'* 7: *lhm* nif. 12: *śrp b'š*.

27) 1 Sam 11:1ff. S: *nhš h'mwny* O: *jbš gl'd* 3: *'lh* 4: *krt lnw wn'bdk* // *bryt* + *'bd* 6: *hnh 'l*

28) 1 Sam 23:8 S: *š'wl* O: *dwd w'nšyw* + *k'lh* 1: *šm'* (pi.) *lmlhmh* 3: *yrd* 6: *swr 'l* (!), aber Objekt David und seine Männer.

29) 2 Sam 11:1 S: *yw'b* + *'bdyw* + *kl-yśr'l* O: *rbh* 5: *šht* hif. 6: *swr 'l*.

30) 2 Sam 11:16 S: *yw'b* O: *rbh* 6: *šmr 'l*.

31) 2 Sam 12:26ff. S: *yw'b* O: *rbh: 'yr hmlwkh* (V. 26), *'yr hmym* (V. 27) 1: *'sp* 7: *lhm* nif., *lhm* nif. 6: *hnh 'l* 8: *lkd, lkd, lkd* 13: *qr' šmy* (negativ).

32) 2 Sam 12:29 S: *dwd* O: [*rbh*] 1: *'sp* 3: *hlk* 7: *lhm* nif. 8: *lkd*.

33) 2 Sam 20:15ff. S: *yw'b* O: *'bl byt hm'kh* 3: *bw'* 6: *swr 'l* 7: *špk sllh, npl* hif. *hwmh* 8: *lkd*.

34) 1 Kön 9:16 S: *pr'h mlk mṣrym* O: *gzr* 3: *'lh* 8: *lkd* 10: *hrg* 12: *śrp b'š*.

35) 1 Kön 15:27 S: *ndb + kl-yśr'l* O: *gbtwn* 6: *swr 'l*.

36) 1 Kön 16:17f. S: *'mry + kl-yśr'l* O: *trṣh* 3: *'lh* 6: *ṣwr 'l* 8: *lkd* 12: *śrp b'š* (*'rmwn*).

37) 1 Kön 20:1ff. S: *bn-hdd mlk-'rm* O: *šmrwn* 1: *qbṣ* 3: *'lh* 4: Verhandlungen : 1. Forderung von den Belagerten akzeptiert, 2. weitergehende Forderung zurückgewiesen. 6: *ṣwr 'l 'l* 7: *lhm* nif.

38) 1 Kön 22:4 S: *mlk yśr'l* [V. 20 *'h'b*] O: *rmt gl'd* 7: *lhm* nif.

39) 2 Kön 6:24ff. S: *bn-hdd mlk-'rm* O: *šmrwn* 1: *qbṣ* 3: *'lh* 6: *swr 'l*.

40) 2 Kön 12:18ff. S: a) *hz'l mlk-'rm* b) *hz'l mlk-'rm* O: a) *gt* b) *yrwšlm* 3: a) *'lh* 4: Tributzahlung durch Joas (Gold aus dem Tempel und aus dem Palast) verhindert Belagerung Jerusalems. 7: a) *lhm* nif. 8: a) *lkd*.

41) 2 Kön 16:5 //51. S: *rṣyn mlk-'rm* O: *yrwšlm* 3: *'lh lmlhmh* 6: *swr 'l 'hz* (!) 7: *l'* (!) *yklw lhlhm*.

42) 2 Kön 16:9 S: *mlk 'šwr* (Tiglat-Pileser III) O: *dmśq* 3: *'lh* 8: *tpś* 10: *mwt* hif. 14: *glh* hif.

43) 2 Kön 17:5f. S: *mlk 'šwr* (*šlmn'sr*) O: *šmrwn* 3: *'lh* 6: *swr 'l* 8: *lkd* 14: *glh* hif.

44) 2 Kön 18:9ff. S: *šlmn'sr mlk-'šwr* O: *šmrwn* 3: *'lh* 6: *swr 'l* 8: *lkd* 14: *glh* hif.

45) 2 Kön 18:13ff. S: a) *snhryb mlk-'šwr* b) *snhryb mlk-'šwr* O: a) *kl-'ry yhwdh* b) *yrwšlm* 3: a) *'lh*: Version, in der Hiskia nach Anfrage an Sanherib von ihm ein Tribut von 300 Talenten Silber und 30 Talenten Gold auferlegt bekommt. 8: a) *tpś*.

46) 2 Kön 24:10ff. S: *'bdy-nbkdnṣr mlk-bbl* O: *yrwšlm* (597) 3: *'lh + bw'* 4: *yṣ' yhwykym* (Übergabe) 6: *swr 'l* 14: *glh* hif.

47) 2 Kön 25:1ff. S: *nbkdnṣr* O: *yrwšlm* (587) 3: *bw'* 6: *hnh 'l; bnh dyq sbyb* 12: *śrp b'š* 14: *glh* hif.

48) 1 Chron 2: 23 // 2. + 3. S: *gšwr + 'rm* O: *hwt y'yr; qnt + bnwt* 8: *lqh*.

49) 1 Chron 20:1 // 29. Var. 49.: David wird nicht im letzten Moment geholt. David ist aber wohl V. 2 der Handelnde. S: *yw'b* O: *rbh* 3: *bw'* 5: *šht* hif. 6: *swr 't* (!) 8: *nkh* (Syr. *lkd*) 9: *hrs*.

50) 2 Chron 32:1ff. // 45. Var. 50.: Hiskia baut Verteidigungsanlagen auf. Der Vorbau ist hier an die zweite Version der Bedrohung Jerusalems durch Sanherib angeglichen worden, in der der Engel JHWHs 185.000 Männer des assyrischen Heeres tötet (1 Kön 19:35f.). S: *snhryb mlk 'šwr* O: *'rym hbṣrwt yhwdh* 3: *bw'* 6: *hnh 'l*.

51) Jes 7:1 // 41. S: *rṣyn mlk-'rm* O: *yrwšlm* 3: *'lh lmlhmh* 7: *l'* (!) *ykl* (Versiones: *yklw*) *lhlhm 'lyh*.

52) Jes 20:1 S: *trtn srgwn mlk-'šwr* O: *'šdwd* 3: *bw'* 7: *lhm* nif. 8: *lkd*.

53) Jes 36:1ff. // 45.,50.,53.: Zweite Version der Bedrohung Jerusalems. S: a) *snhryb mlk-'šwr* b) *rb-šqh* O: a) *kl-'ry yhwdh hbṣrwt* b) *yrwšlm* 3: a) *'lh* 4: b) *'śh brkh; yṣ' 'l* 8: a) *tpś*.

54) Jer 21:4 S: *nbkdnṣr* O: *yrwšlm* 6: *swr 'l*.

55) Jer 21:9 S: *kśdym* O: *yrwšlm* 6: *ṣwr 'l*.

56) Jer 38:28 S: (*nbkdnṣr*) O: *yrwšlm* 8: *lkd*.

57) Jer 39:1 // 47. S: *nbkdnṣr* O: *yrwšlm* (587) 6: *swr 'l*.

58) Jer 52:4 // 47.

59) Dan 1:1 S: *nbkdnṣr* O: *yrwšlm*[14] 3: *bw'* 6: *ṣwr 'l*.

Die vergleichende Zusammenstellung zeigt, daß es längst nicht in allen Fällen, in denen eine Stadt eingenommen wurde, zu einer Belagerung kam. List (Jos 8 - Ai; 2 Sam 5:6-9 - Jerusalem) oder Verrat (Jos 2 - Jericho; Ri 1:23-26 - Bethel) führten schneller und ohne größere Verluste zum Ziel, und öfter konnte eine Stadt beim ersten Angriff eingenommen werden. Von einer Belagerung konstruiert mit *ḥnh 'l* ist die Rede bei den Nummern 11.14.15.26a.27.31.47.50. Die Konstruktion mit *ṣwr 'l* findet sich bei 28.29.33.35.36.37.39.41.43.44.46.49.54.55.57. 59. Sie sind teilweise auswechselbar. Das gleiche Ereignis (Belagerung Jerusalems 587) wird Nr. 47 mit *ḥnh 'l*, Nr. 57 mit *ṣwr 'l* beschrieben. Soweit bei den Bann-Erzählungen mit *lpy ḥrb* en *ḥrm* hif. von einer Belagerung die Rede ist, erscheint immer *ḥnh 'l*,[15] nie *ṣwr 'l*. Daß Belagerung und *ḥrm* selten zusammen erscheinen, liegt am Charakter des Bannes, der mit der Totalität des Sieges auch den direkten, baldigen Triumph verbindet, im Gegensatz zur Belagerung, die meistens einen längeren Prozeß voraussetzt. Die Einnahme einer Stadt wird 31x durch *lkd*, 2x durch *tpś*, 2x durch *lqḥ [bmlḥmh]* und 1x durch *nkh* ausgedrückt.

Die 40 erzählten Versuche zur Einnahme einer Stadt haben folgenden Ausgang:

a) Die Stadt (Städte) wird (werden) erobert:
Nr. 1.4: Städte Sihons, Nr. 2.45: Zeltdörfer Jairs, Nr. 3.48: Kenath und Nebenorte, Nr. 5: Städte Ogs, Nr. 8: Jericho, Nr. 9.10: Ai, Nr. 12: Makkeda, Nr. 13: Libna, Nr. 14: Lachis, Nr. 15: Eglon, Nr. 16: Hebron, Nr. 17. Debir, Nr. 18: Hazor, Nr. 19: "alle Städte dieser Könige", Nr. 22: Jerusalem, Nr. 23.24: Kirjath-Sepher (Debir).

b) Die Belagerung führt zur Eroberung der Stadt:
Nr. 25a.b: Sichem, Migdal-Sichem, Nr. 29.30.31.32.49: Rabba, Nr.34: Gezer, Nr. 40: Gath, Nr. 42: Damaskus (732), Nr. 43.44: Samaria (722), Nr. 45.50.53 "alle Städte Judas" (701), Nr. 52: Asdod (711), Nr. 47.54.55.56.57.58: Jerusalem (587).

c) Die (geplante) Belagerung führt zum gewünschten Ziel und wird abgebrochen:
Nr. 33: Abel-Beth-Maacha, Nr. 36: Thirza, Nr. 40: Jerusalem, [Nr. 44: Jerusalem (701)] Nr. 46.[59]: Jerusalem (597).

---

[14] Für die Verwechslung der Belagerung 597 und der Verbannung Jojachins mit einer hier postulierten Belagerung und Verbannung Jojakims 607/606 vgl. K.Koch, *Daniel* (BKAT XXII/1; Neukirchen, 1986), 25-31.
[15] Jos 10:31f.,34f.

d) Die geplante Belagerung kommt nicht zustande:
   Nr. 28: Kegila, Nr. 38: Ramoth in Gilead (Abwehr in offener Schlacht), Nr. 41.
   51: Jerusalem (733), Nr. 45.50.53 Jerusalem (701) oder Möglichkeit f.

e) Die Stadt wird durch militärisches Eingreifen gerettet:
   Nr. 11: Gibeon, Nr. 27: Jabes in Gilead, Nr. 35: Gibbethon (vgl. auch 1 Kön 16-
   :17 Omri zieht von Gibbethon ab).

f) Die Belagerung mißlingt:
   Nr. 26a.b: Thebez, Migdal-Thebez, Nr. 37: Samaria, Nr. 39: Samaria, [evt. Nr.
   45. 50.53 Jerusalem 701].

In der Aufschlüsselung zeigt sich, daß im allgemeinen die Städte gegen
eine gut geführte Belagerung keine Chance hatten. Abgebrochene oder
mißlungene Belagerungen sind in der Minderheit gegenüber den
gelungenen Versuchen, eine Stadt einzunehmen. Insgesamt 29 (30) x
erreicht der Angreifer sein Ziel. Nur 11 x muß er ohne Erfolg aufge-
ben. Das Bild ändert sich auch nicht, wenn wir die historisch nicht-
verifizierbaren und legendären Erzählungen aus der Aufstellung entfer-
nen. Denn historisch kontrollierbar sind hier nur die wenigsten Berichte. Die Erzählungen über die Landnahme- und Richterzeit können nur
sehr vereinzelt als historische Nachricht gewertet werden. Die Berichte
aus der Zeit der Aramäerkriege können zwar allgemein in ein historisches Bild eingezeichnet werden, eine genaue Datierung ist jedoch
nicht möglich. Außerdem gibt es Verdichtungen auf eine Person (Ben-
Hadad) und zweckdienliche Uminterpretationen. Erst in der assyrischen
und babylonischen Zeit ist es möglich, die Ereignisse mit Jahreszahlen
zu versehen, und erst hier verfügen wir über außerbiblisches Material.
Aber auch dann sind wir trotz reichlich fließender Quellen längst nicht
immer imstande, den historischen Ablauf genau nachzuzeichnen. Trotz
dieser Unsicherheiten stehen auch jetzt—bei den datierbaren und verifizierbaren Texten—6 (7) gelungene Angriffe nur 2 (1) mißlungenen
Belagerungen gegenüber. Eine fortifizierte Stadt hatte der assyrischen
und babylonischen Kriegsmaschinerie nur kurz- oder mittelfristig etwas
entgegenzusetzen. Aber eine Belagerung konnte auch für den Angreifer
eine langwierige, teure Angelegenheit mit erheblichen Verlusten an
Menschen und Material werden. Darauf weist schon die praktizierte
Zweistufigkeit einer Belagerung hin: Zuerst die vollständige Einkreis-
ung der Stadt in der Hoffnung, sie durch Machtdemonstrationen und
Aushungerung zur Übergabe zu bewegen, danach der Sturmangriff mit
Hilfe von Belagerungsmaschinen. In diese abgestufte Aktion paßt
selbstverständlich das Kapitulationsangebot am Anfang als Mittel, ohne
Anstrengung das gewünschte Ziel zu erreichen. Das gleiche gilt umge-
kehrt für das Unterwerfungsangebot der Belagerten, wenn sie im

voraus einschätzen konnten, daß sie gegen den vorrückenden Angreifer keine Chance haben würden.

In welchen Fällen der obenstehenden Auflistung wird nun von einer solchen Verhandlung berichtet? Aufnahmekriterium ist dabei der Versuch zur Verhandlungsführung, nicht die Eingrenzung auf die *šlwm* Formulierung. Auch hier werden die Verhandlungen zuerst ohne Rücksicht auf Historizität aufgelistet, um die Funktion der Verhandlung in den Erzählungen bestimmen zu können.

1) Num 21:21ff.: Anfrage Israels an Sihon von Hesbon, auf der Königsstraße durch sein Land ziehen zu dürfen. Sihon verweigert die Zustimmung.

4) Dtn 2:34f.: Anfrage Israels an Sihon von Hesbon, durch sein Land ziehen zu dürfen. Die Verweigerung wird im deuteronomistischen Rückblick auf eine Verstockung durch JHWH zurückgeführt (V. 30).

27) 1 Sam 11:1ff.: Die Einwohner von Jabes sind im Unterwerfungsangebot an Nahas, den Ammoniter, bereit, ihm zu dienen. Nahas fordert Körperverletzung als Schmachzeichen. Saul befreit Jabes.

33) 2 Sam 20:15ff.: Seba ist nach Abel-Beth-Maacha geflüchtet und wird dort von Joab belagert. Eine Frau nimmt die Verhandlungen auf, und Joab fordert die Auslieferung Sebas. Als dessen Kopf über die Mauer geworfen wird, bricht Joab die Belagerung ab.

37) 1 Kön 20:1ff.: Ben-Hadad stellt während der Belagerung Samarias die Forderung nach Gold und Silber. Ahab willigt ein. Eine erneute, überhöhte Forderung wird abgelehnt.

38) 2 Kön 12:18ff.: Hasael zieht nach der gelungenen Eroberung Gaths gegen Jerusalem, aber Joas kauft sich mit dem Tempel- und Palastschatz frei. Eine Belagerung findet nicht statt.

44) 2 Kön 18:13ff.: a) Hiskia zahlt ein Tribut in der von Sanherib gewünschten Höhe und verhindert damit eine Einnahme Jerusalems. b) In der Fortführung/ zweiten Version der Erzählung soll eine Intimidierungsansprache die Übergabe der Stadt erzwingen.

46) 2 Kön 24:10ff.: Durch frühzeitige Übergabe verhindert Jojachin die Vernichtung der Stadt.

Es zeigt sich, daß das Verhandlungsmoment zwischen dem drohenden Angriff und der tatsächlichen Belagerung in den Texten eine unterschiedliche Funktion hat.

1. Die Verhandlung in den Nrn. 1 und 4 hat seinen Ort in Verbindung mit den *ḥrm*- Vorstellungen. Das Angebot, auf im voraus festgelegtem Wege durch das Land zu ziehen, die Reserven und Existenzmittel des Landes nicht anzutasten, soll die Unschuld Israels an der Vernichtung des Gegners betonen. Nicht Israel, sondern Sihon—und nach demselben Schema Og—ist der eigentliche Agressor. Den Kampf und den *ḥrm* hat der Gegner sich selbst zuzuschreiben. Durch die von JHWH bewirkte Verstockung in der Dtn-Version wird dies nochmals überhöht.

2. Die Verhandlung in den Nrn. 27.37 und 44b dient der Darstellung

der Arroganz der Angreifer. 1 Sam 11:1ff. will Nahas durch die
Körperverletzung die Einwohner von Jabes erniedrigen, und die
Gewährung der Siebentagefrist soll darstellen, daß die Jabesiter seiner
Meinung nach in keiner Weise mit Hilfe rechnen können. Daß es sich
dabei eher um ein narratives Element handelt als um ein kalkuliertes
Risiko von Seiten Nahas', ist wahrscheinlich, es sei denn, Nahas ver-
spricht sich von den Boten eine Panikstimmung im ganzen Land. Die
narrative Funktion drückt aus, daß "menschlich gesehen, keine Hoffnung auf Rettung mehr besteht."[16] Hier wird bewußt die Negativseite
betont, um die Rettungstat Sauls im umso helleren Lichte erscheinen
zu lassen.

1 Kön 20:1ff. zeigt in der Verhandlungsführung eine Steigerung der
Forderungen. Im ersten Angebot von Seiten des Ben-Hadad geht es
dem Angreifer um Silber und Gold (V. 3). Nachdem Ahab allzu
schnell zugestimmt hat, kommt die nächste Forderung: "Alles was in
deinen[17] Augen begehrlich ist, werden meine Knechte mitnehmen"
(V. 6). Darauf folgt die Verweigerung Ahabs und ein Stück psycholo-
gischer Kriegsführung (V. 10f.). Die hier angeschlossene Propheten-
erzählung benutzt die vorangehende Verhandlung als Sprungbrett für
die Übereignungsformel und die Erkenntnisaussage: *ntnw bydk hywm
wyd't ky-'ny yhwh*. Damit wird die Prahlerei des Aramäerkönigs zur
Auflehnung gegen JHWH, wie es die Fortsetzung der Erzählung
deutlich macht (V. 28).

Die gleichen Motive kehren wieder in der zweiten Version der
Sanherib-Erzählung in den Jesajalegenden. Der Rabsake vermittelt das
Verhandlungsangebot: "So spricht der König von Assur: 'Schließt
Frieden mit mir (*'św-'ty brkh*) und ergebt euch mir (*wṣ'w 'ly*), so sollt
ihr ein jeder von seinem Weinstock und von seinem Feigenbaum essen
und ein jeder das Wasser aus seinem Brunnen trinken bis ich komme
und euch hole in ein Land, das eurem Lande gleich ist, ein Land voll
Korn und Wein, ein Land von Brot und Weinbergen, ein Land voller
Ölbäume und Honig. Ihr sollt am Leben bleiben und nicht sterben'" (2
Kön 18:31f.). Kurz zusammengefaßt: Zwar Verbannung, aber am
Leben bleiben. Dieses Angebot wird geschichtstheologisch untermau-
ert: Keiner der Götter der bisher eroberten Städte hat es gegen den
König von Assur aufnehmen können. So verführe Hiskia die Jerusale-
mer, "wenn er spricht: 'JHWH wird uns retten'" (V. 32).[18] Mit dem

---

[16] H.J. Stoebe, *Das erste Buch Samuelis* (KAT VII/1; Gütersloh, 1973), 226.
[17] MT: *'ynyk*, LXX und Vorschlag BHS *'ynyhm*. Die *lectio difficilior* des MT ist
vorzuziehen, denn die dadurch betonte Erniedrigung Ahabs stimmt ausgezeichnet
mit der härter werdenden Verhandlung überein.
[18] Vgl. auch V.30,35; 2 Kön 19:4.10.16.23 // Jes 36:16f.15.18; 37:4.6.10.17.24.

Geist, der Sanherib eingegeben wird, "damit er ein Gerücht hört, in sein Land zurückkehrt und dort eines gewaltsamen Todes stirbt" (2 Kön 19:7, Bestätigung V. 37) und mit dem *ml'k yhwh*, der im Assyrerlager 185.000 Männer tötet (2 Kön 19:35), endet die Erzählung.

3. Die Verhandlung führt zum Ziel. Der Angreifer erreicht das von ihm Gewünschte. Die Belagerung kommt nicht zustande oder wird abgebrochen. Nr.33 zeigt die Einigung zwischen Joab und den Belagerten. Um den Preis der Auslieferung Sebas wird die Belagerung abgebrochen. Auch die erste Version der Sanherib-Erzählung Nr. 44a gehört in diese Kategorie. Sanherib setzt die Höhe des Tributes fest, Hiskia zahlt.

4. Es werden keine formelle Verhandlungen aufgenommen, aber der drohende Angriff wird durch eine Initiative der Angegriffenen, durch Tributzahlung oder durch frühzeitige Übergabe abgewehrt. In diese Kategorie gehört die Hasael-Erzählung Nr. 38, in der Joas sich durch die Abgabe des Tempel- und Palastschatzes freikauft, sowie die Übergabe Jojachins in Nr. 46.

Von den hier gefundenen vier Kategorien haben zwei eine narrative Funktion. Das Verhandlungsmoment wird eingeführt im Rahmen der *hrm*-Vorstellungen, um Israel letztendlich als schuldlos darzustellen. Im zweiten Fall dient das Kapitulationsangebot dazu, die Arroganz der Angreifer zu schildern. Es wird nicht zufällig sein, daß in allen drei Fällen die Belagerung c.q. Eroberung mißlingt. In den Kategorien drei und vier geht es um einen praktischen Zweck. Durch die Verhandlungen wird das Ziel erreicht ohne eine an Menschenleben und Material verlustreiche Belagerung. Oder die Belagerten ergreifen selbst die Initiative, um Schlimmerem zuvorzukommen.

2.2

Wenden wir uns nun dem größeren Kontext der altorientalischen Welt zu, zu der Israel gehörte.

Welche Bilder einer Stadteroberung vermitteln die altorientalischen Texte und Reliefs aus Israels direkter Umgebung in Theorie und Praxis? Zuerst ist zu bedenken, daß es auch in der Umwelt eine große Kluft zwischen der Ideologie einerseits und der Praxis anderseits gab. Denn die Reliefs und Texte aus der Umwelt haben eine andere Funktion als die neutrale Registrierung geschehener Fakten. In der Umwelt sind die Belege, die wir haben, immer Darstellungen des Siegers, und sie dienen der Demonstration der Macht des Pharaos, des Großkönigs, der Reiche Ägyptens, Assurs und Babylons sowie der ihrer Götter. Mißlungene Belagerungen kennt die offizielle Ideologie ebensowenig wie Kompromisse oder verlorene Schlachten. Dagegen sind die Belege des Alten Testaments relativ weit gestreut. Sie reichen von einer idealisierten Darstellung der Frühzeit, in der sie am ehesten den altorientalischen Darstellungen entsprechen, bis hin zu bitterer Niederlage und dem Ende der Staaten Israels und Judas. Auch wenn dort von göttlicher Bewährung und Rettung erzählt wird—die Texte spiegeln die Situation der Bedrängten wider.

Aus dieser Perspektive ist es verständlich, daß es ein institutionalisiertes Verhandlungsangebot in den altorientalischen Darstellungen nicht geben kann. Zugleich aber wird deutlich, daß der wirkliche Geschehensablauf weniger von der Ideologie als von den jeweiligen Interessen der Großmächte zu einer bestimmten Zeit in einer bestimmten Region diktiert wurde. Mit einer Stadt, die er für seinen internationalen Handel braucht, geht der assyrische König anders um als mit einem rebellischen Vasallen, dessen Beispiel andere ermutigen könnte.

Trotzdem bleibt die Frage, ob die Funktion, die das Kapitulationsangebot in den alttestamentlichen Texten hat, der Spielraum zwischen Angreifer und Belagertem, auch in den altorientalischen Darstellungen erscheint.

Wir wenden uns zunächst den ägyptischen Darstellungen zu und beschränken uns dabei auf das Neue Reich, für den theoretischen Zusammenhang dann auf die Ramessidenzeit.

Die Kriegsdarstellungen auf den ägyptischen Reliefs folgen einem bestimmten Muster.[19] Nach der Mitteilung einer feindlichen Aktion, die fast immer als Rebellion dargestellt wird, bekommt der Pharao von der Gottheit den Auftrag, diese Störung des Gleichgewichts zu beseitigen. Nach dem Verlassen des Tempels erfolgt die Mobilmachung der Truppe. Der Pharao besteigt den Streitwagen und marschiert gegen den Feind. Nach einer offenen Schlacht oder nach der Bestürmung befestigter Anlagen werden die Feinde besiegt, vorgeführt und inventarisiert. Kein Ägypter wird verwundet oder kommt zu Tode. Die Rückkehr erfolgt in Triumph. Die Gefangenen werden der Gottheit vorgeführt und geopfert. Meistens schließt die Bildsequenz mit dem Betreten des

---

[19] Vgl. dazu W. Widmer, "Zur Darstellung der Seevölker am Großen Tempel von Medinet Habu", *ZÄS* 102 (1975), 67-77; B. Cifola, "Ramses III and the Sea Peoples: A Structural Analysis of the Medinet Habu Inscriptions", *Or* NS 57 (1988), 275-306; E. Noort, "Seevölker, materielle Kultur und Pantheon. Bemerkungen zur Benutzung archäologischer Daten - ein kritischer Bericht", in: B. Janowski, K. Koch, G. Wilhelm (Hg.), *Religionsgeschichtliche Beziehungen zwischen Kleinasien, Nordsyrien und dem Alten Testament. Internationales Symposion 17.-21. März 1990* (Freiburg-Göttingen, 1993), 363-389, hier 367-372.

Tempels und Palastes durch den Pharao. Anfang (A) und Ende (A')
und damit die ganze Militäraktion sind religiös motiviert.[20] Der zen-
tral stehende Kampf/Sieg (C)[21] wird flankiert durch die militärische
Vorbereitung (B)[22] und durch die militärischen Folgen des Sieges:
Die Inventarisierung der gefangenen und getöteten Feinde (B').[23] Es
handelt sich also um ein Schema: A-B-C-B'-A'.[24] So wird die ganze
Aktion von der Gottheit veranlaßt. Von ihr kommt die Beauftragung,
die Siegeszusage, der Beistand im Kampf, ihr gehört die Beute.[25] Eine
Reihe ägyptischer Reliefs berichtet nun von der Bestürmung kanaanäi-
scher Städte durch den Pharao. O. Keel hat in seiner Auflistung von 34
solcher Reliefdarstellungen zwei Standardtypen ausgemacht: 1. Eine
Reihe von Darstellungen, in denen die Bevölkerung der angegriffenen
Stadt sich zur Wehr setzt, 2. Abbildungen der Einnahme und Bestraf-
ung der rebellischen Stadt.[26] Die Darstellung einer sich zur Wehr
setzenden Stadtbevölkerung bei einer Belagerung bedeutet aber nicht,
daß der Ausgang des Geschehens zweifelhaft sei. Denn auch eine
solche Darstellung fügt sich in das oben beschriebene Schema des
Totalablaufes ein. Außerdem werden die Aktion und die Gefährlichkeit
des Feindes (aus ägyptischer Sicht) sowohl im Text als auch im Bild
öfter überproportional dargestellt. Denn das Ausmaß der Rebellion, die
Größe des Widerstandes betont und verstärkt den dann folgenden Sieg
des Pharaos.[27] In den von Keel eindeutig zum ersten Standardtyp

---

[20] Als Beispiel darf der erste libysche Krieg des Ramses III und die Darstellung
in Medinet Habu gelten. Anfang: (A) Med.Habu Pl.13, 3f.,6f.; 14,3ff.,9ff.,19ff.
(Beauftragung durch Amon-Re); (A') Ende: Pl. 26,1ff. (Anbietung der Beute und
der Gefangenen an Amon-Re und Mut).
[21] (C) Med.Habu Pl.19,1ff. (Kampf des Kriegsgottes Montu und Ramses III).
[22] (B) Med.Habu Pl.16,9ff.; 17,1ff. (Besteigung des Streitwagens, Standarte des
Amon).
[23] (B') Med.Habu Pl.22,2ff.; 23,1ff. (Ansprache des Ramses III und Inventarisierung der Feinde durch abgeschnittene Hände und Phalli).
[24] Widmer 1975, 70.
[25] In der Diskussion um den "Heiligen Krieg" (G. von Rad, *Der Heilige Krieg
im alten Israel*, Göttingen 1951) sind öfter Parallelen aus Mesopotamien angeführt
worden, um die These von Rads zu bestreiten (M. Weippert, *ZAW* 84 [1972],
460ff.). Zu Unrecht hat das ägyptische Material dabei keine Rolle gespielt.
[26] O. Keel, "Kanaanäische Sühneriten auf ägyptischen Tempelreliefs", *VT* 25
(1975), 413-469.
[27] Z.B. heißt es über die "Seevölker" Med.Habu Pl.46,16-18; KRI V 39,14-40,5:
"Nicht hielt irgendein Land vor ihren Armen stand; (und die Länder) von Hatti,
Qadi, Qarqemiš, Arzawa, und Alašia an waren (nun) entwurzelt [auf einen Schlag]
... Sie (die Seevölker) legten ihre Hände auf die Länder bis zum Umkreis der Erde;
ihre Herzen waren zuversichtlich und vertrauensvoll: 'Unsere Pläne werden gelin-
gen!'" Das hier gebotene (unhistorische) Bild einer weltweiten Bedrohung stellt den
Sieg des Ramses III in der See- und Landschlacht in ein umso helleres Licht.

gerechneten drei Darstellungen[28] sind denn auch die Zeichen der
nahenden Übergabe zu sehen. In einem Fall, der den Angriff des
Ramses II auf die Stadt *qdj* zeigt,[29] wird heftig gekämpft. In *šrdn*-
Tracht gekleidete, ägyptische Hilfstruppen greifen den Feind an, von
der Stadt aus werden Projektile auf die Ägypter geschleudert. Zugleich
zeigt das Bild aber stürzende und getötete Belagerte, ein Gefangenen-
zug wird dem Pharao vorgeführt, der bogenschießend auf gefallenen
Feinden steht. Belagerung und Niederlage der Stadt sind gleichzeitig
dargestellt. Die zwei anderen Abbildungen von Ramses II[30] und Ramses IV (?)[31] zeigen beide einen Mann, der dem Pharao ein Räucher-
gefäß entgegenstreckt. Zu Recht hat Keel die Deutungen, die in diesem
Zeichen nur ein allgemeines Kapitulationsangebot sehen, verworfen
und die Szene darüber hinausgehend als Sühneritus für den in der
Theophanie im Zorn erscheinenden göttlichen Pharao gedeutet: "... man
kann das Räuchern auf den Mauerkronen nur dahin deuten, daß die
'Rebellen' damit den Pharao als numinöse Macht anerkennen und
seinen furchtbaren Zorn zu besänftigen suchen."[32] Dies bedeutet, daß
auch in den Darstellungen, in denen der Kampf der Belagerten gegen
den Pharao dargestellt wird, ihre Niederlage und ihre Bitte um
Besänftigung des Zorns des Gott-Königs Teil der Bildaussage ist. Noch
viel stärker ist dies sichtbar in den Bildern des zweiten Standardtyps,
wo nicht der Kampf, sondern die Übergabe im Zentrum steht. Das hier
oft auftauchende Motiv von Kindern,[33] die dem Pharao als Geiseln[34]
dargeboten werden, geht über die Beschwichtigung des göttlichen
Zorns hinaus. Hier geht es um die Zukunft, die in die Hände des
Pharaos gelegt wird. Mit dem "heute" ist die Rebellion beendet und sie
wird nie wieder stattfinden.[35] Von einer gewissen Gleichwertigkeit der

---

[28] Keel 1975, 418.

[29] B. Porter, R.L.B. Moss, *Topographical Bibliography of Ancient Egyptian Hieroglyphic Texts, Reliefs, and Paintings. II. Theban Temples* (Oxford, 1972), 333; W. Wreszinski, *Atlas zur altägyptischen Kulturgeschichte, II. Teil* (Leipzig, 1935), Taf. 72, Keel 1975, 419, Abb. 2, Katalognr. 22.

[30] Porter/Moss 1972, 333; Wreszinski 1935, Taf. 78-80; Keel 1975, Katalognr. 21.

[31] Porter/Moss 1972, 494; Wreszinski 1935, Taf.146f.; Med. Habu II, Taf. 94; *ANEP*, Abb. 346; Keel 1975, Katalognr. 34.

[32] Keel 1975, 431f.

[33] Keel 1975, Katalognrn. 8,13,15,18,26,27,29,31,32,33.

[34] So Keel 1975, 413ff. zurecht gegen Ph. Derchain, "Les plus anciens témoig-
nages de sacrifices d'enfants chez les Sémites occidentaux", *VT* 20 (1970), 351-355.

[35] Keel 1975, 461: "Was die ägyptischen Reliefs auf den Mauern der syro-
palästinischen Städte zeigen, ist das ernste Bemühen ihrer Bewohner, den göttlichen
Pharao, den man durch seine Treulosigkeit und seinen Abfall furchtbar erzürnt hat,
zu besänftigen, indem man ihm räuchert, ihn lobend preist, seine 'Sünden' beklagt

Kontrahenten kann also hier nicht die Rede sein. In der Gestalt des Pharaos erscheint die Gottheit und bestraft die Rebellion. Nur das Räucheropfer, das in den Texten vielfach bezeugte Schuldbekenntnis[36] und das Angebot der Kinder als Geiseln haben nach dem dogmatisch feststehenden Sieg des Pharaos die gleiche Funktion wie die Verhandlung: Das Leben der Belagerten zu retten. Die Belagerten selbst können dazu nichts mehr tun. Ihr Schicksal liegt völlig in den Händen des Pharaos, der sich dann als gnädig erweist.

Dieses Bild des Pharaos, der als Vertreter und Inkarnation der Gottheit nur eine Störung beseitigt, ja auf Grund seiner Überlegenheit auch gnädig sein kann, ist eine Überhöhung, die sich so im mesopotamischen Bereich nicht findet. Hier zeigen die Inschriften zwar auch eine religiöse Legitimierung des königlichen Handelns, auch hier verleihen die Götter und Göttinnen dem König den Sieg und leisten sie Beistand im Krieg, aber die theologische Darstellung ist weniger abgerundet. Dafür treten die Macht und die Härte des Königs umso stärker hervor.

Bei seinem Feldzug nach Karchemis und zum Libanon nähert sich Assurnasirpal II Kunulua, der Residenz Lubarnas, des Patinäers: "Vor meinen zornigen Waffen und meiner wütenden Schlacht fürchtete er sich, und um sein Leben zu retten, umfaßte er meine Füße ... (Aufzählung der Beute) ... Ihm selbst ließ ich Gnade angedeihen ... Ich nahm Geiseln von ihm."[37] Das ist ein Vorgang, wie er auch in einer Reihe der ägyptischen Reliefs dargestellt wird.

Daß es gewöhnlich weniger glimpflich ablief, zeigt der gleiche Text: "Ich eroberte die Städte von Luchutu, richtete dort ein großes Gemetzel an, zerstörte, verwüstete und verbrannte sie mit Feuer. Die überlebenden Männer nahm ich gefangen und spießte sie gegenüber ihren

---

und ihm in den eigenen Kindern seine bedingungslose Unterwerfung, ja sein Leben anbietet, damit er es erhalte und den Odem des Lebens neu schenke, kurzum, sie schildern die Reaktion auf das zerstörische Erscheinen eines erzürnten Gottes."

[36] Vgl. Keel 1975, 439f.

[37] *TUAT* I/4, 359: III 73, 76f.; Prisma B Assurbanipal II 59-64, *TUAT* I/4, 400: "Ich bekam Mitleid mit ihm, und seinen leiblichen Sohn gab ich ihm zurück. Die Schanzen, die ich gegen Baal, den König von Tyrus, aufgeworfen hatte, löste ich auf, zu Wasser und zu Land öffnete ich all seine Wege, die ich besetzt hatte." Im hethitischen Bereich erwähnen die Annalen Mursilis II: III, 14-16, *TUAT* I/5, 477 einen Fall, in dem eine Frauendelegation die Kapitulation anbietet: "Er schickte mir seine Mutter, Greise und Greisinnen voraus [entgegen]. Sie kamen zu mir (und) [fielen] (mir) zu Füßen. Und weil mir die Frauen zu Füßen fielen, gab ich nach um [der Frauen] willen."

Städten auf Pfähle auf."[38]

Meistens aber erscheint eine Notiz, daß die Städte XYZ belagert, erobert, die Beute herausgeholt und die Stadt/Paläste verbrannt wurden.[39] Das gleiche Schema findet sich auch im hethitischen Bereich.[40] Die Brutalität der assyrischen Truppen, die an prominenten

---

[38] *TUAT* I/4, 360: III 83f. So auch die Stierinschrift Salmanassars III, *TUAT* I/4 (92): "Aschtamaku nebst 99 Städten eroberte ich, richtete dort ein Gemetzel an und plünderte sie aus." Die 'Große Prunkinschrift' Sargons II, 34f. beschreibt die Belagerung und Eroberung Qarqars, *TUAT* I/4, 384: "In Qarqaru, seiner Lieblingsstadt, belagerte ich (sc. Sargon II) ihn (sc. Jaubi'di von Hamat) nebst seinen Kriegern und eroberte es. Qarqaru verbrannte ich mit Feuer. Ihm selbst zog ich die Haut ab. In jenen Städten tötete ich die Sünder, und ich erzwang einen Friedensschluß. 200 Streitwagen und 600 Reitpferde hob ich unter den Einwohnern von Hamat auf und fügte sie zu meinem stehenden Heere hinzu." Chicago-Prisma III, 7-14, *TUAT* I/4, 389 über den dritten Feldzug Sanheribs: "Ich näherte mich Ekron. Die Statthalter und Fürsten, die Vergehen begangen hatten, tötete ich, an die Türme der ganzen Stadt hängte ich ihre Leichen. Die Einwohner der Stadt, die Sünde und Frevel begangen hatten, zählte ich als Beute. Die übrigen von ihnen, die nicht durch Sünde und Frevel belastet waren, die sich als schuldlos erwiesen, befahl ich freizulassen." Prisma A Assurbanipals IX, 115ff.: "Ich eroberte Uschu (sc. Tyrus). Die Einwohner ... tötete ich. Unter den unbotmäßigen Einwohnern hielt ich ein Strafgericht ab."; 122ff.: "Die unbotmäßigen Einwohner von Akko tötete ich. Ihre Leichen hängte ich an Stangen rings um die Stadt. Die Übriggebliebenen nahm ich mit nach Assyrien und vereinigte sie zu einer Heeresabteilung." (*TUAT* I/4, 401.)
[39] Salmanassar III beim Feldzug im 6. Regierungsjahr (853a), *TUAT* I/4, 361; Annalenfragment Salmanassar III, *TUAT* I/4 17-20: "Städte ohne Zahl zerstörte, verwüstete und verbrannte ich mit Feuer. Beute machte ich ohne Zahl."; Annalen Sargons II, *TUAT* I/4, 379 (57): "Raphia zerstörte, verwüstete und verbrannte ich mit Feuer. 9033 Einwohner nebst ihrer reichen Habe schleppte ich fort."; *TUAT* I/4, 380 (258-260): "Asdod, Gimtu und Asdod-jam belagerte und eroberte ich. Die Götter, die darin wohnten, ihn selbst (sc. Jamani von Asdod) nebst den Einwohnern seines Landes, Gold, Silber, Besitz seines Palastes zählte ich als Beute." // Nineve-Prisma Sargons II VIIb 37'ff.// 'Große Prunkinschrift' Sargons II, 104f. Nach der 'Großen Prunkinschrift' Sargons II 23f. belagert und erobert er Samaria und deportiert 27290 (Bessere Lesart: 27280.) Einwohner. Zu der These einer zweimaligen Eroberung Samarias: H. Tadmor, "The Campaigns of Sargon II", *JCS* 12 (1958), 22-40, 77-100 und die sorgfältige Revidierung der These durch B. Becking, *The Fall of Samaria. An Historical & Historical Study* (SHANE II; Leiden-New York-Köln, 1992). Nach dem Chicago-Prisma II, 69ff.; III 6ff. geht Sanherib bei seinem dritten Feldzug gegen die Küstenregion Palästinas vor: "Im Verlauf meines Feldzugs belagerte, eroberte und plünderte ich Bit-Daganna, Japho, Banajabarqa und Azuru, Städte des Sidqa, die sich meinen Füßen nicht schleunig unterworfen hatten." ; "Eltheke und Thimna belagerte, eroberte und plünderte ich." (Chicago-Prisma II, 69-71, *TUAT* I/4,389).
[40] Annalen Mursilis II: I, 45-47, *TUAT* I/5, 473: "... griff [die Ortschaft ...] humessena an, und mitsamt Einwohnerschaft, Rind(ern) (und) Schaf(en) [nahm ich] sie (als Beute) und brachte sie fort, her nach Hattusa. Die Ortschaft (selbst) aber [brannte ich] völlig nieder." Die Reihenfolge "Aufziehen zum Kampf", "Angriff", "Vernichtung" ("Auflistung der Beute") findet sich in den Annalen Hattusilis I: I, 46-48; II, 49-52, Rs. III, 34-40, *TUAT* I/5, 461ff.

Stellen in den Texten und in den Reliefs[41] vorhanden ist, wird zweifellos der Abschreckung und der Warnung künftiger Rebellen gedient
haben. Daß es aber längst nicht immer im Interesse der assyrischen
Könige lag, nur wüstes und verbranntes Land zu hinterlassen, zeigen
die ausgeklügelten Deportationsmaßnahmen, die einerseits die Zerset-
zung der nationalen und militärischen Struktur der eroberten Stadt
bezweckten, anderseits für die Stärkung der assyrischen Militär- und
Wirtschaftsmacht gedacht waren.[42] Auch die eroberte Stadt wurde in
den meisten Fällen vom assyrischen König wieder neu besiedelt.

Einige Male wird in den assyrischen Texten das Vorgehen bei einer
Belagerung detailliert dargestellt. Die Stadt wurde entweder durch
einen Sturmangriff oder durch eine Aushungerungstaktik genommen.
Ein Beispiel für den ersten Fall ist der dritte Feldzug Sanheribs nach
dem Chicago-Prisma III, 19ff.: "46 mächtige ummauerte Städte sowie
die zahllosen kleinen Städte ihrer Umgebung belagerte und eroberte ich
durch das Anlegen von Belagerungsdämmen, Einsatz von Sturmwid-
dern, Infanteriekampf, Untergrabungen, Breschen und *Sturmleitern*."[43]
Die zweite Taktik wird von Sanherib auf seinem Feldzug gegen Juda
701 demonstriert: "Schanzen warf ich gegen ihn (sc. Hiskia von Juda)
auf, und das Hinausgehen aus seinem Tor *verleidete* ich ihn."[44] Des-
gleichen von Assurbanipal auf seinem Feldzug gegen — wohl nicht
zufällig — "Baal, den König von Tyrus, der inmitten des Meeres
wohnte"[45]: "Ich warf Schanzen gegen ihn auf. Damit seine Leute
nicht entkämen, bewachte ich (die Stadt) streng. Zu Wasser und zu
Land besetzte ich seine Wege, seinen Zugang schnitt ich ab. Wasser
und Verpflegung, ihren Lebensunterhalt machte ich für ihren Mund
knapp. Mit einer starken, unentrinnbaren Umzingelung schloß ich sie
ein. Ihre Kehle engte ich ein und brachte ich in Bedrängnis."[46] Der
Vorgang des Einschließens ohne Sturmangriff taucht beim Feldzug des
Salmanassar III im Jahre 841 auf: "Ich zog hinter ihm (Hasael von
Damaskus) her und schloß ihn in Damaskus, seiner Residenz, ein.

---

[41] Z.B. Pfählung, Häutung und Tötung der gefangenen Einwohner von Lachis
auf dem Relief von Sanherib: D. Ussishkin, *The Conquest of Lachish* (Tel Aviv,
1982), 82, Segment III en 86, Segment V.
[42] B. Oded, *Mass Deportations and Deportees in the Neo-Assyrian Empire*
(Wiesbaden, 1979), 41ff.
[43] *TUAT* I/4, 389.
[44] Chicago-Prisma III, 29f., *TUAT* I/4, 389.
[45] Prisma B Assurbanipal II, 41ff.
[46] Prisma B Assurbanipal II, 44-51, *TUAT* I/4, 400. Für eine detaillierte Behandlung der unterschiedlichen Formen und Vorgehensweisen vgl. A. van der Kooij,
"Das assyrische Heer vor den Mauern Jerusalems im Jahre 701 v.Chr.", *ZDPV* 102
(1986), 93-109.

Seine Baumgärten schlug ich nieder. Bis zum Hauran-Gebirge zog
ich."[47] Die gleiche Formulierung findet sich bei der Steintafel-In-
schrift Adad-nararis III: "... , den König des *'Eseltreiberlandes'* schloß
ich in Damaskus, seiner Residenz, ein. Furcht vor dem Schreckens-
glanz Assurs, meines Herrn, warf ihn nieder, er ergriff meine Füße und
bezeugte mir seine Untertanigkeit. ... (Beuteaufzählung) nahm ich in
unermeßlicher Menge in Damaskus, seiner Residenz, in seinem Palast
entgegen."[48] Die Notiz des Einschließens des Gegners in seiner Stadt
braucht also nicht auf eine vergebliche Belagerung hinzuweisen. Kann
man beim Feldzug Salmanassars III noch an eine vorübergehende
Bedrohung denken, bei der nur das Land außerhalb der Stadt verwüstet
wird, so führt die Einschließung von Damaskus durch Adad-narari III
zur Übergabe der Stadt.

Die gleiche Kombination: Belagerung und Vernichtung des ökologischen Umfeldes findet sich in den Annalen Tiglatpilesers III: "Ich
schloß ihn ein gleich einem Käfigvogel. Seine Obstgärten ... Pflanzun-
gen ohne Zahl schlug ich nieder und ließ nichts übrig ... *Chadara*, die
Heimatstadt Rachianus vom *'Eseltreierland'*, [... wo] er geboren war,
belagerte und eroberte ich." (folgen Deportationszahlen).[49] Beim
dritten Feldzug des Sanherib in 701 findet sich dann die berühmte
Formulierung: "Ihn selbst (sc. Hiskia von Juda) schloß ich gleich
einem Käfigvogel in Jerusalem, seiner Residenz, ein."[50] Asarhaddon
belagert Sanduarri, den König von Kundu und Abdi-Milkutti, den
König von Sidon: "Ich vertraute auf Assur, Sin, Schamasch, Bel und
Nebo, die großen Götter, meine Herren und belagerte sie mit einer
Umzingelung. Gleich einem Vogel[51] holte ich ihn aus dem Gebirge
und schlug ihm den Kopf ab."[52] Auch die babylonischen Chroniken
zeigen das gleiche Bild: Eroberung, Plünderung, Tötung und Deportation.[53]

---

[47] *TUAT* I/4, 366 Annalenfragment 13-17. So auch die Marmorplatte Salmanassars III, IV 2-4 mit dem Zusatz "sein(e) Getreidegarben / Hinterland verbrannte ich
mit Feuer."
[48] *TUAT* I/4, 368 15-21. So auch die Saba'a-Stele Adad-nararis III (19).
[49] *TUAT* I/4,372 (203-206). Im ägyptischen Bereich ist die Vernichtung des
Baumbestandes u.a. belegt bei Thutmoses III (*ANET* 239a, 240a) und Ramses III
(*ANEP* 344). Für Israel selbst 2 Kön 3:19.25.
[50] Chicago-Prisma III 27-29, *TUAT* I/4,389, van der Kooij 1986, 97.
[51] Weitere Bespiele für das Bild des Vogels: van der Kooij 1986, 97.
[52] Prisma Nineve A Asarhaddons III, 28-31, *TUAT* I/4,396.
[53] IV 3: "Im 4. Jahre wurde Sidon erobert und geplündert"; Z. 17ff.: "Vier
Monate kämpften sie gegen die Stadt (sc. Kimuchu). Sie eroberten die Stadt und
töteten die Garnison des Königs von Akkad."; Z. 21ff.: "Schunadiri, Elammu und
Dachammu, Städte in 'Transmesopotamien' eroberten und plünderten sie"; Rs. Z.
12f.: "Die Stadt Juda (sc. Jerusalem) belagerte er. Am 2. Adar eroberte er die Stadt."

Bei allen Aktionen fehlt die religiöse Legitimation nicht.[54] Nahe an das Alte Testament führt die Inschrift des Königs Zakkur von Hamath, nicht zuletzt weil hier aus der Sicht des belagerten Königs und dessen Gottheit geredet wird: "Und all diese Könige belagerten Hazrak. Und sie richteten einen Wall auf, höher als der Wall von Hazrak; und sie hoben einen Graben aus, tiefer als [sein] Grabe[n]. Aber ich erhob meine Hände zu Be'elsche[may]n, worauf Be'elschemay[n] mir antwortete ... Be'elschemayn [wandte sich] zu mir durch Seher und durch Wahrsager. Be'elschemayn [sagte] zu mir: 'Fürchte dich nicht, denn [ich] habe [dich] zum Köni[g] gemacht [und ich] [werde] dir beiste[hen], und ich werde dich befreien von all [diesen Königen, die] eine Belagerung gegen dich eröffnet haben.'"[55] Und schließlich darf hier die Erwähnung der bekannten, einzigen außerbiblischen Parallele für den Bann in der moabitischen Mesa-Inschrift nicht fehlen: "Kamosch sprach zu mir: 'Geh, nimm Nebo von den Israeliten ein.' Da ging ich (los) in der Nacht und bekämpfte es vom Anbruch der Morgenröte bis zum Mittag. Ich nahm es ein und tötete sie alle, 7000 Mann, Beisassen, Frauen, Beisassinnen und Sklavinnen, denn an Aschtar-Kamosch hatte ich sie geweiht."[56]

Wie stellt sich nun das Bild des Vorgehens bei einer Belagerung, das wir aus den biblischen Texten gewonnen haben, auf dem Hintergrund der altorientalischen Welt dar? Pointiert gesagt: Dtn 20:10-14

Den König (sc. Jojachin im Jahre 598) nahm er gefangen. Einen König nach seinem Herzen (sc. Zedekia) setzte er dort ein. Seinen schweren Tribut nahm er mit und führte ihn nach Babel." (*TUAT* I/4, 402ff.).

[54] "Mit der erhabenen Kraft, die Assur, mein Herr, mir gegeben hat, und mit den mächtigen Waffen, die Nergal, der vor mir hergeht, mir geschenkt hat, kämpfte ich mit ihnen." (Monolith-Inschrift Salmanassar III, *TUAT* I/4,361: II 96f.); Saba'a-Stele Adad-nararis III und Scheich-Hamad-Stele Adad-nararis III, *TUAT* I/4, 369 :... auf Befehl des Assur, des *Marduk*, des Adad und der Ischtar, meiner göttlichen Helfer, warfen *Furcht* und *schrecklicher Nimbus* [sie] nieder und sie ergriffen meine Füße. Tribut und Abgabe ...". Vergleichbar ist die Rolle der Gottheit im kleinasiatischen Raum. Der göttliche Beistand steht hier zwischen der Mitteilung, daß die Stadt X angegriffen wird und ihre Vernichtung. In den Annalen Mursilis II: IV 26-28 und 37-39, *TUAT* I/5, 480f. heißt es: "... [zog ich] meine Sonne, nach Jahressa [und] griff Jahressa an. Und die Sonnengöttin von Arinna, meine Herrin, der Mächtige Wettergott, mein Herr, [Mezz]ulla und alle [Götter] liefen mir (helfend im Kampf) voraus. Ich [be]zwang Jahressa und brannte ihn völlig nieder"; "Nur gegen zwei befestigte Orte, Aripsa und Dukkamma, kämpfte ich. Und die Sonnengöttin von Arinna, meine Herrin, der Mächtige Wettergott, mein Herr, Mezzulla und alle Götter liefen mir (helfend im Kampfe) voraus. Ich nahm Aripsa und Dukamma im Kampfe ein."

[55] *KAI*, Nr. 202, *TUAT* I/6, 627.

[56] *KAI* II 168-167, *TUAT* I/6, 648f. Vgl auch Z. 11f.: "Ich bekämpfte die Stadt (sc. Ataroth), nahm sie ein und tötete die ganze Bevölkerung der Stadt *als Schauspiel* für Kamosch und für Moab."

sind so etwas wie eine Haager Konvention, 20:15ff., wie unvergleich-
lich die Kategorien teilweise auch sein mögen, paßt zu den Darstellungen wie wir sie aus der Umwelt kennen.

Die Gottheit befiehlt den Angriff, führt und schützt den König im
Kampf. Die Rückkehr in den Tempel auf den ägyptischen Reliefs zeigt,
daß in Ägypten ihr der Sieg und die Beute gehören. Verfügen wir
ausnahmsweise über einen Text wie im Falle des Zakkur von Hamath,
in dem der belagerte König die Hauptperson ist, wird auch hier die
Rettung von der Gottheit verheißen, wie groß die Bedrohung auch sein
mag.

Die Behandlung der eroberten Städte ist vom wirtschaftlichen und
politischen Interesse des Königs abhängig. Feuer und Verwüstung
gehören zum Standardrepertoire genau wie die auf Abschreckung
bedachte, grausame Exekution der Anführer und/oder der kampffähigen
Männer, gelegentlich auch der ganzen Stadtbevölkerung. Manchmal
wird unterschieden zwischen denen, die sich aktiv am Aufstand beteiligt haben, und denen, die dies nicht gemacht haben. Deportation
zwecks Verstärkung der eigenen Armee oder für den Aufbau der
eigenen Bau- und Landwirtschaft ist in vielen Fällen erfolgt. Eine
Neubesiedlung der eroberten Stadt im Auftrag des Eroberes wird öfter
berichtet. Einige Male erwähnen die assyrischen Texte die Verwüstung
des ökologischen Umfeldes einer Stadt.

Abgesehen von der spezifischen Bannvorstellung, die nur in Moab
belegt ist, unterscheidet sich die Ideologie und die Durchführung von
Stadtbelagerungen und Stadteroberungen in der Umwelt kaum von der
Theorie und Praxis in Israel, wenn man sich der unterschiedlichen
Dimensionen und Regionen bewußt bleibt.

III

Kehren wir wieder zurück zum Alten Testament und zum Kriegsgesetz
Dtn 20.

Die Gründe, ein diachronisches Relief in Dtn 20:10-18 anzunehmen,
sind wohlbekannt und brauchen hier nur kurz erwähnt zu werden.
Dabei stellt sich aber heraus, daß es nicht so sehr die Gegensätze
zwischen 20:10-14 einerseits und 7:2; 13:13ff. anderseits, sondern
vielmehr die Übereinstimmungen zwischen den beiden letzten Texten
und 20:15ff. sind, die dazu zwingen für 20:15ff. eine spätere Entstehung anzunehmen.

1) Nach Seitz[57] widerspricht die geforderte Tötung der wehrfähigen Männer[58] nach Ablehnung des Kapitulationsangebotes in 20:13f. der Tendenz von Dtn 7. Denn die Formulierung Dtn 7:2 *hḥrm tḥrym* könnte als Befehl zum totalen Bann verstanden werden. Es bleibt aber festzuhalten, daß die Tötung von Frauen und Kindern sowie die Verbrennung der Beute 7:2 nicht ausdrücklich erwähnt wird. Die figura etymologica kann hier sehr wohl die Funktion haben, die Banntheologie an sich gegenüber dem nachfolgenden Verbot zur Bund-schließung und zur Verschwägerung zu betonen.[59]

2) Die Tötung der wehrfähigen Männer in 20:13f. stehe auch im Gegensatz zu 13:13ff. Denn anders als in 7:2 wird 13:16ff. nicht nur von den Einwohnern einer Stadt gesprochen, sondern auch von *w't-kl-'šr-bh w't-bhmth* sowie von der Beute, die verbrannt werden soll. Hier ist also expressis verbis vom totalen Bann die Rede. Aber hier läßt sich die Situation nicht mit 20:13f. vergleichen. Es handelt sich hier nicht um eine Kriegs- und Belagerungssituation, sondern um eine theoretische, innerisraelitische Angelegenheit, bei der eine ganze israelitische Stadt von JHWH abgefallen ist.

Dagegen sind die Verbindungen zwischen den beiden Texten und Dtn 20:15ff. nicht zu übersehen:

1) Dtn 7:2 *hḥrm tḥrym* // 20:17 *hḥrm tḥrymm*
2) Dtn 7:1 *hḥty whgrgšy wh'mry whkn'ny whprzy whḥwy whybwsy* //
Dtn 20:17 *hḥty wh'mry hkn'ny whprzy hḥwy whybwsy*

Sowohl 7:2 als 20:17 benutzen für das Banngebot die Formulierung mit dem Infinitiv als inneres Objekt vor der finiten Verbalform. 20:16 hat als vorangehende Parallelformulierung *l' tḥyh kl-nšmh*, während 7:2 nur ein einfaches *nkh* bietet. Damit betont 20:16f. den vollständigen Bann noch stärker als 7:2. Auffällig ist die Parallelie zwischen den beiden Völkerlisten. Die Reihenfolge ist gleich, 20:17 fehlen nur die Girgasiter, und die Völker sind paarweise verbunden durch zwei fehlende *waws* 7:1 gegenüber. Dtn 20:17 macht einen sekundären Eindruck durch die schon geschehene Zusammenfassung im Suffix bei *tḥrymm*.

---

[57] G. Seitz, *Redaktionsgeschichtliche Studien zum Deuteronomium* (BWANT 93; Stuttgart-Berlin-Köln-Mainz, 1971), 161.
[58] Seitz 1971, 159 u.ö spricht vom "kleinen Bann". Ein solcher Terminus verschleiert, daß in Dtn 20:10-14 *hrm* gar nicht vorkommt.
[59] Labuschagne *Deueronomium IB*, 106 weist zu Recht hin auf die theoretische Funktion des Bannbefehls. Würde der Bann angewendet werden, bräuchte es keine Verschwägerungsverbote mehr. Gerade dieser Widerspruch kann aber zu der betonten Formulierung geführt haben.

3) Auffälliger noch als die gleichlautenden Formulierungen ist die gemeinsame Begründung. Der Bann ist nicht Folge und Zweck der Kriegshandlung, sondern dient der Abwehr der Fremdgötterkulte. Er ist Mittel zum Zweck, nicht der Zweck selbst. Sowohl 7:25f. als 13:15 wird der Fremdgötterkult als *tw'bh* bezeichnet wie auch 20:18. Das damit Gemeinte aus 13:15 kommt näher an 20:18 heran als das Gold und Silber aus 7:25f.

Vor diesem Hintergrund treten nun die Unterschiede zwischen 20:10-14 und 20:15-18 umso deutlicher in Erscheinung. Dtn 20:10-14 setzt im Gegensatz zu Dtn 20:15-18 keine Landnahmesituation voraus. V. 14 redet allgemein von "deinen Feinden", V. 17 nennt die Feindvölker aus der Landnahmedarstellung. V. 14 beschreibt den Casus allgemein: "eine Stadt um gegen sie zu kämpfen", V. 16 dagegen nennt sie: "die Städte dieser Völker, die JHWH, dein Gott dir zum Erbteil geben wird". V. 13f. kennen nur die übliche Übergabeformel, V. 16 verbindet sie mit der Landnahme. V. 13 läßt nach dem Kampf nur die Tötung der männlichen Einwohner zu und nimmt V. 14 die Frauen, Kinder und das Vieh davon ausdrücklich aus. V. 16 dagegen verlangt "nichts, was Atem hat, am Leben zu lassen" und "sie vollständig mit dem Bann zu schlagen". Dtn 20:10-14 nennt keinen Anlaß und kein anderes Ziel als Gewinn von Beute und Arbeitskraft, Dtn 20:15-18 dagegen begründet den Bann mit der Abwehr der Fremdgötterkulte. V. 10-14 hat mit dem Bann nichts zu tun, V. 15-18 wird von der Bannvorstellung bestimmt. Diese Unterschiede werden von V. 15 dahingehend erklärt, daß V. 10-14 sich nur auf Städte bezieht, die "sehr weit entfernt" liegen, näher spezifiziert als die Städte, die nicht zu den Völkern von V. 16f. gehören.

Der Gegensatz zwischen 10-14 und 15-18 läßt sich auch noch an der *hrm*-Vorstellung[60] selbst zeigen. Die deuteronomistische Vorstellung im Rahmen der Landnahmetheorie geht davon aus, daß durch den *hrm* die Vorbewohner des Landes verschwunden sind. Der *hrm* bezieht sich immer auf alle Einwohner einer Stadt: Frauen, Männer und Kinder. Darüber hinaus werden in der Jericho-Erzählung Jos 6:21; 7:1 und in

---

[60] C.H.W. Brekelmans, *De Herem in het Oude Testament* (Nijmegen, 1959); G. Schmitt, *Du sollst keinen Frieden schließen mit den Bewohnern des Landes. Die Weisungen gegen die Kanaanäer in Israels Geschichte und Geschichtsschreibung* (BWANT 91; Stuttgart-Berlin-Köln-Mainz, 1970); M. Rose, *Der Ausschließlichkeitsanspruch Jahwes* (BWANT 106; Stuttgart-Berlin-Köln-Mainz, 1975), 112ff.; N. Lohfink, *hrm*, *TWAT* III, 1978, 192-213; N. Lohfink, "'Gewalt' als Thema alttestamentlicher Forschung", in: N. Lohfink (Hrsg.), *Gewalt und Gewaltlosigkeit im Alten Testament* (QD 96; Freiburg-Basel-Wien, 1983), 15-50; G. Braulik, *Deuteronomium II* (NEB; Würzburg, 1992), 147ff.

der Saul-Erzählung 1 Sam 15:3 auch Vieh und Beute in die *ḥrm*-Weihe einbezogen. In der Ai-Erzählung Jos 8:21ff. bedarf es eines besonderen JHWH-Wortes, Jos 8:2, damit Vieh und Beute Israel zufällt. Alle anderen deuteronomistischen Darstellungen[61] gehen davon aus, daß sämtliche Einwohner getötet werden, Vieh und Beute aber Israel gehört. Die Vorstellungen schwanken also in Blick auf Vieh und Beute, nie auf die Radikalität der Tötung der gesamten Einwohnerschaft. Damit fällt Dtn 20:10-14 mit seiner Beschränkung auf die wehrfähigen Männer definitiv aus dem Kreis der *ḥrm*-Vorstellungen heraus. Schließlich muß bedacht werden, daß V. 10-14 ein Kapitulationsangebot beinhaltet. Wir haben schon gesehen, daß auch in der Umwelt Theorie und Praxis weit auseinander klaffen können und daß weder in den ägyptischen noch in den mesopotamischen Texten im Rahmen der Ideologie für ein solches Angebot ein offizieller Platz eingeräumt werden kann. Trotzdem wird es in der Praxis öfter zu solchen Verhandlungen gekommen sein. In den alttestamentlichen Texten gilt, daß Kapitulationsangebot und *ḥrm*-Vorstellung sich gegenseitig ausschließen. Deswegen erscheint der Bann nicht in 20:10-14 und dort wo der Bann herrscht, gibt es keinen Verhandlungsspielraum.

Die Brücke zwischen den beiden Teilen wird von V. 15 gebildet. Labuschagne rechnet ihn aufgrund seiner logotechnischen Analyse zu V. 10ff.[62] Die Struktur der Verse scheint aber dagegen zu sprechen. Braulik hat auf den gleichlautenden Beginn von V. 10 und V. 19 sowie auf die chiastische Verbindung zwischen V. 12a und 20b; 12b und 19a und auf die sachliche Zusammenbindung von *'kl šll 'ybk* (V. 14) mit V. 19b, 20a hingewiesen.[63] Das spricht für eine ursprüngliche Verbindung von 20:10-14 mit 20:19-20 ohne 15-18. Außerdem bringt V. 15 nicht nur den regionalen Unterschied, sondern wechselt auch von *'ybym* zu *hgwym-h'lh*, die V. 16 wieder aufgenommen und V. 17 listenmäßig erfaßt werden. Damit ist auch V. 15-18 eine strukturelle Einheit.[64]

Dtn 20:10-14.19-20 sind also zunächst für sich zu nehmen. Das Kriegsgesetz spiegelt einen normalen Vorgang wider. Es ist nicht einmal besonders human, wie immer betont wird, sondern eher pragmatisch. Die Annahme eines Verhandlungsangebotes bringt Tribut und Herrendienst ohne eine ermüdende und verlustreiche Belagerung. Wird

---

[61] Dtn 2:34f.; 3:4-7; Jos 10:28ff.; 11:11,14
[62] Labuschagne 1990, 159, 161, 164, Anhang 46.
[63] G. Braulik, *Die deuteronomischen Gesetze und der Dekalog. Studien zum Aufbau von Deuteronomium 12-26* (SBS 145; Stuttgart, 1991), 68.
[64] Labuschagne 1990, 161 ist rechtzugeben, daß der Plural V. 18 eine Signalfunktion hat.

die Belagerung doch nötig, weil der Feind sich wehrt, ist danach nur die kämpfende Truppe auszuschalten, Stadt, Bewohner und Beute gehören dem Angreifer. Das Verbot, das ökologische Umfeld zu zerstören, wirkt letztendlich auch zum Vorteil des Angreifers. Gewinnt er die Stadt, so sind die Infrastruktur und die Versorgungsmöglichkeit intakt geblieben, ein nicht unbeträchtlicher Vorteil für die Tributerhebung.

In welcher Zeit kann ein solches Gesetz entstanden sein? Die Frage wird meistens mit einem Verweis in die Josiazeit beantwortet.[65] Dort sei die Politik des Königs als Emanzipation und Annexion zu beschreiben. Zum ersten Mal greife ein judäischer König in der assyrischen Zeit wieder über die Grenzen Judas hinaus. Oder mit den Worten Donners: "Er legte seine Hand, wahrscheinlich nicht einmal mit militärischen Mitteln, auf die praktisch herrenlos gewordene Provinz Samerīna ... In seinem letzten Regierungs- und Lebensjahr operierte Josia, wenn auch nur aus gegebenem Anlaß, sogar auf dem Boden der Provinz Magiddū. Es ist nicht auszudenken, wohin das noch hätte führen können, wenn dem Leben des Königs nicht im Jahre 609 bei Megiddo ein plötzliches und gewaltsames Ende bereit worden wäre."[66] Dieses Bild des expansionistischen Josias muß aber um einiges reduziert werden. Denn die Beweislage für eine solche Rekonstruktion ist dürftig. Die Reformtätigkeiten Josias außerhalb Judas sind nur in zwei angehängten Teilen[67] von deuteronomistischen Händen nachgetragen.[68] Und die Fortsetzung des Reformberichtes 2 Kön 23:2-4 belegt, daß Josias Aktion gegen Totenbeschwörer und Wahrsager, gegen Teraphim und Götzen nur in Jerusalem und Juda stattfindet. Weiter kann die These einer politischen Annektion Samarias sich nicht auf einen direkten Bericht stützen. Sie kommt durch eine Rekonstruktion der Gaue unter Josia nach dem einflußreichen Aufsatz Alts[69] zustande. Durch eine Verbindung von Jos 15:45 (Gau 5).61b.62a (Gau 12) mit Jos 18:21b-24a; 19:41-46 wird eine außerjudäische Lokalisierung der beiden Gaue erreicht,[70] die dann mit der postulierten Annexion Josias erklärt wird.[71] Wenn aber die Annexion der Nord- und Westgebiete selbst zur Disposition steht, liegt hier ein Zirkelschluß vor.

---

[65] Schmitt 1970, 138 und viele andere.

[66] H. Donner, *Geschichte des Volkes Israel und seiner Nachbarn in Grundzügen* (GAT 4/2; Göttingen, 1986), 348.

[67] 2 Kön 23:15ff.,19f.

[68] Vgl. H. Spieckermann, *Juda unter Assur in der Sargonidenzeit* (FRLANT 129; Göttingen, 1982), 112ff.

[69] A. Alt, "Judas Gaue unter Josia" *PJB* 21 (1925), 100-116 = *KS* II, 276-288.

[70] Für die Problematik: Spieckermann 1982, 24f.,150f.,A.268.

[71] Alt 1953,283.

Denn die generelle Datierung der Listen aus Jos 15 in die Josiazeit ist längst nicht mehr gesichert.[72] Auch die Aktion Josias bei Megiddo, die zu seinem Tod führte, braucht nicht unbedingt eine Herrschaft über die Nordprovinz zu bedeuten. Wenn die Expedition schon militärischen Charakter hatte,[73] dann muß sie doch eher als Zeichen militärischer Schwäche gedeutet werden. Denn eine Chance, Necho aufzuhalten, bestand für Josia im Falle militärischer Schwäche, wenn überhaupt, dann nur am Paß von Megiddo. Verfügte er dagegen über politische und militärische Stärke, so hätte er die Reise nach Megiddo unterlassen und z.B. von Gezer aus operieren können. Aber selbst dort in Megiddo ging Josia sang- und klanglos unter. Es scheint also eher das spätere Bild des Josia zu sein, das ihn grenzüberschreitend tätig sein läßt.

Trotzdem ist es geraten, für Dtn 20:10-14 in der vorexilischen Zeit zu bleiben. Die Zeit der rigiden Assur-Treue unter Manasse kommt dafür nicht in Frage. Bleibt zu fragen, ob ein Ansatz in der Hiskiazeit gefunden werden kann. Daß seine Regierungszeit auch ein Stück Hoffnung auf nationale Befreiung widerspiegelt, wird nicht zunichte gemacht durch das katastrophale Ende dieser Politik. Welche Anstöße werden hier sichtbar? Aus den ersten Aufstandsbewegungen nach dem Thronwechsel von Salmanassar V auf Sargon II (722) hält Hiskia sich heraus.[74] Die Folgen geben ihm recht. 720 reicht der Feldzug des Sargon II bis Rapihu, südwestlich von Gaza. Der Aufstand wird niedergeschlagen, 716 wird dort eine assyrische Kolonie eingerichtet. An der 713 einsetzenden Aufstandsbewegung, die den Feldzug des Sargons von 711 zur Folge hatte, hat Hiskia sich wohl beteiligt. Als aber der Kern des Aufstandsgebietes, Philistäa, in eine assyrische Provinz umgewandelt wurde, zog er sich rechtzeitig zurück und kam unbehelligt davon. Seine Stunde schlägt sechs Jahre später beim Thronwechsel Sargon/Sanherib. Hiskia organisiert die bis dann größte Koalition gegen Assyrien unter Beteiligung von Philistäa, Phönikien und den ostjordanischen Staaten mit Unterstützung von Ägypten. Das Ende kommt erst vier Jahre später mit dem Feldzug Sanheribs in 701. Die wiederholten Aufstandsbewegungen zeigen aber, daß sich die südwestliche Regio Palästinas kurz nach dem Fall des Nordreiches noch lange nicht mit der Assyrerherrschaft abgefunden hatte. Jedesmal, wenn die Gelegenheit günstig erschien, flammten die Aufstandsbewegungen auf. Und im

---

[72] Nach der Debatte aus den fünfziger Jahren (Aharoni, Kallai, Cross, Wright), die unterschiedliche höhere Datierungen befürworteten, scheint ein Vergleich mit Neh 3 eher in die Persische Zeit zu weisen.

[73] Vgl. P. Welten, *Die Königs-Stempel. Ein Beitrag zur Militärpolitik Judas unter Hiskia und Josia* (ADPV; Wiesbaden, 1969), 161ff.

[74] Jes 14:28-32.

Juda des Hiskia scheinen Kräfte vorhanden gewesen zu sein, die eine
führende Rolle zu übernehmen in der Lage waren. Daß Hiskia, vorsichtig taktierend im ersten Jahrzehnt, 705 zum Anführer einer Groß-
koalition werden konnte, die die ganze Landbrücke Palästinas umfaßte,
zeigt, daß es einen Boden gab für nationale Befreiung und Expansion.[75] Es ist nicht unwahrscheinlich, daß Teile der deuteronomischen
Gesetzgebung, u.a das Kriegsgesetz 20:10-14 in diesem Klima entstanden sind. Sicherheit ist über eine solche Ansetzung nicht zu be-
kommen. Wenn aber bei Josia fraglich ist, ob er sich, abgesehen von
seinem katastrophalen letzten Abenteuer, überhaupt außerhalb Judas
bewegt hat, dann scheint die Hiskiazeit vor 701 mit der großen internationalen Aktion zur zeitlichen Ansetzung von Dtn 20:10-14 durchaus
geeignet.

Dtn 20:15-20 gehört zu den späteren deuteronomistischen Bearbeitungen. Dtn 20:10-14 wird dann umgearbeitet und als programmatische
Rückschau für einen möglichen Neuanfang in ein Landnahmerahmen
hineingezwängt.

---

[75] Vielleicht darf hier auch die einsame Notiz untergebracht werden, Hiskia habe
Philistäa geschlagen (2 Kön 18:8).

THE USE OF DEUTERONOMY 32:39 IN MONOTHEISTIC CONTROVERSIES IN RABBINIC LITERATURE

J.T.A.G.M. VAN RUITEN

Rijksuniversiteit Groningen

The central theme of Deuteronomy can be stated in a single sentence: it is a call to the service of one God by an elect people centered around one sanctuary, through obedience to the law in the land which God has given.[1] The belief in the one God is the central issue in the theology of Deuteronomy. In later times, the monotheistic statements of Deuteronomy (especially Deut 4:35.39; 6:4; 7:9; 32:39) are used by the monotheistic religions of Late Antiquity, Judaism and Christianity, to support their argument against those who did not believe in one God. In this article we shall concentrate on one of the most important monotheistic texts of Deuteronomy, namely 32:39. Firstly, we study the form and meaning of Deut 32:39 in its literary context. Secondly, we examine the *Wirkungsgeschichte* of this text in rabbinic literature. Because of the abundance of the material we confine ourselves to those texts in which one can identify some sort of controversy about the belief in one God.

Deuteronomy 32:39 in Its Literary Context

As far as the belief in one God is concerned, Deuteronomy is not concerned with a theoretical monotheism, but rather gives a confession of faith. The monotheism of Deuteronomy emerged from the struggle against idolatry.[2] Moreover, the decline of Israel is attributed to the following of other gods.[3] The existence of other gods is not denied, however, only their power and significance for Israel. Deuteronomy stresses the incomparability of YHWH (e. g. 3:24; 4:7-8; 10:17) or the uniqueness of YHWH for *Israel* (e.g. 4:19; 5:6-7 [= Ex 20:2-3]. Israel

---

[1] A.D.H. Mayes, *Deuteronomy* (NCBC; Grand Rapids-London, 1979), 57-58. Compare: O. Kaiser, *Einleitung in das Alte Testament. Eine Einführung in ihre Ergebnisse und Probleme* (Gütersloh, 1984⁵) 136.

[2] C.J. Labuschagne, *The Incomparability of Yahweh in the Old Testament* (POS 5; Leiden, 1966), 72.

[3] M. Hutter, "Das Werden des Monotheismus im alten Israel", in: E. Brox et al. (eds.), *Anfänge der Theologie. Fs. J.B. Bauer* (Graz, 1987) 36. In many places the following of other gods is condemned: Deut 5:7; 8:9-10; 13; 31:16; 31:17.

came to know YHWH as the God who interferes in history, who transcends the forces of nature and of other gods, and therefore this God demanded the exclusive worship of Israel. The recognition of his uniqueness and exclusiveness for Israel could only lead to the recognition of his absoluteness.

In Deut 32:39 one finds one of the affirmations of the absolute uniqueness of YHWH (compare: 4:35, 39; 6:4; 7:9). The text is part of the large poem Deut 32:1-43, which is commonly called *the Song of Moses*.[4] After the 'introduction' (v. 1-6: the loyalty of YHWH versus the disloyalty of Israel) the text continues with a looking back on the beginning of the relation between YHWH and Israel (v. 7-18). YHWH's mercy is outlined in connection with Israel's apostasy. The reaction of YHWH against Israel is one of judgment with a foreign nation as his instrument (v. 19-25). However, the judgment is being restrained and changes into a complaint against Israel's enemies (v. 26-36), that results in revenge and recompense (v. 37-42). The text ends with a call to joy because of the judgement (v. 43).

Deut 32:37-42 is the third speech of YHWH in the Song of Moses,[5] introduced by ויאמר.[6] The nations are probably the addressees, alt-

---

[4] For an analysis of Deut 32:1-43 see C.J. Labuschagne, "The Song of Moses. Its Framework and Structure", in: I.H. Eybers et al., *De Fructu Oris Sui. Festschrift A. van Selms* (POS 9; Leiden, 1971), 85-98. See also O. Eissfeldt, *Das Lied Moses Deuteronomium 32 1-43 und das Lehrgedicht Asaphs Psalm 78 samt einer Analyse der Umgebung des Mose-Liedes* (BVSAW.PH 104/5; Berlin, 1958); W.F. Albright, "Some Remarks on the Song of Moses", *VT 9* (1959), 339-346; R. Meyer, "Die Bedeutung von Deuteronomium 32, 8f.43 (4Q) für die Auslegung des Moseliedes", in: A. Kuschke (ed.), *Verbannung und Heimkehr. Festschrift W. Rudolph* (Tübingen, 1961), 197-209; S. Carillo Alday, *El Cántico de Moisés (Dt 32)* (Madrid, 1970); St. Hidal, "Some Reflections on Deuteronomy 32", *ASTI* 11 (1978), 15ff; T. Trapp, *Dispute and Display. The Song of Moses in Deut 32:1-43*, Diss. Heidelberg 1980; M. Lana, "Deuteronomio e Angelologia alla Luce di una Variante Qumranica (4Q Dt 32,8)", *Henoch* 5 (1983), 179-205; P.-M. Bogaert, "Les trois rédactions conservées et la forme originale de l'envoi du Cantique de Moïse (Dt 32:43)", in: N. Lohfink (ed.), *Das Deuteronomium. Entstehung, Gestalt und Botschaft* (BETL 68; Leuven, 1985), 329-339; J. Luyten, "The Song of Moses (Dt 32:1-43)", in: Lohfink, *Das Deuteronomium*, 341-347; A. Reichert, "The Song of Moses (Dt. 32) and the Quest for Early Deuteronomic Psalmody", in: *Proceedings of the Ninth World Congress of Jewish Studies, Jerusalem, August 4-12, 1985* (Jerusalem, 1986), 53-60; J.C. de Moor, *The Rise of Yahwism. The Roots of Israelite Monotheism* (BETL 91; Leuven, 1990), 155-160.

[5] The first speech of YHWH begins in v. 20 (ויאמר), the second in v. 26 (אמרתי)

[6] Both LXX and Qumran reads YHWH as subject of the verb אמר in v. 37. The targumim on v. 37, however, have another subject: 'the nations of the world' (Neofiti 1; Fragment-Targums), 'the enemy' (Add. 27031). According to these targumim אלהימו in v. 37 refers therefore to the God of Israël! Targum Onkelos

hough it is not stated quite clearly. These verses continue the thought of YHWH's destruction of the enemies, described in v. 26-36, with the ironical questioning after the power of their gods in whom they have trusted.[7] The climax of the passage is v. 39:

ראו עתה כי אני אני הוא	aA	See now, that I, I, am He,
ואין אלהים עמדי	aB	and there is no god with me;
אני אמית ואחיה	bA'	I kill and make alive;
מחצתי ואני ארפא	bA"	I wound and I heal;
ואין מידי מציל	bB	and there is none that can deliver out of my hand.

We consider Deut 32:39 as a form of divine self-predication within a lyric self-praise.[8] Prosodically, the verse is made up out of two lines, a bicolon and a tricolon. The first line (v. 39a) contains four plus three stresses, the second line (v. 39b) three plus three plus three stresses.[9] Both lines are joined together by way of external parallelism. The first colon of the first line (v. 39aA), in which occurs the personal pronoun אני two times, is balanced by the first two cola of the second line (v. 39bA), in which the personal pronoun אני occurs also two times, one time in each colon. The second colon of the first line (v. 39aB) is balanced by the third colon of the second line (v. 39bB) in that in both cola the negative אין preceded by the copulativum ו occurs, as well as the suffix 1st sg m (v. 39aB: עמדי; v. 39bB: מידי).

In v. 39aA (כי אני אני הוא) the doubling of the personal pronoun אני is striking. Outside our text it occurs only in Is 43:11.25; 51:12 (each time with אנכי). The function of the doubling is probably one of stress

---

does not make explicit who is the subject of אמר in v. 37.

[7] Mayes, o.c., 392.

[8] M. Dijkstra, Gods voorstelling. Predikatieve expressie van zelfopenbaring in Oudoosterse teksten en Deutero-Jesaja (Dissertationes Neerlandicae, Series Theologica 2; Kampen, 1980), 40-41.

[9] As far as syntax is concerned it is not impossible to read v. 39a as a tricolon (two plus two plus three stresses). The object-clause starts with כי and exists out of two parts, the second part introduced by ו. If v. 39a is read as one colon (of four stresses), as we do, the syntactical unit of the object-clause is slightly neglected. However, the rhythmical pattern 2+2+3 followed by 3+3+3 is quite exceptional. Moreover, the first colon ('See now') would be unbalanced. For the prosodic theory of classical Hebrew, especially as far as rhythm and metrum is concerned, see H. van Grol, De versbouw in het klassieke Hebreeuws. I. Metriek (Amsterdam, 1986). Compare: L. Alonso Schökel, Das Alte Testament als literarisches Kunstwerk (Köln, 1971); J.C.L. Gibson, "Stress and Vocalic Change in Hebrew: A Diachronic Study", Journal of Linguistics 2 (1966), 35-56.

and contrast.[10] Therefore, the best translation of the phrase כי אני אני הוא would be: 'that I alone am He'. The phrase אני הוא does not occur on many places,[11] outside Deut 32:39 only in Deutero-Isaiah (41:4; 43:10.13; 46:4; 48:12).[12] In many cases הוא functions as demonstrative.[13] In Is 41:4; 43:10 אני הוא functions as derivation of and substitution for the phrase אני יהוה, in Is 43:13 as derivation of אני אל. Some consider the independent use of the phrase in Deut 32:39 and Is 48:12 as a special monotheistic revelation formula.[14] However, we should be reserved with this designation, because the phrase does not occur in many places, and is also used in polytheistic contexts.[15] Probably, also in Deut 32:39 we can take the phrase אני הוא as a substitution of the phrase אני יהוה. The meaning of the phrase is made explicit in the same verse. First, by the next colon in the same line 'and there is no god with me' (v. 39aB), and second by the cola with which Deut 32:39aA has external balance, namely v. 39bA: 'I kill and make alive; I wound and I heal'.

In the second colon of the first line (v. 39aB: 'and there is no god with me') אין functions as adverb. It expresses the non-existence of something or somebody. In this text it concerns the non-existence of a god in company (עמדי) of YHWH. On the basis of this colon alone it is difficult to decide if it is a claim for absoluteness of YHWH (i.e. the existence of other gods is being denied), or of incomparability of YHWH (i.e. the existence of other gods is not being denied, only their effectiveness is incomparable to that of YHWH).[16] However, the

---

[10] L. Köhler, *Deuterojesaja (Jes 40-55) stilkritisch untersucht* (BZAW 37; Giessen, 1923), 59; D. Michel, "Nur ich bin Jahwe. Erwägungen zur sogenannten Selbstvorstellungsformel", *Theologia Viatorum* 11 (1973), 150; H.-J. Fabry, art. הוא, *TWAT* II, 367; C. Brockelmann, *Hebräische Syntax* (Neukirchen, 1956), § 129b; GK § 133kl; Dijkstra, *o.c.*, 249-250.

[11] See R. Rendtorff, "Die Offenbarungsvorstellungen im Alten Israel", in: *Offenbarung als Geschichte*, 34; W. Zimmerli, "'Offenbarung' im Alten Testament. Ein Gespräch mit R. Rendtorff", *EvTh* 22 (1962), 21; J. Morgenstern, "Deutero-Isaiah's Terminology for 'universal God'", *JBL* 62 (1943), 273; N. Walker, "Concerning HU' and 'ANI HU'", *ZAW* 74 (1962), 205-206. For an evaluation of the different positions see Dijkstra, *o.c.*, 76-77.

[12] Compare also Ps 102:28 (אתה הוא).

[13] GK § 136a.

[14] C.R. North, *The Second Isaiah, Chapters XL-LV* (Oxford, 1964), 94; K. Elliger, *Deuterojesaja. I: Jesaja 40,1-45,7* (BKAT XI/1; Neukirchen, 1978), 124-125; H.-J. Fabry, *TWAT*, I, 367; H. Wildberger, "Der Monotheismus Deuterojesajas", in: H. Donner et al. (eds.), *Beiträge zur Alttestamentlichen Theologie. Festschrift für Walter Zimmerli zum 70. Geburtstag* (Göttingen, 1977), 527.

[15] Dijkstra, *o. c.*, 248.

[16] Labuschagne, *Incomparability*, 114, note 3, prefers the second opinion: 'There is no god like me'.

phrase 'and there is no god with me' (v. 39aB) has its balance in the third colon of the second line: 'and there is none that can deliver out of my hand' (v. 39bB). That is to say, the other gods are powerless. There may exist gods outside YHWH, they may accept offerings, they are powerless gods (v. 37-38), and with that actually 'no god' (v. 21). The incomparability of YHWH confessed in the first line (v. 39a) is strengthened by the *merismus*[17] of the first two cola of the second line (v. 39bA). The polar wordpairs חיה / מות (to kill; to make alive) and חצה / רפא (to wound; to heal) expresses the totality of this incomparability. There is no area in life where YHWH does not exercise his power. The phrase of the incomparability of YHWH becomes in fact a statement about his uniqueness.[18] It is the acknowledgement that YHWH is the only God. He has control over life and death, and no one can deliver out of his hand.[19]

The Use of Deuteronomy 32:39 in Rabbinic Literature

The text of Deut 32:39 is quoted on several places in rabbinic literature. The following texts can be pointed out:[20]

> bPes 68a; bSanh 91b; 104a; Mek, *bo'* 12; *Shirta* 4; *bahodesh Yitro* 5; MRS, 81; Sifre Deut 329; Midrash Tannaim Deut 32:39; Ex r 21:3; Lev r 18:5; Deut r 11:10; Eccl r 1:4,2-3; Gen Rabbati, 29; Eccl z 1:4; M Ps 95; SER, 130; PRE 34; 'Otiyot de Rabbi Aqiba, I:249; Mishnat Rabbi Eliezar, 94; Midrash Hadash, 175, Midrash Haggadol, *wa'era*, 138.

---

[17] J. Krasovec, *Der Merismus im Biblisch-Hebräischen und Nordwest-semitischen* (Bib Or 33; Rome, 1977); E. Noort, "JHWH und das Böse. Bemerkungen zu einer Verhältnisbestimmung", *OTS* 23 (1984), 121-122.

[18] Compare Labuschagne, *Incomparability*, 114: "The vindication of Yahweh's incomparable position with regard to the gods attests to His uniqueness, and the obvious conclusion to be drawn from His Incomparability is His 'singleness'." Elsewhere in Deut 32, however, the author speeks freely about other gods. See especially the original text of v. 8 and v. 43 ('sons of god' in stead of 'sons of Israel'; compare LXX and Qumran). In Deut 32:8 it is described how Elyon divided the nations under his sons, giving Jacob/Israel to YHWH (v. 9). According to De Moor, *o. c.*, 156-157 the song of Moses shows the features of a text in transition from polytheism to the recognition of one god above all others.

[19] Deut 32:39 is firmly embedded in the context. The rhetorical question of v. 37 ('Where are their gods') gets an answer in v. 39aB ('and there is no god beside me'), whereas the rhetorical invitation v. 38b ('Let them rise up and help you') is proved powerless in v. 39bB ('and there is none that can deliver out of my hand'). Moreover, compare 'in my hand' (v. 39bB) with 'refuge' (v. 37b) and 'protection' (v. 38b).

[20] We made use of A. Hyman, תורה הכתבה והמסורה. *A Reference Book of the Scriptural Passages Quoted in Talmudic, Midrashic and Early Rabbinic Literature. Second Edition Revised by his Son A.B. Hyman*, I-III (Tel Aviv, 1979), for the collection of the loci in rabbinic literature. In addition to this we made use of indices and notes in editions and translations of rabbinic works.

In most texts in which Deut 32:39 is quoted doctrinal concerns can be observed. Different parts of Deut 32:39 are used as prooftext against some five different heresies. The first part of the verse (v. 39a) is used: 1. against those who believe in no power in heaven (Sifre Deut 329); 2. against those who believe in two powers in heaven (Sifre Deut 329; Mek, *Shirta* 4; *bahodesh Yitro* 5; MRS, 81; Midrash Tannaim on Deut 32:39; SER, 130); 3. and against those who believe that God does not interfere in human affairs (Sifre Deut 329). The second part of the verse (v. 39bA) is quoted against those who do not believe in the resurrection and the world to come (Sifre Deut 329; bPes 68a; bSanh 91b; Midrash Tannaim Deut 32:39; Ex r 21:3; Eccl r 1:4,2-3; SER, 130). Finally, the last part of the verse (v. 39bB) is quoted against those who believe in the merits of the fathers (Sifre Deut 32:39).[21]

In this article we confine ourselves to those texts in which there is some sort of polemic concerning the belief in God: Mek, *bahodesh Yitro* 5 (parallels in Mek, *Shirta* 4 and MRS, 81) and Sifre Deut 329. In the first place we shall go into the content of the pericope of the texts in which Deut 32:39 is quoted. Attention will be paid to the biblical texts quoted, especially to Deut 32:39. In the second place, we shall try to identify the heresies with actual groups in Late Antiquity.

Mekilta de Rabbi Yisma'el, bahodesh Yitro 5

Three texts in rabbinic literature in which Deut 32:39 is quoted in a monotheistic context are very much parallel to each other. Two texts are found in Mek, namely in *Shirta* 4, an explanation related to Ex 15:3-4, and in *bahodesh Yitro* 5, an explanation related to Ex 20:2. The third text is found in MRS, 81, an explanation related to Ex 15:3.[22] We confine ourselves to the text in Mek, *bahodesh Yitro* 5, because it is the most elaborated one:[23]

---

[21] It is the view of R. Aqiba that a father 'merits' certain blessings for his son. See mishna Edduyyot 2:9. Compare Tosefta ySanh 10:1 (27d); mishna Abot 2:2; yBer 4:1 (7d); bBer 27b; bSota 10b; Gen r 55:8; Ex r 44:3, 7; Lev r 36:3, 5; Deut r 3:15; Eccl r 10:9,1; Song r 1:14. For the concept of the merit of the fathers see A. Marmorstein, *The Doctrine of Merits in Old Rabbinic Literature and the Old Rabbinic Doctrine of God*, I-II (New York, 1968), 38; E.E. Urbach, *The Sages - Their Concepts and Beliefs* (English Translation) (Jerusalem, 1975), 499-501.

[22] A parallel is also found in Pesikta Rabbati 21, 100b. However, Deut 32:39 is not quoted there.

[23] A critical edition of the text can be found in H.S. Horovitz - I.A. Rabin, *Mechilta de Rabbi Ismael cum variis lectionibus et adnotationibus* (Frankfurt a. M., 1931 [reprint Jerusalem 1960]), 219-220. See also J. Z. Lauterbach, *Mekilta de Rabbi Ishmael. A Critical Edition on the Basis of the Manuscripts and Early Editions with an English Translation - Introduction and Notes*, II (Philadelphia,

'I am YHWH your God' (Ex 20:2). Why is this said? For He was revealed at the sea as a mighty hero making war, as it is said: *'YHWH is a man of war'* (Ex 15:3), and He was revealed at Sinai as an old man full of mercy, as it is said: *'And they saw the God of Israel etc.'* (Ex 24:10). And for the time when they were redeemed, what does it say? *'Like the very heaven for clearness'* (Ex 24:10). And it says: *'As I looked, thrones were placed'* (Dan 7:9). And it says: *'A stream of fire issued and came forth from before him etc.'* (Dan 7:10)

Scripture does not give the nations of the world an opportunity for saying that there are two powers; but (it declares): *'I am YHWH your God'* (Ex 20:2). I was in Egypt, I was at the sea. I was at Sinai. I was in the past, I will be in the future to come. I am in this world, I am in the world to come, as it is said: *'See now that I, even I, am He etc.'* (Deut 32:39). And it says: *'Even to old age I am He'* (Is 46:4). And it says: *'Thus says YHWH, the King of Israel and his Redeemer, YHWH of hosts: I am the first and I am the last'* (Is 44:6). And it says: *'Who has performed and done this, calling the generations from the beginning? I, YHWH, the first, and with the last, I am He.'* (Is 41:4)

The unity of God is the central issue in this midrash.[24] The text is introduced with the question: 'Why is this said?' related to the text of Ex 20:2. According to the author of the Midrash a problem is raised by the fact that Ex 20:2 gives two different designations for God: יהוה ('YHWH') and אלהיך ('your God'). Moreover, אלהיך ('your *God*') is a plural form. However, the text does speak in singular about God: 'I am YHWH your God, *who brought* you out of the land of Egypt' (אנכי ... אשר הוצאתיך). Despite the two different designations and the plural form there are not two gods. God manifests himself in different situations in history in different ways, nevertheless He is one and the same God.

Scriptural quotations are used to describe the different manifestations of God (Ex 15:3; 24:10a; 24:10b; Dan 7:9, 10; Deut 32:39; Is 46:4; 44:6; 41:4). The first two quotations are Ex 15:3a and Ex 24:10a. In these biblical texts two different, even contrasting, manifestations of God can be seen. God can manifest himself as a mighty hero making war, but also as an old man, full of mercy. The text of Ex 15:3a, part

---

1933 [reprint 1976]), 231-232. According to J. Neusner (*A History of the Jews in Babylonia*, I [London, 1965], 179) the Mekilta de Rabbi Yismael was originally compiled on the basis of discussions between 135 and 150 C.E. According to Strack-Stemberger the final redaction took place in the second half of the third century (H.L. Strack - G. Stemberger, *Einleitung in Talmud und Midrasch* [München 1982[7]] 240). P. Schäfer, "Israel und die Völker der Welt. Zur Auslegung von Mekilta de Rabbi Yisma'el, bahodesh Yitro 5", *FJB* 4 (1976), 62, suggests even an earlier date, namely at the end of the second century C. E., whereas others argues for a much later date for the final redaction (B. Z. Wacholder, "The Date of the Mekilta de-Rabbi Ishmael", *HUCA* 39 [1968], 117-144).

[24] In the edition of Horovitz - Rabin this is the third paragraph of the fifth *parasha* of *bahodesh Yitro*. The fifth *parasha* consists of nine paragraphs. Schäfer, *o.c.*, 32-62, demonstrates the redactional unity and arrangement of the paragraphs.

of the song at the Red Sea, which remembers the deliverance out of Egypt, proves the first manifestation: 'YHWH is a man of war'. The text of Ex 24:10a ('And they saw the God of Israel') is used as proof-text for the second manifestation of God. The quotation of Ex 24:10a as a prooftext for the merciful manifestation of God is at first sight obscure. However, Ex 24:10 is in the first place part of the Sinai-story. In rabbinic tradition the image of an old sage who teaches is used to describe the giving of the Torah at Sinai.[25] In the second place, it must be noted that the second designation for God in Ex 20:2, i. e. 'God' ('the God of Israel') is used in Ex 24:10. In the third place, God's attribute of mercy can, indirectly, be found in Ex 24:10-11 itself. The attitude of God towards the elders of Israel shows his mercy.[26] Although the elders of Israel had looked upon God, 'He did not lay his hand on the chief man of the people of Israel' (Ex 24:11a). Although 'they saw God, they ate and drank' (Ex 24:11b). Elsewhere in Scripture it is stated that no man may see God and live (Ex 33:20: 'For no man shall see me and live'). In the fourth place, God's compassion can also be found in a rabbinic interpretation of Ex 24:10. The expression 'the brick-work of sapphire stone' which occurs in the same verse (Ex 24:10b), but which is not quoted in our midrash, refers in rabbinic tradition to the work in bricks in which the Israelites were engaged in Egypt. The compassion of God is showed by the fact that before they were redeemed, the brickwork was placed as a mark in heaven, under the throne of God[27] or under his feet.[28] In other texts the compassion of God is showed by the fact that the Shekinah was with the Israelites in their slavery. After Israel was redeemed from Egypt the brickwork was placed where the brick was generally kept and it was seen no more in heaven.[29] This gives an explanation for the obscure reference to Ex 24:10b in our midrash ('And as the very heaven for clearness'). The brightness of the heaven symbolises the end of the slavery, and the joy of God.

It is not clear why the text of this midrash is as obscure as it is here.

---

[25] Compare Pes r 21 (100b) ('as an old man'); *Midrash Haggadol. Exodus*, 295 ('an old man wrapped in his cloak').

[26] This is the opinion of J. Goldin, *The Song at the Sea. Being a Commentary on a Commentary in Two Parts* (New Haven, 1971), 127, and A.F. Segal, *Two Powers in Heaven. Early Rabbinic Reports about Christianity and Gnosticism* (Leiden, 1977), 38, n. 5, and 40.

[27] Targum Pseudo-Yonathan on Ex 24:9-10.

[28] Lev r 23:8. Compare ySuk 4:3 (54c), and Song r 4:8,1, with the same tradents. Close parallels can be found in PRE 48 (116a, b); Sifre Zuta Num 10:35 (267); Tanh B, *beshallah* 11.

[29] Mek, *Pisha Bo'* 14.

It could have been mistakenly reproduced from other passages.[30] However, it remains unclear then why the first part of the text in other passages ('Whenever Israel is enslaved the Shekinah, as it were, is enslaved with them') is missing here, and in the parallel text *Shirta* 4. One could simply suggests that the midrash of the brick-work of sapphire stone under God's throne as a symbol for the slavery in Egypt, and for the compassion of God with Israel was well-known. It was therefore not necessary to give the complete version of the midrash.[31] This suggestion is not really convincing since in other contemporary sources this particular midrash is quoted completely indeed. The best explanation is that by way of *homoioteleuton* this passage has fallen out. Originally *bahodesh Yitro* 5 contained the following passage after the quotation of Ex 24:10a ('And they saw the God of Israel etc.'): *Another interpretation of 'And they saw the God of Israel etc.' (Ex 24:10). Such was the view until they were redeemed,*[32] or simply: *Such was the view until they were redeemed.*

After the quotation of Ex 15:3 and Ex 24:10 two texts from the book of Daniel are used: '*As I looked, thrones were placed*' (Dan 7:9); '*A stream of fire issued and came forth from before him* etc.' (Dan 7:10). The point of the quotation of Dan 7:9-10 is, as Goldin[33] states rightly, that the verses of Daniel serve to demonstrate that it is one and the same God who appears in different aspects. The text of Dan 7:9 suggests that he is an old man (a merciful aspect), and in the following verse there is something fiery (a militant aspect). So this prooftext is on line with both Ex 15:3 and Ex 24:10.[34]

The unity of God is the central issue in every part of this midrash.

---

[30] So I. Lewy (*Ein Wort über die Mechilta des R. Simon* [Breslau, 1889], 9, n. 1); compare Horovitz - Rabin (*Mechilta*, 219, note on line 16), who agree with Lewy as far as the parallel passage *Shirta* 4 is concerned.

[31] So Schäfer, *o. c.*, 40.

[32] This is the explanation of Goldin (*o. c.*, 127) for the omission in the parallel text *Shirta* 4.

[33] Goldin, *o. c.*, 128.

[34] In other texts in rabbinic literature the text of Dan 7:9 is used to show the misconception that the belief in more gods is described by Daniel. The text states 'thrones (plural) were placed'. In bSanh 38b this text is used as a passage 'which the *minim* have taken as grounds for their heresy'. However, the talmud teaches also that 'their refutation is found near at hand', namely 'one that was ancient did sit' (singular) (Dan 7:9). Segal, *Two Powers*, 40, in his interpretation of *bahodesh Yitro* 5, states that in Dan 7:9 two thrones in heaven 'imply two different figures to fill them'. In his opinion this is a reference to the conception of the two powers in heaven. In this interpretation it remains unclear, however, why Dan 7:10 is quoted to make the point of the singular form, when the singular is so near at hand in Dan 7:9 ('one that was ancient did sit').

Those who say that Scripture itself teaches the doctrine of the two powers by quoting different passages from Scripture (Ex 15:3 against Ex 24:10; Dan 7:9 against Dan 7:10) are counteracted by the quotation of Ex 20:2 in which the different designations and the plural forms point to one and the same God. Also the second part of the midrash shows clearly that the singular forms of the sentence in Ex 20:2 are used as an argument against those who declare the existence of more than one God on the basis of the same and other texts from the Old Testament. Seven statements are made in which God is referred to by the personal pronoun 1st person singular ('I was in Egypt, I was at the sea. I was at Sinai. I was in the past, I will be in the future to come. I am in this world, I am in the world to come'),[35] and four texts are quoted at first sight to illustrate these statements: Deut 32:39; Is 46:4; Is 44:6; Is 41:4.[36]

The biblical texts quoted correspond to the seven statements in that the personal pronoun 1st singular (אני) is used seven times. In the quoted part of Deut 32:39 (כי אני אני הוא) it occurs twice, in Is 46:4 once (ועד זקנה אני הוא), in Is 44:6 twice (אני ראשון ואני אחרון), and in Is 41:4 again twice (אני יהוה ראשון ואת אחרנים אני הוא). Moreover, the texts quoted occur in a context of polemic against idolatry. In Deut 32:39 (ואין אלהים עמדי) and in Is 44:6 (ומבלעדי אין אלהים) it is explicitly quoted that there is no other god. These texts show that wherever 'I' is repeated twice in Scripture it refers to one God. Besides, the texts of Deut 32:39, Is 46:4 and Is 41:4 have the expression אני הוא ('I [am] He') in common.

A closer examination of the seven statements, however, shows that the first three of them are already proved in the first part of the midrash. Ex 20:2 is a prooftext of the first statement ('I was in Egypt'), Ex 15:3 of the second ('I was at the sea') and Ex 24:10 of the third ('I was at Sinai'). It is likely therefore that the four texts which follow the seven statements (Deut 32:39; Is 46:4; Is 44:6; Is 41:4) are used as prooftexts for the remaining four statements ('I was in the past, I will be in the future to come. I am in this world, I am in the world to come'). Four texts are used to prove four statements. The case is not,

---

[35] In the parallel texts (Mek, *Shirta* 4; MRS, 81) the 1st person singular is replaced by the 3rd person singular ('He was in Egypt etc.)

[36] For the importance of numerical sayings see A. Wünsche, "Die Zahlensprüche in Talmud und Midrasch", *ZDMG* 65 (1911), 57-100, 395-421; 66 (1912), 414-459; G. Nádor, "Some Numeral Categories in Ancient Rabbinical Literature: The Numbers Ten, Seven and four", *Acta Orientalia* 14 (1962), 301-315; W.S. Towner, *The Rabbinic 'Enumeration of Scriptural Examples'* (Leiden, 1973); K. -E. Grözinger, "Der Gesang in der Theologie der Rabbinen. Der Midrasch von den zehn Liedern", *FJB* 4 (1976), 81-99.

however, that one text proves one statement. It is our opinion that each
text here functions as a proof for the four statements all together. The
text of Is 44:6 ('*I am the first and I am the last*') and Is 41:4 ('*I,
YHWH, the first, and with the last, I am He*') contain the polar word-
pair ראשון ('first') and אחרון ('last'). The correspondence with the four
statements is evident. The word ראשון corresponds with 'the past' and
'this world', whereas אחרון corresponds with 'the future to come' and
'the world to come'. Also Is 46:3-4 contain a polar expression. In v. 3
it is stated that God was with Israel 'from the birth' and 'from the
womb'; in v. 4 God assures that he will be with them 'even to old age'
and 'until grey hairs'. So God was with Israel in the past, and he will
be with them in the future. Finally, also Deut 32:39 is used as prooftext. Anyhow, it is a proof for the last statement 'I am in the world to
come'. In rabbinic literature the phrase '*I kill and make alive*' (Deut
32:39bA') is one of four promises which contain an allusion to the
resurrection of the dead.[37] However, when the Isaianic texts quoted
function as prooftexts for all the four statements, one might suppose
the same function for Deut 32:39. Probably, the midrash interprets the
activity of killing as referring to the past and to this world, whereas the
activity of making alive refers to the future to come and to the world
to come. One can find a confirmation of this interpretation of Deut
32:39 in Targum Neofiti 1, which renders Deut 32:39bA' as follows:
'It is I who puts to death *in this world* the living and who makes alive
the dead *in the world to come*'.[38] There is still another possibility.
The midrash might be referring to a tradition of interpretation of Deut
32:39 which is found in the Targum of Pseudo-Yonathan.[39] The
Targum renders Deut 32:39aA as follows: 'See now that I am He *who
is* and *who was* and I am He *who will be*'.[40] We might assume that
the author of Mek, *bahodesh Yitro* 5, was acquainted with either one or
both tradition(s) of interpretation of Deut 32:39aA contained in the
targumim. The affinity of Deut 32:39 with the Isaianic texts quoted in
the midrash is most evident when we read Deut 32:39 with the targu-
mic renderings.

---

[37] The other texts are: Num 23:10; Deut 33:6; Hos 6:2. See Sifre Deut 329; bPes
68a; bSanh 91b; Midrash Tannaim Deut 32:39; Ex r 21:3; Eccl r 1:4,2-3; SER, 130.
[38] See: R. Le Déaut, *Targum du Pentateuque. Traduction des deux recensions
palestiniennes complètes. Tome IV. Deutéronome* (Paris, 1980), 276. Compare also
the Fragment-Targum of the Pentateuch (MS Vatican Ebr. 440).
[39] We find this tradition also in the Palestinian Targum contained in the
manuscript Add. 27031 of the British Museum. See Le Déaut, *o.c.*, 277.
[40] The Aramaic of Targum Pseudo-Yonathan reads as follows אנה הוא דהוי והוית
ואנה הוא דעתיד למהוי. See M. McNamara, *The New Testament and the Palestinian
Targum to the Pentateuch* (AnBib 27; Rome, 1967), 111.

The prooftexts Deut 32:39; Is 46:4; Is 44:6; Is 41:4 are joined together with the other prooftexts (Ex 20:2; 15:3; 24:10) by the mentioning of the seven statements. The first three refer to the first part of the midrash, the last four to the second part. If this interpretation is correct the isolated position of Dan 7:9, 10 is striking. Possibly, it forms a later interpolation, due to the popularity of Dan 7:9 with regard to the belief in two gods.

The central theme of the midrash can be described as counteracting the belief in two gods. The midrash states that the biblical texts are quoted in order not to give the nations of the world an opportunity for saying that there are two powers. In the first part of the midrash texts are quoted which show different aspects of God, and which seem to contradict each other (Ex 15:3 against Ex 24:10; Dan 7:9 against Dan 7:10). This can result in the opinion that Scripture states that there is more than one God. However, Ex 20:2 and the last four texts (Deut 32:39; Is 46:4; Is 44:6; Is 41:4) are quoted to counteract this opinion. The text speaks of two different *attributes* of God: that of mercy and that of justice,[41] and not of two gods. It is striking that the formulation in our midrash is exactly the opposite of the standard rabbinic identification. Usually the attribute of mercy is connected with the name YHWH, and that of justice with the designation Elohim. YHWH is in our midrash, however, 'a man of war' and Elohim 'an old man full of mercy'. This specific formulation of the attributes of God helps to refute those who think that there are two divine principles instead of two attributes. By connecting an aspect of justice to YHWH, and an aspect of mercy to Elohim, the danger of isolating two divine principles is diminished.[42]

Different answers have been given to the question if the nations of the world (those who believe in two powers) denotes a specific group in history. According to some the text is a polemic against Christians,[43] according to others against certain Gnostic groups,[44] or the

---

[41] A thorough discussion about the attribute of mercy and of justice in Urbach, *o.c.*, 448-461.

[42] Urbach, *o.c.*, 451-452: 'The use of a Name that denotes one attribute does not annul the existence of the other. Both attributes are of equal importance'.

[43] So R.T. Herford, *Christianity in Talmud und Midrash* (London, 1903 [reprint New York-London, 1966]), 301; M. Goldstein, *Jesus in the Jewish Tradition* (New York, 1950), 86; K. Hruby, *Die Stellung der jüdischen Gesetzeslehrer zur werdenden Kirche* (Zürich, 1971), 59 ff.

[44] A. Marmorstein, "The Unity of God in Rabbinic Literature", *HUCA* 1 (1924), 489; K. Rudolph, "Randerscheinungen des Judentums und das Problem der Entstehung der Gnosis", in: *Gnosis und Gnostizismus* (Darmstad, 1975), 786; Segal, *Two Powers*, 57-59; A.N. Dahl - A.F. Segal, "Philo and the Rabbis on the Names of

pagan-hellenistic world in general.[45] According to Segal the situation is very complex. The conception of the 'two powers in heaven' goes back to early hellenistic Judaism, which was acquainted with the doctrine of the *logos* and with the idea of a mediator of creation. Philo used the term 'second god' to describe the *logos*.[46] In rabbinic literature it may once have designated a specific group of sectarians (e. g. Christianity, Gnosticism, Jewish apocalyptic and mystical groups), but it appears to have become a stock characterization of heresy toward the end of the tannaitic period. It was understood as a title for all binitarian or dualistic heresies and no longer referred to one particular sect.[47]

To this we can add that the character of our text is less polemic than has been suggested. The midrash is part of a great redactional unity, i.e. *bahodesh Yitro* 5. The theme of this redactional unit of nine midrashim is the relationship of Israel and the nations of the world, as regards the Tora and the Revelation at Sinai. The third paragraph (the text under consideration) is concerned with the most important aspect of the Revelation, the belief in one God. The tone of the whole text of *bahodesh Yitro* 5 is much more apologetic than polemic.[48]

Sifre Deuteronomy 329 (on Deut 32:39)[49]

'*See now that I, I, am he*' (Deut 32:39aA). This is a response to those who say there is no power in heaven. He who says there are two powers in heaven is answered: "Has it not yet been written: '*And there is no god beside me*'" (Deut 32:39aB). And similarly (for one who says) he has not the strength to kill nor to revive, (he has not the strength) to do evil nor to make good, Scripture says: '*See now that I, I, am he ... I kill and make alive*' (Deut 32:39aA, bA'). And also: '*Thus says YHWH, the King of Israel and his Redeemer, YHWH of hosts: I am the first and I am the last; besides me there is no god*' (Is 44:6).

God", *JSJ* 9 (1978), 16ff.

[45] Schäfer, *o.c.*, 60-61. Schäfer is possibly right in saying that the opponents are not the Christians, Gnostics or pagans themselves, but Jews who were influenced by one system or another.

[46] E.g. Philo, *Quaestiones et Solutiones in Genesis* 2:62; cf. Segal, *o.c.*, 159-181.

[47] Segal, *o.c.*, 153-154. Compare J. Maier, *Jüdische Auseinandersetzung mit dem Christentum in der Antike* (EdF 177; Darmstadt, 1982), 166-169.

[48] The conceptions of these midrashim can be put between the extremes of particularism (the revelation is just for Israel) and universalism (the torah is for all the nations). The text of *bahodesh Yitro* 5 gives several possible answers to the question as to the relation of Israel and the nations in connection with the revelation on Sinai. Compare Schäfer, *o.c.* 59.

[49] L. Finkelstein, *Siphre ad Deuteronomium H.S. Horovitzii schedis usuis cum variis lectionibus et adnotationibus* (Berlin, 1939 [reprint New York, 1969]), 379-380. Because Siphre is not homogeneous it is difficult to date the midrash. According to Strack - Stemberger (*o.c.*, 254) the final redaction took place at the end of the third century CE.

Another interpretation: '*I kill and make alive*' (Deut 32:39bA'). This is one of four promises which contain an allusion to the resurrection of the dead: '*I kill and make alive*' (Deut 32:39bA'); '*Let me die the death of the righteous*' (Num 23:10); '*Let Reuben live, and not die*' (Deut 33:6); '*After two days he will revive us*' (Hos 6:2). I might think that death was for one while life was for another. (Therefore) Scripture says: '*I wound and I heal*' (Deut 32:39bA''). Just as wounding and healing is for one (and the same), so is death and life for one (and the same).

'*And there is none that can deliver out of my hand*' (Deut 32:39bB). No father can deliver his sons. Abraham could not deliver Ishmael, and Isaac could not deliver Esau. From this I know only that fathers cannot deliver their sons. From where do I learn that brothers may not deliver their brothers? Scripture teaches: '*No man can ransom his brother*' (Ps 49:8). Isaac did not deliver Ishmael, Jacob did not deliver Esau. Even if a man were to give all the money in the world, it would not give him atonement, as it is said: '*No man can ransom his brother ... his ransom would cost too much ...*' (Ps 49:8-9). A soul is dear. When a man sins with it, there is no compensation.

The text of Sifre Deut 329 consists of three paragraphs. Each paragraph is linked up with a part of Deut 32:39. The first paragraph is connected especially with Deut 32:39a, and is concerned with the belief in one God. The thought of the paragraph is developed in three steps. Firstly, the writer of the midrash finds here a connection between v. 39 and the rhetorical question of v. 37. Those who say *in the text of Deuteronomy* 'Where is (are) their god(s)' are those who deny any power in heaven.[50] They are refuted by the presentation of the evidence. God himself answers those who deny his existence by saying '*See now that I, I, am he*' (Deut 32:39aA). Secondly, there may be others, continues the midrash, who believe in more powers in heaven, since אלהימו ('Their god[s]') in Deut 32:37 could be read as a plural, as if there were more gods. Moreover, the plural verbforms in Deut 32:38bA could refer to the gods in v. 37 indeed. Apparently, Deut 32:39aA seems to confirm that there are more powers, since the personal pronoun (אני: 'I') is repeated twice. But God corrects the impression that there might be two gods by saying: '*And there is no god beside me*' (Deut 32:39aB). This is confirmed in the Midrash by the quotation of Is 44:6. This text shows that wherever 'I' is repeated twice in Scripture ('*I am the first and I am the last*') it refers to one God ('*Besides me there is no God*'), He is the first, the last, and there is no other. Thirdly, Deut 32:39 is seen by the midrash as an answer to the ironical call in v. 38b ('*Let them rise up and help you, let them be your protection*'). The ironical call of v. 38b is made explicit in the

---

[50] Notice that for the author of Sifre Deut 329 it is not God who is the speaker in Deut 32:37 as is the case in MT and LXX. Compare note 6.

midrash ('He has not the strength to kill nor to revive, [he has not the strength] to do evil nor to make good'). These are those who do recognise a power in heaven, but who deny that it interferes in human affairs. They are refuted here by Deut 32:39bA. God is omnipotent, and he does interfer in the life of people.[51]

The second paragraph of *piska* 329 is not concerned with the belief in the one God. Its subject is the resurrection of the dead. It is linked up with Deut 32:39bA ('*I kill and make alive; I wound and I heal*'), which contains, according to the midrash, an allusion to the resurrection of the dead, like Num 23:10; Deut 33:6, and Hos 6:2. The second part of the paragraph opposes those who deny the resurrection of the dead on the basis of Deut 32:39bA. The passage might be interpreted in a way that God kills one person and gives life to another. But the passage goes on by saying: '*I wound and I heal*'. Just as the wounding and healing refer to the same person (healthy people need not be healed), so putting to death and bringing to life refer to the same person.[52] This interpretation of the phrase in Deut 32:39 is also found in bPes 68b and bSanh 91b.[53]

The third paragraph, finally, is linked up with Deut 32:39bB ('*And there is none that can deliver out of my hand*'). The midrash uses this

---

[51] The passage introduced by 'And similarly' (או כענין) until the quotation of Is 44:6, i. e. the third step of the first paragraph, is seen by R.T. Herford (*Christianity in Talmud and Midrash* [London, 1903], 299) and H.W. Basser (*Midrashic Interpretation of the Song of Moses* [American University Studies, Series VII Theology and Religion, Vol. 2; New York-Frankfurt a. M.-Bern, 1984], 241) as an interpolation. It is true that this passage interrupts the basic idea of the paragraph. The basic idea is concerned with the belief in one God, and Is 44:6 forms an appropriate conclusion.

[52] Segal, *Two Powers*, 86-87, interprets this text as a reference to a doctrine which is either dualistic or polytheistic. According to him Deut 32:39b proves that there are not two Powers in heaven, but only one. On p. 84 Segal translates this part of the text as follows: 'I might think that death was by one (power) while life was by another. Scripture teaches: '*I wound and I heal*' (Deut 32:39). Just as wounding and healing is by one (power), so is death and life by one (power alone)'. Although Segal's translation 'by one' for באחד is not impossible (ב can indicate who or what has caused an effect) it gives a very unlikely interpretation of the text. It does not explain why the verse proves that wounding and healing are done by one God, any more than it proves that killing and giving life are done by one God. Cfr. Basser, *o.c.*, 241-242.

[53] The text of bPes 68b reads: 'Our Rabbis taught: '*I kill and make alive*' (Deut 32:39). I might interpret, I kill one person and give life to another, as the world goes on: therefore Scripture teaches: '*I wound and I heal*' (Deut 32:39). Just as the wounding and healing refer to the same person, so putting to death and bringing to life refer to the same person. This refutes those who maintain that resurrection is not intimated in the Torah' (parallel in bSanh 91b). Compare Gen r 95:1; Eccl r 1:4,2.

phrase against those who claim that fathers can save their sons. This claim is possibly also based on contextual exegesis, as far as 'the rock in which they took refuge' (v. 37) is taken to refer to Abraham.[54] The second part of this paragraph shows that brothers cannot save one another by reference to Ps 49:8. This verse is explained as if it is referring to two pairs of brothers: Isaac and Ishmael, and Jacob and Esau. The last paragraph of this *piska* thus says that Ishmael and Esau cannot be saved by the merit of their fathers (Deut 32:39) nor by the merit of their brothers (Ps 49:8-9).

Sifre Deut 329 contains opposition against deviant views. According to some scholars Sifre Deut 329 is a polemic against certain Christian groups,[55] according to others against certain gnostic groups.[56] The exegesis of Deut 32:39 in Sifre Deut 329 contains a polemic background, but one should add immediately that this polemic does not concern only one view, but some distinguished heretical views.[57] The passage seems to be an anthology of arguments against various attitudes which the rabbis opposed, united by the use of the quotation from Deut 32:39. At least five types of heresies can be discerned, each heresy countered by a quotation from Deut 32:39: 1. those who say there is no power ('atheists'); 2. those who say there are two powers; 3. those who deny that God interferes in human affairs; 4. those who do not believe in the resurrection of the dead; 5. those who believe that an ancestor can save a son ('merit of the fathers') or a brother can save a brother.

Some different groups can be considered as candidates for these heresies. The first heresy ('atheism') is possibly directed against certain views among the pagan-Roman world, as will be shown below. As we have seen above, the doctrine of the two powers may once have designated a specific group of sectarians, but it appears to have become a stock characterization of heresy toward the end of the tannaitic period.[58] Another heresy, the *denial that God interferes in human affairs*, could be aimed at the Epicureans, who were probably members of the Sadducean group. According to Josephus the Epicureans deny providence, and assert that the world is without a ruler and provider.

---

[54] Compare Is 51:1-2. See Basser, *o.c.*, 242-244.

[55] Herford, *o.c.*, 289-290; A. Büchler, "Über die Minim von Sepphoris und Tiberias im zweiten und dritten Jahrhundert", in: *Judaica. Festschrift H. Cohen* (Berlin, 1912), 289-290; Goldstein, *o.c.*, 86-87; Hruby, *o.c.*, 60.

[56] Marmorstein, *o.c.* 488.

[57] So rightly Segal, *o.c.*, 89.

[58] See note 47.

They deny God's involvement in the affairs of men and the world.[59] Well-known is the attribution of the *denial of the resurrection* to the Sadducees. According to Josephus the Sadducees did not accept either the immortality of the soul or the idea of reward and punishment after death.[60] Also in rabbinic literature the denial of the resurrection is attributed to the Sadducees.[61] However, also other groups are condemned by the rabbis because they deny the resurrection. According to R. Simeon ben Elazar in Sifre Num 112 the books of the Samaritans are wrong because they say 'the dead will not resurrect',[62] and according to bSanh 90b-91 the denial of the resurrection is attributed also to the *minim*. Finally, the belief in the *merit of the fathers* is rooted deeply in rabbinic Judaism.[63] Opposition against abuse of the conception of the merit of the fathers is found, outside Sifre Deut 329, also elsewhere in rabbinic literature.[64]

The author of Sifre 329 himself seems not to be interested in identifying one group or another with the heretical views. The midrash is mainly concerned with the *exegesis* of Deut 32:39 in its literary context. Therefore, vague indications as 'those who say' (אומרים) and 'he who says' (האמר) should not be interpreted primarily as referring to extra-textual groups or persons, but as referring to the text of Deut 32. It is probable that 'those who say' and 'he who says' refer to the subject of אמר in Deut 32:37.[65] However, the context of the midrash

---

[59] Josephus, *Antiquitates Judaicae*, X, 9,7 (277-278).

[60] Josephus, *Antiquitates Judaicae*, XVIII, 1,4 (16); *Bellum Judaicum* II, 8,14 (164-165). Compare: Hippolytus, *Refutatio Omnium Haeresium* IX, 29:1-2; Matt 22:23; Mc 12:18; Luc 20:27; Acts 23:8.

[61] According to most interpreters the first statement in mishna Sanh 10:1 ('the one who says there is no resurrection of the dead') is referring to the Sadducees. See L.H. Schiffman, *Who Was a Jew. Rabbinic and Halakhic Perspectives on the Jewish-Christian Schism* (Hoboken, NJ, 1985), 42; H. Sysling, *Techiyyat Ha-Metim. De opstanding van de doden in de Palestijnse Targumim op de Pentateuch en de overeenkomstige tradities in de klassieke rabbijnse bronnen* (Zutphen, 1991), 126-128. Compare: J.H. Maier, *Jesus von Nazareth in der talmudischen Überlieferung* (EdF 82; Darmstadt, 1978), 51-62.

[62] It is not likely that the Samaritans themselves denied the resurrection. See their interpretation of Gen 3:19 and Deut 32:39 in *Hilluk* 10, *Mimar Marqa* 4:12, and *Malef* 190. Probably the rabbis meant that according to the Samaritans the resurrection cannot be derived *from the Tora*. Compare bSanh 90b. See: R. Bóid, "Use, Authority and Exegesis of Mikra in the Samaritan Tradition", in: M. Mulder - H. Sysling (eds.), *Mikra* (Compendia II.1; Assen-Maastricht-Philadelphia, 1988), 608-609; Sysling, *o.c.*, 76-78.

[63] See note 21.

[64] See bSanh 104a; Mek, *pisha* V (16); *beshallah* 4 (98); Midrash Tannaim, 62; M Ps 46:1; 146:2; ARN B 27 (54). Compare 4 Ezra 7:102-105; Pseudo Philo's *Liber Antiquitatum Biblicarum* 33:4-5.

[65] In MT an explicit subject of the verb אמר is lacking. See note 6.

suggests some sort of actualisation of the heresies mentioned in Sifre Deut 329. For in the preceding *piska'ot* v. 37-38 is put into the mouth of the 'the Nations of the World' (*piska* 327) by R. Nehemiah, and of 'evil Titus, the son of Vespasian's wife' (*piska* 328). Titus "entered the Holy of Holies and slashed two curtains with a sword and said: 'If He be God let Him come (אם אם אלוה הוא יבוא) and oppose this'." *Piska* 328 ends with the words: 'The Holy One, Blessed be He, is forgiving towards everything. He exacts immediate punishment for the desecration of His name'. The beginning of Deut 32:39aA ('*See, now*') proves that the punishment of God is executed immediately. Since R. Nehemia proposes in Sifre Deut 327-328 'the nations of the world', i. e. Titus, as subject of אמר, it is possible to regard Sifre Deut 329 as a polemic against different views among the pagan-Roman world.

In Jewish literature the Roman Empire is denoted by the name Esau. For the first time it is found in 4 Ezra 6:7-10 (end first century C.E.). In rabbinic literature this denotation leads to a detailed explanation and actualisation of the Jacob-Esau story. In bBaba Batra 16b, Ex r 1:1 and Tanh Ex 1 'the rejection of the fundamental principle of religion' and 'the denial of the resurrection' are two of the five sins of Esau.[66] The rejection of the fundamental principle of religion (כופר בעיקר) is a *terminus technicus* for different kinds of blasphemy. It has a connotation of the denial of God, of the belief in more than one god, and of the denying that God takes notice of man.[67] In Sifre Deut 329 the term כופר בעיקר is not used. However, the heresies of the denial of God, of the belief in more than one god, and of the denying that God takes notice of man[68] are mentioned indeed. Moreover, also the denial of the resurrection is mentioned in Sifre Deut 329. This means that four of the five heresies in our midrash could be attributed to Esau (= Rome). The fifth heresy ('the belief in the merit of the fathers') is not attributed to Esau; it is, however, the name of Esau which is mentioned two times in the third paragraph. Esau could not be delivered by his father Isaac nor by his brother Jacob (= Israel).

Conclusion

In this article we studied the form and function of Deut 32:39 in its

---

[66] The others are 'seduction of a betrothed maiden', 'killing of a man' and 'despising his birthright'.

[67] M. Hadas-Lebel, "Jacob et Esaü ou Israël et Rome dans le Talmud et le Midrash", *Revue de l'histoire des religions* 201 (1984), 374. Compare Sysling, *o. c.*, 108-109.

[68] Urbach, *o. c.*, 26-30.

literary context. The verse is well embedded in its context (especially v. 37-39) and expresses the totality of the incomparability of YHWH. There is no area in life where YHWH does not exercise his power. The phrase of the incomparability of YHWH attests to his uniqueness. The verse does not contain a statement about the resurrection of the dead. Subsequently we studied the *Wirkungsgeschichte* of Deut 32:39 in rabbinic literature. Because of the abundance of the material we confined ourselves to those texts in which one can identify some sort of controversy about the belief in one god. In two texts Deut 32:39 plays a part in the controversy about monotheism: in Mek, *bahodesh Yitro* 5 (parallels in Mek, *Shirta* 4, and MRS, p. 81) and in Siphre Deut 329. In Mek, *bahodesh Yitro* 5 Deut 32:39 functions as prooftext that there are not two gods. Only one God exists in the past and in the future, in this world and in the world to come. Sifre Deut 329 is an anthology of arguments against various attitudes which the rabbis opposed, united by the use of the quotation from Deut 32:39.

THE QUESTION OF 'DEUTERONOMIC' ELEMENTS
IN GENESIS TO NUMBERS

MARC VERVENNE

Leuven

In a superb essay written in 1978, Prof. C.J. Labuschagne briefly
developed his ideas about the origin of the books Genesis to Kings.[1]
The literary development of this Hebrew composition is divided into
four main stages, i.e. the Yahwistic History (10-9th century B.C.E.),
the *proto-deuteronomic reworking* of J (end of the 8th century B.C.E.)
as well as the *deuteronomistic revisions* of this new synthesis (7th
century B.C.E. and later), and the Priestly final redaction (7th-2nd
century B.C.E.). With respect to the 'deuteronomic' elements in
Genesis to Numbers, Labuschagne maintains that the distinction
between proto-dt and dtr parts remains a difficult problem to solve.[2]
To this we may add a remark made by Peter Weimar in his 1985 study
of the Sea Narrative: "Die Probleme der Redaktionsgeschichte des
deuteronomistischen Werkes sind erst in jüngerer Zeit wiederum
stärker in Fluß gekommen (...) Ist dabei immer deutlicher die Mehr-
schichtigkeit des deuteronomistisches Werkes sichtbar geworden, so
fehlen im Rahmen des Pentateuch noch weitgehend entsprechende
Untersuchungen zu den als deuteronomistisch zu qualifizierenden
Texten, ganz abgesehen davon, daß das schwierige Problem der
Zuordnung der einzelnen Redaktionsschichten innerhalb des deuteronomistischen Werkes und des Pentateuch überhaupt noch nicht ernst-

---

[1] C.J. Labuschagne, *Gods oude plakboek. Visie op het Oude Testament* ('s-Gravenhage, 1978), 93-119. See also C.J. Labuschagne, "Redactie en theologie van het
boek Deuteronomium", *Vox Theologica* 43 (1973), 174.

[2] Labuschagne, *Gods oude plakboek*, 106: "Aangezien wij in de proto-deutero-
nomische bewerking te maken hebben met het begin van een hele serie bewerkin-
gen, en omdat de straks te bespreken heruitgave [= dtr re-edition] een voortzetting
is van deze eerste bewerking, is het moeilijk te zeggen wat proto-deuteronomisch,
en wat *deuteronomistisch* is, dat wil zeggen onder invloed staat van de schrijvers
van het boek Deuteronomium." In Labuschagne's view, texts such as Gen 20:1-17;
21:8-21; 22:1-18; Exod 3:1.4b.6b.10-15 are proto-dt, whereas Exod 19:3-8; 20:22-
24; 23:13-33; 24:3-8; 32-34; Num 12; 14; 22-24; 33:50-56 reveal dtr redactional
editing.

haft verfolgt worden ist."[3]

In line with these statements the present paper will deal with the question of 'deuteronomic' elements in the Pentateuch, and, more particularly, in the collection of texts contained in Genesis to Numbers (the so-called Tetrateuch). The main focus will be on some methodological issues, which I will try to clarify with reference to the Sea Narrative as found in Exod 13:17-14:31 (MT).

I. *Trends in Current Pentateuchal Studies*[4]

Present-day scholarly publications display a great diversity of literary approaches to the Pentateuch. In respect of methodology, it is sufficiently well known that one has to distinguish between studies directed to diachrony and those focusing on synchrony. Such a useful, if somewhat simplified, differentiation reveals that a 'diachronic' approach deals with the evolutionary phases of the Pentateuch, whereas a 'synchronic' one studies its final state,[5] disregarding the process of growth.[6]

---

[3] P. Weimar, *Die Meerwundererzählung. Eine redaktionskritische Analyse von Ex 13,17-14,31* (Ägypten und Altes Testament 9; Wiesbaden, 1985), 156, n. 24.

[4] Cf. C. Houtman, *Inleiding in de Pentateuch* (Kampen, 1980); Id. "The Pentateuch", in: A.S. van der Woude (ed.), *The World of the Bible, Bible Handbook* II (Grand Rapids, MI, 1989), 165-205; R.N. Whybray, *The Making of the Pentateuch. A Methodological Study* (JSOTS 53; Sheffield, 1987); A. de Pury - Th. Römer, "Le Pentateuque en question: position du problème et brève histoire de la recherche", in: A. de Pury (ed.), *Le Pentateuque en question. Les origines et la composition des cinq premiers livres de la Bible à la lumière des recherches récentes, Le monde de la Bible* (Genève, 1989), 9-80; J. Briend, "Lecture du Pentateuque et hypothèse documentaire", in: P. Haudebert (ed.), *Le Pentateuque. Débats et recherches. XIVe congrès de l'ACFEB (Angers, 1991)* (Lectio divina 151; Paris, 1992), 9-32; E.W. Nicholson, "The Pentateuch in Recent Research: A Time for Caution", in: J.A. Emerton (ed.), *Congress Volume. Leuven 1989* (SVT 43; Leiden, 1991), 10-21; W.H. Schmidt, "Elementare Erwägungen zur Quellenscheidung im Pentateuch", in: Emerton (ed.), 22-45; C. Levin, *Der Jahwist* (FRLANT 157; Göttingen, 1993), 9-35.

[5] According to E. Blum, "the" final form of the Pentateuch only exists as an hypothesis, since the Pentateuch does not have a homogeneous structural design but is a multi-dimensional composition in which a variety of intentions are generated. Consequently, diachronic clarifications only can prepare for an understanding of the final form. See, E. Blum, "Gibt es die Endgestalt des Pentateuch?", in Emerton (ed.), *Congress Volume. Leuven 1989*, 46-57.

[6] For a more articulated treatment of this classification, especially with regard to the Sea Narrative, see M. Vervenne, "The Sea Narrative Revisited", *Biblica* 74 (1993) (forthcoming). In this article, the methodology applied in four recent studies of the Sea Narrative is discussed: P. Weimar, *Die Meerwundererzählung* (1985, supra, n. 3); J.L. Ska, *Le passage de la Mer. Étude de la construction, du style et de la symbolique d'Ex 14,1-31* (AnBib 109; Rome, 1986); M. Vervenne, *Het*

Concentrating on the complex issue of the origins and literary history of the Pentateuch, it is obvious that ever since the appearance of R. Rendtorff's critical assessment of the established understanding of the 'Yahwist' as a theologian, Pentateuchal studies have been surging forward.[7] Following N. Lohfink, one could say that different hypotheses are generated by circular movements.[8] Current research obviously relies on classical approaches to the literary history of the Pentateuch, and, more particularly, makes use of well-known models, some of which had already been developed in the 18th century.[9] It seems to me that there are basically three models which, however, unfold variant types: (1) Source Critical model, to which a strong redaction-critical impetus is given (e.g., W.H. Schmidt); (2) Traditio-historical model (e.g., R. Rendtorff), of which the composition critical model is a variant (e.g., E. Blum); (3) Redaction Critical model, which displays a "documentary type" (e.g., P. Weimar), a "supplementary type" (e.g., J. Van Seters, S. Tengström, C. Levin), and a "fragmentary type" (e.g., C. Houtman, R.N. Whybray).

Recent criticism, then, questions the validity of the classical "Four Source Hypothesis" in general and its constituents in particular.[10] A

Zeeverhaal (Exodus 13,17-14,31). Een literaire studie (Leuven, 1986); U.F.W. Bauer, כל הדברים האלה. *All diese Worte. Impulse zur Schriftauslegung aus Amsterdam. Expliziert an der Schilfmeererzählung in Exodus 13,17-14,31,* (Europäische Hochschulschriften 23/442; Bern-New York-Frankfurt am Main-Paris, 1992).

[7] R. Rendtorff, "Der «Jahwist» als Theologe? Zum Dilemma der Pentateuchkritik", *Congress Volume Edinburg 1974* (SVT 28; Leiden, 1975), 158-166. See also a series of other contributions by R. Rendtorff: "Literarkritik und Traditionsgeschichte", *EvTh* 27 (1967), 138-153; "Traditio-Historical Method and the Documentary Hypothesis", *Proceedings of the Fifth World Congress of Jewisch Studies (1969)* I (Jerusalem, 1973), 5-11; *Das überlieferungsgeschichtliche Problem des Pentateuch* (BZAW 147) (Berlin and New York, 1977); "Pentateuchal Studies on the Move", *JSOT* 3 (1977), 43-45; *Das Alte Testament. Eine Einführung* (Neukirchen-Vluyn, 1983), 166-173; "The Future of Pentateuchal Criticism", *Henoch* 6 (1984), 1-16.

[8] N. Lohfink, "Deutéronome et Pentateuque. État de la recherche", in Haudebert (ed.) *(supra,* n. 4), 35: "En domaine scientifique, les hypothèses peuvent faire l'objet de mouvements circulaires. Ces circuits d'hypothèses surgissent pour une problématique donnée, lorsque trop peu de données sont connues. Dans ce cas, souvent, plusieurs explications peuvent entrer en concurrence sans être contradictoires pour autant. On vérifie une façon de voir après l'autre, et, tôt ou tard, on retrouve la première approche."

[9] On this, see also W.H. Schmidt, "Elementare Erwägungen", 1, n. 1; Nicholson, "The Pentateuch" *(supra,* n. 4), 10-13; Levin, 9-35 *(supra,* n. 4).

[10] For literature, see *supra,* n. 4, as well as the various volumes of the *Elenchus bibliographicus* of *Biblica* (1967ff.). C. Levin's 1993 study of the Yahwist may serve as a paradigm of a recent survey and critical assessment of Pentateuchal studies.

number of scholars have their doubts about the origin and nature of the J tradition, to say nothing of its existence. With regard to E, though the fragmentary character of the so-called Elohistic materials has been generally admitted, the available evidence no longer seems to tangibly support the claim that E can be conjectured as an autonomous tradition. Furthermore, biblical scholars differ about the nature and range of the 'deuteronomic' component in Genesis to Numbers. I shall discuss this problem more extensively in the next section of this paper. Finally, the classic view that a unified and distinct Priestly document can be reconstructed in the Pentateuch has been criticized. This discussion can generally be summarized in this way: is P to be regarded as an originally independent source or is it a revision of an earlier non-Priestly composition?[11]

II. *The Question of a 'Deuteronomic' Redaction of the Pentateuch*[12]

The starting point of the discussion on the presence of 'deuteronomic' materials in the collection Genesis to Numbers is W.M.L. De Wette's *Dissertatio critico-exegetica* (1805). This study was undoubtedly a turning point in Pentateuchal research. De Wette not only connected the book of Deuteronomy with the report of 2 Kgs 22-23, but also compared it with corresponding texts in Genesis to Numbers. In his view, these Pentateuchal traditions served as source texts for the Deuteronomic composition as found in the book of the same name. The idea of a 'deuteronomic' reworking of the Pentateuch/Hexateuch

---

[11] Cf. M. Vervenne, "The 'P' Tradition in the Pentateuch: Document and/or Redaction? The 'Sea Narrative' (Exodus 13,17-14,31) as a Testcase", in: C. Brekelmans - J. Lust (eds.), *Pentateuchal Studies and Deuteronomistic History* (BETL 94; Leuven, 1990), 67-90 (bibliography, 67-68, note 3); E. Blum, *Studien zur Komposition des Pentateuch* (BZAW 189; Berlin-New York, 1990), 219-360; L. Schmidt, *Studien zur Priesterschrift* (BZAW 214; Berlin-New York, 1993).

[12] See especially R. Smend, *Die Entstehung des Alten Testaments* (Stuttgart-Berlin-Köln-Mainz, 1984³), 62-69; W.H. Schmidt, *Einführung in das Alte Testament* (Berlin-New York, 1989⁴), 53-55; J. Van Seters, "The So-Called Deuteronomistic Redaction of the Pentateuch", in: Emerton (ed.), 58-77; J.A. Soggin, *Introduction to the Old Testament* (London, 1989), 143-145; De Pury - Römer, 48-50, 72-73; Blum, *Studien*, 164-188; E. Talstra, *Solomon's Prayer. Synchrony and Diachrony in the Composition of I Kings 8,14-61* (Kampen, 1992), 54-68. — An exhaustive critical assessment of the history of research into the question of a deuteronomic redaction, viz. dt/dtr elements in the Pentateuch is currently done at K.U. Leuven by Hans Ausloos. This doctoral project is funded by the Belgian National Fund for Scientific Research (*Nationaal Fonds voor Wetenschappelijk Onderzoek*) (promotor: M. Vervenne). See also his unpublished licentiate thesis: *De deuteronomische redactie van de Pentateuch. Een kritische status quaestionis van het onderzoek naar het boek Exodus* (Leuven, 1992).

was introduced by F. Bleek in his 1822 study *Einige aphoristische Beiträge zu den Untersuchungen über den Pentateuch*. According to Bleek, a first comprehensive redaction of the Hexateuch found place in the time before the Jerusalem-based kingdom split apart following Solomon's death. A second redaction was achieved by the author of Deuteronomy at the end of the kingdom of Judah. This editor connected his own work with the existing composition Genesis-Numbers and slightly retouched a few passages in order to tune the new literary work to 'deuteronomic' views. J.W. Colenso (1865) contended that a thoroughly 'deuteronomic' revision and updating of Genesis to Numbers was done by the author of Deuteronomy. In the seventh volume of *The Pentateuch* (1879), Colenso identified about 140 'deuteronomic' verses in the book of Exodus!

With regard to the question of a 'deuteronomic' redaction of the Pentateuch, it is worth mentioning that the pioneering and innovative scholarly work of the first half of the 19th century launched the idea of affiliating the so-called (pre-Wellhausenian, so to speak) 'Jehovist' (JE) to the 'deuteronomic' author (cf. J.J. Stähelin, A. Knobel). This idea was taken up again by A. Kuenen and J. Wellhausen.[13] It, moreover, occurs more explicitly in H. Holzinger's *Einleitung* (1893) and in S.R. Driver's commentaries on Deuteronomy (1902³) and Exodus (1911):

> Der Verwandschaft [between Rje and Rd] ist so gross, dass man im einzelnen oft schwanken kann, ob ein sekundäres Stück Rje oder dem dt'ischen Bearbeiter zuzuweisen ist. (...) Man muss sich fragen, ob es unter diesen Umständen nicht überhaupt einfacher ist, Rje mit Rd zu identifizieren. (Holzinger, *Einleitung*, 490)

> [There are] certain sections of JE (in particular Gn. 26,5   Ex. 13,3-16   15,26   19,3-6, parts of 20,2-17   23,20-33   34,10-26), in which the author (or compiler) adopts a parenetic tone, and where his style displays what may be termed an approximation to the style of Dt.; and these sections appear to have been the source from which the author of Dt. adopted some of the expressions currently used by him. (Driver, *Deuteronomy*, LXXVII-LXXVIII)

> Many of these [Rje passages] *approximate* in style and tone to Deuteronomy; these are, no doubt, pre-Deuteronomic; but those with a *strong* Deuteronomic colouring (as XX.2b, 4b, 5a, 10b, 12) will have been written under the influence of Dt., and be post-Deuteronomic. (Driver, *Exodus*, XVII-XVIII)

---

[13] A. Kuenen, *Historisch-critisch onderzoek naar het ontstaan en de verzameling van de boeken des ouden verbonds. Eerste deel. De Thora en de historische boeken des ouden verbonds* (Leiden, 1887²), 135-136, 235, 237-241 ["... in een verband, dat bijna deuteronomisch klinkt ..." (240)], 242, 249 ["... ook het spraakgebruik van JE getuigt van zijne nauwe verwantschap met D¹ en diens navolgers."], 251; J. Wellhausen, *Die Composition des Hexateuchs und der historischen Bücher des Alten Testaments* (Berlin, 1899³), 73-74, 79, 85-86, 94 ["Dessen (= 'Jehovist') Geistesverwandtschaft mit dem Deuteronomium tritt wiederum auffallend hervor — wenn nicht ausser ihm noch ein Deuteronomist aunzunehmen ist." (n. 2)], 115.

Twentieth-century scholarship, however, did not give much attention to the complicated question of the 'deuteronomic' elements in Genesis-Numbers. The occurring of dt passages or fragments in these books was simply accepted without any further argumentation or discussion. Moreover, biblical scholars were more and more convinced that it was unacceptable to imagine the author(s) of Deuteronomy taking materials from non-deuteronomic traditions. Consequently, correspondences with the dt/dtr language, style and thinking as found in Genesis to Numbers were treated from the point of view of Deut and not vice versa (cf. M. Noth, Th.C. Vriezen).

J.A. Soggin notes that this approach did not produce any significant difficulties. The question, however, "changed once the number of passages involved proved to be greater and their content to be relevant from a historical and religious point of view. In this case we find ourselves confronted with a problem of undeniable importance, which is certainly not marginal and therefore cannot be brushed aside ...".[14] Soggin, moreover, points to L. Perlitt's calculation of so-called 'deuteronomic' passages in Genesis to Numbers, which would face us with a situation simular to the dtr redaction in Joshua and Samuel.[15]

The omnipresence of 'deuteronomic' elements in the Tetrateuch inevitably led to a re-defining of the issue. In the early sixties, C. Brekelmans and N. Lohfink pointed out difficulties in relating the passages in question to the author of Deuteronomy.[16] They therefore

---

[14] Soggin (*supra*, n. 12), 143.

[15] Cf. L. Perlitt, *Bundestheologie im Alten Testament* (WMANT 36; Neukirchen, 1969). − According to A. de Pury and Th. Römer, Perlitt has clearly pointed out the problem of 'deuteronomism' in the Tetrateuch. Besides Perlitt they also refer to M. Weinfeld's *Deuteronomy and the Deuteronomic School* (1972) as a pioneering work with respect to the description of theological and stylistic characteristics of the dt/dtr texts. Strangely enough, they seem to suggest that C. Brekelmans, whose publications on the so-called 'deuteronomic' elements in Genesis to Numbers appeared in 1966 and 1967 (= 1963 lecture!) respectively (see *infra*, n. 16), has made use of both Perlitt (1969) and Weinfeld (1972): cf. "Les études de Perlitt et de Weinfeld eurent tout de suite un grand écho. Mais les uns − comme C.A. *(sic!)* Brekelmans [1966], A. Reichert [1972] et d'autres − *utilisèrent* ces travaux pour postuler dans le Tétrateuque une couche rédactionnelle prédeutéronomique ou protodeutéronomique, ..." (49) (italics mine).

[16] C.H.W. Brekelmans, "Éléments deutéronomiques dans le Pentateuque", *Recherches Bibliques* 8 (1967), 77-91; Id. , "Die sogenannten deuteronomischen Elemente in Genesis bis Numeri", (SVT 15; Leiden, 1966), 90-96; N. Lohfink, *Das Hauptgebot. Eine Untersuching literarischer Einleitungsfragen zu Dtn 5-11* (AnBib 20; Rome, 1963), 121-124. See, furthermore, N. Lohfink, "Gibt es eine deuteronomistische Bearbeitung im Bundesbuch?", in: Brekelmans - Lust (eds.), *Pentateuchal Studies and Deuteronomistic History*, 91-113. Cf. also H. Cazelles, "Connexions et structure de Gen. XV", *RB* 69 (1962); D.E. Skweres, *Die Rückverweise im Buch*

proposed the terminology 'proto-deuteronomic' which allows an earlier dating. Other scholars, however, assert that there is no evidence for an early deuteronomic redaction.[17] More recently, there seems to be a strong tendency to explain the close affinities in language, style and theology between non-Priestly portions in the Tetrateuch and dt/dtr traditions in a different way. Several scholars hold the opinion that the dtr redactors also revised and expanded the Pentateuchal tradition outside the book of Deuteronomy. Consequently, they reject the contention that the author(s) of Deuteronomy would have made use of traditional materials as contained in Genesis to Numbers.[18] Others

---

Deuteronomium (AnBib 79; Rome, 1979), 99-101.

According to Talstra, 57, Lohfink would have introduced the term 'proto-deuteronomisch' "a little earlier than Brekelmans". Brekelmans and Lohfink, in fact, brought in this terminology independently of one another in 1963. In that same year, Brekelmans gave a lecture at the 15th *Colloquium Biblicum Lovaniense*. This paper was under the title "Éléments deutéronomiques dans le Pentateuque" (1967). Rendtorff, in referring to the question of a 'deuteronomic' *Bearbeitungsschicht* in the Pentateuch does not refer to Brekelmans at all when pointing to those who support an early, viz. proto-dt redaction (*Das überlieferungsgeschichtliche Problem*, 79, n. 9 [Lohfink] and 10 [Plöger]).

Besides Brekelmans and Lohfink, mention should be made of the following studies: A. Reichert, *Der Jehowist und die sogenannten deuteronomischen Erweiterungen im Buch Exodus*, Unpublished dissertation (Tübingen, 1972); J. Halbe, *Das Privilegrecht Jahwes Ex 34,10-26. Gestalt und Wesen, Herkunft und Wirken in vordeuteronomischer Zeit* (FRLANT 114; Göttingen, 1975); C. Begg, "The Destruction of the Calf (Exod. 32,20 / Dt 9,21)", in N. Lohfink (ed.), *Das Deuteronomium. Entstehung, Gestalt und Botschaft* (BETL 68; Leuven, 1985), 208-251; F. Langlamet, "Israël et "l'habitant du pays"', *RB* 76 (1969), 321-350; J. Loza, "Les catéchèses étiologiques dans l'Ancien Testament", *RB* 78 (1971), 481-500; M. Caloz, "Exode, XIII,3-16 et son rapport au Deutéronome", *RB* 75 (1968), 5-62; G. Schmitt, *Du sollst keinen Frieden schliessen mit den Bewohnern des Landes. Die Weisungen gegen die Kanaanäer in Israels Geschichte und Geschichtsschreibung* (BWANT 91; Stuttgart-Berlin-Köln-Mainz, 1970); D.J. McCarthy, *Treaty and Covenant* (AnBib 21; Rome, 1963; 1978²); Skweres, *Die Rückverweise*; Vervenne, *Het Zeeverhaal*; Id., "The Protest Motive in the Sea Narrative (Ex 14,11-12). Form and Structure of a Pentateuchal Pattern", *ETL* 63 (1987), 257-271; Id., "De uittocht uit Egypte: 'verdrijving' of 'vlucht'?, *Bijdragen* 49 (1988), 402-409; Id., "The 'P' Tradition" (*supra*, n. 11). See also H.D. Preuß, *Deuteronomium* (EdF 164; Darmstadt, 1982), 30, 43, 175; F. Postma, E. Talstra, M. Vervenne, *Exodus. Materials in Automatic Text Processing. Part I: Morphological, Syntactic and Literary Case Studies*, (Instrumenta Biblica 1/I; Amsterdam-Turnhout, 1983), 98-108; R.E. Clements, *Deuteronomy, Old Testament Guides* (Sheffield, 1989), 96-97.

[17] Cf. G. Fohrer, *Überlieferung und Geschichte des Exodus. Eine Analyse von Ex 1-15* (BZAW 91; Berlin, 1964); Smend, *Die Entstehung*.

[18] Cf. Th.C. Vriezen - A.S. van der Woude, *De literatuur van Oud-Israël* (Wassenaar, 1976⁵), 197-198; Rendtorff, *Das überlieferungsgeschichtliche Problem*, 75-79, 163-173; Soggin, 145; Smend, *Die Entstehung*, 62-69; J. Vermeylen, "L'affaire du veau d'or (Ex 32-34). Une clé pour la 'question deutéronomiste'?", *ZAW* 97 (1985), 1-22; Id., "Les sections narratives de Deut 5-11 et leur relation à

regard the classical J portion of the Pentateuch as a late literary work which has supplemented the DtrH and, therefore, can be labeled as a post-dtr composition.[19] 'Deuteronomic' elements in the Tetrateuch are also identified as post-dtr by E. Blum. His argumentation essentially reflects the classical view of the history of Genesis to Kings, though he does introduce one significant modification with his assumption of five successive stages: ancient traditions (formerly J/E/JE), D (Deuteronomy), DtrH, KD (post-dtr composition), KP (priestly composition).[20]

No doubt these hypotheses of the last thirty years remind us of the 'circular movements' referred to by Lohfink. The proto-dt theory takes up the thread of "JE approximating Deut." (Kuenen, Wellhausen, Driver), whereas the adherents of a dtr and post-dtr redaction of the Tetrateuch breathe new life into the view which, at the turn of the century, rejected the notion that the writers of Deuteronomy took materials from the Tetrateuch.

In summary, one can say that present-day Pentateuchal research deals in three different ways with the question of the nature and extent of 'deuteronomic' elements in Genesis-Numbers:[21]

1° Proto-dt redaction: Non-Priestly Tetrateuchal texts displaying 'deuteronomic' — in the most general sense of the word — affinities belong to a 'deuteronomic' redaction previous to Deut and should therefore be characterized as *proto-* or *early-deuteronomic*. This redaction, moreover, is often identified as being the work of the author/redactor of the so-called "JE composition". It seems that this school of writers launched, sometime around the end of the 8th century B.C.E., the language, style and theology characteristic of the estab-

---

Ex 19-34", in: Lohfink (ed.), *Das Deuteronomium*, 174-207; Blum, *Studien*, 7-218.

[19] Cf. J. Van Seters, *Abraham in History and Tradition* (New Haven-London, 1975); Id., "The So-Called Deuteronomistic Redaction"; H.H. Schmid, *Der sogenannte Jahwist. Beobachtungen und Fragen zur Pentateuchforschung* (Zürich, 1976); H.-C. Schmitt, "'Priesterliches' und 'prophetisches' Geschichtsverständnis in der Meerwundererzählung Ex 13,17-14,31. Beobachtungen zur Endredaktion des Pentateuch", in: A. Gunneweg - O. Kaiser (eds.), *Textgemäss. Aufsätze und Beiträge zur Hermeneutik des Alten Testaments. Festschrift für Ernst Würthwein zum 70. Geburtstag* (Göttingen, 1979), 139-155; M. Rose, *Deuteronomist und Jahwist. Untersuchungen zu den Berührungspunkten beider Literaturwerke* (ATANT 67; Zürich, 1981); A.D.H. Mayes, *The Story of Israel between Settlement and Exile. A Redactional Study of the Deuteronomic History* (London, 1983); F.V. Winnett, "Re-Examining the Foundations", *JBL* 84 (1965), 1-19; Levin, *Der Jahwist*.

[20] Blum, *Studien*. On this, see J.L. Ska, "Un nouveau Wellhausen?", *Biblica* 72 (1991), 253-263.

[21] Compare also Van Seters, "The So-Called Deuteronomistic Redaction", 58.

lished dt/dtr traditions. Proto-dt texts *approximate* but do not attain the fullness and fixity of the dt/dtr strata in Deuteronomy and Joshua-Kings.[22]

2° Dtr redaction: The 'deuteronomic' affinities in Genesis to Numbers are considered as part of a (late) *deuteronomistic* redaction of the Pentateuch as a whole, and, more particularly, the redaction which was also responsible for composing the so-called 'Deuteronomistic History' (DtrH).

3° Post-dtr redaction: 'Deuteronomic' elements in the Tetrateuch do not stem from a dtr redaction, but result from *post-dtr* reworkings, which can be identified with either a late J, i.e. a creative author imbued with the spirit of DtrH, or a post-exilic theological composer.

III. *Methodology*

J. Van Seters states that current approaches to the question of 'deuteronomic' elements in Genesis-Numbers represent "such a variety of viewpoints and possibilities that the question arises how to make any progress in the debate."[23] He then raises the subject of methodology, and, more particularly, the question of how to decide whether a Tetrateuchal text is proto-dt, dtr or post-dtr. According to Van Seters, it is "methodologically dubious to use the language and terminology of Dtn/Dtr to identify a group of texts as 'proto-D' simply because they are embedded within that part of the Pentateuch that has been considered by the documentary hypothesis as earlier than Dtn."[24] Following on this, he suggests that the only way to properly make "such judgments would be to see how the Pentateuchal texts fit into a stream of development or history of tradition in non-Pentateuchal texts that clearly begins before Deuteronomy and proceeds beyond Dtr into the exilic and post-exilic periods."[25] In this respect, he refers to Hosea as

---

[22] Cf. Begg, 249 and compare also Labuschagne, 104-105: "Wij noemen deze heruitgave 'proto-deuteronomisch' omdat de nieuwe elementen erin sterke verwantschap vertonen met het enige tijd later ontstane boek Deuteronomium. De meer gangbare term waarmee deze bewerking wordt aangeduid, '*elohistisch*', is mijns inziens eenzijdig en dus minder juist."

[23] Van Seters, 58.

[24] Van Seters, "The So-Called Deuteronomistic Redaction", 59. To this one could remark that it is "methodologically dubious to use the language and terminology of Dtn/Dtr to identify a group of texts as" *post-Dtr* "simply because they are embedded within that part of the Pentateuch that has been considered by the documentary hypothesis as" J which is now regarded by several scholars as a late, post-exilic literary composition.

[25] Van Seters, 59.

a starting point and Jeremiah, Ezekiel and Second Isaiah as important representatives of the exilic traditions.

Van Seters is right to claim that critical scholarship should approach the question of a 'deuteronomic' redaction of the Pentateuch within a controlling framework, especially one built upon more or less datable prophetic traditions. Such an approach, in exceeding the boundaries of the complex Genesis to Numbers, has to focus on *all* non-Priestly texts in this collection of narratives, laws and prescriptions. The precise nature of these texts needs, of course, to be determined. With respect to the characterisation of Tetrateuchal passages or textual elements as proto-dt, dt/dtr or post-dtr, the method proposed by C. Brekelmans is workable.[26] In line with this approach, I would state that genuine 'deuteronomic' elements in Genesis-Numbers can be recognized by their *typical* dt/dtr theology, style and vocabulary.[27] If these are lacking, there is every indication that the so-called dt elements of the text under consideration are either proto-dt or post-dtr. This distinction, however, can only be made in comparing them with other Old Testament traditions which are clearly pre-dt and post-dtr respectively. Especially in this respect, the application of the criterion of the "con-

---

[26] Cf. Brekelmans, "Éléments", 80; Id., "Die sogenannten deuteronomischen Elemente", 93-94.

[27] Compare also W.H. Schmidt, 37: "Bestimmung des — umstrittenen, nicht selten zu weit gefaßten — "Deuteronomistischen" ist allerdings strikt dem Grundsatz zu folgen, daß es an der Sprache ausgewiesen sein muß. Bezieht man Gesichtspunkte der Komposition, d.h. der Funktion von Versen wie Abschnitten im Kontext, oder geistesgeschichtliche Erwägungen ein, dann läßt sich, möchte man nicht jede Eindeutigkeit preisgeben, allein auf Grund der Sprache entscheiden, ob der entsprechende Zusammenhang "deuteronomistisch" ist oder nicht."

A clear exposition of Brekelman's methodology regarding the identification of proto-dt elements in Genesis to Numbers can be found in Talstra, 55:

"(1) The dtr theology in its more elaborated form should be absent in the texts concerned. (...)

(2) One should be able to find words and expressions in the texts which are similar to the formulations in Deut., but not yet so stereotypical (...).

(3) Likewise one should be able to find formulations in the text which are not used in Deut. or in the DtrH, but do have parallels in texts which are generally regarded as pre-dtr." It should be said, however, that the terminology which Talstra uses in relating to Brekelman's approach is rather confusing. As a matter of fact, Brekelmans consistently speaks about "éléments prédeutéro*miques* / postdeutéro*miques*" (1967), "protodeutero*nomisch* / postdeutero*nomisch*", whereas Talstra labels these as "proto-*dtr*" and "post-*dtr*" respectively, i.e. proto/post-deuterono*mistic*. Compare, however, the above-mentioned "(1) The *dtr* theology ..." (italics mine) with the original Dutch edition (E. Talstra, *Het gebed van Salomo. Synchronie en diachronie in de kompositie van I Kon. 8,14-61* [Amsterdam, 1987], 41): "1. De *dtn.* theologie ..." (italics mine). As regards the dt/dtr phraseology, see M. Weinfeld, *Deuteronomy and the Deuteronomic School* (Oxford, 1972).

trolling" framework could be validated. We should, furthermore, (critically) take account of the fierce criticism which has been voiced by E. Blum of the application of stylistic criteria by those adhering the theory of a proto-dt redaction of (parts of) the Tetrateuch.[28] Blum asserts that the arguments in support of such a redaction reveal some methodological inconsistencies.[29] First, the concordances of style and vocabulary between non-Priestly portions of the Pentateuch and genuine deuteronomic texts seem to be determined in terms of literal agreements. Phrases which are not fully dt are mechanically labeled as proto-dt, without taking into consideration a dtr or even post-dtr origin. It should be noted, however, that Blum's judgement does not do justice to the close study of language and style undertaken by those scholars who defend the thesis that dtr speech was not introduced suddenly but is possessed of a pre-history. As Talstra rightly states, the approach of Brekelmans and Langlamet, to mention only these two, "not only uses linguistic arguments more extensively and carefully, but above all with priority".[30] Clearly, meticulous linguistic analysis of the text as a meaningful composition is essential to literary and redactional investigations.[31] Linguistic affinities between texts should be subjected to a detailed analysis concerning their formal correspondences and differences, and the way these are to be accounted for. Linguistic determination of the nature of 'deuteronomic' elements in Genesis-Numbers must also take account of the physical form of the text (text-criticism).[32] Second, the stylistic comparison, Blum says, is restricted to the book of Deuteronomy while excluding DtrG and Jer-D. It is true that the research model explaining the process of growth of both Deuteronomy and the dtr literature should be validated when examining the nature of the so-called 'deuteronomic' elements in Genesis to Numbers.[33] This widening of the methodological perspective, how-

---

[28] E. Blum, *Die Komposition der Vätergeschichte* (WMANT 57; Neukirchen-Vluyn, 1984), 374-375; Id., *Studien*, 164-176.

[29] Blum, *Studien*, 167-168.

[30] Talstra, 80.

[31] On this, see especially Talstra, 53-82. Compare also Lohfink, "Deutéronome et Pentateuque", 46, as well as Z. Zevit, "Clio, I Presume", *BASOR* 260 (1985), 76-77 (criticizes the lack of linguistic argumentation in Van Seters, *In Search of History* [1983]).

[32] Cf. Lohfink, "Deutéronome et Pentateuque", 45. See also E. Tov, *Textual Criticism of the Hebrew Bible* (Minneapolis-Assen-Maastricht, 1992), 313-349.

[33] As far as the study of DtrH is concerned, see E. Jenni, "Zwei Jahrzehnte Forschung an den Büchern Josua bis Könige", *ThR*, n. F. 27 (1961), 1-32, 97-146; A.N. Radjawane, "Das deuteronomistische Geschichtswerk. Ein Forschungsbericht", *ThR*, n. F. 38 (1974), 177-216; H. Weippert, "Das deuteronomistische Geschichtswerk. Sein Ziel und Ende in der neueren Forschung", *ThR*, n. F. 50 (1985), 213-

ever, is not completely absent from the well-known proto-dt orientated studies, and is, more particularly, explicitly present in the analysis made, for example, by Caloz and Begg.[34] Third, it appears to Blum that one unconsciously postulates some sort of linear development of the 'deuteronomic' tradition from 'simple' to 'complex', from 'concise' to 'lengthy'.[35] This opinion, however, would need to be confronted with the detailed analyses made by various scholars. The studies of Begg (Exod 32-34) and Lohfink (Exod 20:22-23:33), for example, show that expressions and formulae are studied as being part of a (theological) 'system' and not as isolated phenomena reflecting some sort of evolutionary process.[36]

IV. *The Sea Narrative as a Paradigm*

Current discussions on the nature and origin of 'deuteronomic' elements in Genesis to Numbers are primarily conducted on the basis of the classic *cruces* as found in Exod 12:24-27a; 13:3-16; 20:1-17; 23:20-33; 32-34.[37] In addition to these well-known passages, there are other texts in the book of Exodus which seem to reveal affinities with 'deuteronomic' thought, language and style. In this section I would like to concentrate on another *crux interpretum* of Old Testament criticism,

---

249; H.D. Preuß, "Zum deuteronomistischen Geschichtswerk", *ThR*, n. F. 58 (1993), 229-264; M.A. O'Brien, *The Deuteronomistic History Hypothesis: A Reassessment*, (OBO 92; Freiburg-Göttingen, 1989). See, furthermore, A.D.H. Mayes, *Deuteronomy* (NCBC; Grand Rapids-London, 1981), 25-110; Preuß, *Deuteronomium* (*supra*, n. 16); C.J. Labuschagne, *Deuteronomium*. Deel I A-B (POT; Nijkerk, 1987), 16-48; Clements, *Deuteronomy* (*supra*, n. 16); M. Weinfeld, *Deuteronomy 1-11: A New Translation with Introduction and Commentary* (AB 5; New York, 1991), 1-122.

[34] Caloz, 35-41; Begg, 233-251 and see, e.g., 249: "... Exod 32-34*, and 32,20 in particular, approximate, but do not attain, the fullness, and fixity of the *Deuteronomic* and *Deuteronomistic* strata in Deuteronomy and the Former Prophets." (italics mine). See also Lohfink, "Deutéronome et Pentateuque", 37 ("... on n'y trouve [in Blum, *Studien*] qu'une seule note de bas de page concernant la critique interne et l'histoire rédactionnelle du Deutéronome!").

[35] Blum, 168: "Als entsprechende Denkvoraussetzung fungieren häufig die Annahmen einer linearen Entwicklung von »einfach« zu »komplex«, von »knapp« zu »breit« oder einer zunehmenden Normierung und Verfestigung des Sprachgebrauchs. Im Grunde sind es aber solche Postulate, die je und je zur Diskussion stehen müßten, lassen sich doch auch ihre genaue Umkehrungen im Einzelfalle denken."

[36] Begg, 233-251; Lohfink, "Gibt es eine deuteronomistische Bearbeitung", 104: "Sowohl im Bundesbuch als auch im Deuteronomium sind die Begriffe festgelegt. Doch sind sie verschieden festgelegt, weil sie in verschiedenen Systemen stehen. Vergleicht man diese, dann zeigt sich: Das deuteronomische System ist das Ausgeklügeltere."

[37] See the overview in Ausloos (*supra*, n. 12), 28-92.

namely, the Sea Narrative, which has, of course, generated much discussion among biblical scholars. My aim here is not to provide an exhaustive analysis of the redaction history of the pericope but to illustrate the way in which we might go about determining the nature of 'deuteronomic' elements in a Tetrateuchal composition.

1. *Types of Analysis*

Biblical scholars agree that the Sea Narrative is not an original literary unit, but the product of the combination of autonomous traditions to form a genuine theological composition.[38] Ever since the emergence of the historical critical approach within biblical studies, the idea of the complexity of this narrative was founded on recording formal data, such as are repetitions, doublets and other irregularities. Referring to these textual phenomena, exegetes have continued till the present day to separate the final edition of the narrative into two or more originally independent accounts, which are characterized as source texts of the story as we now have it.

Until very recently, literary criticism of the Sea Narrative was primarily source criticism. This type of analysis interprets the double (triple) versions of the events narrated as source doublets (triplets), whereas the various irregularities in the text are explained as resulting

---

[38] For a survey on the different opinions regarding the nature and development of the Sea Narrative, see Vervenne, *Het Zeeverhaal*, 11-59; Bauer, *All diese Worte*, 198-209. For a redaction-critical analysis of Exod 13:17-14:31, see Weimar, *Die Meerwundererzählung*; F. Kohata, *Jahwist und Priesterschrift in Exodus 3-14* (BZAW 166) (Berlin/New York, 1986), 277-301; Id., "Die Endredaktion (R^P) der Meerwundererzählung", *Annual of the Japanese Biblical Institute* 14 (1988), 10-37; A.F. Campbell - M.A. O'Brien, *Sources of the Pentateuch. Texts, Introductions, Annotations* (Minneapolis, 1993), 238-254; Blum, *Studien*, 9-43, 256-262; L. Schmidt, *Studien*, 19-34; Levin, *Der Jahwist*, 341-347; H. Lamberty-Zielinski, *Das »Schilfmeer«. Herkunft, Bedeutung und Funktion eines alttestamentlichen Exodusbegriffs* (BBB 78; Frankfurt am Main, 1993), 57-133. See, moreover, M. Vervenne, "The Sea Narrative Revisited", *Biblica* 74 (1993) − H. Lamberty-Zielinski states that P. Weimar's analysis of the Sea Narrative "eine der jüngsten (neben Kohata [...]) und umfangreichsten Darstellungen zu diesem Textkomplex ist" (57, n. 3). She does not seem to be aware of my 1986 study, though it has been mentioned, and partially published, in several articles of mine: see, for example, "The Protest Motif" (*supra*, n. 16), 257, n. 1; "The 'P' Tradition" (*supra*, n. 11), 77, n. 28. See also Bauer, 203-205, 210-348 (Bauer has made ample use of my study for his literary analysis of Exod 13:17-14:31). My own study of the Sea Narrative will be extended to the preceding 'Plague Composition' (Exod 7-11) by Bénédicte Lemmelijn, a doctoral student of mine. The project is entitled "The Plagues of Egypt (Exodus 7:14-11:10). A Text-Critical, Linguistic and Literary Study" and funded by the Belgian National Fund for Scientific Research (*Nationaal Fonds voor Wetenschappelijk Onderzoek*).

from merging originally independent traditions. Classical scholarship used to distinguish within the Sea Narrative two main narrative layers, which correspond to the sources J and P, as well as fragments of the so-called E tradition. A few remarkable variations, however, should be noticed. J. Wellhausen and O. Procksch[39] attribute a large part of the narrative to E, whereas W. Rudolph, K. von Rabenau and B. Halpern[40] disavow an Elohistic contribution in the literary history of the pericope. While most scholars point to an important number of Priestly elements, Wellhausen and H. Gressmann[41] minimize the P portion in Exod 13:17-14:31. R. Smend, O. Eissfeldt and G. Fohrer even deny that P is present in this narrative.[42]

To conclude this brief survey of classical source-critical approaches to the Sea Narrative it should be said that Wellhausen's analysis was not followed by many scholars. The nature and extent of the so-called 'JE' redaction, however, has been more influential, at least until the beginning of this century and, as stated above, again in recent years within the framework of the study of 'deuteronomic' elements in Genesis-Numbers. The source-critical division worked out by M. Noth, and, to a lesser degree, the one by Eissfeldt, has proved more successful.[43] It is noteworthy that, after the publication of Noth's *Überlieferungsgeschichte des Pentateuch* in 1948, many exegetes no longer attributed Exod 13:20 to P but followed Noth in ascribing this verse to J.

Recent diachronic inquiries into Exod 13:17-14:31 reflect the current trends in Pentateuchal studies as discussed above. Since they can only be briefly presented here, suffice it to say that one can distinguish three types of research.

The scholarly work of people like F. Kohata and A.F. Campbell / M.A. O'Brien displays a "Source Critical Model" which basically

[39] Wellhausen, *Die Composition*, 75-77; O. Procksch, *Das nordhebräische Sagenbuch. Die Elohimquelle übersetzt und untersucht* (Leipzig, 1906), 77-81.

[40] W. Rudolph, *Der "Elohist" von Exodus bis Josua* (BZAW 68) (Berlin, 1938), 27-33; K. von Rabenau, "Die beiden Erzählungen vom Schilfmeerwunder in Ex. 13,17-14,31", *Theologische Versuche* 1 (1966) 7-29; B. Halpern, *The Emergence of Israel in Canaan* (SBL Monograph Series 29; California, 1983), 36-43.

[41] Wellhausen, *Die Composition*, 75-77; H. Gressmann, *Mose und seine Zeit. Ein Commentar zu den Mosesagen* (Göttingen, 1913), 108-112.

[42] R. Smend, *Die Erzählung des Hexateuch auf ihre Quellen untersucht* (Berlin, 1912), 137-144; O. Eissfeldt, *Hexateuchsynopse* (Leipzig, 1922), 30-36; Fohrer, *Überlieferung*, 97-110, 124-125.

[43] M. Noth, *Überlieferungsgeschichte des Pentateuch* (Stuttgart, 1948), 18, 32, 39; Id., *Das zweite Buch Mose. Exodus übersetzt und erklärt* (ATD 5; Göttingen, 1959), 80-95; Eissfeldt, *Hexateuchsynopse*, 133-137, 271.

adheres to the classical source division.[44] Kohata, for example, although he attends to the redactional process of assembling the originally independent source-texts JE and P, does not have much regard for the "creative" work of the redactors ($R^{je/d(tr)/p}$). This opinion, which definitely reflects 19th century scepticism about the contribution of redactors to the formation of the Pentateuch, views the presumed final redactor R^P principally as a *Sammler*.[45] On the other hand, Kohata appears to be fully aware of the complexity of the redaction history of the Pentateuch, and, more especially, he points up the puzzling relationship between dt/dtr and priestly (re-)editing of existing narratives.[46] As far as the JE edition of the Sea Narrative is concerned, he suggests its possible reworking by a redactor who "der dtr Tradition nahesteht".[47]

A second type of approach employs a "Redaction Critical Model", which gives particular attention to the redactional work of creative authors who shaped new compositions on the basis of existing narratives. In this respect, mention should be made of the analyses of the Sea Narrative offered by H. Lamberty-Zielinski, C. Levin, M. Vervenne, and P. Weimar.[48] Both Lamberty-Zielinski and Vervenne propose

---

[44] Kohata, *Jahwist*, 277-301; Id., "Die Endredaktion":
   J: 14:5b-6.10bα.13(-14?).20.21aß.27aßb.(28b?).30
   E: 13:17aß-19; 14:5a.19a
   P^g: 13:20; 14:1-4.8-9.10abß.15.16*.17-18.21aαb.22-23.26.27aα.28a(b?).29
   $R^{(je/d(tr)/p)}$: 13:17aα.21-22; 14:7.11-12.(14?).19b.24-25.31
   Campbell and O'Brien, 238-254:
   J: 13:20-22; 14:5b-6.9aα.10bα.13-14.19b-20.21aß.24.25b.27aßb.30-31
   E: 13:17-19; 14:5a.7.11-12.19a.25a
   P: 14:1-4.8.9aßb.10abß.15-18.21aαb.22-23.26-27aα.28-29.

[45] See, for example, Kohata, "Die Endredaktion", 29-30: "So geht der sachlich genaue Charakter der Priesterschrift durch die Redaktion verloren."; "Das Ergebnis der Redaktion läßt sich zwar als eine fortlaufende Geschichte lesen, aber es mangelt ihm an innere Folgerichtigkeit sowie an literarische Qualität."; "Der Redaktor nimmt sich kaum die Freiheit, den Text nach seiner eigenen theologischen Intention zu gestalten.'

[46] Kohata, *Jahwist*, 37: "Erfolgte die dtr Redaktion ($R^{D<tr>}$) vor der Einarbeitung von P? (...) Oder gebrauchte R^P, der in einer seiner Vorlagen das Dtn bzw. dtr Geschichtswerk vorfand, dtn-dtr Sprache? Oder wurden alle Quellenschriften nach R^P noch einmal dtn-dtr bearbeitet?"; 294: "So führt unser Teilproblem zur Frage nach der Redaktion des gesamten Pentateuch, vor allem nach der Beziehung von $R^{D(tr)}$ zu seinen Redaktionen. Ist $R^{D(tr)}$ mit einer von ihnen (R^{JE} oder R^P) identisch oder unabhängig? Oder ist $R^{D(tr)}$ eine mehrstufige Bearbeitung, die die Redaktion des Pentateuch wie auch die Bearbeitung der Texte umfaßt?"

[47] Kohata, 292.

[48] Redaction history of the Sea Narrative:
Lamberty-Zielinski, 90 (see also my remark on this study, *supra*, n. 38):
   J (*Grundschicht*): 14:5a.6.9aα.10bα.13a.14.24aαßb.25b.27b.28b.30.31aß

a pre-exilic "JE" redaction approximating the dt/dtr line of tradition, while Weimar allows for a late 8th century thorough "JE" revision which is *theologiegeschichtlich* related to the "Deuteronomic School",[49] and, moreover, was *punktuell* updated by an exilic dtr redactor. Blum, on the other hand, argues in support of a post-exilic partial D-composition (KD) of the Sea Narrative, which would presuppose DtrH.[50] The latter approach, in fact, represents a third research pattern, viz. the "Composition Critical Model". Blum rejects recent *redaktionsgeschichtlich*-oriented studies of the Pentateuch (cf. Weimar, et al.), since he claims that, though it should be taken for granted that

---

R^je (pre-dt/dtr *Fortschreibung*): 13:17.18 (minus ים סוף).19.21.22; 14:5b.11.12. 13b.19.20. 21aßγ.24aγ.25a.27aα"ß.31aαb

P^g: 13:20; 14:1.2a.3.4.8 (minus מלך מצרים).10abß.15.16 (minus ו הרם את מטך). 17abα.18a. 21aαb.22.23aα.26abα.27aα'.28a.29

R^P: 13:18 * (only ים סוף); 14:2b.7.8* (מלך מצרים).9aßb.16* (הרם את מטך). 17bß.18b. 23aßγb.26bß

Levin, 341-347:

J^Q: 13:20; 14:10bα.13 (to תיראו).14.21a (from ויולך).24aαß.b.25b.27 (from ויסב)
J^R: 13:21a; 14:5a;6.10bß.13 (from התיצבו).19b-20aα.b.24aγ.30
J^S: 14:5b.7.19a.20aßγ.25a
P: 14:1-4.8-9.15aα.b.16-18.21aα (to first הים).b.22-23.26.27 (to first הים).28-29
R: 14:10a.15aß
R^S: 13:17-19.21b-22; 14:11.12.31

Vervenne, "The 'P' Tradition", 77-79, 79-87 (the letters a, b, c, etc. mark clause boundaries):

R^JE (proto-dt): 13:17-19.21-22; 14:5-7.8c.9ab*.10b-e.11-12*.13-14.19-20.21bc*. 24-25.27b-d*. 28c.30.31*
R^P: 13:20; 14:1-4.8ab.9b*.10a.11-12*.15-18.21a.21bc*.21d.22-23.26.27a.27b-d*.-28ab.29.31*

Weimar, *Die Meerwunderzählung*, 269-274:

Pre-J: 14:5a.9aα.10bα* (only ויראו מאד).13aα.14.24aßb.25a.27b.28b.30a* (minus ביום ההוא). 31aß.
J^R: 14:10bα* (minus ויראו מאד).25b.30b.
R^je: 13:17aα.19; 14:5b.6.11aα* (ויאמרו אל משה).11b.21aß.24aα.27aß.31b (+ 15:20.21).
R^Dtr: 13:21a.22; 14:19b.20aγb.24aγ.
Pre-P (Priestly *Vorlage*): 14:8b.15aα.16aß.16b.21aα.21b.22.23aα.23b.26abα.-27aα.28a* (minus את הרכב ואת הפרשים לכל חיל פרעה).29.
P^g: 14:1.2a.4.8aα*ß.10bß.15b.16aα.17abα.18a.28a* (את הרכב ואת הפרשים לכל חיל פרעה).
R^P: 13:17aßb.18.20.21b; 14:2b.3.7aα.7b.8aα* (מצרים מלך).9aß* (minus רכב). 9b.11a* (minus ויאמרו אל משה).12.13aßb.15aß.17bß.18b.19a.20aα.23aßγ. 26bß.30a* (ביום הוא). 31aα.
Glosses: 14:7aß.9aß* (only רכב).20aß.

[49] Weimar, 130, n. 56.
[50] Blum, *Studien*, 256-257:
KD: 14:13-14.30-31
KP: 14:1-4.7-8.10bß.15-18.21aαß*.22-23.26.27aα*.28-29
Nachträge: 13:19; 14:19a

the Pentateuch contains a large number of original independent texts, it is no longer possible to unravel "tradition" and "composition".[51] In line with this, my own "redaction critical" approach to the Sea Narrative could also be classified as "composition critical". To clarify this I will offer, in the next section, a brief representation of my view on the literary history of the Sea Narrative with special reference to Weimar's detailed redaction critical study of the pericope.[52]

A literary analysis of the Sea Narrative based on a careful linguistic analysis shows a well-structured account composed of two narrative layers, which represent two different but interrelated compositional levels reflecting on the "Sea Event".

It appears that a first composition constitutes a relatively self-sufficient story and apparently resulted from redactional reworking of existing textual materials and traditions by (an) author/s who, sometime around the fall of the Northern kingdom, introduced the religious ideas, language and style of what is usually called the "Deuteronomic School".[53] In view of its compound character, this composition may conventionally be designated with the acronym "JE". It is a didactic story with a view to convincing the Isaelite readers of divine power acting against the "enemy". To that end the redactor/composer simulated the theme of YHWH war. War, however, is only a staged event, since the Israelites are portrayed as an army at rest whereas the Egyptians fight windmills. The narrative, moreover, is mainly aligned with the Wilderness tradition (Exod 15ff).

The (proto-dt) "JE" composition, in its turn, served as a source for the 6th century Priestly school, which composed a new narrative. I have defended elsewhere the thesis that the P portion of Exod 13:17-14:31 cannot be read as an independent and coherent literary unit but should be typified as a redactional reworking based on the existing "JE" narrative.[54] The Priestly composers, more particularly, inserted their stereotypical pattern of YHWH speech and execution, as well as revised and rewrote various parts of the existing account. Moreover, they adjusted Sea and Plagues, and also connected these with Creation and Flood. The violent "JE" story is thus converted into a divine

---

[51] Blum, *Studien*, 208-215.
[52] See also Vervenne, "The Sea Narrative Revisited".
[53] Compare to Lamberty-Zielinski, 99-116, 122-125.
[54] Cf. Vervenne, "The P Tradition". Compare with Blum, *Studien*, 260 and L. Schmidt, *Studien*, 19-34. As regards the discussion of the unexpected statement in 14:15 (מה תצעק אלי), Blum does not seem to know my 1987 treatment of this peculiar passage: "The Protest Motif", 260-261, 267-269. See also Vervenne, "The 'P' Tradition", 86-87.

judgment which predominately concerns the "enemy" (Egypt) but also ultimately serves as a warning addressed to Israel to remain faithful.

The analysis I have made of the redaction, viz. composition history of Exod 13:17-14:31, concurs with Weimar's hypothesis in that neither the non-Priestly (JE) nor the Priestly redactional layer is considered as an original unity. Consequently, I do accept the artificial nature of both compositions, which certainly resulted from reworking traditional materials and texts. As opposed to Weimar and in line with Blum, I do not accept that the process of growth of these compositions can be wholly reconstructed. Since the (proto-dt) JE as well as the P composers have reworked heterogeneous materials in such a radical and creative way, that it is no longer possible to unravel the original form of the source texts/traditions of which they made use. It should be repeated again that reliable literary analysis ought to rest on discernible significant texts, rather than being developed from reconstructed source-texts which, in turn, serve as the basis for all kinds of hypotheses about the possible compositional levels of the text. As regards the Sea account, reconstructing an underlying, independent JE narrative, as well as patterned Priestly portions, should not move away from the final Hebrew composition.

2. 'Deuteronomic' Elements in the Sea Narrative

Until recently, most scholars did not seriously take into consideration the appearance of 'deuteronomic' elements in Exod 13:17-14:31. Wellhausen and Kuenen confined the "nearly deuteronomic" constituents within the JE parts of the Tetrateuch to well-known passages, such as Exod 12:24-27 and 13:3-16. A. Jülicher, on the other hand, while attributing Exod 13:3-16 to a dt author (D), also remarked on the combination of 13:3-16 and 13:17-14:31 to form a unity. As a consequence, he ascribed the transitional statement in 13:17a to the dt redactor (R^D) who composed 13:3-16.[55] At the turn of the century, B. Baentsch questioned the 'deuteronomic' character of 14:31. He assumed this verse to be a J passage on the one hand and to contain R^D elements on the other.[56] Driver, then, clearly labeled 14:31 as J,

---

[55] A. Jülicher, "Die Quellen von Exodus VII,8–XXIV,11. Ein Beitrag zur Hexateuchfrage", *Jahrbücher für Protestantische Theologie* 8 (1882), 119.

[56] B. Baentsch, *Exodus - Leviticus* (HK 1; Göttingen, 1900), 127: "Doch ist manches in diesem v. für J auch wieder auffällig. Die Bezeichnung Moses als Knecht Gottes ist bei J beispiellos, findet sich aber bei E, Num 12,7f. Dtn 34,5 Jos 1,1f. (...), und besonders häufig bei Rd im Buche Josua, Jos 1,7.13.15 8,31.33 9,24 11,12.15 12,6 13,8 14,7 18,7 22,2.4.5. Auch היד הגדולה, im Sinne von »Grossthat«, erinnert stark an Rd, vgl. Dtn 34,12 (...)." Compare to Jülicher, 123:

though his comment adds the affinities with "the work of the Deuteronomic editor" in Joshua, as listed by Baentsch.[57]
Apart from G. Hölscher, and C.A. Simpson,[58] who put the case for
14:31 R[D] very succinctly by referring to Baentsch, there were, until the
1980's, very few scholars who considered the matter of 'deuteronomic'
elements in the Sea Narrative. Then, in 1976, H. Donner seemed to
hint at the possibility of a proto-dt origin of Exod 13:19E,[59] while O.
Kaiser, for his part, suggested that this verse, which should be connected with Gen 50:24-26 and Josh 24:32, appears to result from a
dt/dtr reworking.[60] Furthermore, G.I. Davies defends the thesis that
Exod 13:20 as well as other itinerary-notes in Exodus to Numbers were
inserted by a redactor who apparently belonged to the same circle as
the dtr editors of Judges.[61]. E. Zenger, in his 1978 commentary on the
book of Exodus,[62] is the first to consider 14:19a and 20a as exilic
deuteronomistic ('d') insertions, while assigning a number of passages
to the "jehowistischen Geschichtsdarstellung" (Je), which, in his view,
served Hezekiah's reform (727-701 B.C.E.) and could, therefore, be
regarded as approaching deuteronomism.[63] Finally, in a survey of the
question of the redaction of the pre-Priestly Tetrateuch, R. Smend

---

"V. f. gehören fragelos zu J, das abschliessende ובמשה עבדו schmeckt ein wenig
nach Redaktion, aber wenn V. 11.12 echt sind, so wäre mindestens ובמשה in J sehr
wohl haltbar."

[57] Driver, 123.4.

[58] G. Hölscher, *Die Anfänge der hebräischen Geschichtsschreibung* (Heidelberg,
1942), 21 [contrast, however, with *Geschichtsschreibung in Israel. Untersuchungen
zum Jahvisten und Elohisten* (SKHVL 50; Lund, 1952), 307: "14:31 wird also von
zweiter Hand stammen."]; C.A. Simpson, *The Early Traditions of Israel. A Critical
Analysis of the Predeuteronomic Narrative of the Hexateuch* (Oxford, 1948), 186.

[59] H. Donner, *Die literarische Gestalt der alttestamentliche Josephgeschichte*
(Heidelberg, 1976), 35: "Der Sprachgebrauch [of Gen 50:23-25] deutet auf den
Elohisten. Zu erwägen wäre allenfalls eine protodeuteronomische Konstruktion, was
freilich zur Folge haben würde, daß man auch Ex. 13,19 als protodeuteronomischen
Eintrag ansehen müßte. Das wird sich kaum mit Sicherheit aufklären lassen."

[60] O. Kaiser, *Einleitung in das Alte Testament. Eine Einführung in ihre Ergebnisse und Probleme* (Gütersloh, 1978⁴), 97 ("vermutlich in den Umkreis der
deuteronomisch-deuteronomistischen Schule gehörenden Bearbeitung zu beurtei-
len."); *Ibid.* (Gütersloh, 1984⁵), 105 ("eine in den Umkreis der deuteronomistischen
Schule gehörenden Zusatz").

[61] G.I. Davies, "The Wilderness Itineraries and the Composition of the Pentateuch", *VT* 33 (1983), 9-12.

[62] E. Zenger, *Das Buch Exodus* (Geistliche Schriftlesung 7; Düsseldorf, 1978),
144-145 (Je: 13:17-19.21-22; 14:5b-7.11-12.19b.20b.24a.30b.31b / d: 14:19a.20a).

[63] Cf. Weimar's approach, *supra* and n. 49. See, moreover, P. Weimar, *Untersuchungen zur Redaktionsgeschichte des Pentateuch* (BZAW 146; Berlin-New York,
1977), 168-169. In *Die Meerwundererzählung*, 144-147, Weimar casts doubt on the
presumed Hezekian origin of Je.

assigns Exod 14,31 to a dtr redactor.[64]

Other textual elements have gradually been added to the 'deuterono-mic' part of the Sea Narrative. F. Stolz relates various passages, which used to be considered as J, to the so-called "Jahwekriegsideologie" (14:13-14.24b.25b.28b.30a.31). As the wording of these elements is reminiscent of dt/dtr phraseology and thought, he argues that they should be attributed to the *Überarbeitungsschicht* J[sek], which Stolz seems to characterize as proto-dt.[65] W. Fuss, on the other hand, asserts that the redaction (R[JE]) which combined the J and E versions of the Sea event has verbal, stylistic and conceptual features to be found exclusively in dtr texts.[66] The theological work (JE) resulting from this literary activity could, therefore, only be oriented to fifth-century readers. According to Fuss, meticulous stylistic and linguistic analysis reveals that this dtr redaction is obviously present, or at least latent (*), in Exod 13:17-19.21-22; 14:3-5*.7.9*.10-15a.16b.19a.20a.21a*.23-25*.27.30-31a. H.H. Schmid, in his re-examination of the Yahwistic tradition in the Pentateuch, also maintains the dtr nature of a signifi-cant portion of the J version of Exod 13:17-14:31, i.e., 14:10.14.24-25.30-31.[67]

P. Weimar's 1985 study of the Sea Narrative marks the beginning of a more painstaking analysis of 'deuteronomic' elements and passages in the biblical account. Weimar claims that the pre-Priestly R[je] account (13:17aα.19; 14:5b.6.11aα*.11b.21aß. 24aα.27aß.31b) has undergone a limited, but, theologically speaking, important reworking by a 6th century dtr redactor.[68] It has been recomposed as a programmatic prelude to the Wilderness complex by adding the topic of the pillar of cloud and fire. In addition, the inclusion of the motif הלך לפני, binds together the Sea and *Landnahme* traditions. The exilic theme of "unfaithfulness", moreover, could serve Dtr's model of justifying the loss of the "promised land". This dtr 'updating' of the R[je] Sea Narra-tive is found, more particularly, in 13:21a.22; 14:19b.20aγb.24aγ. Such

---

[64] Smend, 66.

[65] F. Stolz, *Jahwes und Israels Kriege. Kriegstheorien und Kriegserfahrungen im Glauben des alten Israels* (ATANT 60; Zürich, 1972), 94-97 and see also 70 on the relationship between Num 14:9 (J[s] and compare Exod 14:13) and Judg 1:19 (proto-dt).

[66] W. Fuss, *Die deuteronomistische Pentateuchredaktion in Exodus 3-17* (BZAW 126; Berlin-New York, 1972), 297-327. An excellent review of this rather confused, but provocative analysis of Exod 3-17, appeared in *RB* 80 (1973), 92-99 (F. Langlamet).

[67] H.H. Schmid, *Der sogenannte Jahwist. Beobachtungen und Fragen zur Pentateuchforschung* (Zürich, 1976), 54-60.

[68] Weimar, *Die Meerwundererzählung*, 148-164.

redactional modifications are also related by F. Kohata to the dtr tradition.[69] He recognizes, though not without hesitation, redactional elements (13:21-22; 14:7.11-12. (14?).19b.24-25.31) which have close affinities with the dtr tradition. It should be remembered, however, that Weimar's R^{je} seems to approximate the 'deuteronomic' tradition, as already stated above.

In my 1986 analysis of Exod 13:17-14:31, I defend the thesis that the first and, thus, oldest version of the Sea Narrative which could be reconstructed on reliable grounds resulted from a late 8th century B.C.E. proto-dt redaction.[70] These redactors reworked traditional materials and, hence, I maintain the conventional label "JE" for the composition they shaped.[71] It appears to me that the proto-dt Sea Narrative emerges as a self-contained account in 13:17-19.21-22; 14:5-7.8c.9ab*.10b-e.11-12*. 13-14.19-20.21bc*.24-25.27b-d*.28c.30. 31*. As already mentioned above, the 1993 study of H. Lamberty-Zielinski also takes into consideration the existence of a pre-dt/dtr reworking of an existing Yahwistic Sea Narrative. She, more particularly, points to 13:17.18*.19.21.22; 14:5b.11.12.13b.19.20.21aβγ. 24aγ.25a.27aα"ß.31aαb.

Finally, E. Blum's critical examination of the Sea Narrative shows two *kompositionelle Textelemente*, namely 14:13-14 and 14:30-31, which are to be related to the "KD" or D-composition, as described above[72] He points out that one should regard these textual elements neither as *Ergänzungen* nor as *Einschübe*, but as substantial constituents resulting from a "partielle kompositionelle Bearbeitung" of a pre-Priestly tradition.[73]

3. *Proto-dt, dt/dtr or post-dtr?*

In the foregoing we have seen how scholars differ in their approach to the problem of 'deuteronomic' elements in the Sea Narrative. Apart from the fact that this question has been ignored until very recently, it

---

[69] Kohata, *Jahwist*, 287-289, 292-294.

[70] Cf. *supra* and n. 6.

[71] With regard to this, I would like to cite a remark made by G.W. Coats, in his review of Fuss' study: "Everyone knows of the excesses in source analysis from past generations; and we should rejoice over rejection of such procedure. (...) But we should also avoid a corresponding error, i.e., rejection of the methodology rather than the excesses. If evidence exists that a narrative is composite, that evidence must be evaluated. My appeal is that we must more carefully sort through methods and their assumptions in order to determine whether what we think is evidence for a composite narrative is really that."

[72] Blum, *Studien*, 30-32, 39-40, 43.

[73] Blum, 40. On 30 he calls these verses "programmatische Rahmenverse".

appears that discussions focus on the extent of such components in Exod 13:17-14:31 as well as on the precise specification of their 'deuteronomic' nature. The latter issue, more particularly, raises the question of whether or not there is evidence to differentiate proto-dt elements from dt/dtr and post-dtr ones. At this point, the matter of methodology, which was discussed in the preceding section (III), reappears. Since the present paper aims to survey in a more general way the problem of 'deuteronomic' elements in the Tetrateuch, with special attention to the Sea Narrative, I will now only employ one specific case to briefly illustrate my contention.[74] It particularly concerns the relationship between Deut 21:30-33 and different parts of the Sea Narrative.

Textual parallels[75]

Deut 1:30a:	יהוה אלהיכם ההלך לפניכם
Exod 13:21a:	ויהוה הלך לפניהם
Num 14:14e:	אתה הלך לפניהם

Deut 1:30b:	הוא ילחם לכם
Exod 14:14a:	יהוה ילחם לכם
Exod 14:25d:	יהוה נלחם להם במצרים

Deut 1:33a:	ההלך לפניכם בדרך לתור לכם מקום לחנתכם
	באש לילה לראתכם בדרך אשר תלכו בה
	ובענן יומם
Exod 13:21-22:	ויהוה הלך לפניהם יומם בעמוד ענן לנחתם הדרך
	ולילה בעמוד אש להאיר להם
	ללכת יומם ולילה
	לא ימיש עמוד הענן יומם ועמוד האש לילה לפני העם
Num 14:14e:	ובעמד ענן אתה הלך לפניהם יומם
	ובעמוד אש לילה

Brief analysis

The classical view of the relationship between these texts is well represented by M. Weinfeld's comment on Deut 1:33: "It seems that in this verse the author drew heavily on Exod 13:21, Num 10:33, and Num 14:14, but occasionally paraphrased the idioms of his sources."[76]

---

[74] An article containing a complete analysis of the proto-dt redaction of Exod 13:17-14:31 is in preparation and will appear in 1994. See also the research project of H. Ausloos as mentioned *supra*, n. 12.

[75] Cf. S.R. Driver, *A Critical and Exegetical Commentary on Deuteronomy* (ICC; Edinburgh, 1895, 1903³), 24.

[76] Weinfeld, *Deuteronomy 1-11*, 149. See also Driver, *Deuteronomy*, 25 and N. Lohfink, "Darstellungskunst und Theologie in Dtn 1,6-3,29", *Biblica* 41 (1960), 114-115.

Recent studies, however, stress that Exod 13:21-22 (+ 14:19a.20a.24); Num 14:14 [שא + ענן] and Exod 14:14.25 [יהוה נלחם], on the one hand, and Deut 1:30-33, on the other, reflect a common 'deuteronomic' tradition. As we saw above, the 'deuteronomic' origin of the texts under concern has been determined in two different ways. Some consider Exod 14* and Num 14* as an early and hence proto-dt stage in the process of developing an established dt/dtr literature (Lamberty-Zielinski, Vervenne, Kohata?), whereas others claim a dtr (Weimar, Kohata?) and even post-dtr origin (Blum) for the Tetrateuchal texts in question.[77]

From the analysis offered by most of these scholars, it is clear that the definition of the 'deuteronomic' nature of Exod 13:21-22 and 14:14 (.25) relies on either diachronic literary-critical arguments (Lamberty-Zielinski, Kohata, Weimar) or synchronic composition-critical evidence (Blum).

Weimar argues that the *Grundschicht* of Num 14:13-19 is dtr, while attributing Deut 1:33 to a late-dtr layer in 1:19-46. He then concludes that this is also the case for the related passage Exod 13:21-22. Kohata, on the other hand, is more cautious when proposing that Exod 13:21-22 is "höchstwahrscheinlich redaktioneller Zusatz, der der dtr Tradition nahesteht", whereas Lamberty-Zielinski identifies Num 14:14 as "vordtr (= jehowistisch)" and, hence, characterises Exod 13:21-22 as pre-dtr. The textual relationships, however, which these scholars put forward as an argument to support the (pre-)dtr character of Exod 13:21f. are not convincing, since their approach is mainly based on the hypothetical results of a diachronic literary-critical analysis. One cannot escape the impression that they pile up hypotheses.[78]

Unlike the scholars mentioned before, Blum denies any *Rückverweis* of Deut 1:30-32 to Exod 14:13-14 (יהוה ילחם / ראה)(KD). First, he claims that the theme of "to see what Yhwh performed" is a central dtr topic (Deut 3:21-22; 6:21 *(sic!)*; 7:18-19; 10:21; 11:2-7; 29:1-2; Josh 23:3; 1 Sam 12:16 etc.). Next, Deut 1:30b does not specifically refer to

---

[77] Lamberty-Zielinski, 106-110; Vervenne, *Het Zeeverhaal*, 807-808; Kohata, *Jahwist*, 292-293 ("höchstwahrscheinlich redaktioneller Zusatz, der der dtr Tradition nahesteht"); Weimar, *Die Meerwundererzählung*, 151-156; Blum, *Studien*, 175-176.

[78] A typical example of this approach by Weimar is to be found in *Die Meer-wundererzählung*, 111-112, n. 7, where he deals with Exod 14:31b. Weimar states that the phrase ובמשה עבדו predominantly occurs in dtr texts, including Num 12:7.8. A dtr characterization of Exod 14:31b, however, seems to be difficult, since this fragment cannot be identified as a redactional element. Weimar then finds a way out of the difficulties in claiming that a few texts from the DtrH, such as Josh 1:1.2, which seem to expose a literary relationship with Exod 14:31b, might be pre-dtr.

the Sea event but to the Exodus as a whole or even the Plagues (cf. Deut 4:34; 6:22; 7:19; 11:3; 29:1-2). Finally, the האמין motif (cf. Exod 14:31) has its parallel within Deuteronomy, viz. Deut 9:23. Although I sympathize with Blum's approach to the problem of the composition of the Pentateuch, it appears that even this scholar does not succeed in bringing forward any very cogent arguments either against the pre-dt nature of Exod 14:13-14 or in support of its post-dtr origin. What is conspicuously absent is a meticulous inquiry into the phraseology of the related texts. First, the phrase "to see what Yhwh performed" is expressed in a variety of wordings, which are not limited to apparent dt/dtr traditions.[79] One should clearly distinguish four patterns of expressions, i.e., ראה את (object) אשר עשה יהוה (Exod 14:13.31; Num 14:22; Deut 3:21; 29:1; Josh 23:3; Judg 2:7; 1 Sam 12:15-16; Ezek 39:21) — ראה את אשר עשה יהוה (Exod 6:1; 19:4; Deut 4:3; Josh 24:7) — ראה את (object) יהוה אשר — יהוה (Exod 9:16; 34:10; Deut 3:24; 11:2.7) — ראה X (Deut 1:30-31; 7:19; 10:21; 29:2). The formula עשה יהוה ב, moreover, only occurs in Exod 14:31 and Josh 24:7. Second, the two other remarks made by Blum do not take serious account of the varying function and meaning of expressions and themes within different contexts. If Exod 14:13-14 were the source-text of Deut 1:30-33, the latter would not necessarily have to echo the "original" focus of the former. Furthermore, it is incomprehensible why Deut 1:32 (האמין) could be related only to Deut 9:23. Regarding the latter, Weinfeld rightly states that the "whole verse looks like an epitome of the episode of the spies in Deut 1:19b-32".[80] Likewise one could say that Deut 1:30-33 epitomizes Exod 13:17-14:31 and Num 14:11-14.

The question still remains whether Exod 13:21-22 and 14:13-14 are proto-dt, dt/dtr or post-dtr. The Sea Narrative contains motifs which are characteristic of the "Wilderness tradition"(cf. Exod 13:21-22; 14:19-20.24). One could distinguish three groups of textual relationships, namely Exod 23:20-33; 32-34 / Num 14:14 / Deut 1:33. The pre-dt character of Exod 23 and 32-34 has been plausibly demonstrated by Brekelmans and Begg, to mention only these.[81] With regard to Num 14, the arguments put forward by Skweres and Lohfink in support of its early dt character are more convincing than Weimar's hypothesis or Blum's objections, since the former carefully analyse the passage in

---

[79] Cf. Vervenne, *Het Zeeverhaal*, 669-673.

[80] Weinfeld, *Deuteronomy 1-11*, 414.

[81] Brekelmans, "Les éléments", 84-90; Begg, 233-250. See also G. Schmitt, *Du sollst keinen Frieden schließen mit den Bewohnern des Landes* (BWANT 91; Stuttgart, 1970), 15; Halbe, 483-505; A.W. Jenks, *The Elohist and North Israelite Traditions* (SBL Monograph Series 22; Missoula, MT, 1977).

question according to the methodological procedure mentioned before (III).[82]

Finally, some textual data could be relevant for determining the nature of 'deuteronomic' elements in the Sea Narrative (cf. *supra*, III). It affects in particular the relationship between the longer text Exod 13:21MT and the shorter text as found in Exod 13:21LXX. The former agrees with Neh 9:12.19MT, while the latter corresponds to Deut 1:33MT:[83]

Exod 13:21LXX-*Vorlage*:

והאלהים הלך לפניהם
יומם בעמוד ענן לראתם בדרך
ולילה בעמוד אש

Deut 1:33aMT:

ההלך לפניכם בדרך לתור לכם מקום לחנתכם
באש לילה לראתכם בדרך אשר תלכו בה
ובענן יומם

Exod 13:21-22MT:

ויהוה הלך לפניהם יומם בעמוד ענן לנחתם הדרך
ולילה בעמוד אש להאיר להם
ללכת יומם ולילה
לא ימיש עמוד הענן יומם ועמוד האש לילה לפני העם

Neh 9:12MT:

ובעמוד ענן הנחיתם יומם
ובעמוד אש לילה להאיר להם את הדרך אשר ילכו בה

Neh 9:19MT:

את עמוד הענן לא סר מעליהם ביומם להנחתם בהדרך
ואת עמוד האש בלילה להאיר להם ואת הדרך אשר ילכו בה

The textual witness in Exod 13:21LXX *approximates* Deut 1:33MT, while Exod 13:21(-22)MT is closer to Neh 9:12.19. Deut 1:33MT, on the other hand, *partly* corresponds to Exod 13:21MT (Deut: לחנתכם and compare with 1:33LXX: ולנחתכם? / Exod: לנחתם) and Neh 9:12.19 (Deut: תלכו בה / Neh: ילכו בה; Deut: לחנתכם / Neh: להנחתם). As a consequence, Exod 13:21-22MT might reflect a redactionally reworked text by a final (Priestly?) editor. After all, Exod 13:21-22 and Deut 1:33 function in a completely different context. Contrary to Exod 13:21-22, the passage in Deuteronomy concentrates on a sort of 'anti-exodus'. For the time being, we may say with Weinfeld that the author of Deut 1:33 "develops his style by bringing in phrases from other Exodus traditions, such as Exod 13:21 and Num 10:33."[84]

---

[82] Skweres, 168-169; Lohfink, "Darstellungskunst"; Weimar, 153, n. 13; Blum, *Studien*, 172-174.

[83] A detailed analysis is offered in Vervenne, *Het Zeeverhaal*, 124-127.

[84] Weinfeld, *Deuteronomy 1-11*, 153. See also *supra*, n. 74.

V. *Much Ado about Nothing?*

In a recent contribution on the Pentateuch, J. Briend says that "refuser une attribution documentaire ne signifie pas pour autant que l'on ait comme unique solution de qualifier le texte de deutéronomique, ce qui est malheureusement trop souvent le cas dans les recherches actuelles.".[85] The main purpose of the present paper was to offer some reflections on the complicated question of 'deuteronomic' elements in the complex Genesis to Numbers. It goes without saying that there is not yet a safe hypothesis available. A great deal of research remains to be done. Outsiders, however, may obtain the impression that there is "much ado about nothing". It should, therefore, be said that despite the undeniable importance of either reader-response or biblical-theological, viz. canonical approaches, it does not seem that diachronic questions are not at all essential. Pentateuchal texts built up a network of meanings which primarily ask for an historical approach in the broadest sense of the word. As regards the question about 'deuteronomism' in the Tetrateuch, we are reminded of the reflection offered by M. Weinfeld in his epoch-making study on *Deuteronomy and the Deuteronomic School*:

> The main characteristic of deuteronomic phraseology is not the employment of new idioms and expressions, because many of these could be found in the earlier sources and especially in the Elohistic source. Indeed, it would be nonsense to say that all of a sudden in the seventh century a new vocabulary and new expressions were created. Language grows in an organic and natural way and is not created artificially. What constitutes the novelty of the deuteronomic style therefore is not new idioms and new expressions, but a specific jargon reflecting the religious upheaval of this time. (...) What makes a phrase deuteronomic is not its mere occurrence in Deuteronomy, but its meaning within the framework of deuteronomic theology.[86]

---

[85] Briend, "Lecture" (*supra*, n. 4), 27.
[86] Weinfeld, 1-2.

YAHWEH AND ITS APPOSITIVES
IN LXX DEUTERONOMIUM

JOHN WILLIAM WEVERS

University of Toronto

The tetragrammaton occurs 561 times in Deut, of which it stands alone in 233 cases, i.e. without appositives. It is accompanied by *'lhyk* 233 times, by *'lhykm* 48 times, by *'lhynw,* 23 times, by *'lhy 'b(w)tyk(m),* *'btynw* or *'btm* 10 times, by *'lhy,* 3 times and *'lhyw* 2 times. κύριος is the normal substitute for *yhwh,* and the appositives are correctly rendered by ὁ θεός + σου, ὑμῶν, ἡμῶν, τῶν πατέρων..., μου and αὐτοῦ resp.

Deviations from the normal renderings are as follows: for *yhwh* 41 cases; for Yahweh thy[1] God, 30 cases; for Yahweh God of ... fathers, 10; for Yahweh your God, 7; for Yahweh my God, 2 times, and for Yahweh our God, 1 time. It is these deviations which are the subject of this essay.

I

Some of these deviations are undoubtedly textual in origin; this is particularly the case where the Samaritan Pentateuch (Sam) supports the LXX variant. Of the 41 cases in which *yhwh* is not rendered by a simple κύριος, 24 add ὁ θεός σου. Seven of these cases (6:12.18; 10:13; 16:2.15; 17:10; 18:12) are clearly textual since Sam reads *yhwh 'lhyk.* One might also include 1:8 where God is speaking: "I have given ... the land ... which ...*nšb'* to your fathers." LXX has ὤμοσα which equals Sam.

1.1. Parallel passages often influence the Deut translator, particularly in view of the repetitive Deuteronomistic language. E.g. at 12:14 reference is made in MT to "the place which Yahweh chooses". The context changes to the singular with v. 13: *hšmr lk.* If one examines this collocation throughout the book it appears that in 17 cases of a relative clause with the verb ἐκλέγω the subject is κύριος ὁ θεός σου; three times

---

[1] Since Modern English does not distinguish between the second singular and second plural I shall be using the Elizabethan "thou" to distinguish the singular from the plural "you" throughout this paper.

it becomes κύριος without an appositive; twice it is κύριος ὁ θεὸς ὑμῶν, and once (17:15) it appears as κύριος ὁ θεός. Not only at 12:14, but also at v. 26, 14:2; 15:20 does MT have *yhwh* but LXX adds the popular appositive; in fact, at 14:23(22)[2]; 16:16 *bḥr* has no explicit subject given but LXX has κύριος and κύριος ὁ θεός σου stated as expressed subject resp.

1.1.2. Such paradigmatic pressure also influenced the recurring collocation "do the upright and the good before *yhwh*". At 12:25 MT has a shorter version: *t'šh hyšr b'yny yhwh*,[3] whereas LXX has the fuller ποιήσῃς τὸ καλὸν καὶ τὸ ἀρεστὸν ἔναντι κυρίου τοῦ θεοῦ σου. The collocation also occurs at 6:18; 12:28; 13:19(18); 21:9 (at 6:18 and 21:9 MT only has *yhwh)* and the reference is always to κυρίου τοῦ θεοῦ σου. The deviant text is created ex par (i.e. from parallel passages).

1.1.3. In fact, most of the changes from *yhwh* to κύριος ὁ θεός σου could be explained as being ex par. At 15:2 MT speaks of a release being called *lyhwh,* whereas LXX has κυρίῳ τῷ θεῷ σου. But two verses earlier "Lord thy God" also occurred, and probably influenced the translator. In v. 4 MT has *ybrkk yhwh* which LXX translates by εὐλογήσει σε κύριος ὁ θεός σου but this takes place in the land which *yhwh 'lhyk* is giving thee, and again the influence is obvious. At 16:16 one reads "not shall one appear empty before *yhwh*", though LXX has "(before) the Lord thy God," but this longer text also obtains in v. 16a as well as three times in v. 15. At 24:4 MT has "it is an abomination before *yhwh* and not shalt thou defile (LXX and Sam have a plural verb!) the land which *yhwh 'lhyk* is giving thee"; LXX levels the text with "Lord thy God" in both clauses. This same type of contextualization to "Lord thy God" occurs at 28:7.11.13.64; 30:8.9b.

1.1.4. Seldom if ever does it seem reasonable to reconstruct a possible exegetical reason for the change. At 4:35 MT has "*yhwh* is God, there is none else beside him." Since Israel is addressed by Moses in a context where the great redemptive acts are being recalled, it is not inappropriate that the text should insist on the covenant relationship, viz. that it is Israel's God who alone is God. Similarly at v. 39 there obtains in an amplified form: "*yhwh* is God in heaven above and on the earth below; there is none else". LXX insists that it is the "Lord thy God who is in heaven above ... and there is none else beside him".

---

[2] Throughout this essay whenever the verse numbering of MT and LXX disagree, the verse number of LXX is placed in parentheses.

[3] I use the grapheme *š* for both *sin* and *shin,* since the two were not distinguished in writing before the time of the Masoretes.

1.2. At 29:3(4) Moses is addressing Israel and recalling the great trials, signs and wonders performed in Egypt "and not did *yhwh* give you a heart to understand", but LXX has κύριος ὁ θεός. This cannot be textual, since the collocation *yhwh 'lhym* does not occur anywhere in Deut; in fact, the double name occurs in the Pentateuch only in Gen 2 and 3 and in Exod 9:30. Could not its use here be a reflection of Gen 3:22 over against 2:16-17, i.e. of the temptation of Adam by which humanity, ὁ Ἀδάμ, yielded to the desire to know good and evil, and thereby lost the ability to understand the divine actions on his own? In the Gen story it was the Lord God who was the actor when man sinned. As a result his eyes were opened to his own nakedness, but a heart to understand was no longer his.

1.3. In two cases MT's *yhwh* appears as κύριος ὁ θεὸς ὑμῶν. At 3:20 "until *yhwh* gives rest to your brothers" is contextualized by LXX by including the appositive, since *yhwh 'lhykm* appears later in the verse as well as in v. 21; the variant is then ex par.

At 9:18 Moses states that he had besought *yhwh* . . . "concerning all your sins which you sinned in doing evil before *yhwh* so as to provoke him". Moses had smashed the two tablets of the ten words in anger, but he still intercedes; it is fitting that in spite of their idolatrous actions *yhwh* should still be called τοῦ θεοῦ ὑμῶν. It should be said that this fits in with v. 16: "you sinned before the Lord your God" as well.

1.4. At 4:3 the Israelites are reminded that "your eyes have seen what *yhwh* did at Baal Peor", but LXX has κύριος ὁ θεὸς ἡμῶν. This is contextually possible, since Moses is speaking to the people, but I suspect that the text is not original, and that ὑμῶν should be read; this is the reading of A 376-oI 73*-551* 343-730 71' 59 646 Arab, whereas the first plural pronoun is impressively supported by almost all the other witnesses. The context is second plural throughout vv. 1-6. Within v. 3 itself note οἱ ὀφθαλμοὶ ὑμῶν in v. a and κύριος ὁ θεὸς ὑμῶν ἐξ ὑμῶν in v. b. The change to the longer text is then a case of leveling to the context.

1.5. Much more difficult to understand are changes from *yhwh* to ὁ θεός σου, ὁ θεὸς ὑμῶν or simply ὁ θεός. Their Hebrew equivalents occur without *yhwh* so infrequently that it is unlikely that these were textually conditioned. *'lhyk* or *'lhykm* do not occur at all (i.e. as sole titles), whereas *'lhym* or *'lwh* or *'l* occur a total of only 29 times.

1.5.1. At 12:21 MT makes reference to cattle and flock "which *yhwh* gave to thee". Earlier in the verse there occurred "the place which *yhwh 'lhyk* chooses," which LXX quite correctly rendered by κύριος ὁ θεός σου, but for *yhwh* 2° LXX has ὁ θεός σου. A variant text κυριος ο θεος σου is supported by 58-376' *b d* 246 *s t* 318 *z* 28 407' Eth Arm^ap Co. This occurs frequently throughout the chapter and is ex par. It is, however, not original, since it would be difficult to explain the loss of an original κύριος. The LXX text may simply be a case of the translator occasionally reminding the reader of who κύριος is; he is thy/your God.

1.5.2. A similar situation obtains earlier in v. 11 where for *lyhwh* LXX reads τῷ θεῷ ὑμῶν. Again there is a variant tradition supporting the prefixing of κυριω, this time by *d* 246 *s* 619 *z* ^Lat Spec 59 Syh; this is almost certainly rooted in the hexaplaric (hex) correction of LXX τω κυριω υμων. One suspects that here the translator is reminding the reader that their vows are with their covenant partner, i.e. with their God (who is of course κύριος).

1.5.3. Of particular interest but difficult is a number of cases where MT has *yhwh* but LXX has ὁ θεός. To suggest that these were due to a parent text having *'lhym* really solves nothing, since one would then ask an explanation for the parent Hebrew text. It could also be maintained that the translator made a mistake, was careless, but this seems to me to dodge the issue.

The first of these occurs at 2:15. Yahweh had sworn that the generation of warriors should perish and not enter Canaan; in fact, they perished during the 38 years of wandering as Yahweh had sworn to them. Then v. 15 explains that "the hand of *yhwh* was on them to destroy them," but in LXX this becomes (ἡ χεὶρ) τοῦ θεοῦ. What the change to "the divine hand" does is to avoid stating bluntly that Israel's covenant deity killed the Israelite men; making the hand of God responsible might seem somewhat more appropriate.

At 4:20 the substitution of ὁ θεός for *yhwh* is particularly strange, since it involves a redemptive context. The Israelites were warned against all forms of astral worship which "Yahweh thy God had assigned to the nations, which are under the sky". Then v. 20 continues with "and you *yhwh* took and brought you out from the iron furnace ... to be his special people". Then Moses continues with his own lot — Yahweh was so angry with him "because of your words" and he swore .... LXX, however, has for v. 20 "but you ὁ θεός took and brought out ..." Why did LXX change to "God took you ...," especially in view of your becoming a λαὸν ἔγκληρον for him? Is this a case of the translator being highly ironic?

At 8:3 Yahweh had fed the Israelites with manna in the wilderness to teach them a lesson; it is not only by bread but by everything that goes forth from the mouth of *yhwh* that humanity lives. LXX has it that by every word that goes forth from the mouth θεοῦ shall humanity live. What the Greek says is that the feeding with manna is a matter of divine sustenance; it is a display of God's power and providence, a divine rather than a covenantal matter.

At 9:26 the substitution of κύριος is probably propelled by the urge to avoid repetition. MT says "I prayed to *yhwh* and I said *'dny yhwh*". Since the vocatives are rendered by κύριε κύριε the translator avoided another κύριος by his καὶ ηὐξάμην πρὸς τὸν θεόν.

The case of 26:17 is much more difficult to explain. V. 16 began with "on this day *yhwh 'lhyk* commands," and v. 17, with "thou didst declare *'t yhwh* this day that he is thy God ...," and v. 18 states that "*yhwh* declared this day about thee that thou art his special people". In this account of the covenant formation through mutual declaration one might have expected LXX to use κύριος throughout, but instead the divine commandment comes from κύριος ὁ θεός σου; as for the people "thou didst choose this day τὸν θεόν to be thy God," just as κύριος chose thee today to be his special people. Since v. 16 had identified Israel's God as κύριος, it was no longer necessary to use the personal name in v. 17; that God was chosen to be Israel's God.

At 29:19(20) the statement is made that "*yhwh* is not willing to forgive him (the idolator)". This comes in the larger context of the covenant made with Israel in Moab, and more immediately in the context of a diatribe against any form of idolatry. LXX has changed what MT says to "not will ὁ θεὸς εὐιλατεῦσαι him," i.e. God will not be merciful to him, though the text does continue with "but the anger of *yhwh* / κύριος and his zeal will burn against that man". Why should LXX avoid the use of κύριος in the opening clause? I suggest that it is intended to avoid any conflict with the characterization of κύριος ὁ θεός σου at 4:31 as a merciful God, one who will not forsake nor destroy thee, nor forget the covenant of thy fathers.

Most puzzling is the case of τὰ πρὸς τὸν θεόν for *'m yhwh* at 31:27. Moses is making his farewell address to the people and reminding them as he had done at 9:7.24 of their perpetual rebellious actions in matters that pertain to *yhwh*. In the earlier contexts the phrase had been rendered more literally by τὰ πρὸς κύριον, but in the farewell statement LXX has changed it to τὰ πρὸς τὸν θεόν. It should be mentioned that ms 848 has [τ]α προς *yhwh* τον θεον here,[4] but this may well be due to

---

[4] See Plate 44, fr. 103, line 5 in Z. Aly, *Three Rolls of the Early Septuagint. Genesis and Deuteronomy,* with preface, introduction, and notes by L. Koenen. (Papyrologische Texte und Abhandlungen 27; Bonn, 1980).

secondary Hebrew influence, or ex par;[5] in any event, it is secondary. Why LXX should have here generalized the statement on Israel's rebellious propensities is not clear; what it has done is to place Israel's mutinous nature even more starkly in perspective — not just as rebellious against their own God, but against deity; it was humanity pitted against God.

1.6. In two cases *yhwh* in MT is omitted by LXX. The omission as 23:3(2) is irrelevant to this enquiry, since the name occurred in v. 3b, all of which had been omitted due to homoioteleuton, i.e. the text from *yhwh* 1° through *yhwh* 2° is lacking in LXX. At 6:19 MT has *k'šr dbr yhwh,* but LXX simply has καθὰ ἐλάλησεν.[6] The shorter text does not impede the reader's understanding, and the omission may be stylistic.[7]

1.7. In 16:1 the translator has changed a third person construction into a direct address to the people, thereby eliminating *yhwh* from the translation. The command to observe the pascha feast is rationalized by a *ky* clause: "for in the month of Abib *yhwh* brought you out of Egypt". LXX describes the exodus as ἐξῆλθες from Egypt.

At 31:23 κύριος is introduced through a change in construction.. V. 22 had said that "Moses wrote this song ... and taught it to the Israelites". Then v. 24 says "And it happened when Moses finished writing .... " V. 23 interrupts this sequence rather oddly by "And he commanded Joshua ... and said ... thou shalt bring the Israelites into the land which I swore to them and I shall be with thee". Obviously the subject is the *yhwh* who was speaking from vv. 16-21. But the translator has changed the relative clause in v. 23 into third person: ἣν ὤμοσεν κύριος αὐτοῖς καὶ αὐτὸς ἔσται μετὰ σοῦ. In other words, v. 23 continues Moses as subject, thereby making a consistent narrative.

II

yhwh 'lhyk would normally be rendered by κύριος ὁ θεός σου; in fact 202 instances of the 233 occurrences of *yhwh 'lhyk* are so rendered. In seven cases LXX represents the plural κύριος ὁ θεὸς ὑμῶν, and in three

---

[5] See J.W. Wevers, *Text History of the Greek Deuteronomy* [hereafter THGD] (MSU 13; Göttingen, 1978), 71.

[6] As might be expected hex has added κυριος at the end.

[7] An interesting occurrence of κύριος is found at 32:4d, which is technically not part of our subject since it does not involve *yhwh*. The phrase in question is "righteous and upright is *hw'*." In the parallel hemistichs *hṣwr* "the rock" occurs in line a and is correctly interpreted as being used figuratively for God, thus θεός, and in line c *'l* obtains, and is also rendered by θεός. It remained then for LXX to identify who was intended by the pronoun as κύριος.

cases κύριος ὁ θεὸς ἡμῶν, i.e. a first plural pronoun.[8]

2.0.1. Of the seven cases of κύριος ὁ θεὸς ὑμῶν the one at 12:9 is probably textual in nature, since LXX follows the number of Sam throughout the verse. Another five represent attempts to make the text somewhat more consistent in number. In 1:19-30 MT constitutes a plural context except for v. 21 which is in the singular for all its nine second person references. LXX contextualizes by making this verse plural throughout as well. Similarly at 4:3 the context is plural throughout except for the odd *yhwh 'lhyk mqrbk* at the end of the verse; LXX levels this to κύριος ὁ θεὸς ὑμῶν ἐξ ὑμῶν. A similar leveling to the plural obtains in vv. 25 and 29. So too at 28:62 the inconsistent singular *šm't bqwl yhwh 'lhyk* is put into the plural to conform to the rest of the verse and v. 63.

The case of 15:5 is puzzling. The entire chapter is in the singular in MT as well as in LXX except for the first part of v. 5 which reads ἐὰν δὲ ἀκοῇ εἰσακούσητε ... κυρίου τοῦ θεοῦ ὑμῶν, but it ends with ἐντολὰς ταύτας ὅσας ἐγὼ ἐντέλλομαί σοι σήμερον. The text is assured with only two mss witnessing a consistent singular text, an obvious scribal correction. There seems to be no clear reason why LXX (or its parent text?) should have changed to the singular for this conditional statement appended to v. 4, and I for one am baffled by it.

2.0.2. At 2:30 MT reads: "And Sihon king of Heshbon was unwilling to let us pass through, because *yhwh 'lhyk* had hardened his heart". LXX has κύριος ὁ θεὸς ἡμῶν which makes it agree with "let us pass" earlier in the verse. The case at 7:19 probably witnesses to an exegetical interpretation by the translator. The relevant context in MT is "'*šr hws'k yhwh 'lhyk*, so shall *yhwh 'lhyk* do to all the nations". LXX interprets the collocation as a ὡς ... οὕτως construction, but then changes the subject of the "so" clause to κύριος ὁ θεὸς ἡμῶν. This can only be an intentional change by which the comparison with "as the Lord

---

[8] This might be taken as part of the larger and highly controversial problem of change in number on which much has been written. One might consult a recent statement in G. Braulik, *Die Mittel deuteronomischer Rhetorik* (AnBib 68; Rome, 1978), 146-149, or *idem*, review of D. Knapp, *Deuteronomium 4: Literarische Analyse und theologische Interpretation* (Göttinger Theologische Arbeiten 35; Göttingen, 1987) in *RB* 96 (1989), 272-273. A thorough discussion basing the change in number on literary analysis obtained in G. Minette de Tillesse, "Sections 'tu' et sections 'vous' dans le Deutéronome", *VT* 12 (1962), 29-87. See also the more recent study of C.T. Begg, "The Significance of the Numeruswechsel in Deuteronomy", *ETL* 55 (1979), 116-124. This essay is not intended to deal with that problem except insofar as the translator's treatment of the singular vs plural suffixes on the appositives of *yhwh* is concerned.

thy God brought thee out", is balanced by the Lord our God identified as operating on "all the nations". The point is that "thy God" delivered "thee", but it is "our God" over against the nations.

A final instance of *yhwh 'lhyk* being rendered by κύριος ὁ θεὸς ἡμῶν obtains at 2:7. A first person plural reference had obtained in v. 1, and then recurs in v. 8. Vv. 3-6 occur in second plural, and MT has v. 7 completely in second singular. LXX follows MT in its second singular references except for the opening *(ky) yhwh 'lhyk* which LXX renders by κύριος ὁ θεὸς ἡμῶν. There is some uncertainty about the original text, since a substantially supported A variant reading witnesses to υμων. Both are contextually possible. It might be argued that υμων continues the plural from vv. 4-6, i.e. not changing to the singular until the next reference: "(Yahweh your God blessed) thee, etc." On the other hand, the first person fits much better, and was probably promoted by the παρήλθομεν τοὺς ἀδελφοὺς ἡμῶν of v. 8.

2.1. In eight cases MT's *yhwh 'lhyk is* shortened to κύριος in LXX. At 9:5 this is probably a textual matter, since Sam lacks *'lhyk*. Both at 18:5 and 25:16 it seems likely that the parent text had only *yhwh*.[9] In both cases mss actually omit *'lhyk*.[10] It is suggested that MT is itself the product of leveling. At 25:16 *yhwh 'lhyk* occurs in the clause immediately before it, and may well have created MT. At 18:5 the text seems to be in some disarray. LXX has a much fuller text; instead of *lšrt* it has ἔναντι κυρίου τοῦ θεοῦ σου λειτουργεῖν καὶ εὐλογεῖν. It should be noted that v. 6 read *'šr ybhr yhwh*, i.e. without an appositive.

At 28:53 *yhwh 'lhyk* occurs in the context of a curse. The siege of the enemy will be so severe that "thou shalt eat ... the flesh of thy sons and daughters which *yhwh 'lhyk* gave thee", which LXX rendered by κύριος. Throughout the curse materials *yhwh* has occurred without appositive whenever he has acted, but when the people's actions are mentioned it is κύριος ὁ θεός σου. And then in v. 53 this same pattern is followed: thou shalt eat ... the flesh of thy son and thy daughter whom κύριος has given thee. LXX is consistent over against MT.

In the first six verses of chapter 30 the phrase *yhwh 'lhyk* occurs eight times; in four cases LXX has only κύριος (vv. 1.3.3.6), and in four cases it has the full κύριος ὁ θεός σου. MT also has the double designation in v. 7, but only *yhwh* in v. 8, and both the double name and the single *yhwh* in v. 9 and the double name twice in v. 10. It seems clear that the trend from a single *yhwh* to *yhwh* plus *'lhyk* was

---

[9] See the statement in *THGD* 76-77.
[10] At 25:16 six Kenn mss (9,80,111,150,177 and 199) do omit *'lhyk;* at 18:5 only Kenn 9 omits *'lhyk*.

established, and the possibility remains that instances of the longer designation are not always to be preferred.

2.2. At 26:3 in MT the worshiper is told to go to the officiating priest and say "I declare today to *yhwh 'lhyk ky* I entered the land ...." LXX has κυρίῳ τῷ θεῷ μου ὅτι. This is clearly a case of haplography/dittography, with the translator reading *'lhy ky* rather than *'lhyk ky*. I suspect the former to be the preferable text.

2.3. In seven cases *yhwh 'lhyk* is represented in LXX by κύριος ὁ θεός, i.e. with the suffix unrepresented. At 4:21 I suspect the change to be intentional. The collocation occurs in the context of Yahweh being angry with me (i.e. Moses) and he swore that I would not cross the Jordan, i.e. enter the land "which *yhwh 'lhyk* is giving thee". LXX has κύριος ὁ θεός; after all, κύριος was also the God of Moses, and the omission of μου makes a neat point.

At 19:2 κύριος ὁ θεός occurs in the clause "which the Lord God is giving thee". The fuller κύριος ὁ θεός σου both in vv. 1 and 3, and the omission of σου in v. 2 is stylistic; it's better Greek. In the other five cases, 17:14.15; 19:8; 21:5; 24:9, the shorter text is clearly original LXX as the witness of ms 848 shows. The σου is omitted as a matter of Greek style.[11]

2.4. At 27:3 MT reads "the land which *yhwh 'lhyk* is giving thee", but LXX substitutes "κύριος ὁ θεὸς τῶν πατέρων σου is giving to thee". The change is due to the last clause which reads "as said the Lord the God of thy fathers to thee".

And at 10:9 LXX simplifies MT which says concerning the Levite that he has no tribal assignment among his fellows, but rather "Yahweh is his inheritance as *yhwh 'lhyk* spoke to him". LXX omits the divine name and appositive in the "as" clause by its καθὰ εἶπεν αὐτῷ.

III

In a few cases the plural suffix of *'lhykm* appears in LXX in the singular. At 5:32-33 MT has a consistent plural reference: "you shall be careful ... Yahweh your God commanded you; not shall you turn ... way which Yahweh your God commanded you you shall walk ... you may live and it may be well to you and you may lengthen ... land which you shall inherit". LXX only has three plural verbs: the first one, φυλάξεσθε, and the last two, μακροημερεύσητε and κληρονομήσετε;

[11] See *THGD* 76-77.

all the intervening text has been put into the singular. Earlier (vv. 24-27) the people were reported as speaking to Moses. Then in v. 28 Moses refers to the people in the plural, and in vv. 30-31 God speaks to Moses, perforce in the singular. Why LXX changes to the singular in vv. 32-33 is not at all clear. At 11:13 a similar situation obtains. There MT is also plural throughout and continuing through 14a, and only thereafter changing to the singular. LXX follows MT in the opening verb with a plural ἀκούσητε, but then changes to the singular through 16a, switching to the plural with 16b. Meanwhile MT has the singular in 14b-15, but has the plural for all of v. 16. The reason for the deviations is not clear.

At v. 2 *yhwh 'lhykm* also appears in the singular in LXX: κυρίου τοῦ θεοῦ σου. V. 1 had been in the singular with "and thou shalt love the Lord thy God and observe" in both texts. MT is consistently plural in vv. 2-7, and LXX imitates MT except for the σου in v. 2. The translator may have been influenced by the (ὁ θεός) σου of v. 1.

MT is consistently plural in 13:4b-5(3b-4) which it continues into the next verse through the *ky* clause, after which the text becomes singular. LXX has switched to the singular with v. 6a(5a) retaining only a plural at the end of the verse: "thou shalt remove the evil ἐξ ὑμῶν αὐτῶν"; accordingly, "Lord thy God" appears twice in the verse instead of MT's *yhwh 'lhykm* and *yhwh 'lhyk*.

Both MT and LXX use the second singular reference throughout 6:15. MT then changes to the plural for vv. 16-17a, after which it reverts to the singular. LXX only has a plural for the verb ἐξεπειράσασθε in v. 16b, otherwise retaining the singular. Thus v. 16a reads οὐκ ἐκπειράσεις κύριον τὸν θεόν σου instead of the plural of MT For v. 17 MT has a peculiarly inconsistent text with v. a reading *tšmrwn ... yhwh 'lhykm,* but then continuing with a reference to the testimonies and statutes which *swk* "he commanded thee". LXX does a fine job of rationalizing the text by not rendering the suffix of the divine appositive with its κύριος ὁ θεός. This allows the reader to read a consistent singular text for vv. 16-19 (except for the verb in v. 16b).

IV

Two cases of *yhwh 'lhy* are worthy of mention. At 18:16 LXX simplifies the narrative by changing the reported speech of the people in the plural rather than in the singular with MT. The singular of MT is consistent with Moses' address to the people in the singular in v. 16a: *š'lt ... yhwh 'lhyk;* LXX interprets the speech in v. 16b *ad sensum.*

At 4:5 Moses says: "I taught you statutes and judgments as *yhwh 'lhy* commanded me". The reference to "my God" might be thought somewhat inappropriate; either a change to "our God" as at 18:16 or omitting the appositive altogether would remove any notion that *yhwh* was only Moses' God over against the Israelites being addressed. LXX opted for the latter alternative: καθὰ ἐνετείλατό μοι κύριος.

4.1. One instance of *yhwh 'lhynw* which LXX did not render literally obtains at 5:2. MT represents an inconsistent text in vv. 1-4 with "your ears ... you shall teach ... you shall be careful ... *yhwh 'lhynw* ... with us ... with our fathers ... with us, even we here today all of us ... spoke with you ...." LXX not only changes the divine appellative to κύριος ὁ θεὸς ὑμῶν (which by itself might be adjudged a homophonic spelling for the first person) but changes all the first person references to the second person, making a consistent second plural text throughout.

V

There remain a few cases in which MT does not mention *yhwh* but LXX introduces κύριος. The verb *nšbʿ* "swore" occurs 22 times in Deut, and in exactly half of these cases MT names *yhwh* as subject. LXX follows MT everywhere except at 7:13, where Sam has *yhwh* but MT does not, and 13:18(17) where MT lacks *yhwh* but LXX has κύριος. It must be adjudged as an ex par reading.

At 31:11 reference is made to the place *'šr ybhr*, but LXX identifies the subject as κύριος. For a discussion of the verb ἐκλέγω and its subject in relative clauses see 1.1. above. The verb does occur in first person, i.e. in the context of Yahweh speaking as well (1:35; 10:11; 31:20.21.23; 34:4). At 31:23 it refers to "the land which I swore to them (the Israelites) and I shall be with thee (i.e. Joshua)". LXX has changed the relative clause into a third person construction: ἣν ὤμοσεν κύριος αὐτοῖς καὶ αὐτὸς ἔσται μετὰ σοῦ, thereby introducing the divine name.

Twice within the Song of Moses (ch.32) κύριος is added as subject of a verb against the witness of MT. V. 37 reads: "And *'mr*: Where are their gods, the *ṣwr* in whom they sought refuge".[12] This may well be

---

[12] The word *ṣwr* "rock" occurs six times in this poem (vv. 4,15,18,30,31 and 37) as a vigorous figure for God, and is except for v. 37 always translated by θεός, demonstrating thereby that the translator fully understood the reference to be to God. The term is applied to God 33 (or 32) times in MT and is usually (18 times) rendered by θεός. In the Psalter βοηθός is used four times, and once ἀντιλήμπτωρ occurs. Other renderings are κτίστης, φύλαξ, κύριος, ὁ μέγας and in Hab 1:12 it is misunderstood as a verb, ἔπλασέν με. The figure is never literally rendered when the reference is to God.

textual, since a Qumran fragment reads *[w']mr yh[wh]*.[13] At v. 43 the
LXX text is considerably longer; it has eight lines rather than the four
of MT. The relevant hemistich, however, is the last one which has
"and he expiates his land (even) his people". LXX follows the Qumran
fragment referred to at v. 37: *wykpr 'dmt 'mw* in omitting the first
"his", which is more sensible, but also adds κύριος. This identification
of the subject is helpful, since there has been no such actual identification within the verse, although six cases of αὐτῷ/αὐτοῦ obtain as well
as three verbal forms, ἐκδικήσει, ἀνταποδώσει (bis) all of which must
all refer to κύριος.

VI

As a general rule the translator is faithful to his parent text. Since
yhwh as well as *yhwh* plus appositive occur extremely frequently
throughout the book, deviations from MT are often ex par; such
influence must have been hard to withstand. Other deviations often
arise through contextualization; the translator does try for some measure of consistency, particularly in the matter of number, though only
here and there; there was no attempt such as that of Targum Neophyte
which simply used the plural throughout the book. Occasionally,
however, the translator does go his own way; he does translate with
sense; in this way his exegesis is at times betrayed even in his use of
κύριος and θεός, and close attention to such deviations from MT proves
to be a worthwhile exercise.

---

[13] Published in transcription in P.W. Skehan, "A Fragment of the 'Song of
Moses' (Deut 32) from Qumran", *BASOR* 136 (1954), 12-15.

ERWÄGUNGEN ZUM RAHMENPSALM
VON DEUTERONOMIUM 33

A.S. VAN DER WOUDE

Groningen

Allgemein wird angenommen, daß der Segen Moses (Dtn 33)[1] nach dem einleitenden Vers zwei verschiedene, aus der vorköniglichen Zeit Israels herrührende literarische Kompositionen beinhaltet, die ursprünglich separat kursierten: einen Psalm (V. 2-5; 26-29)[2] und die von

---

[1] Abgesehen von den Dtn-Kommentaren ist auf folgende Veröffentlichungen hinzuweisen: K.H. Graf, *Der Segen Mose's (Deuteronomium c. XXXIII) erklärt* (Leipzig, 1857); A.G.J. van der Flier, *Deuteronomium 33*, Diss. Leiden, 1895; C. J. Ball, "The Blessing of Moses", *PSBA* 18 (1896), 118-137; H. Hayman, "The Blessing of Moses: Its Genesis and Structure", *AJSL* 17 (1900-1901), 96-106; P. Riessler, "Das Moseslied und der Mosessegen, II. Der Mosessegen", *BZ* 12 (1914), 125-134; K. Budde, *Der Segen Mose's* (Tübingen, 1922); U. Cassuto, "Il capitolo 33 del Deuteronomio e la festa del Capo d'anno nell'antico Israele", *Rivista degli Studi Orientali* 11 (1926-1928), 233-253; A. van Hoonacker, "Notes sur le texte de la »Bénédiction de Moïse« (Deut. XXXIII)", *Le Muséon* 42 (1929), 42-60; Th.H. Gaster, "Ancient Eulogy of Israel", *JBL* 66 (1947), 53-62; F.M. Cross - D.N. Freedman, "The Blessing of Moses", *JBL* 67 (1948), 191-210; C. Armerding, "The Last Words of Moses: Deuteronomy 33", *Bibliotheca Sacra* 114 (1957), 225-234; R. Tournay, "Le Psaume et les Bénédictions de Moïse", *RB* 65 (1958), 181-213; I. L. Seeligmann, "A Psalm from Pre-regnal Times", *VT* 14 (1964), 75-92; P.D. Miller, "Two Critical Notes on Psalm 68 and Deuteronomy 33", *HTR* 57 (1964), 240-243; H.-J. Zobel, *Stammesspruch und Geschichte* (BZAW 95; Berlin, 1965); B. Margulis, "Genesis XLIX 10/Deut. XXXIII 2-3. A New Look at Old Problems", *VT* 19 (1969), 202-210; C.J. Labuschagne, "The Tribes in the Blessing of Moses", *OTS* 19 (1974), 97-112; F.M. Cross - D.N. Freedman, *Studies in Ancient Yahwistic Poetry* (Missoula, Mont., 1975); H. Seebass, "Die Stammesliste von Dtn XXXIII", *VT* 27 (1977), 158-169; D.N. Freedman, "The Poetic Structure of the Framework of Deuteronomy 33", in: G. Rendsburg, Ruth Adler, M. Arfa, N.H. Winter (eds.), *The Bible World. Essays in Honor of C.H. Gordon* (New York, 1980), 25-46; D.L. Christensen, "Two Stanzas of a Hymn in Deuteronomy 33", *Biblica* 65 (1984), 382-389; J. Sanmartín, "Problemas de textología en las «Bendiciones» de Moisés (Dt 33) y de Jacob (Gn 49)", in: V. Collado - E. Zurro (eds.), *El misterio de la palabra. Homenaje de sus alumnos al profesor D. Luis Alonso Schökel* (Madrid, 1983), 75-96; J. Jeremias, *Das Königtum Gottes in den Psalmen* (FRLANT 141; Göttingen, 1987), 82ff.; J.C. de Moor, *The Rise of Yahwism. The Roots of Israelite Monotheism* (BETL 91; Leuven, 1990), 161-164.

[2] Die Frage, ob im ursprünglichen Rahmenpsalm V. 26 unmittelbar auf V. 5 folgte, braucht hier nicht gelöst zu werden. Vgl. I. L. Seeligmann (*a.a.O.* [Anm. 1], 84ff.), der im Text von V. 21b Spuren einer Brücke zwischen beiden Versen findet und V. 26-29 mit Gaster als den Hymnus betrachtet, der von der V. 5 erwähnten

diesem eingerahmten Stammessprüche (V. 6-25).[3] Ich wende mich hier dem Psalm zu, indem ich davon eine annotierte Übersetzung biete, seine Gattung zu bestimmen versuche und mich bemühe ihn (religions)geschichtlich einzuordnen.

Übersetzung und Anmerkungen

[2]Jahwe kam vom Sinai
und glänzte «seinem Volke» auf von Seir.
Er strahlte auf vom Gebirge Paran
und rückte heran von «Meribat Kades»,
zu seiner Rechten Ihm Lichtstrahlen.
[3]Ja, Er liebte die Sippen:
alle seine Heiligen waren an deiner Seite;
sie sammelten sich an zu deinen Füßen,
machten sich auf den Weg hinter dir.
[4][Ein Gesetz befahl uns Mose.]
«Sein» Besitz wurde die Gemeinde Jakobs
[5]und es kam auf in Jeschurun ein König,
als sich die Häupter des Volkes versammelten,
die Stämme Israels insgesamt.
[26]Keiner ist wie der Gott Jeschuruns,
der über den Himmel fuhr zu deiner Hilfe,
in seiner Erhabenheit auf den Wolken;
[27]der die uralten Götter «demütigte»
und die Mächte der Urzeit «zerbrach».
Er vertrieb den Feind vor dir her
und befahl: Vertilge!
[28]So konnte Israel in Sicherheit wohnen,
Jakob in Abgesondertheit «lagern»
in einem Land von Getreide und Most;
ja, der Himmel über ihm träufelt Tau.
[29]Heil dir, Israel! Wer ist wie du,
ein Volk, dem durch YHWH geholfen wird,
den Schild deiner Hilfe
und deinen erhabenen Schwertträger.
So müssen dir deine Feinde heucheln;
du aber wirst auf ihren Rücken treten.

Anmerkungen zum Text:

V. 2. Wenn man *lmw* nicht in לעמו ändern möchte, könnte man *lnw* (vgl. LXX, S, V und T) lesen. Daß hier vielleicht Sinai und Lim als

---

Gemeinde gesungen wurde. S. auch Z. Weisman, *VT* 28 (1978), 365-368, der vermutet, daß V. 19a ebenfalls Reste eines ursprünglichen, zwischen V. 5 und V. 26 liegenden Textes enthält.
[3] C. J. Labuschagne, *a.a.O.* [Anm. 1], kritisiert die Bezeichnung der Verse 6-25 als "Stammessprüche". Wir verwenden den Ausdruck hier aus traditionellen Gründen.

Mond-Sonnen-Zweiheit nebeneinandergestellt seien[4], ist schon aus formkritischen Gründen abzulehnen.

Obgleich (Meribat) Kades im AT nirgendwo als Ausgangspunkt der göttlichen Epiphanie erscheint, empfiehlt sich wegen der chiastischen Struktur der vier Halbverse, der historischen Umdeutung der Epiphanieschilderung und der Tatsache, daß anscheinend erst in V. 3 von Gottes Engeln die Rede ist, doch die Lesart "(er kam / rückte heran) von Meribat Kades".[5] Weniger überzeugend ist die Lesart "von der Wüste von Kades" (so Seeligmann) oder "mit den Myriaden von Kades" (so LXX). Greßmann[6], der der Ansicht war, daß der Sinaigott Jahwe in Kades zum Volksgott Israels erhoben wurde, schlug "nach Meribat Kades" vor. Diese Deutung ist aber ungesichert. Der Übersetzung von J. C. de Moor: "from the ten thousands of Kadesh" (im Sinne von "human warriors") vermag ich ebenfalls nicht zu folgen. S liest *w'mh mn rbwt' dqdyš'* (vgl. V: et cum eo sanctorum milia; T: *w'mh rbwt qdyšyn*). Dieser Übersetzung folgen manche Kommentatoren. Doch scheint (wie gesagt) von Gottes Engeln erst in V. 3 die Rede zu sein.

Schon die alten Versiones haben *'šdt* nicht mehr verstanden (vgl. LXX: ἐκ δεξιῶν αὐτοῦ ἄγγελοι μετ' αὐτοῦ; V: in dextera eius ignea lex; T: "seine Rechte schrieb inmitten von Feuer das Gesetz und gab es uns"). Der geistvolle Vorschlag von Labuschagne *'šdt lmw'b* ("the slopes of Moab"), vgl. *'ap* (V. 3), zu lesen, wirkt verführerisch, greift aber wohl zu stark in den überlieferten Text ein. Wir schlagen mit Ball und Seeligmann vor, das Wort im Sinne von "streams of light" zu erklären, vgl. syr. *'šd*, "ausgiessen" (auch vom Licht gesagt), und die Parallelstelle Hab. 3:4 (*qrnym mydw lw*). Das folgende *lmw* kann als Präposition mit dem Suffix der 3. Pers. masc. *Singular* gedeutet werden.[7] Daß danach ein Halbvers fehle, weil dem "rechts" ein "links" entsprechen sollte (so Greßmann; vgl. auch Seeligmann), ist logisch nicht notwendig und bei unserer begrenzten Kenntnis der hebräischen Poesie alles andere als sicher.

V. 3. Wir fassen עמים als "Sippen" bzw. "Stämme", vgl. V. 19a und Gen. 28:3.[8]

Es gibt keinen genügenden Grund, die Suffixe der 2. Pers. Sing.

---

[4] E. Lipiński, "Le dieu Lim", *XVe Rencontre assyriologique internationale* (Liège, 4-8 juillet 1966), éd. par J.-R. Kupper, 151-160; s. auch G. Dossin, "A propos du dieu Lim", *Syria* 55 (1978), 327-332.

[5] So u. a. Von Rad, *Das fünfte Buch Mose. Deuteronomium* (ATD 8; Göttingen, 1964), 144; Labuschagne.

[6] *Die Anfänge Israels* (Die Schriften des AT I/2; Göttingen, 1922), 173.

[7] Vgl. Joüon, *Grammaire*, § 103f.

[8] Vgl. Labuschagne, *a.a.O.* [Anm. 1], 99, Anm. 4.

masc. in Suffixe der 3. Pers. Sing. masc. (auf Gott bezogen) zu ändern,
weil angedeutet sein dürfte, daß die Engel dem Volk auf Schritt und
Tritt zur Seite standen. "Seine Heiligen" meint wohl nicht die Mit-
glieder des von Gott erwählten Volkes (weil von Israel als einem für
Jahwe heiligen Volk erst seit dem Deuteronomium programmatisch
gesprochen wird),[9] sondern die Engel Gottes (Hos. 12:1, Ps. 89:6;
Hiob 15:15; Sach. 14:5 usw.; KAI 4,4/5; 26 A III, 19). Wenn "seine
(zum Krieg) Geheiligten" gemeint wären, hätte der Autor wohl das
Part. Pu. verwendet.

Rätselhaft sind die Worte וכו חם והם, die Änderungsvorschläge daher
zahllos. Eine befriedigende Erklärung ist bislang nicht gefunden
worden. Wir deuten *tkk* mit J.T. Milik, *Biblica* 38 (1957), 252-255 und
Seeligmann, *a.a.O.* [Anm. 1], 80 als "to crowd together",[10] fassen die
folgende Verbalform als Plural, übersetzen sie aufgrund von Gen. 29:1
mit "sich (auf den Weg) begeben" und erklären *mdbrt(y)k* mit Seeligmann als "hinter dir", "dir folgend".

V. 4. Man betrachtet die erste Hälfte von V. 4 (oder auch den ganzen
Vers; so noch Seeligmann und Jeremias) meistens als sekundären
Zusatz, weil ein neues Thema angeschnitten wird, das weder im
Vorangehenden noch im Folgenden angesprochen ist. Vgl. dazu die
nachfolgenden Überlegungen. Weil das *He* von *mwršh* offenbar als auf
Gott bezogenes Pron. poss. der 3. Pers. Sing. masc. gedeutet werden
muß, ist im Falle der Authenzität von V. 4a als (gedachtes) Subjekt
von צוה ursprünglich Gott, nicht "Mose" anzunehmen (vgl. Labuschagne, *a.a.O.* [Anm. 1], 99, Anm. 6). Die Erwähnung Moses wäre
dann sekundär (vgl. Budde, Gaster und Tournay; anders Von Rad).

V. 27. Statt *m[e]'ona* ist wohl *ma'[a]nœ* zu lesen. Sodann ist מחחת als
Verschreibung für מחתת (Part. Pi'el) zu betrachten.

V. 28. Statt עין ist entweder *'ân* (Partizip) oder *yâ'ôn* (Imperfekt) zu
lesen (von *'wn*, "wohnen").

V. 29. Der Ausdruck אשר חרב ist wohl ähnlich der akkadischen
Wendung *ša* mit Substantiv im Sinne einer Person, die mit etwas zu
tun hat bzw. für eine Sache verantwortlich oder zuständig ist, zu
deuten.

Die Gegner heucheln, indem sie sich unfreiwillig dem Sieger unter-
werfen. Für *bmwt* im Sinne von "Rücken" vgl. ugar. *bmt*.

---

[9] Vgl. H.-P. Müller, *THAT* II, 606.
[10] Vgl. auch O. Komlós, *VT* 4 (1954), 435f.

Die Gattung des Liedes

Trotz des auf Epiphanieschilderungen basierenden Wortlauts der ersten drei Halbzeilen von V. 2 bildet der Rahmenpsalm nicht ein aus aktuellem Anlaß komponiertes Siegeslied, sondern einen Hymnus. Dieser hat Gottes geschichtliche Heilstaten und ständiges Eintreten für Israel im Blick. Die Epiphanieschilderung, die in babylonischen Quellen ein kosmisch-mythologisches Geschehen beschreibt, ist hier geschichtlich umgedeutet und dient der Verkündigung, daß Jahwe herangekommen ist um seinem Volk zu helfen.[11] Daraus ergibt sich auch die in einer Epiphanieschilderung nicht zu erwartende Rede vom Heranrücken Gottes von Meribat Kades her. Diese Vorstellung vom Kommen Gottes ist spezifisch frühisraelitisch. Ob sie allerdings ihre Entstehung den Einflüssen der Sinaiüberlieferung verdankt,[12] ist zweifelhaft, weil im Rahmen der Sinaitheophanie[13] von ירד (Ex. 19:18; 34:5) die Rede ist und die Sinaitradition auf die Ausformung der Epiphanieschilderungen nicht eingewirkt hat. Im Hymnus Dtn 33:2-5.26-29 "kommt Jahwe nicht nur zur Vertreibung der Feinde (V. 27.29), sondern zu einer ganzen Reihe von Heilstaten der Frühzeit" (Jenni)[14]. Dabei ist zunächst seine Führung in der Wüste angesprochen (V. 2 und 3).

Inzwischen ist die Bestimmung des Liedes als Hymnus nicht allgemein akzeptiert worden. Seebass[15] möchte den ursprünglichen Psalm auf die Verse 2, 3, 27-29 beschränken und nennt ihn folglich ein Kriegslied. Seiner Meinung nach bilden V. 4-5 und 26 den Rahmentext der Sprüchesammlung.

Der (religions)historische Hintergrund des Liedes

Die Verse 4 und 5 bereiten uns ernsthafte Schwierigkeiten. Manche Kommentatoren möchten V. 4 als späteren Zusatz betrachten, weil seine Thematik weder im Vorangehenden noch im Folgenden aufge-

---

[11] Vgl. J. Jeremias, *Theophanie. Die Geschichte einer alttestamentlichen Gattung* (WMANT 10; Neukirchen-Vluyn, 1965), 152ff.; E. Jenni, "«Kommen» im theologischen Sprachgebrauch des Alten Testaments", in: J. J. Stamm - E. Jenni - H. J. Stoebe (Hrsg.), *Wort-Gebot-Glaube. Walter Eichrodt zum 80. Geburtstag* (ATANT 59; Zürich, 1970), 251-261, bes. 256; C. J. Labuschagne, *a.a.O.*, 99ff.

[12] Erwogen von J. Jeremias, *a.a.O.*, 154f.

[13] Ich möchte mit C. Westermann, *Das Loben Gottes in den Psalmen* (Göttingen, 1963³), 69-76 zwischen Theophanie und Epiphanie einen Unterschied machen, obgleich ich die Kritik von G. W. Ahlström, *Joel and the Temple Cult of Jerusalem* (SVT 21; Leiden, 1971), 84 teile, daß "what Westermann has seen as the difference between theophany and epiphany seems rather to be a difference of acting than of literary forms".

[14] E. Jenni, *a. a. O.*, 256.

[15] *A.a.O.* [Anm. 1], 160f.

griffen wird und *lnw* im Liede sonst nicht erscheine. Ersteres Argument ist kaum durchschlaggebend. Wenn der Hymnus tatsächlich eine Reihe von Heilstaten der Frühzeit Israels nennt, ist nicht zu erwarten, daß diese auch im Vorangehenden oder im Folgenden erwähnt werden. Der Gebrauch von *lnw* mutet jedoch deuteronomisch an. Mit der Mehrzahl der Ausleger betrachten wir daher V. 4a als späteren Zusatz, zumal im Lied sonst nur die Wüstenwanderung und Themen, die sich mit der Landnahme und Gottes Eigentumsvolk befassen, angesprochen werden. Das bedeutet aber noch nicht, daß ganz V. 4 sekundär ist. Wäre das der Fall, so ließe sich das Imperf. consec. *wyhy* (V. 5a) grammatikalisch nur schwer mit dem Imperf. *yś'(w)* von V. 3 verbinden. Diese Schwierigkeit stellt sich nicht ein, wenn man V. 4b als authentisch betrachtet: dann folgt das Imperf. consec. *wyhy* einem Nominalsatz, vgl. V. 27b nach V. 26-27a. Ist V. 4a sekundär, muß *mwrśh* (V. 4b) im Sinne von "sein (= Gottes) Besitz" gedeutet werden: die Gemeinde Jakobs wurde Gottes Eigentum, vgl. Dtn 32:8.

Viele ältere Ausleger haben die Anfangsworte von V. 5 auf das Aufkommen des irdischen Königtums in Israel, nicht auf das Königtum Jahwes bezogen. Budde ist mit anderen Auslegern entschieden dafür eingetreten, daß die Worte *wyhy byśrwn mlk* nur "Und es kam in Jeschurun ein König" bedeuten können. In seinem Dtn-Kommentar bezweifelt von Rad, ob man mit der Mehrzahl der Kommentatoren V. 5 auf Jahwe beziehen darf in dem Sinne, daß der Hauptgedanke des Liedes der wäre, daß Jahwe vom Sinai gekommen ist, um in Israel sein Königtum anzutreten. Seiner Meinung nach "ist es ... sehr fraglich, ob das so (wie in V. 5 geschieht) ausgedrückt werden konnte, und - war denn Jahwe König in «Israel»?" Die Jahwe-Königsvorstellung sei sonst als ein Königtum über die Götter und über die Völker verstanden worden (das mag für die frühisraelitische Zeit zutreffen; in späterer Zeit wird Jahwe jedoch "König Israels" (Jes 44:6; Zeph 3:15), "König Jakobs" (Jes 41:21), Israels "König" (Ps 149:2); "unser König" (Jes 33:22; Ps 47:7) und "euer König" (1 Sam 12:12; Jes 43:15) genannt). Crüsemann[16] räumt ein, daß es grammatikalisch nicht möglich sei, eine Entscheidung zwischen der Übersetzung "es kam ein König" und "Er wurde König" zu fällen, ist aber der Meinung, daß "ein in V. 5 genannter irdischer König .. in den zentralen Gedankengang des Psalms nicht integriert" ist und daß "eine königsfreundliche Hand ... wohl kaum das Königtum bloß auf die Aktivität der רָאשֵׁי עָם zurückführen" würde statt auf Jahwe selbst. Zu dieser Stellungnahme läßt sich bemer-

---

[16] F. Crüsemann, *Der Widerstand gegen das Königtum* (WMANT 49; Neukirchen-Vluyn, 1978), 80ff.

ken, daß *wyhy* mit folgendem Substantiv im Biblisch-Hebräischen zwar
"er wurde X" bedeuten kann, daß aber diese Wendung (abgesehen von
ל mit Personalsuffix, vgl. 1 Kön 1:2) immer das, wozu einer wurde,
gleich nach der Verbalform ohne zwischenliegende adverbiale Bestimmung zum Ausdruck bringt. Diese syntaktische Feststellung dürfte für
die Erklärung von V. 5a entscheidend sein. Es ist schon richtig, daß
das, wozu einer wird, im Biblisch-Hebräischen auch ohne die Präposition ל vor dem betreffenden Substantiv zum Ausdruck gebracht werden
kann (vgl. Gen 4:2; Jos 9:21; 2 Sam 7:8; 19:14; 20:26; 1 Kön 4:1
usw.). Schiebt sich zwischen *wyhy* und dem, wozu eine(r) oder etwas
wurde, jedoch eine adverbiale Bestimmung ein, dann ist mit "er/es
kam", nicht "er/es wurde ... zu" zu übersetzen, vgl. Ps 76:3.

Inhaltlich muß Crüsemann eingestehen, daß die Nennung der Häupter des Volkes und der Versammlung der Stämme im diesem Zusammenhang seltsam ist, weil es "nach all unserer Kenntnis historisch unmöglich (ist), daß eine Versammlung des vorstaatlichen Israel Jahwe
zum König über sich proklamiert hätte".[17] Ein Rekurs auf ein außer-
jerusalemisches Thronbesteigungsfest lehnt er mit Recht ab, aber seine
These, daß Deut 33:5 nur als Antikonzeption des Königwerdens Sauls
und Davids zu verstehen sei, ist alles andere als überzeugend.[18] Ihm
zufolge handle es sich bei der Aussage, daß Gott König in Jeschurun
wurde, um "ein bewußtes Gegenbild zur Entstehung der ersten israelitischen Königtümer, das von diesen Erfahrungen lebt". Es sei zum Ausdruck gebracht worden, daß weder Saul noch David, noch ein anderer,
sondern nur Jahwe selbst legitimerweise König über Israel wurde und
ist.[19] Diese Folgerung läßt sich jedoch dem Vers kaum entnehmen.
Sie stelle (wenn sie richtig wäre) nicht nur einen komplizierten Gedankengang, sondern auch implizite eine in religionsgeschichtlicher Hin-
sicht bedenkliche Aussage dar. "Jahwes »Königtum« ist ein Erbe
Kanaans" (W. H. Schmidt) und als König der Völker und der ganzen
Welt wurde Er König Israels.[20] Daß Jahwe sein Königtum über Israel
einer Proklamierung einer Versammlung des vorstaatlichen Israel zu
verdanken habe, weist Crüsemann selber als historisch unmöglich ab.
Dann aber kann sich der Autor von Dtn 33 bei der von Crüsemann

---

[17] *A. a. O.*, 81. Anders urteilt allerdings J. C. de Moor, *a.a.O.* [Anm. 1], 163
("In v. 4b-5 it is stipulated that it was the assembly of the tribes of Israel that
attributed the title of "King" to YHWH, not the other gods, as in Tablet IV of
Enuma Elish").
[18] Vgl. auch die Kritik von J. Jeremias, *a. a. O.* [Anm. 1], 89, Anm. 24.
[19] *A. a. O.*, 82.
[20] W. (H.) Schmidt, *Königtum Gottes in Ugarit und Israel* (BZAW 80; Berlin,
1961), 72.

befürworteten Aussage, daß Jahwe König in Jeshurun *wurde*, kaum eines Gegenbildes zur Entstehung der ersten israelitischen Königtümer bedient haben. Auch die Bemerkung von W. H. Schmidt[21], daß der Anschluß von V. 26 an V. 5 keinen Zweifel daran zulasse, daß mit dem König von V. 5 Jahwe selbst gemeint sei, weil V. 26 den, der in V. 5 König in Jeschurun wurde, nun Gott Jeschuruns nenne, überzeugt nicht, weil Jeschurun lediglich ein Ehrenname Israels bzw. Jakobs ist, also über Jahwes Gottsein oder Königtum an sich nichts aussagt. Auch Schmidts Bemerkung, daß Jahwe von V. 2a an die handelnde Person bleibt, dürfte nicht für die Übersetzung "Er wurde König in Jeshurun" sprechen. Denn einmal ist es unsicher, ob Jahwe in den vorangehenden Versen immer grammatikalisches Subjekt ist (vgl. V. 3b und 4b). Zweitens ist Gott bei der Übersetzung "Er wurde König ..." zwar grammatikalisches Subjekt, inhaltlich aber Objekt der in dem Falle vorauszusetzenden Wahl der Stämme Israels.

Wie gesagt, weisen grammatikalische Überlegungen darauf hin, daß *wyhy byšrwn mlk* nicht "Er wurde König in Jeschurun", sondern "es kam ein König in Jeschurun" bedeutet (vgl. auch LXX: καὶ ἔσται ἐν τῷ ἠγαπημένῳ ἄρχων; V: erit apud rectissimum rex; S: *wnhw' b'ysryl mlk'*). Mit dieser Übersetzung läßt sich die Aussage, daß dies während einer Versammlung der israelitischen Stämme geschah, zwanglos verbinden: Saul wurde in einer Zusammenkunft der Stämme Israels zum König erwählt (1 Sam. 10:20ff.) und die Ältesten Israels salbten David in Hebron zum König (2 Sam. 5:3). Man könnte V. 5 allenfalls als Gelenkpunkt des Lobliedes betrachten, in dem die Wahl eines irdischen Königs (offenbar im Sinne eines Fürsten über Gottes Erbe, vgl. 1. Sam. 10:1) als Höhepunkt der Heilsgeschichte dargestellt wird.

Obige Überlegungen führen dazu, den Psalm *nicht als vorstaatlich* zu betrachten, sondern ihn frühestens in die Zeit Sauls anzusetzen. Daß der dtn Autor den nordisraelitischen Hymnus zusammen mit nordisraelitischen Stammessprüchen in sein Buch aufgenommen hat, dürfte ein wichtiger Hinweis auf die nordisraelitische Herkunft der deuteronomischen Bewegung sein.

---

[21] *A.a.O.*, 68.

A BIBLIOGRAPHY OF C.J. LABUSCHAGNE

A. HILHORST

Rijksuniversiteit Groningen

1959
"Die gebruik van die Godsaanduidinge *'ēl* en *'ĕlōhîm* in die geskrifte van die Profete", *Hervormde Teologiese Studies* 14 (1959), 67-78.

1960
"Some Remarks on the Prayer of David in II Sam. 7", *Studies on the Books of Samuel. Papers Read at 3rd Meeting Held at Stellenbosch 26-28 January 1960* (Pretoria, no year), 28-35.

1961
Die onvergelyklikheid van Jahwè in die Ou Testament, Diss. Universiteit van Pretoria, 1961.

1962
"Some Remarks on the Translation and Meaning of *'āmartî* in the Psalms", *New Light on Some Old Testament Problems. Papers Read at 5th Meeting Held at the University of South Africa, Pretoria 30 January - 2 February 1962*, 27-33.

1963
"Geloof en voortbestaan volgens die Ou Testament", *Pro Veritate* 1,10 (Febr. 1963), 7-8 and 1,11 (March 1963), 7.

1964
"Ugaritic *blt* and *biltî* in Is. X 4", *VT* 14 (1964), 97-99.

1965
"The Similes in the Book of Hosea", *Studies on the Books of Hosea and Amos. Papers Read at 7th and 8th Meetings of Die O.T. Werkgemeenskap in Suid-Afrika 1964-1965* (Potchefstroom, no year), 64-76.
"Amos' Conception of God and the Popular Theology of His Time", *Studies on the Books of Hosea and Amos. Papers Read at 7th and 8th Meetings of Die O.T. Werkgemeenskap in Suid-Afrika 1964-1965* (Potchefstroom, no year), 122-133.
"Did Elisha Deliberately Lie? - A Note on II Kings 8 10", *ZAW* 77 (1965), 327-328.

1966
The Incomparability of Yahweh in the Old Testament (POS 5; Leiden, 1966).
"Fanaticism and Extremism Unmasked and Cured. The Story of a Man Who Learned to Ask "What Shall I Do, Lord?"", *Pro Veritate* 5,7 (Nov. 1966), 4-5.

"What Does It Mean to Be a Human Being?", *Pro Veritate* 5,8 (Dec. 1966), 8-10.

"*Teraphim* - A New Proposal for Its Etymology", *VT* 16 (1966), 115-117.

1967

"The Crux in Ruth 4 11", *ZAW* 79 (1967), 364-367.

"The Communion of Saints. The Early Church's First Lesson in Ecumenism-", *Pro Veritate* 5,12 (April 1967), 4-6.

"Die Triomflied van Verworpenes. 'n Besinning oor Handelinge 16:9-40", *Pro Veritate* 6,2 (15 June 1967), 6-9.

"Wie Meen dat hy Staan, moet Oppas dat hy nie Val nie", *Pro Veritate* 6,5 (15 Sept. 1967), 6-8.

"Wie is die Voorbok onder die Sondaars?", *Pro Veritate* 6,7 (15 Nov. 1967), 9-12.

1968

Hebreeuse Spraakkuns. Vormleer, sinsleer en oefeninge deur Dr. B. Gemser. 3de verbeterde druk versorg deur Dr. C.J. Labuschagne (Pretoria 1968).

Schriftprofetie en volksideologie. Openbare les gegeven ter gelegenheid van de aanvaarding van het ambt van lector in de Israëlitische letterkunde en de uitlegging van het Oude Testament aan de rijksuniversiteit te Groningen op dinsdag 29 oktober 1968 (Nijkerk, no year).

1969

"De valse profetie in Israël", *Rondom het Woord* 11 (1969), 142-152.

"Openbaring, schepping en verbond. Kanttekeningen van een oudtestamenticus bij H.A.M. Fiolet, *Vreemde Verleiding*", *Kerk en Theologie* 20 (1969), 266-276.

1970

"De bijbel en het probleem van de homofilie", *Kerk en theologie* 21 (1970), 55-65.

"Die Nederlandse Jeug in Opstand", *St. Andrew's News/Nuus* No. 719 (March 1970), last page.

1971

Israëls Jabroer-profeten. Zes radiolezingen over spanningen tussen ware en valse profeten in het Oude Testament (Verken de Bijbel 18; Amsterdam - Driebergen, 1971).

"The Song of Moses: Its Framework and Structure", *De fructu oris sui. Essays in Honour of Adrianus van Selms* (POS 9; Leiden, 1971), 85-98.

"Original Shaph'el-Forms in Biblical Hebrew", *Old Testament Studies. Papers Read at the Tenth Meeting of Die O.T. Werkgemeenskap in Suid-Afrika 1967* (Pretoria, 1971), 51-64.

"Het spreken Gods en het spreken over God", *Theocreet* 3,1 (Oct. 1971), 9-14.

"Ware en valse profeten. Hoe ze te onderscheiden", *De Bijbel* 4,52 (Dec. 1971), 1633-1634.

Editor: *De fructu oris sui. Essays in Honour of Adrianus van Selms* (POS 9; Leiden 1971) (with I.H. Eybers, F.C. Fensham, W.C. van Wyk, and A.H. van Zyl).

1972
"Botsing met het establishment (over Amos 7:10-17)", *De Bijbel* 4,59 (Febr. 1972), 1858-1859.

1973
"The Particles הֵן and הִנֵּה", *Syntax and Meaning. Studies in Hebrew Syntax and Biblical Exegesis* (OTS 18; Leiden, 1973), 1-14.
"Redactie en theologie van het boek Deuteronomium", *Vox theologica* 43 (1973), 171-184.
"De verhouding tussen het Oude en het Nieuwe Testament", *Rondom het Woord* 15 (1973), 118-132.

1974
"The Tribes in the Blessing of Moses", *Language and Meaning. Studies in Hebrew Language and Biblical Exegesis. Papers Read at the Joint British-Dutch Old Testament Conference Held at London, 1973* (OTS 19; Leiden, 1974), 97-112.
"Gebod en zedelijk handelen", *Rondom het Woord* 16 (1974), 95-108.
"The *našû–nadānu* Formula and Its Biblical Equivalent", *Travels in the World of the Old Testament. Studies Presented to Professor M.A. Beek on the Occasion of His 65th Birthday* (Studia Semitica Neerlandica 16; Assen, 1974), 176-180.

1975
"Geloven in het spreken Gods", *Rondom het Woord* 17 (1975), 64-81.
"De godsdienst van Israel en de andere godsdiensten. Op zoek naar een bijbelse fundering van de theologia religionum", *Wereld en Zending* 4 (1975), 4-16.
"Inzichten om dankbaar voor te zijn; een oudtestamenticus kijkt terug", *Gratias agimus. Opstellen over Danken en Loven, aangeboden aan Prof.Dr. W.F. Dankbaar* (Studies van het Instituut voor Liturgiewetenschap 2; Groningen, 1975), 54-57.

1976
Aramaic Texts from Qumran with translations and annotations I (Semitic Study Series N.S. 4; Leiden, 1976) (with B. Jongeling and A.S. van der Woude).
"נתן *ntn* geben", *THAT* II (München - Zürich, 1976), 117-141.
"ענה *'nh* I antworten", *ibid.*, 335-341.
"פה *pæ* Mund", *ibid.*, 406-411.
"קול *qōl* Stimme", *ibid.*, 629-634.
"קרא *qr'* rufen", *ibid.*, 666-674.

1977
Wat zegt de bijbel in GODS naam? Nieuwe bijbeluitleg en modern godsgeloof ('s-Gravenhage, 1977[1], 1977[2]).

"Zondag 24 juli: Genesis 12:4a. Zondag 31 juli: Genesis 22:1. Zondag 7 augustus: Numeri 22:20 en 35. Zondag 14 augustus: Deuteronomium 8:3b", *Postille* 1976-1977, 129-138.

1978

Wat zegt de bijbel in GODS naam? Nieuwe bijbeluitleg en modern godsgeloof ('s-Gravenhage, 1978³).
Gods oude plakboek. Visie op het Oude Testament ('s-Gravenhage, 1978¹).
"Theologie in Groningen. Labuschagne antwoordt Geense", *Theocreet* 10,3 (Febr. 1978), 34-38.

1979

Wat zegt de bijbel in GODS naam? Nieuwe bijbeluitleg en modern godsgeloof ('s-Gravenhage, 1979⁴)
Gods oude plakboek. Visie op het Oude Testament ('s-Gravenhage, 1979²).

1980

Wat zegt de bijbel in GODS naam? Nieuwe bijbeluitleg en modern godsgeloof ('s-Gravenhage, 1980⁵).
"Racisme volstrekt tegenstrijdig met het evangelie", *Racisme* (Utrecht, 1980), 22-27.

1981

"De Messiasverwachtingen in het Oude Testament", *Groninger Kerkbode* 257,22 (Nov. 1981), 1.
"Kritisch lezen, een historisch-kritische leeswijze", *Rondom het Woord* 23 (1981), 16-27 and 46-51.

1982

"The Pattern of the Divine Speech Formulas in the Pentateuch. The Key to Its Literary Structure", *VT* 32 (1982), 268-296.
"The Meaning of *b⁽ᵉ⁾yād rāmā* in the Old Testament", *Von Kanaan bis Kerala. Festschrift für Prof.Mag.Dr.Dr. J.P.M. van der Ploeg O.P. zur Vollendung des siebzigsten Lebensjahres am 4. Juli 1979 überreicht von Kollegen, Freunden und Schülern* (AOAT 211; Kevelaer - Neukirchen-Vluyn, 1982), 143-148.

1984

Wat zegt de bijbel in GODS naam? Nieuwe bijbeluitleg en modern godsgeloof ('s-Gravenhage, 1984⁶).
"Additional Remarks on the Pattern of the Divine Speech Formulas in the Pentateuch", *VT* 34 (1984), 91-95.
"Pentateuchal Patterns: A Reply to P.R. Davies and D.M. Gunn", *VT* 34 (1984), 407-413.
"Nieuwe perspectieven voor een zinvolle dialoog", *Summa* 16,4 (Dec. 1984), 18-19.
"Saul en David in historisch perspectief. Trudi Klijn in gesprek met Prof.dr. C.J. Labuschagne", K. Deurloo - K. Eykman (eds.), *Sjofele koning. David en Saul in profetisch perspectief* (Baarn, 1984), 42-46.

1985

Gods oude plakboek. Visie op het Oude Testament ('s-Gravenhage 1985³).
"Divine Speech in Deuteronomy", N. Lohfink (ed.), *Das Deuteronomium. Entstehung, Gestalt und Botschaft* (BETL 68; Leuven 1985), 111-126.
"The Literary and Theological Function of Divine Speech in the Pentateuch" J.A. Emerton (ed.), *Congress Volume, Salamanca 1983* (SVT 36; Leiden, 1985), 154-173.
"Enkele moderne hulpmiddelen bij de bestudering van de bijbel", *NTT* 39 (1985), 327-331.

1986

"On the Structural Use of Numbers as a Composition Technique", *JNSL* 12 (1984 [1986]), 87-99.
"Neue Wege und Perspektiven in der Pentateuchforschung", *VT* 36 (1986), 146-162.
"Some Significant Composition Techniques in Deuteronomy", *Scripta Signa Vocis. Studies about Scripts, Scriptures, Scribes and Languages in the Near East Presented to J.H. Hospers by His Pupils, Colleagues and Friends* (Groningen, 1986), 121-131.
"De functie van getallen in de bijbelse oudheid", *Intensief* 12/8 (1986), 6-11.
"De literairkritische methode", A.S. van der Woude (ed.), *Inleiding tot de studie van het Oude Testament* (Kampen, 1986), 102-127.
"Het derde gebod", *Theocreet* 17,4 (1986), 2-5.

1987

Deuteronomium deel I A (POT; Nijkerk 1987).
Logotechnische analyse bij Deuteronomium 1:1-4:49 [read *43*] (POT; Nijkerk, 1987).
Deuteronomium deel I B (POT; Nijkerk, 1987).
Logotechnische analyse bij Deuteronomium 4:44-11:32 (POT; Nijkerk, 1987).
"De numerieke structuuranalyse van de bijbelse geschriften", *NTT* 41 (1987), 1-16.
"Opmerkelijke compositietechnieken in het boek Micha", F. García Martínez - C.H.J. de Geus - A.F.J. Klijn (eds.), *Profeten en profetische geschriften* (Kampen - Nijkerk [1987]), 100-116.

1988

"Priesters en Profeten in het Oude Testament", *Schrift* No. 119 (Oct. 1988), 170-176.

1989

"The Life Spans of the Patriarchs", A.S. van der Woude (ed.), *New Avenues in the Study of the Old Testament. A Collection of Old Testament Studies Published on the Occasion of the Fiftieth Anniversary of the Oudtestamentisch Werkgezelschap and the Retirement of Prof.Dr. M.J. Mulder* (OTS 25; Leiden - New York - København - Köln, 1989), 121-127.
"Woord vooraf", S. de Jong, *Onvruchtbare moeders. Een feministische lezing van Genesis* (Boxtel - Brugge, 1989), 5-6.

1990

Deuteronomium deel II (POT; Nijkerk, 1990).
Logotechnische analyse bij Deuteronomium 12:1-26:19 (POT; Nijkerk, 1990).
Gods oude plakboek. Visie op het Oude Testament ('s-Gravenhage, 1990⁴).
"Het bijbelse scheppingsgeloof in ecologisch perspectief", *Tijdschrift voor theologie* 30 (1990), 5-17.
"De cruciale beslissing (Joz. 24)", *Jota* No. 5 (1990), 13-21.
"Apartheid en Europees racisme", *Amandla* (Aug. - Sept. 1990), 23-24.

1991

Hoe heilzaam is de bijbelwetenschap? De bijdrage van de bijbel(wetenschap) aan de cultuur. Rede uitgesproken op 17 september 1991 ter gelegenheid van het afscheid als hoogleraar Oude Testament aan de Rijksuniversiteit te Groningen (Nijkerk, no year).
"Europees racisme en het geweld tegen de natuur", *Amandla* (April 1991), 23-24.
"Creation and the Status of Humanity in the Bible", V. Brümmer (ed.), *Interpreting the Universe as Creation. A Dialogue of Science and Religion* (Kampen, 1991), 123-131.

1992

Vertellen met getallen. Functie en symboliek van getallen in de bijbelse oudheid (Zoetermeer, 1992).
"You Shall Not Boil a Kid in Its Mother's Milk. A New Proposal for the Origin of the Prohibition", *The Scriptures and the Scrolls. Studies in Honour of A.S. van der Woude on the Occasion of His 65th Birthday* (SVT 49; Leiden - New York - Köln, 1992), 6-17.
Editor: *The Scriptures and the Scrolls. Studies in Honour of A.S. van der Woude on the Occasion of His 65th Birthday* (SVT 49; Leiden - New York - Köln, 1992) (with F. García Martínez and A. Hilhorst).

INDEXES

I. Index of Authors

Olsen, D.T. 37f.
Oost, R. 31
Otto, E. 186
Ottoson, M. 186, 193

Paran, M. 187
Pardee, D. 189
Paul, M.J. 195
Perlitt, L. 39, 56, 60, 147, 152, 19-7f., 248
Pfann, S.J. 63, 95
Pfeiffer, C.F. 183
Phillips, A. 197
Pienaar, P.J. 14
Ploeg, J.P.M. van der 65
Plöger, O. 249
Polzin, R. 51, 57
Porter, B. 210
Postma, F. 249
Potgieter, F.J.M. 24, 26
Preuss, H.D. 37f., 48, 135, 143, 152, 155, 197, 249, 254
Procksch, O. 256
Puukko, F. 6

Rabenau, K. von 197, 256
Rabin, I.A. 229, 231
Rad, G. von 34, 38, 140, 152f., 167ff., 189, 197, 209, 283f.
Radjawane, A.N. 253
Rashi 104, 121
Reed, J.A. 64
Rehm 104
Reichert, A. 224, 248f.
Reid, T. 18f.
Rendsburg, G. 281
Rendtorff, R. 31f., 48ff., 226, 245, 249
Richter, H.-F. 123, 127, 130
Richter, W. 101f., 105f., 189
Riessler, P. 281
Rinaldi, G. 91
Ringgren, H. 53, 60
Robertson, D.A. 185
Römer, Th. 33, 39, 45, 55, 57, 155, 244, 246, 248
Roersma, L. 184
Roos, J.H. 14
Rose, M. 218, 250
Rost 120
Roux, L.A.D. 22
Rowley, H.H. 124, 128

Rudolph, K. 235
Rudolph, W. 256
Ruiten, J.T.A.G.M. van 90, 223-241
Ruppert, L. 48

Sanders, P. 189
Sanderson, J.E. 65
Sanmartín, J. 281
Sasson, J.M. 123, 129, 133
Sauer, G. 130
Schäfer, P. 229, 231, 235
Schäfer-Lichtenberger, C. 45, 200
Schedl, C. 32, 101f., 119
Schiffman, L.H. 239
Schloegl 105
Schmauch, W. 7
Schmid, H.H. 200, 250, 262
Schmidt, L. 246, 255, 259
Schmidt, W.H. 244ff., 252, 287f.
Schmitt, G. 218, 220, 249, 266
Schmitt, H.-C. 250
Schreckenberg, H. 90
Schüssler Fiorenza, E. 29
Schult, H. 33
Schulz 104
Seebass, H. 281, 285
Seeligmann, I.L. 43f., 281, 283f.
Segal, A.F. 230f., 234, 237f.
Seitz, G. 216f.
Seybold, K. 120
Shepard, G.T. 24
Shepard, W. 18
Simpson, C.A. 261
Ska, J.L. 54, 244, 250
Skehan, P.W. 65, 95, 99, 158, 185, 280
Skweres, D.E. 56f., 248f., 266f.
Smend, R.Sr 256
Smend, R.Jr 246, 249, 261f.
Smick, E.B. 24
Smith, G.A. 104, 153
Soggin, J.A. 39, 185f., 246, 248f.
Soler, J. 178f.
Speiser, E.A. 24
Spieckermann, H. 220
Stade, B. 41
Staerk, W. 1-7, 9ff.
Stähelin, J.J. 247
Stamm, J.J. 285
Stange, E. 1
Stegemann, H. 79
Steiner, M. 85

II. Index of biblical references

The index does not include biblical passages mentioned in the footnotes. Also the lists on pp. 80-82 and 201-202 are not referred to.

SUPPLEMENTS TO VETUS TESTAMENTUM

2. POPE, M.H. *El in the Ugaritic texts.* 1955. ISBN 90 04 04000 5
3. *Wisdom in Israel and in the Ancient Near East.* Presented to Harold Henry Rowley by the Editorial Board of Vetus Testamentum in celebration of his 65th birthday, 24 March 1955. Edited by M. NOTH and D. WINTON THOMAS. 2nd reprint of the first (1955) ed. 1969. ISBN 90 04 02326 7
4. *Volume du Congrès* [International pour l'étude de l'Ancien Testament]. Strasbourg 1956. 1957. ISBN 90 04 02327 5
8. BERNHARDT, K.-H. *Das Problem der alt-orientalischen Königsideologie im Alten Testament.* Unter besonderer Berücksichtigung der Geschichte der Psalmenexegese dargestellt und kritisch gewürdigt. 1961. ISBN 90 04 02331 3
9. *Congress Volume,* Bonn 1962. 1963. ISBN 90 04 02332 1
11. DONNER, H. *Israel unter den Völkern.* Die Stellung der klassischen Propheten des 8. Jahrhunderts v. Chr. zur Aussenpolitik der Könige von Israel und Juda. 1964. ISBN 90 04 02334 8
12. REIDER, J. *An Index to Aquila.* Completed and revised by N. Turner. 1966. ISBN 90 04 02335 6
13. ROTH, W.M.W. *Numerical sayings in the Old Testament.* A form-critical study. 1965. ISBN 90 04 02336 4
14. ORLINSKY, H.M. *Studies on the second part of the Book of Isaiah.* — The so-called 'Servant of the Lord' and 'Suffering Servant' in Second Isaiah. — Snaith, N.H. Isaiah 40-66. A study of the teaching of the Second Isaiah and its consequences. Repr. with additions and corrections. 1977. ISBN 90 04 05437 5
15. *Volume du Congrès* [International pour l'étude de l'Ancien Testament]. Genève 1965. 1966. ISBN 90 04 02337 2
17. *Congress Volume,* Rome 1968. 1969. ISBN 90 04 02339 9
19. THOMPSON, R.J. *Moses and the Law in a century of criticism since Graf.* 1970. ISBN 90 04 02341 0
20. REDFORD, D.B. *A study of the biblical story of Joseph.* 1970. ISBN 90 04 02342 9
21. AHLSTRÖM, G.W. *Joel and the temple cult of Jerusalem.* 1971. ISBN 90 04 02620 7
22. *Congress Volume,* Uppsala 1971. 1972. ISBN 90 04 03521 4
23. *Studies in the religion of ancient Israel.* 1972. ISBN 90 04 03525 7
24. SCHOORS, A. *I am God your Saviour.* A form-critical study of the main genres in Is. xl-lv. 1973. ISBN 90 04 03792 2
25. ALLEN, L.C. *The Greek Chronicles.* The relation of the Septuagint I and II Chronicles to the Massoretic text. Part 1. The translator's craft. 1974. ISBN 90 04 03913 9
26. *Studies on prophecy.* A collection of twelve papers. 1974. ISBN 90 04 03877 9
27. ALLEN, L.C. *The Greek Chronicles.* Part 2. Textual criticism. 1974. ISBN 90 04 03933 3
28. *Congress Volume,* Edinburgh 1974. 1975. ISBN 90 04 04321 7
29. *Congress Volume,* Göttingen 1977. 1978. ISBN 90 04 05835 4
30. EMERTON, J.A. (ed.). *Studies in the historical books of the Old Testament.* 1979. ISBN 90 04 06017 0
31. MEREDINO, R.P. *Der Erste und der Letzte.* Eine Untersuchung von Jes 40-48. 1981. ISBN 90 04 06199 1
32. EMERTON, J.A. (ed.). *Congress Vienna* 1980. 1981. ISBN 90 04 06514 8
33. KOENIG, J. *L'herméneutique analogique du Judaïsme antique d'après les témoins textuels d'Isaïe.* 1982. ISBN 90 04 06762 0

34. Barstad, H.M. *The religious polemics of Amos*. Studies in the preachings of Amos ii 7B-8, iv 1-13, v 1-27, vi 4-7, viii 14. 1984. ISBN 90 04 07017 6
35. Krašovec, J. *Antithetic structure in Biblical Hebrew poetry*. 1984. ISBN 90 04 07244 6
36. Emerton, J.A. (ed.). *Congress Volume*, Salamanca 1983. 1985. ISBN 90 04 07281 0
37. Lemche, N.P. *Early Israel*. Anthropological and historical studies on the Israelite society before the monarchy. 1985. ISBN 90 04 07853 3
38. Nielsen, K. *Incense in Ancient Israel*. 1986. ISBN 90 04 07702 2
39. Pardee, D. *Ugaritic and Hebrew poetic parallelism*. A trial cut. 1988. ISBN 90 04 08368 5
40. Emerton, J.A. (ed.). *Congress Volume*, Jerusalem 1986. 1988. ISBN 90 04 08499 1
41. Emerton, J.A. (ed.). *Studies in the Pentateuch*. 1990. ISBN 90 04 09195 5
42. McKenzie, S.L. *The trouble with Kings*. The composition of the Book of Kings in the Deuteronomistic History. 1991. ISBN 90 04 09402 4
43. Emerton, J.A. (ed.). *Congress Volume*, Leuven 1989. 1991. ISBN 90 04 09398 2
44. Haak, R.D. *Habakkuk*. 1992. ISBN 90 04 09506 3
45. Beyerlin, W. *Im Licht der Traditionen*. Psalm LXVII und CXV. Ein Entwicklungs-zusammenhang. 1992. ISBN 90 04 09635 3
46. Meier, S.A. *Speaking of Speaking*. Marking direct discourse in the Hebrew Bible. 1992. ISBN 90 04 09602 7
47. Kessler, R. *Staat und Gesellschaft im vorexilischen Juda*. Vom 8. Jahrhundert bis zum Exil. 1992. ISBN 90 04 09646 9
48. Auffret, P. *Voyez de vos yeux*. Étude structurelle de vingt psaumes, dont le psaume 119. 1993. ISBN 90 04 09707 4
49. García Martínez, F., A. Hilhorst and C.J. Labuschagne (eds.). *The Scriptures and the Scrolls*. Studies in honour of A.S. van der Woude on the occasion of his 65th birthday. 1992. ISBN 90 04 09746 5
50. Lemaire, A. and B. Otzen (eds.). *History and Traditions of Early Israel*. Studies presented to Eduard Nielsen, May 8th, 1993. 1993. ISBN 90 04 09851 8
51. Gordon, R.P. *Studies in the Targum to the Twelve Prophets*. From Nahum to Malachi. 1994. ISBN 90 04 09987 5
52. Hugenberger, G.P. *Marriage as a Covenant*. A Study of Biblical Law and Ethics Governing Marriage Developed from the Perspective of Malachi. 1994. ISBN 90 04 09977 8
53. García Martínez, F., A. Hilhorst, J.T.A.G.M. van Ruiten, A.S. van der Woude. *Studies in Deuteronomy*. In Honour of C.J. Labuschagne on the Occasion of His 65th Birthday. 1994. ISBN 90 04 10052 0